JOURNEYS

A Reading and Literature Program

JOURNEYS

A Reading and Literature Program

Arrivals

Curriculum and Writing

Richard J. Smith

Professor of Curriculum and Instruction,
University of Wisconsin.
Formerly, Director of Reading Development,
Public Schools of Madison, Wisconsin.
Formerly, Reading Coordinator, Public Schools
of Ripon, Wisconsin.

Max F. Schulz

Professor of English,
University of Southern California.

HBJ HARCOURT BRACE JOVANOVICH, PUBLISHERS

New York   Chicago   San Francisco   Atlanta   Dallas   *and*   London

Printed in the United States of America

ISBN 0-15-337100-5

Acknowledgments

For permission to reprint copyrighted material, grateful acknowledgment is given to the following sources:

Samuel W. Allen: "To Satch" by Samuel W. Allen.

Isaac Asimov: "The Fun They Had" by Isaac Asimov. Copyright © 1951 by NEA Service, Inc.

Isaac Asimov and Boys' Life: "The Disappearing Man" by Isaac Asimov from *Boys' Life*, June 1978, published by the Boy Scouts of America.

Bantam Books, Inc.: "Jacks" from *Girlsports* by Karen Folger Jacobs. Copyright © 1978 by Karen Folger Jacobs. All rights reserved.

Bill Berger Associates, Inc.: "The Dinner Party" by Mona Gardner. Reprinted by permission of *Saturday Review,* January 31, 1942.

The Christian Science Monitor: "Unfolding Bud" by Naoshi Koriyama from *The Christian Science Monitor.* Copyright © 1957 The Christian Science Publishing Society.

Barbara Corcoran and American Girl: "The Cherub and My Sainted Grandmother" by Barbara Corcoran from *American Girl* magazine, a magazine for all girls, published by Girl Scouts of the U.S.A.

Curtis Brown, Ltd.: "The Word" from *Short Story 18* by Mildred Clingerman. Copyright © 1953 by Mildred Clingerman.

Dodd, Mead & Company, Inc. and McGraw-Hill Ryerson Limited: "The Cremation of Sam McGee" from *The Collected Poems of Robert Service* by Robert Service.

Doubleday & Company, Inc.: "The Whale" and "The Hippo" from *The Collected Poems of Theodore Roethke* by Theodore Roethke. Copyright © 1961 by Theodore Roethke. "Gilead" from *Pilgrimage: The Book of the People* by Zenna Henderson. Copyright © 1954 by Mercury Press, Inc.

Grace Nies Fletcher: "The Fallen Star" by Grace Nies Fletcher, published in *Woman's Day,* October 1952.

Dorothy R. Geiger: "In the Fog" from *Plays to Enjoy* by Milton Geiger. Copyright © 1939, renewed 1967 by Milton Geiger.

Arthur Hailey: "Flight Into Danger" a TV play by Arthur Hailey. Copyright © 1956, 1957, 1960 by Arthur Hailey. This play is the sole property of the author and is fully protected by copyright. All inquiries should be addressed to Seaway Authors Ltd., 1 Place Ville Marie, Suite 1609, Montreal, Canada H3B 2B6.

Harcourt Brace Jovanovich, Inc.: From "Eugenie Clark and the Sleeping Sharks" (retitled "Eugenie Clark and the Sharks") in *Wild Animals, Gentle Women,* copyright © 1978 by Margery Facklam.

Esther R. Heuman and Boys' Life: "It's Not a Game for Girls" by William Heuman from *Boys' Life,* April 1970, published by the Boy Scouts of America.

Houghton Mifflin Company: "The Boomer Fireman's Fast Sooner Hound" from *The Fast Sooner Hound* by Arna Bontemps and Jack Conroy. Copyright © 1942 by Arna Bontemps and Jack Conroy. "Ghost Town" from *The Collected Stories of Jack Schaefer.* Copyright © 1966 by Jack Schaefer. "The Shark" from *Fast and Slow* by John Ciardi. Copyright © 1975 by John Ciardi.

Evelyn Tooley Hunt: "Mama Is a Sunrise" by Evelyn Tooley Hunt from *The Lyric,* 1972.

Robert Lescher Literary Agency: "The Power of Light" by Isaac Bashevis Singer from *Cricket Magazine,* December 1976. Copyright © 1976 by Isaac Bashevis Singer.

J. B. Lippincott Company: "The Sea—The Key to Man's Future" (retitled "The Sea—The Key to Our Future") from *Harvesting the Sea* by D.X. Fenten. Copyright © 1970 by D.X. Fenten.

Little, Brown and Co.: "The Boy Who Laughed at Santa Claus" from *Good Intentions* by Ogden Nash. Copyright © 1937 by Ogden Nash.

Zoltan Malocsay and Boys' Life: "My Hero" by Zoltan Malocsay from *Boys' Life,* June 1976, published by the Boy Scouts of America.

Critical Readers

We wish to thank the following
people, who helped to evaluate materials
for this book.

REBECCA CLARK
Egypt Elementary School, Memphis, Tennessee

DONNA ENGEL
Iroquois Junior High School, Des Plaines, Illinois

ANN FALLON
Blessed Agnes School, Chicago, Illinois

AGNES GREGG
Hixson Junior High School, St. Louis, Missouri

SHELLEY UMANS
Columbia University, New York, New York
Formerly with New York City Public School System, New York, New York

JOAN WILLIAMSON
Marshall University High School, Minneapolis, Minnesota

MARY WINFIELD
Wooster Junior High School, Stratford, Connecticut

JOAN YESNER
Marshall University High School, Minneapolis, Minnesota

CONTENTS

Discoveries

Experience

Visions

Flight Into Danger

by Arthur Hailey   **210**

Landscapes

Diversity

Gilead

by Zenna Henderson **449**

Turn to page xiv for **Outline of Skills**

OUTLINE OF SKILLS

Literature Skills

Reading Skills

Word Attack Skills

Composition Skills

DISCOVERIES

The Disappearing Man

Isaac Asimov

I'm not often on the spot when Dad's on one of his cases, but I couldn't help it this time.

I was coming home from the library that afternoon, when a man dashed by me and ran full speed into an alley between two buildings. It was rather late, and I figured the best thing to do was to keep on moving toward home. Dad says a nosy fourteen-year-old isn't likely to make it to fifteen.

But in less than a minute, two policemen came running. I didn't wait for them to ask. "He went in there," I said.

One of them rushed in, came out, and shouted, "There's a door open. He went inside. Go 'round to the front."

They must have given the alarm, because in a few minutes, three police cars drove up, there were plainclothesmen on the scene, and the building was surrounded.

I knew I shouldn't be hanging around. Innocent bystanders get in the way of the police. Just the same, I was there when it started and, from what I heard the police saying, I knew they were after this man, Stockton. He was a loner who'd pulled off some pretty spectacular jewel robberies over the last few months. I knew about it because Dad is a detective on the force, and he was on the case.

"Slippery fellow," he said, "but when you work alone, there's no one to double-cross you."

I said, "Doesn't he have to work with someone, Dad? He's got to have a fence—someone to peddle the jewels."

"If he has," said Dad, "we haven't located him. And why don't you get on with your homework?" (He always says that when he thinks I'm getting too interested in his cases.)

Well, they had him now. Some jeweler must have pushed the alarm button.

The alley he ran into was closed on all sides but the street, and he hadn't come out. There was a door there that was open, and he must have gone in. The police had the possible exits guarded. They even had a couple of men on the roof.

I was just beginning to wonder if Dad would be involved, when another car came up, and he got out. First thing he saw me and stopped dead. "Larry! What are you doing here?"

"I was on the spot, Dad. Stockton ran past me into the alley."

"Well, get out of here. There's liable to be shooting."

I backed away, but I didn't back off all the way. Once my father went into the building, I got into his car. The driver knew me, and he said, "You better go home, Larry. I'm going to have to help with the search, so I can't stay here to keep an eye on you."

"Sure, you go on," I said. "I'll be leaving in a minute." But I didn't. I wanted to do some thinking first.

Nobody leaves doors open in New York City. If that door into the alley was open, Stockton must have opened it. That meant he had to have a key; there wasn't time to pick the lock. That must mean he worked out of that building.

I looked at the building. It was an old one, four stories high. It had small businesses in it, and you could still see the painted signs in the windows in the fading light.

On the second-floor window, it said, "Klein and Levy, Tailors." Above that was a theatrical costumer, and on the top floor was a jeweler's. That jeweler's made sense out of it.

If Stockton had a key to the building, he probably worked with that jeweler. Dad would figure all that out.

I waited for the sound of shots, pretty scared Dad might get hurt. But nothing happened. Maybe Stockton would see he was cornered and just give in. I hoped so. At least they didn't have to evacuate the building. Late on Saturday, I supposed it would be deserted.

After a while, I got tired of waiting. I chose a moment when no policemen were looking and moved quickly to the building entrance. Dad would be hopping mad when he saw me, but I was curious. I figured they had Stockton, and I wanted to see him.

They didn't have him.

There was a fat man in a vest in the lobby. He looked scared, and I guess he was the watchman. He kept saying, "I didn't see anybody."

Policemen were coming down the stairs and out of the old elevator, all shaking their heads.

My father was pretty angry. He said, "No one has anything?"

A police sergeant said, "Donovan said no one got out on the roof. All the doors and windows are covered."

"If he didn't get out," said my father, in a low voice that carried, "then he's in the building."

"We can't find him," said the sergeant. "He's nowhere inside."

My father said, "It isn't a big building——"

"We had the watchman's keys. We've looked everywhere."

"Then how do we know he went into the building in the first place? Who saw him go in?"

There was a silence. A lot of policemen were milling about the lobby now, but no one said anything. So I spoke up. "I did, Dad."

Dad whirled and looked at me and made a funny sound in the back of his throat that meant I was in for it for still

being there. "You said you saw him run into the alley," he said. "That's not the same thing."

"He didn't come out, Dad. There was no place else for him to go."

"But you didn't actually *see* him go in, did you?"

"He couldn't go up the side of the buildings. There wouldn't have been time for him to reach the roof before the police——"

But Dad wasn't listening. "Did *anyone* actually see him go in?"

Of course no one said anything, and I could see my father was going to call the whole thing off, and then when he got me home I was going to get the talking-to of my life.

The thought of that talking-to must have stimulated my brain, I guess. I looked about the lobby desperately, and said, "But, Dad, he *did* go into the building, and he didn't disappear. There he is right now. That man there." I pointed, and then I dropped down and rolled out of the way.

There wasn't any shooting. The man I pointed to was close to the door—he must have been edging toward it—and now he made a dash for it. He almost made it, but a policeman who had been knocked down grabbed his leg and then everyone piled on him. Later they had the jeweler, too.

I went home after Stockton was caught, and when my father got home much later, he did have some things to say about my risking my life. But he also said, "You got onto that theatrical costume bit very nicely, Larry."

I said, "Well, I was sure he went into the building and was familiar with it. He could get into the costumer's if he had to, and they would be bound to have police-

men's uniforms. I figured if he could dump his jacket and pants and get into a policeman's uniform quickly, he could just walk out of the building."

Dad said, "You're right. Even after he got outside, he could pretend he was dealing with the crowd and then just walk away."

Mom said, "But how did you know which policeman it was, Larry? Don't tell me you know every policeman by sight."

"I didn't have to, Mom," I said. "I figured if he got a policeman's uniform at the costumer's, he had to work fast and grab any one he saw. And they wouldn't have much of an assortment of sizes anyway. So I just looked around for a policeman whose uniform didn't fit, and when I saw one with trouser legs stopping above his ankles, I knew he was Stockton."

Close Up

1. Larry sees Stockton, a notorious jewel thief, run into an alley. (a) Why does he assume Stockton went into the building? (b) What two facts make him think Stockton has a key to the building?

2. Larry notices signs for three small businesses located in the building. Which business does he think is Stockton's fence?

3. The police can't find Stockton in the building. (a) How do the business signs give Larry a clue to Stockton's whereabouts? (b) How does he identify Stockton?

The Short Story

A short story is a brief work of fiction about made-up characters and events. The characters often face a problem that they struggle to overcome or *resolve* by the end of the story.

1. Larry is the most important character in this story. Name two other important characters.

2. Larry has a problem. What does he know he must do to avoid getting a talking-to from his father?

3. Find the two paragraphs that describe the point at which Larry resolves his problem.

Activities

1. Imagine you are your favorite story detective (for example, Nancy Drew, Frank or Joe Hardy, Miss Marple, Sherlock Holmes). Tell the class about your life and about one of the cases you solved.

2. Make a book cover for your favorite mystery story.

SENTENCE MEANING

Using Quotation Marks

Opening (") and closing (") quotation marks set off the exact words a character says from the rest of the story. For example, notice the quotation marks around the exact words the father says in the following: "If he didn't get out," said my father, in a low voice that carried, "then he's in the building."

1. In each of the following items, find the exact words of the speaker. Notice that these words are enclosed in quotation marks. Write these words on a separate piece of paper.
   a. One of them rushed in, came out, and shouted, "There's a door open. He went inside. Go 'round to the front."
   b. "Slippery fellow," he said, "but when you work alone, there's no one to double-cross you."
   c. "If he has," said Dad, "we haven't located him. And why don't you get on with your homework?"
   d. "Sure, you go on," I said. "I'll be leaving in a minute."
   e. A police sergeant said, "Donovan said no one got out on the roof. All the doors and windows are covered."

2. Sometimes the speaker's exact words are quoted, but the speaker is not identified. In the lines below, Larry and his father talk to each other. Find who is speaking by noting the order in which the two characters speak.

   > Dad whirled and looked at me and made a funny sound in the back of his throat that meant I was in for it for still being there. "You said you saw him run into the alley," he said. "That's not the same thing."
   > "He didn't come out, Dad. There was no place else for him to go."
   > "But you didn't actually *see* him go in, did you?"
   > "He couldn't go up the side of the buildings. There wouldn't have been time for him to reach the roof before the police——"
   > But Dad wasn't listening. "Did *anyone* actually see him go in?"

   a. Who says that Stockton didn't come out?
   b. Who asks, "But you didn't actually see him go in, did you?"
   c. Who says that Stockton couldn't go up the side of buildings?
   d. Who asks if anyone actually saw Stockton?

WORD ATTACK

Using a Glossary

The glossary appears at the back of this book. It lists in alphabetical order many of the words you may be unfamiliar with in the selections. It gives the pronunciation, part of speech, and meaning of each word.

Take the word *stimulate* from the following sentence. "The thought of that talking-to must have *stimulated* my brain, I guess." The glossary entry reads:

stim u late (stĭm′yə-lāt′) *v.*: To excite, rouse, or spur to action.

The letters in parentheses (stĭm′yə-lāt′) are the special marks that tell you how to pronounce the word. You can find the key to these marks on the first page of the glossary.

The abbreviation *v.* tells you the word *stimulate* is a verb. (The abbreviation *n.* means noun, *adj.* means adjective, and *adv.* means adverb.) You probably know that the ending *-d* or *-ed* is a past-tense verb ending. To find the meaning of *stimulated*, simply add *-d* or *-ed* to the verbs in the definition (excited, roused, spurred).

▶ On a separate piece of paper, copy the glossary entry for each of the *italicized words* below.
   a. "Innocent *bystanders* get in the way of the police."
   b. "He was a loner who'd pulled off some pretty *spectacular* jewel robberies."
   c. "There's *liable* to be shooting."
   d. "At least they didn't have to *evacuate* the building."
   e. "And they wouldn't have much of an *assortment* of sizes anyway."

Eugenie Clark and the Sharks

Margery Facklam

Sunlight sparkled on bright blue-green water as a small boat dropped anchor. Three divers wearing black wetsuits adjusted their scuba gear. One diver leaned over the side of the boat and peered into the water. It was so clear he could see the rainbow assortment of fishes swimming around the coral reef.

"Sharks below," he called.

"No problem," a second diver answered calmly. "Use this," she said, handing cans of shark repellent to the others.

When they had sprayed themselves all over with the repellent, the divers put on their masks and flipped backward out of the boat into the warm water. Two tiger sharks began to circle the divers. Silently, they picked up speed to attack, but as they closed in on the swimmers, they slammed on invisible brakes. Suddenly, their mouths seemed to be frozen open. They shook their heads, as though trying to get rid of something. And the divers went about exploring the coral reef, unconcerned about the sharks.

So far, the scene is only make-believe. There is no shark repellent that really keeps sharks away, but there may be soon, because Dr. Eugenie Clark was curious about a little fish called the Moses sole.

In 1960, Eugenie was netting fish in the Red Sea, when she came across the fish known scientifically as *Pardachirus;* local fishermen called it the Moses sole. When she touched the fish, a milky substance oozed from the pores along its fins. It was slippery, and her fingers felt tingly and tight, the way they might feel if they fell asleep.

The Moses sole is a flatfish, like the flounder you buy at the market, and it got its name from a traditional story told in Israel. According to the legend, when Moses parted the Red Sea, this little fish was caught in the middle and split in half. Each half became a sole.

Eugenie is an ichthyologist, a scientist who studies fish. She was working at the Marine Laboratory at the Hebrew University in Elat, Israel, when she decided to find out more about the sole's poison. A scientist had reported the poisonous substance in 1871, but no one had studied it further. When Eugenie tested it on sea urchins, starfish, and reef fishes, she found that small doses killed these creatures quickly. She began to wonder how it would work on larger fishes, especially sharks.

Three reef whitetip sharks lived in a tank at the laboratory, and they ate anything dropped into the water. One day as Eugenie was experimenting with the fish, she found one small Moses sole that had not been completely "milked" of its poison. She put a string through its gills, which did not hurt it, and lowered the fish into the sharks' tank. The moment the sole touched the water, the sharks swept toward it with mouths open wide. But when they got within a few feet of the fish on the string, the sharks' jaws seemed to be frozen open. They dashed away, shaking their heads as though trying to get rid of something awful. For six hours, Eugenie watched the sharks approach the sole, and the reactions were the same each time the sharks swam near the poisonous fish.

The use of this poison as a shark repellent was an exciting idea. So far, everything invented to keep sharks away has not worked on all sharks all the time. Streams of air bubbles used as a barrier along beaches eventually attracted sharks, who seemed to enjoy the feeling of the bubbles as they swam through them. Different dyes that swimmers can release in the water only hide the swimmer from the shark temporarily but cannot keep a really hungry shark away. Lifeboats on ships and Navy planes are sometimes equipped with plastic bags large enough to hold a person. Stranded in the water, the person inflates the top ring and crawls into the tubelike bag. A shark cannot follow the scent of a human inside this bag, nor can it see kicking legs or blood from a wound. But such bags are not carried as regular equipment by swimmers at an ocean beach. A substance that can be sprayed on, the way mosquito repellent is, would be perfect.

But before Eugenie could experiment further on the Moses sole, she had to leave the Elat laboratory, and other work claimed her attention for many years. It wasn't until 1974 that she was able to collect some of the fish and test the shark-stopping poison. After dozens of experiments in tanks and in the sea, a final test was arranged to find out how free-swimming sharks reacted to the live Moses sole.

An eighty-foot shark line, with ten shorter lines dropping from it, was stretched close to the rocky Israeli coastline three feet underwater, at a point where a ledge dropped off to a depth of one thousand feet. Each of the ten dropper lines was baited with parrot fish, groupers, nonpoisonous flatfish, and the Moses sole. As Eugenie, her fourteen-year-old son, and other assistants snorkled quietly along the underwater ledge and watched the sharks approach the bait at dawn or sunset, they saw the poison at work.

One by one the fish were gulped down by hungry sharks, but the Moses sole remained untouched. When Eugenie wiped the skin of a Moses sole with alcohol to remove the poison and tossed the fish into the water, a shark would instantly eat it. It was an exciting discovery—a substance that could really stop a shark. Further work is being done now to make a chemical compound like the poison of the Moses sole that can be used as a reliable commercial shark repellent.

Close Up

1. What did Eugenie Clark discover when she tested the Moses sole's poison on small fish?

2. Eugenie Clark put a Moses sole into a tank with three sharks. (a) How did the sharks react when they saw the Moses sole? (b) Why didn't they eat the sole?

3. (a) List the three methods used today to keep sharks away. (b) Why would a shark-stopping spray be better than these methods?

The Essay

An essay is a short composition about one topic. In an essay, the author examines the topic and reaches conclusions about it.

1. What is the topic of this essay?
    a. Becoming an ichthyologist.
    b. Finding a shark repellent.
    c. Naming the Moses sole.

2. Reread the last sentence of this essay. What conclusions does the author make about her topic?

Activities

1. You are a magazine writer. Your assignment is to interview Eugenie Clark. Make a list of questions you would ask her to get a good story.

2. Find out how you can become an ichthyologist and report your findings to your class. (You might gain information from a book on careers, the vertical file in the library, and your guidance counselor.)

SENTENCE MEANING

Using Punctuation Marks

Certain punctuation marks tell you when to pause when reading a sentence. A comma (,) tells you to take a slight pause. A semicolon (;) tells you to take a longer pause to separate two complete ideas that are closely related. A period (.) tells you to come to a full stop, since one sentence is ending.

---

1. Copy each sentence below on a separate piece of paper. Then find each sentence in the essay and add the correct punctuation marks to your paper. (If you add a period, capitalize the first letter after the period.)

    a. Silently they picked up speed to attack but as they closed in on the swimmers they slammed on invisible brakes.

    b. In 1960 Eugenie was netting fish in the Red Sea when she came across the fish known scientifically as *Pardachirus* local fishermen called it the Moses sole.

    c. She put a string through its gills which did not hurt it and lowered the fish into the sharks' tank.

    d. It wasn't until 1974 that she was able to collect some of the fish and test the shark-stopping poison after dozens of experiments in tanks and in the sea a final test was arranged to find out how free-swimming sharks reacted to the live Moses sole.

2. Read aloud each sentence in Exercise **1**. Make sure to take the pause indicated by the punctuation you have added.

3. The words in the following two groups of sentences are exactly the same.

    They dashed away, shaking their heads as though trying to get rid of something awful. For six hours, Eugenie watched the sharks approach the sole, and the reactions were the same each time the sharks swam near the poisonous fish.

    They dashed away, shaking their heads as though trying to get rid of something awful for six hours. Eugenie watched the sharks approach the sole, and the reactions were the same each time the sharks swam near the poisonous fish.

    a. Which group of sentences says that the sharks tried to get rid of something awful for six hours—the first or the second?

    b. Which group of sentences says that Eugenie watched the sharks for six hours—the first or the second?

WORD ATTACK

Using Root Words to Build Words

The root, or base part of a word, is often used to build other words. For example, *graph* is a root word that means "writing." This root is used to build the words *phonograph*, *telegraph*, *photograph*, and *graphology*. Do you know what each of these words has to do with writing?

1. Each of the following words was built from the root *ichthyo*, meaning "fish." Find the meaning of each of these words in the dictionary.
    a. ichthyologist
    b. ichthyology
    c. ichthyornis
    d. ichthyosaur
    e. ichthyic

2. Use each word above in an original sentence.

The Shark

John Ciardi

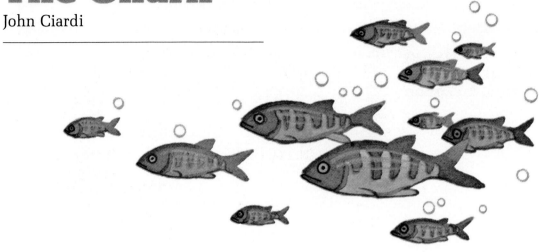

My sweet, let me tell you about the Shark.
Though his eyes are bright, his thought is dark.
He's quiet—that speaks well of him.
So does the fact that he can swim.
5   But though he swims without a sound,
Wherever he swims he looks around
With those two bright eyes and that one dark thought.
He has only one but he thinks it a lot.
And the thought he thinks but can never complete
10   Is his long dark thought of something to eat.
Most anything does. And I have to add
That when he eats, his manners are bad.
He's a gulper, a ripper, a snatcher, a grabber.
Yes, his manners are drab. But his thought is drabber.
15   That one dark thought he can never complete
Of something—anything—somehow to eat.

Be careful when you swim, my sweet.

Close Up

1. (a) What is "that one dark thought that he (the shark) can never complete"? (b) Why does the poem warn you to "be careful when you swim"?

2. The shark has two good qualities—he's quiet and he can swim. How do these qualities make the shark dangerous?

The Poem

A poem is usually arranged in lines. Sometimes these lines have a definite rhythm and a definite rhyme. Rhythm is the pattern of stressed (ˊ) and unstressed (˘) sounds within a line. For example,

"Be careful when you swim, my sweet."

Rhyme is the repetition of sounds. Rhyme usually occurs at the end of lines, but it may also occur within a line.

1. Read "The Shark" aloud. Let your voice carry the rhythm of the poem.

2. Find the words in the poem that rhyme with each word below.
   a. shark
   b. him
   c. sound
   d. complete
   e. grabber

The Invisible Man

H. G. Wells

Dramatized by Lewy Olfson

Characters

Narrator

Griffin

Mrs. Hall

Jimson

Millie

First Man

Woman

Second Man

Cuss

Mrs. Mallory

Kemp

Constable Adye

Narrator: The stranger appeared early in February, late one stormy night, carrying a black suitcase in his thickly gloved hand. He was wrapped up from head to foot, and the brim of his soft felt hat hid every inch of his face, except for his eyes, which were covered by dark glasses. He staggered into the Coach and Horses Inn, more dead than alive, with snow piled on his shoulders. Mrs. Hall, the innkeeper's wife, thought she had never seen so strange-looking a man. But at this time of the year, travelers were few and far between, and she was in no mood to question her guest's appearance.

Griffin (roaring out): A fire, in the name of charity! I want a room and a fire!

Mrs. Hall: If you can pay, sir, I'm sure you'll find my inn comfortable.

Griffin: I can pay well enough. Here are three gold pieces.

Mrs. Hall (taken aback): Three gold pieces! Yes, sir. Right away, sir. Please step this way, and I'll show you the finest room we have.

Griffin: It needn't be fine. Just so long as there's a fire—and a good stout door with a lock. I wish to be warmed and fed and left alone.

Mrs. Hall: Yes, sir. I'll have the

porter light a fire immediately. *(Pause)* Will this room suit?

Griffin: Yes, perfectly. Perfectly.

Mrs. Hall *(calling out):* Jimson! A gentleman in Room Eight, Jimson! Come light a fire! *(On mike)* He'll be here directly, sir.

Griffin: He can't get here soon enough to suit me. I'm half-frozen.

Mrs. Hall: I should think so, sir, traveling on such a night as this. If you'll excuse me, I'll see to some supper for you.

Griffin: I'll excuse you, right enough. I don't want people hanging about.

Mrs. Hall: May I take your hat and cloak, sir, to dry them out by the kitchen fire? You're soaked through, I shouldn't wonder.

Griffin *(haughtily):* Don't touch me, madam. I shall dry my clothes at my own fire—if I ever *get* a fire.

Mrs. Hall *(offended):* Very good, sir. You needn't be so touchy. I was only trying to be friendly. No harm in that, I hope, sir?

Griffin: I do not look to innkeepers' wives for friendship. Indeed, I do not look for friendship at all. I will pay you well for my room, never fear. For the rest, you have only to leave me alone. I am expecting my belongings in a day or two. The instant they arrive, you are to knock on my door and tell me. They are very important to me—to my work.

Mrs. Hall: Your work, sir?

Griffin *(coldly):* Yes, madam, my work. I have a great deal of work to do, and I wish to be left alone. Utterly—wholly—completely alone.

Narrator: The stranger got his wish. Except for the delivery of his meals, his door remained closed. For two days,

none but the porter had so much as a glimpse of him. And even the porter had strange things to tell of what he had seen.

Jimson: Kept his back to me the whole time, he did. Wouldn't let me see so much as an inch of his face. Got me wondering, I tell you. I kept asking him questions, and making observations about the weather until I thought he'd burst. He was so anxious for me to get out. At last he couldn't control his anger, and he whirled around. Would you believe it? He talked to me through a handkerchief? Held the thing right up to his face. Like he didn't want me to see him! *(In an awesome whisper)* You know what I think? I think he's invisible!

Mrs. Hall *(laughing):* Did you hear that, Millie, my girl? Invisible, you say? You're a superstitious fool, Jimson. Your mind's wandering.

Millie *(laughing):* I suspect we should send a letter to the Queen, Mrs. Hall, inviting her down to meet our special guest. It isn't every inn that has the privilege of playing host to an invisible man.

Narrator: But though the women scoffed at Jimson, their curiosity about the stranger changed to fear. On the third day after his arrival, the stranger's belongings arrived. Completely muffled, as was his custom, the stranger supervised the unloading.

Griffin *(sternly):* Come along with those boxes there. I've been waiting long enough.

Mrs. Hall: There certainly are a great many boxes, sir.

Griffin: Perhaps I should explain, Mrs. Hall, that I am an experimental investigator. The boxes contain my apparatus and appliances.

Mrs. Hall: Oh, yes, sir. Only there are so many boxes—well, it certainly will make a great deal of trouble cleaning up after you.

Griffin: Put it down on the bill. A shilling—put down a shilling for cleaning up the packing straw. That ought to be enough. And for heaven's sake, don't be forever worrying me. If there's damage, put it on the bill. Charge me whatever you like—but stop asking me questions. *Leave me alone!*

Narrator: The little town of Iping quickly came to accept the man at the inn as a standing topic of conversation. But after a week, a new mystery broke out, which occupied everyone's attention. Conversation was now given over to the rash of burglaries that had erupted in the neighborhood.

First Man: It's the most amazing thing. Nobody's broken into the post office for years—and it must have been during the daytime, too. Seven pounds sixpence[1] was taken!

Woman: And what about the business down at old Mrs. Harney's? Went out of the kitchen for five minutes, and when she came back, a fresh-baked kidney pie was gone.

Mrs. Hall: That's nothing to what happened at Dr. Huntington's. Had a bank note in front of him on his desk. Turned his back a moment—and when he looked around it was gone! And the window closed the whole time!

Second Man: Have you heard the latest? It was at the hospital. Three folks were sitting in the front waiting room, while old Mrs. Hopkins was paying her bill. Nurse Craig had just put the money

down on the counter, when it rose straight up in the air—all by itself—and walked out.

Narrator: The robberies increased, but the police found themselves helpless. There were no clues of any kind; sums of money just seemed to vanish into thin air. Several weeks went by, and then one day, Dr. Cuss, who had been going from house to house taking up a collection for the new nursing home, came running down the stairs of the Coach and Horses, his eyes ablaze with fright.

Mrs. Hall (*frightened*): Why, Dr. Cuss! You look as though you'd seen a ghost!

Cuss (*frightened*): Worse, Mrs. Hall! Worse! The man—the man in Room Eight!

Mrs. Hall: Scared you off, did he? He's very particular about being left alone. I should have warned you.

Cuss: I—I thought I'd go in to see him for a minute. I heard he was rich—thought he might give me something for the collection. I knocked on the door, and waited. There was no answer.

Mrs. Hall: Perhaps he didn't hear you.

Cuss: Just what I thought myself, so I—I took the liberty of walking in. He was working, and the minute he heard me behind him, he jammed both of his hands into his coat. But not before I was able to see—to see——

Mrs. Hall (*breathlessly*): To see what, Dr. Cuss?

Cuss (*terrified*): He has no hands, Mrs. Hall. There were just two empty sleeves! And—and when he turned around, I—I saw something else. He has no face! The man in Room Eight—no hands—no face! You can see right

---

1. Seven pounds six pence: About thirty-five dollars.

through him, except where there's clothing covering him. Jimson was right—he's an invisible man!

Narrator: The strange story told by Dr. Cuss spread like wildfire. Suddenly it seemed to explain the petty thefts that had been going on. Townsmen were soon deputized, with one purpose in mind: to arrest and capture the incredible Invisible Man.

Cuss (in a whisper): Should we knock on the door, or shove right in?

Jimson: No use knocking—it would only warn him.

First Man: Jimson's right. He'd have a chance to make himself invisible.

Second Man: We'll do better to rush in—take him by surprise.

Cuss: Very well. Courage, men. We'll capture him—if there's anything to capture. Now then: one, two, three, push!

Sound: Door being flung open.

Jimson (loudly): We've got you now, Invisible Man!

Griffin: Oho, my secret is out, is it?

Cuss (alarmed): I don't see him!

First Man: Where is he?

Second Man: The voice came from that direction!

Jimson: Look. That bandage hanging in midair! Hurry!

First Man: He's moving too fast!

Griffin (with an evil laugh): Is it a fight you want? Fools, you're no match for me!

First Man: The bandage has dropped to the floor.

Second Man: Look, he's taking off the other one!

Cuss: We'll never catch him once he gets them off. He'll be invisible again!

Griffin (laughing): There, that's the last of it. Now, come and catch me if you can. Fools, all of you! Here, Dr. Cuss—a blow with the poker to teach you to meddle where you aren't wanted.

Sound: Sharp blow, followed by body falling.

Jimson: He's killed the doctor!

Griffin: I'll kill all of you before I'm through. You may have found out my secret, but you'll never track me down. (Fading, laughing) You'll never catch me. Nobody can catch the Invisible Man! Ha-ha, ha-ha!

Narrator: Now there could be no doubt. The whole of Iping was convinced that they had been visited by an invisible man. Word spread rapidly from town to town. In neighboring Burdock, the story was presented in the evening paper, where it caught the eye of Dr. Kemp.

Mrs. Mallory: Have you heard about the strange goings-on at Iping, Dr. Kemp? An invisible man, they say.

Kemp: Yes, Mrs. Mallory, I have just been reading about it. Rubbish! Superstitious rubbish!

Mrs. Mallory: I thought so myself, Dr. Kemp. But they say——

Kemp: I don't care what they say. It's simply a case of mass hysteria—a readily explainable phenomenon, I can assure you.

Mrs. Mallory: All the same sir, I thought I'd leave a bit earlier than usual tonight, if you don't mind. Just in case the Invisible Man is walking around. I shouldn't like to meet him, you know.

Kemp: I tell you it's impossible, Mrs. Mallory. Still and all, you may leave if you like. Just see that the windows are all closed in the library. I'm going there in a moment to do some work.

Mrs. Mallory: I've already closed them, sir, and turned down your bed too.

(Fading) I'm sure you think I'm foolish, Dr. Kemp.

Kemp (lightly): That you are, Mrs. Mallory. If you should bump into this invisible man, you must be certain to give him my regards.

Narrator: It was two o'clock before Dr. Kemp had finished his work for the night. He rose, yawned, and went upstairs to bed. He had already removed his coat and vest, when suddenly he noticed that something seemed odd in the room.

Kemp: Strange . . . something . . . seems not quite right. Hello, what's this? The bed is depressed—as though someone had been sitting on it. And there *is* a sound—as though someone were breathing heavily. (Laughs) My imagination's playing tricks on me. All that talk of an invisible man has even rattled *me*.

Sound: Door slam, slightly off mike.

Kemp (startled): How did that door come to fly shut? There's no breeze—the

window isn't open. *(Firmly)* Is there someone in this room?

Griffin *(amazed)*: By Jove, it's Kemp!

Kemp *(quickly)*: Who said that? Where are you?

Griffin: I say, this *is* a piece of luck. Fancy seeing Kemp again, after all these years.

Kemp *(a bit frightened)*: How do you know my name? Who is it?

Griffin: I should think you'd be able to guess who I am, after all the talk you've heard. I'm the Invisible Man. *(Pause)* That doesn't frighten you?

Kemp *(formally)*: I am a scientist. I am never frightened by testimony of my own senses. I did not believe you existed until now; but as I have been forced to change my mind, I see no reason to lose hold of my senses.

Griffin: You were always a man of nerve, Kemp. Don't you recognize my voice? I'm Griffin, of University College. We were students there.

Kemp: Griffin?

Griffin: I was a bit younger than you were. You must remember me—I was an albino[2] with white hair, pale skin. I am still a man like yourself, only now I am invisible.

Kemp: I think I do remember you, Griffin. But how did all this come about?

Griffin: It's horrible enough, but I shall tell you the whole story. But you must promise not to tell a soul.

Kemp *(scolding)*: My dear fellow, I make no bargains with anyone.

---

2. albino (ăl-bī′nō) n. A person who lacks normal coloration. Usually this person has abnormally light skin and hair and abnormal eye coloring (usually pink or red).

Griffin *(intensely)*: You will make a bargain with *me*, Dr. Kemp. Do not forget for an instant that though you cannot see me, I can see you all the time. One false move—one sign of giving warning to anyone—and you are as good as dead. There, I see by your face you understand. Now get me some food. I must eat. Then I shall tell you my story.

Narrator: Thus it happened that in the middle of the night, Dr. Kemp found himself a prisoner by his own fire, listening to the most incredible story he had ever heard.

Griffin: You may remember that at the college I was much interested in problems of light. As an albino, I suppose, I was naturally attracted to the subject of pigments. I began to do some experiments in changing the color of various substances. Finally, quite by accident, I hit on a method of rendering any inert object—a piece of wood, a bit of meat, even a lump of coal—absolutely as colorless, as transparent, as water. Suddenly, I had a brilliant idea: If I could transform inert matter, why not a living animal? A human being? In short—why not make myself invisible?

Kemp: It must have taken you endless research, my dear fellow.

Griffin: I worked at it for years—and at last I succeeded. I will not bore you with the details of my experiments. I am too tired, and besides, they are all written down in my notebooks, and you shall read them. I was forced to leave those precious notebooks behind in Iping when I made my escape; but with your help, I shall recover them.

Kemp: You must have had many adventures as an invisible man.

Griffin: Many, many adventures. But it is not going as I had planned. I am invisible only when I am undressed. With clothes on, I can be seen as easily as you. Do you know what it is like to run through the streets and fields on a night like this, without a stitch on one's back? I may die of cold. Ah, yes, you nod your head. I cannot eat unless I am alone, for I would be found out by the spoon floating in midair. In short, I am confounded at every turn. Dogs nip at me; they pick up my scent, even if they don't see me. There is no end of trouble. That is why this is such a stroke of luck, my running into you.

Kemp (startled): I! What have I to do with it?

Griffin (intensely): With you in on my secret, I can take refuge in your house. I can sleep in your bed, eat at your table, warm myself by your fire, and none will be the wiser. Alone, there is so little I can do. But with a confederate, a thousand things are possible.

Kemp: What things?

Griffin (eagerly): Together, Kemp, we will rule the world. All who disobey us, we shall kill.

Kemp: Kill! Surely you jest!

Griffin: No jest at all. Suppose a message were slipped under the door of the mayor's house, saying, "Deliver ten thousand pounds to the first empty table at the inn by tomorrow noon, or you will die." He wouldn't do it, would he? So, the Invisible Man kills him. Rest assured, Kemp, that the next instructions from the Invisible Man will be carried out to the letter.

Kemp: You're mad, Griffin, mad! I'll report you!

Griffin (quickly, in close): You shall do nothing of the kind, Kemp. Either you will do my bidding, or you will become my first victim.

Narrator: That night, the terrified Kemp was unable to sleep. He could not escape the knowledge that he was truly in the power of this invisible madman, Griffin. One thought became clearer and clearer: He must get help.

Tiptoeing to the door of the room in which Griffin lay, Kemp was reassured, by the steady sound of breathing, that the Invisible Man was asleep. Quickly he returned to the library, where he wrote an urgent note.

Kemp (in a whisper, close on mike): "Mrs. Mallory, I . . . am a prisoner . . . of the . . . Invisible Man. Do not enter . . . the house. Send . . . help . . . at once."

Narrator: Slipping the note around the outside doorknob, where his housekeeper would be sure to see it, Kemp made his way back to his room, and for the first time that night, managed to fall asleep.

Narrator: The Invisible Man, tired from his adventures, slept late. When at last he entered the dining room—Kemp knew he had come in by the rustling of the drapes—his voice was calmer than it had been the night before.

Griffin: Well, Kemp, have you thought over what I have said?

Kemp: Yes, Griffin, I have—and I can't say I like it.

Griffin: No one asked you to like it.

Sound: Door opening, and several male voices, off mike.

Griffin (startled): What was that?

Kemp (trying to maintain his calm): Nothing, Griffin, nothing.

Griffin (agitated): I heard a door open. Betrayed me, have you?

Kemp: No, Griffin, no.

Griffin: You are a liar. They'll never catch me, Kemp. No one will ever catch me. I swear to you, I shall pay you for this treachery.

Constable Adye (fading on): Dr. Kemp, your housekeeper told us to come.

Kemp (quickly): There's no time to lose, Constable! He's by the door!

Adye (calling out): Surround the door, men. Don't let him through!

Sound: Dull thud.

Kemp: Throwing books, are you, Griffin? He must be somewhere by the bookcase!

Griffin (laughing): You'll never catch me, Kemp. Never!

Adye: Something's brushed past me!

Kemp: Surround the room, men. Feel through the air with your hands—it's the only way.

Adye: He must be by the door again. To the door!

Sound: Crash of glass.

Adye: He's broken the window. Look, Dr. Kemp. In the mud beneath your windowsill. A footprint.

Kemp (in despair): Escaped! Heaven help us all, Constable Adye. The Invisible Man has escaped. His reign of terror has begun.

Narrator: Now that the truth about the Invisible Man was known, Dr. Kemp resolved to combat him with every tool at his disposal. Griffin had told what it was like to live the life of an invisible man, and Kemp was able to present this information to the deputies.

Kemp: First, we must set a watch on every train and carriage leaving the countryside. He must not get through. Then we must prevent him from eating or sleeping. Food must be locked up. Houses must be barred against him. Clothes are not to be put out to dry, but must be kept indoors. Pray heaven it freezes tonight! Spread the roads with broken glass—he is barefoot. Go through the fields with sticks, beating the air and ground for every inch. There is no telling where he may be. And bloodhounds—we must get out the dogs, for they can smell what cannot be seen. These things sound cruel, I know. But it is our only chance.

Narrator: Days went by with no results. Suddenly, on the fourth night of the strange siege, a note was pushed under Dr. Kemp's locked door.

Kemp (reading): "Doctor Kemp. You have brought this situation about. By now, another man would have been caught—or starved. But I am no ordinary man. Be warned: I shall have my revenge. You cannot escape me. I shall kill you tonight at nine o'clock. No matter where you are, no matter what you are doing, you cannot escape."

Mrs. Mallory (terrified): Is there nothing we can do, Dr. Kemp? Surely you are not going to sit back and wait for him to kill you.

Kemp: That is precisely what I am going to do: sit back and wait. But he will not kill me. The man is mad, and in his madness, he does not see that he is giving us the very chance we need.

Adye (confused): What chance, Dr. Kemp? It seems to me that all is lost.

Kemp: Not lost, Constable Adye. Listen, I have a plan . . .

Narrator: Dr. Kemp outlined his plan to Constable Adye, who immediately saw how practical it was.

Adye: But let us not forget, Dr. Kemp, there is great risk to you.

Kemp: The risk cannot be helped. If we do not do as I have suggested, I am a doomed man in any case.

Narrator: That night——

Sound: Clock striking nine in background, under following speech.

Narrator: —as the clock strikes nine, Dr. Kemp opens his front door, and slowly, unaccompanied and unarmed, begins to walk down the path. When he has reached the street—dark and empty—he addresses the sky.

Kemp *(in an even voice):* Griffin, I know when I am beaten. You have sworn to kill me tonight, and I cannot escape you. I have come here to keep my appointment with you.

Narrator *(in close):* Suddenly Kemp feels a pair of man's hands circling his throat. Slowly, slowly, they intensify in pressure.

Kemp *(gasping):* Harder—harder, Griffin. Soon—it will—be over.

Narrator: Slowly Kemp's body bends beneath the pressure of the murderer's strength.

Griffin *(in close):* You were a fool to try to capture me, Kemp. If you had listened to me, you might have ruled the world. But now you have brought about only your own destruction.

Sound: A volley of pistol shots, followed by the thud of a body falling and a moan from Griffin.

Adye *(fading on quickly):* Kemp! Are you all right?

Kemp *(gasping, weakly):* Yes—yes. What about Griffin? Did you get him?

Adye *(soberly):* I can feel his body here on the gravel. There is no heartbeat.

Mrs. Mallory *(fading on):* Oh, Dr. Kemp. I've never been so frightened in my life. Are you all right?

Kemp *(breathing heavily):* Thank heavens I am, Mrs. Mallory.

Adye: It was a stroke of genius, Doctor. Genius!

Kemp: I knew that he would try to kill me with his bare hands. If he had used a weapon, he would have revealed himself to you—and he must have guessed I would be watched. But what he did not realize was that, by watching what happened to me, you would be able to guess his position and could take careful aim.

Adye: Poor madman! To think he was brilliant enough to make such an important scientific discovery, but then he couldn't use it for his own good or for the benefit of mankind.

Mrs. Mallory *(shrieking in horror):* Look, Dr. Kemp. The dead man!

Adye *(in awe):* He—he's becoming visible again.

Kemp: How horrible. Look at the face. Such madness—such torment— such pain and grief reflected in its twisted features.

Mrs. Mallory: I cannot bear to look. It's so hideous! I—I almost wish he were invisible again.

Kemp *(soberly):* Ah, if the world can learn its lesson from the story of this evil genius, we will never again know anyone mad enough to try to become what Griffin became. He has proved, only too conclusively, that there can never be any happiness for anyone who wishes to rule the world. Certainly not for an invisible man.

Close Up

1. Why do Mrs. Hall and Millie laugh when Jimson tells them that Griffin is invisible?

2. (a) How do the townspeople learn that Griffin is really invisible? (b) What do they suspect Griffin has done?

3. Griffin visits Kemp and reveals how he discovered the formula. What does Griffin plan to do with this powerful weapon?

4. Griffin's hunger for power has turned him into a mad, tormented man, who is finally destroyed. (a) How is Griffin's fate a lesson for all those who seek happiness through misuse of power? (b) Do you agree with the lesson? Why or why not?

The Play

A play is meant to be performed. Actors and actresses take the parts of the various characters. Through their words and their actions, you learn what the characters are like, what happens to them, and how they resolve their problems. When you read a play, you should try to hear the words in your mind—just as you think the actors and actresses would say them.

"The Invisible Man" is a radio play. It includes directions for sound effects. These directions are printed in *italics*. For example, "*Sound: Sharp blow followed by body falling.*" These sound effects help you to picture what is happening.

1. Who is the most important character in this play?

2. You learn what the characters are like through dialogue—what they say to one another. What does the following statement tell you about Griffin? "I do not look to innkeepers' wives for friendship. Indeed, I do not look for friendship at all."

3. Information about events that happened before the time when the play takes place (outside the action of the play) is also important. Which character tells you this information?

4. The directions say that Griffin laughs when he says, "I'll kill all of you before I'm through. You may have found out my secret, but you'll never track me down." Do you think Griffin laughs as though something is funny or as though he is insane? Why?

5. Find three directions for sound effects.

SENTENCE MEANING

Finding Core Parts

The core parts of a sentence contain the basic message. The other parts of the sentence give information about the core parts. Every sentence has at least two core parts. One part, *the simple subject*, answers the question "Who?" or "What?" The second part, *the simple predicate* or verb, answers the question "Did what?" For example, notice the two core parts printed in *italics*, in the following sentence: Later that evening, *the stranger appeared* at the Coach and Horses.

Some sentences have a third core part that completes the simple predicate. For example: *Griffin dried his clothes* at his own fire. Who? *Griffin.* Did what? *Dried.* What did he dry? *His clothes.*

---

1. Find the two core parts in each sentence below. Write them on a separate piece of paper.
   a. After three days, Griffin's belongings arrived at the inn.
   b. Within a short time, several burglaries occurred in the neighborhood.
   c. Griffin's experiment succeeded after many tries and much research.
   d. He ran through the streets without a stitch of clothes on his back.

2. Find the three core parts in each sentence below. Write them on a separate piece of paper.
   a. The boxes contained all of the apparatus for Griffin's experiments.
   b. Someone stole a bank note from Dr. Huntington.
   c. After learning Griffin's secret, townspeople pursued him.
   d. At 2 A.M. Dr. Kemp finished his work for the night.

WORD ATTACK

Fitting the Context

Many words have more than one meaning. The word "hit" means one thing if you are reading about a baseball game, but something very different if you are reading about a "hit and run" police report. When you find a word that has more than one meaning, look at the context—the other words in the sentence. They usually will help you decide the meaning to use.

▶ Read each of the following sentences. Choose the meaning of the word in *italics* that fits the context.

a. "And what about the *business* down at old Mrs. Harney's?"
  (1) activity
  (2) place to sell things

b. "The bed is *depressed*—as though someone had been sitting on it."
  (1) unhappy
  (2) sunken

c. "But after a week, a new mystery broke out, which *occupied* everyone's attention."
  (1) took up
  (2) lived in

d. "Nurse Craig had just put the money down on the *counter*. . . ."
  (1) shelf
  (2) person in a factory who counts parts

e. "Conversation was now given over to the *rash* of burglaries. . . ."
  (1) a reddish skin disease
  (2) an outbreak of several incidents during a short period of time

My Search for Roots

Alex Haley

My earliest memory is of Grandma, Cousin Georgia, Aunt Plus, Aunt Liz and Aunt Till talking on our front porch in Henning, Tennessee. At dusk, these wrinkled, graying old ladies would sit in rocking chairs and talk about slaves and massas and plantations—pieces and patches of family history, passed down across the generations by word of mouth. "Old-timey stuff," Mama would exclaim. She wanted no part of it.

The furthest-back person Grandma and the others ever mentioned was "the African." They would tell how he was brought here on a ship to a place called "Naplis" and sold as a slave in Virginia. There he mated with another slave, and had a little girl named Kizzy.

When Kizzy became four or five, the old ladies said, her father would point out to her various objects and name them in his native tongue. For example, he would point to a guitar and make a single-syllable sound, *ko*. Pointing to a river that ran near the plantation, he'd say, "Kamby Bolongo." And when other slaves addressed him as Toby—the name given him by his massa—the African would strenuously reject it, insisting that his name was "Kin-tay."

Kin-tay often told Kizzy stories about himself. He said that he had been near his village in Africa, chopping wood to make a drum, when he had been set upon by four men, overwhelmed, and kidnapped into slavery. When Kizzy grew up and became a mother, she told her son these stories, and he in turn would tell *his* children.

His granddaughter became my grandmother, and she pumped that saga into me as if it were plasma, until I knew by rote the story of the African, and the wending of our family through cotton and tobacco plantations into the Civil War and then freedom.

I remembered still the vivid highlights of my family's story. Could this account possibly be documented for a book? During 1962, between other assignments, I began following the story's trail. In plantation records, wills, census records, I documented bits here, shreds there. By now, Grandma was dead; repeatedly I visited other close sources, most notably "Cousin Georgia" Anderson in Kansas City, Kansas. I went as often as I could to the National Archives in Washington, and the Library of Congress, and the Daughters of the American Revolution Library.

By 1967, I felt that I had the seven generations of the U.S. side (of the family) documented. But the unknown quotient in the riddle of the past continued to be those strange, sharp, angular sounds spoken by the African himself. Since I lived in New York City, I began going to the United Nations lobby, stopping Africans and asking if they recognized the sounds. Every one of them

listened to me, then quickly took off. I can well understand; me with a Tennessee accent, trying to imitate African sounds!

Finally, I sought out a linguistics expert who specialized in African languages. To him I repeated the phrases. The sound "Kin-tay" he said was a Mandinka tribe surname (family name). And "Kamby Bolongo" was probably the Gambia River in Mandinka dialect. Three days later, I was in Africa.

In Banjul, the capital of Gambia, I met with a group of Gambians. They told me how, for centuries, the history of Africa has been preserved. In the older villages of the back country, there are old men, called *griots* (gree-ohs), who are, in effect, living archives. Such men know and, on special occasions, tell the histories of clans, or families, or villages, as those histories have long been told. Since my forefather had said his name

was Kin-tay (properly spelled Kinte), and since the Kinte clan was known in Gambia, they would see what they could do to help me.

I was back in New York when a registered letter came from Gambia. Word had been passed in the back country, and a *griot* of the Kinte clan had, indeed, been found. His name, the letter said, was Kebba Kanga Fofana. I returned to Gambia and organized a safari to locate him.

There is an experience called "the peak experience," a moment which, emotionally, can never again be equaled in your life. I had mine, that first day in the village of Juffure, in the back country in black West Africa.

When our fourteen-man safari arrived within sight of the village, the people came flocking out of their circular mud huts. From a distance, I could see a small, old man with a pillbox hat, an off-white robe, and an aura of "somebodiness" about him. The people quickly gathered around me in a kind of horseshoe pattern. The old man looked piercingly into my eyes, and he spoke in Mandinka. Translation came from the interpreters I had brought with me.

"Yes, we have been told by the forefathers that there are many of us from this place who are in exile, in that place called America," said the old man.

Then the old man, who was seventy-three rains of age—the Gambian way of saying seventy-three years old, based upon the one rainy season per year—began to tell me the lengthy ancestral history of the Kinte clan. It was clearly a formal occasion for the villagers. They had grown mouse-quiet, and stood rigidly.

Out of the *griot's* head came spilling details incredible to hear. He recited who married whom, two or even three

centuries back. I was struck not only by the profusion of details, but also by the biblical pattern of the way he was speaking. It was something like, "—and so-and-so took as a wife so-and-so, and begat so-and-so. . ."

The *griot* had talked for some hours and had got to about 1750 in our calendar. Now he said, through an interpreter, "About the time the king's soldiers came, the eldest of Omoro's four sons, Kunta, went away from this village to chop wood—and he was never seen again. . ."

Goose pimples came out on me the size of marbles. He just had no way in the world of knowing that what he told me meshed with what I'd heard from the old ladies on the front porch in Henning, Tennessee. I got out my notebook, which had in it what Grandma had said about the African. One of the interpreters showed it to the others, and they went to the *griot,* and they all got agitated. Then the *griot* went to the people, and *they* all got agitated.

I don't remember anyone giving an order; but those seventy-odd people formed a ring around me, moving counterclockwise, chanting, their bodies close together. I can't begin to describe how I felt. A woman broke from the circle, a scowl on her jet-black face, and came charging toward me. She took her baby and almost roughly thrust it out at me. The gesture meant, "Take it!" and I did, clasping the baby to me. Whereupon the woman all but snatched the baby away. Another woman did the same with her baby, and then another, and another.

A year later, a famous professor at Harvard would tell me: "You were participating in one of the oldest ceremonies of humankind, called 'the laying on of hands.' In their way, these tribespeople were saying to you, 'Through this flesh, which is us, we are you and you are us.' "

Later, as we drove out over the back-country road, I heard the staccato sound of drums. When we approached the next village, people were packed alongside the dusty road, waving, and the din from them welled louder as we came closer. As I stood up in the Land Rover, I finally realized what it was they were all shouting: "Meester Kinte! Meester Kinte!" In their eyes, I was the symbol of all black people in the United States whose forefathers had been torn out of Africa while theirs remained.

Hands before my face, I began crying—crying as I have never cried in my life. Right at that time, crying was all I could do.

Close Up

1. (a) When Alex Haley's relatives talk about their family history, who is the "furthest-back" person they mention? (b) What two things did this person do that show he did not want to forget his African roots?

2. Haley wants to learn more about his roots. (a) Where does he research his family history? (b) How do the African words which Kizzy learned from her father help him find out more about his family?

3. Why does Haley want to meet a *griot?*

4. Haley has a peak experience during the laying on of hands ceremony. (a) What do the tribespeople say through this ceremony? (b) What does Haley represent to the tribespeople?

5. Why do you think Haley cried?

The Personal Narrative

A narrative is a story. **A personal narrative is a true story or account of the author's own experiences or of an event in the author's life.** The author identifies himself by the pronoun "I," and seems to speak directly to the reader: "I began following the story's trail."

1. (a) What event first made Haley interested in tracing his roots? (b) What event made him think he would be successful in finding his roots?

2. All of the events lead to the peak experience. (a) When does Haley have his peak experience? (b) Find the sentence in the story that shows why he had goose pimples.

3. Haley uses the pronoun "I" throughout this story. Which of the following sentences would not belong in his personal narrative?
   a. I listened as the *griot* recounted the history of the Kinte clan.
   b. After many weeks, I found an answer to the puzzle of my ancestor's language.
   c. A mini-safari was arranged to take Haley to the village of Juffure.

Activity

▶ **Composition.** Write your own personal narrative. Center it on one event—an experience with an interesting person you know, or something you liked to do, or something that made you feel good. Share this narrative with your class.

SENTENCE MEANING

Understanding Pronoun Referents

Pronouns are words used in place of nouns—words that name persons, places, or things. Commonly used pronouns are *it, you, he–his, she–her–hers,* and *they–them.*

By using pronouns, authors don't have to use the same noun again and again. For example: The old man was seventy-three rains of age. *He* knew the history of the Kinte clan. (*He* replaces "the old man.") But sometimes, the word the pronoun replaces is unclear. Using the context of the whole sentence or paragraph will help you decide what word or words a pronoun is replacing.

▶ In each of the following paragraphs, pronouns that could confuse you are underlined. Use the context to help you find the word each underlined pronoun replaces.

a. "Kin-tay often told Kizzy stories about himself. He said that he had been near his village in Africa, chopping wood to make a drum, when he had been set upon by four men, overwhelmed, and kidnapped into slavery. When Kizzy grew up and became a mother, she told her son these stories, and he in turn would tell <u>his</u> children."

Does <u>his</u> replace Kin-tay's or Kizzy's?

b. "The griot had talked for some hours and had got to about 1750 in our calendar. Now he said, through an interpreter, 'About the time the king's soldiers came, the eldest of Omoro's four sons, Kunta, went away from this village to chop wood—and <u>he</u> was never seen again. . . .'"

Does <u>he</u> replace the griot, Omoro, or Kunta?

c. "One of the interpreters showed it to the others, and they went to the griot, and they all got agitated. Then the griot went to the people, and <u>they</u> all got agitated."

Does <u>they</u> replace the interpreters, the others, or the people?

WORD ATTACK

Using Direct Context Clues

Authors sometimes give direct clues to the meanings of the words they think their readers might not know. Sometimes they simply define the word: "My grandmother pumped that *saga*, or history, into me." Sometimes they give examples that help define the word: "I found *documents* for the story—plantation records, wills, census records."

▶ Use direct context clues—definitions and examples—to define the *italicized* word or words in each sentence below.

   a. "In the older villages of the back country, there are old men, called *griots* (gree-ohs), who are, in effect, living archives."

   b. "The sound 'Kin-tay' he said was a Mandinka tribe *surname* (family name)."

   c. "Finally, I sought out a *linguistics* expert who specialized in African languages."

   d. "There is an experience called '*the peak experience*,' a moment which, emotionally, can never again be equaled in your life."

   e. "Then the old man, who was seventy-three *rains of age*— the Gambian way of saying seventy-three years old, based upon the one rainy season per year—began to tell me the lengthy ancestral history of the Kinte clan."

Keeping Hair

Ramona Wilson

My grandmother had braids
at the thickest, pencil wide
held with bright wool
cut from her bed shawl.
5 No teeth left but white hair
combed and wet carefully
early each morning.
The small wild plants found among stones
on the windy and brown plateaus
10 revealed their secrets to her hand
and yielded to her cooking pots.
She made a sweet amber water
from willows,
boiling the life out
15 to pour onto her old head.
"It will keep your hair."
She bathed my head once
rain water not sweeter.
The thought that once
20 when I was so very young
her work-bent hands
very gently and smoothly
washed my hair in willows
may also keep my heart.

Close Up ▶ The grandmother taught the narrator how to keep hair. (a) Do you think she also taught the narrator love? (b) Which words in the poem support your answer?

The Boy Who Laughed at Santa Claus

Ogden Nash

In Baltimore there lived a boy.
He wasn't anybody's joy.
Although his name was Jabez Dawes,
His character was full of flaws.
5 In school he never led his classes,
He hid old ladies' reading glasses,
His mouth was open when he chewed,
And elbows to the table glued.

He stole the milk of hungry kittens,
10 And walked through doors marked NO ADMITTANCE.
He said he acted thus because
There wasn't any Santa Claus.
Another trick that tickled Jabez
Was crying "Boo!" at little babies.
15 He brushed his teeth, they said in town.
Sideways instead of up and down.

Yet people pardoned every sin,
And viewed his antics with a grin,
Till they were told by Jabez Dawes,
20 "There isn't any Santa Claus!"
Deploring how he did behave,
His parents swiftly sought their grave.
They hurried through the portals pearly,
And Jabez left the funeral early.

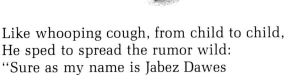

25 Like whooping cough, from child to child,
He sped to spread the rumor wild:
"Sure as my name is Jabez Dawes
There isn't any Santa Claus!"
Slunk like a weasel or a marten
30 Through nursery and kindergarten,
Whispering low to every tot,
"There isn't any, no there's not!"

The children wept all Christmas Eve
And Jabez chortled up his sleeve.
35 No infant dared hang up his stocking
For fear of Jabez' ribald mocking.
He sprawled on his untidy bed,
Fresh malice dancing in his head,
When presently with scalp a-tingling,
40 Jabez heard a distant jingling;
He heard the crunch of sleigh and hoof
Crisply alighting on the roof.

What good to rise and bar the door?
A shower of soot was on the floor.
45 What was beheld by Jabez Dawes?
The fireplace full of Santa Claus!
Then Jabez fell upon his knees
With cries of "Don't," and "Pretty please."
He howled, "I don't know where you read it,
50 But anyhow, I never said it!"

"Jabez," replied the angry saint,
"It isn't I, it's you that ain't.
Although there is a Santa Claus,
There isn't any Jabez Dawes!"
55 Said Jabez then with impudent vim,
"Oh, yes there is; and I am him!
Your magic don't scare me, it doesn't"——
And suddenly he found he wasn't!

The Boy Who Laughed at Santa Claus   **43**

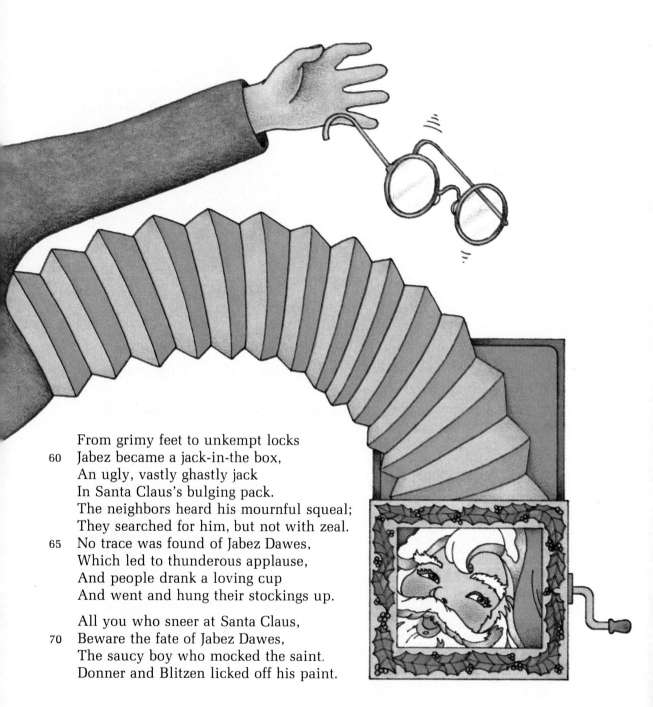

From grimy feet to unkempt locks
60 Jabez became a jack-in-the box,
An ugly, vastly ghastly jack
In Santa Claus's bulging pack.
The neighbors heard his mournful squeal;
They searched for him, but not with zeal.
65 No trace was found of Jabez Dawes,
Which led to thunderous applause,
And people drank a loving cup
And went and hung their stockings up.

All you who sneer at Santa Claus,
70 Beware the fate of Jabez Dawes,
The saucy boy who mocked the saint.
Donner and Blitzen licked off his paint.

1. What reason does Jabez give for his shocking behavior?

2. Jabez spreads the wild rumor that there isn't any Santa Claus. (a) How do you know this rumor made the children feel sad? (b) Why didn't the children hang up their stockings on Christmas Eve?

3. (a) What does Jabez do to show Santa he is sorry? (b) How do you know Jabez really isn't sorry?

4. (a) What will happen to all those people who sneer at Santa Claus? (b) Do you think the poet wants you to take this warning seriously? Why or why not?

The Narrative Poem

A narrative poem tells a story. It may contain rhythm and rhyme. Rhythm is the beat of each line of poetry—that is, the pattern of stressed and unstressed sounds. Rhyme is the repetition of sounds in words, for example, boy-joy, classes-glasses. Rhyme usually occurs at the end of lines.

1. This poem tells the story of Jabez Dawes. (a) What did Jabez do that angered Santa Claus? (b) What did Santa Claus do to Jabez?

2. Read one stanza of this poem aloud. Does it have a definite rhythm?

3. Every two lines are rhymed. What word does the poet rhyme with *chewed*? What does he rhyme with *kittens*?

4. You may think you can pronounce the boy's name, Jabez. But look at the following two rhymed lines:

    "Another trick that tickled Jabez
    Was crying 'Boo!' at little babies."

    How does Ogden Nash want you to pronounce Jabez?

Activities

1. This poem has nine stanzas. You might want to get together with eight students and each prepare one stanza for oral reading.

2. **Composition.** Think of a simple story and see if you can write a short, narrative poem that tells the story. Read it to a friend.

SENTENCE MEANING

Reading Poetry

Poetry is written to be read aloud with a certain rhythm. To help you catch and hold the rhythm, poets write their words in lines, with their sentences spilling over, one line into another. The sentences carry the meaning; but the lines carry the rhythm.

Sometimes to create rhymes that sound good, poets change the word order people usually use. For example, the poet may say:

"Like whooping cough, from child to child,
He sped to spread the rumor wild:"

The natural word order for this sentence would be: "He sped to spread the wild rumor like whooping cough from child to child."

▶ Decide which of the following groups of words is not in natural word order. Put these words into natural order. For example: "They hurried through the portals pearly," becomes "They hurried through the pearly portals."
   a. "In school he never led his classes."
   b. "There wasn't any Santa Claus."
   c. "And elbows to the table glued."
   d. "He brushed his teeth, they said in town."
   e. "Yet people pardoned every sin."

WORD ATTACK

Using Guide Words

Sometimes, you need to look up the meaning of an unfamiliar word in a dictionary or glossary. The words in dictionaries are arranged in alphabetical order. There are usually guide words—two words at the top of each page in the dictionary. The guide words tell you that all words in alphabetical order that come between these two words can be found on this page. For example, the guide words 'faith'' and ''falsehood'' tell you that the word ''fall'' can be found on that page.

1. Look up each of the following words from the poem in a dictionary. What are the guide words on the top of the page where you find each word?
   a. antics
   b. portals
   c. slunk
   d. marten
   e. ribald

2. **Composition.** Choose three of the words you looked up. For each word, write an original sentence.

3. Choose the guide words that would appear on the page where you would find each of the following *italicized* words.
   a. *Flaws* would appear on the page with the guide words:
      (1) flat—flower   (2) flag—flake   (3) fix—flap
   b. *Deplore* would appear on the page with the guide words:
      (1) dead—deliver   (2) delight—destroy   (3) date—decrease
   c. *Chortle* would appear on the page with the guide words:
      (1) chore—citrus   (2) chuckle—cider   (3) case—cease
   d. *Malice* would appear on the page with the guide words:
      (1) maze—mean   (2) meager—mental   (3) make—maybe

REVIEW QUIZ

On the Selections

1. In "The Disappearing Man," Larry knows that Stockton must have a fence. What is a fence?

2. How does Larry know that Stockton must be within the building?

3. Eugenie Clark is an ichthyologist. Why would she use scuba equipment?

4. How did the Moses sole get its name?

5. In "The Invisible Man," Griffin finds the secret of invisibility while he is looking for the solution to a different problem. What is this problem?

6. Kemp does not believe in the invisible man. What happens that forces Kemp to change his mind?

7. In "My Search for Roots," Alex Haley wishes to document his family history. Name one source Haley uses to find a written record of his roots.

8. How is a *griot* like a library?

9. In "Keeping Hair," does the grandmother use the secrets of nature or store-bought products?

10. What is the moral, or lesson, you learn from "The Boy Who Laughed at Santa Claus"?

On Sentence Meaning

1. Put quotation marks around the exact words Dad said. Write your answer on a separate piece of paper.
    Go home, Larry, Dad barked. I don't want you to get hurt.

2. The following words are really two sentences. Add a period and capital letter to show that the sharks picked up speed silently. Write your answer on a separate piece of paper.
    "Two tiger sharks began to circle the divers silently, they picked up speed to attack, but as they closed in on the swimmers, they slammed on invisible breaks."

3. Find the core parts in the following sentence.
    Quite by accident, Griffin found a method of making an inert object colorless and transparent.

4. In the following sentence, the pronoun they is underlined. What noun does this pronoun refer to?
    "One of the interpreters showed it to the others, and they went to the griot, and they all got agitated. Then the griot went to the people, and they all got agitated."

5. Rewrite the following sentence in natural word order:
    "They hurried through the portals pearly."

COMPOSITION

Sentence Combining

Varying the length of your sentences is a key to good writing. Often, you can build a more interesting sentence by combining two short related sentences. For example, you can combine the two short sentences below by using the comma and connecting word in the parentheses that follow the second sentence.

> The police guarded all possible exits.
> Two officers covered the roof. (, and)

> *becomes*

> The police guarded all possible exits, and two officers covered the roof.

▶ Combine each pair of sentences by using the comma and connecting word in the parentheses that follow the second sentence.

a. The sharks gulped down the other fish.
   They did not eat the Moses sole. (, but)

b. The robberies increased.
   The police could find no clues. (, but)

c. The policemen came down the stairs.
   They were all shaking their heads. (, and)

d. The Moses sole is a flatfish.
   It gets its strange name from a traditional Israeli story. (, and)

e. Eugenie Clark had to leave the Elat laboratory.
   She could not complete her experiments. (, and)

f. The stranger appeared one stormy night.
   He was wrapped up in clothing from head to toe. (, and)

g. Mrs. Hall tried to be friendly.
   Griffin roared at her and told her to go away. (, but)

h. Griffin was an old schoolmate.
   Kemp did not want to help him. (, but)

i. Alex Haley wanted to document his family's history.
   At first, he couldn't find anyone to help him. (, but)

j. All the children cried Christmas Eve.
   Jabez Dawes laughed at their distress. (, but)

BEFORE GOING ON

Setting a Purpose for Reading

How fast or how slow you read a selection depends on why you are reading it. For example, if you are reading to find the special information in the selection, you will read slowly and carefully. If you are searching for a particular fact, you will scan it until you come to the few words you need. If you want only a general idea of what the selection is about, you will read the whole selection quickly, without stopping to examine the specific points you might find.

▶ Below are some purposes you might have for reading "The Loch Ness Monster." In each case, decide whether you would read the whole article slowly and carefully, scan it to find certain information, or read the whole article quickly.

a. Your teacher will give you a test on the information in "The Loch Ness Monster."

b. You've heard about the Loch Ness Monster, and you wonder why there is so much interest in it.

c. You've read a lot about the Loch Ness Monster and are especially interested in its size. You wonder what this story says just about size.

d. You want to know the speed at which John Cobb's boat, the *Crusader*, was traveling when it exploded.

e. You are an amateur photographer, and you want to write a paper about different uses of photography. You've heard that the Loch Ness Monster has been photographed, and you wonder if this article talks about those photographs.

f. You are a scientist who has studied the Loch Ness Monster. You want to see if this author has written an accurate article.

g. You're bored, looking for something to read. You find the article in a magazine. After reading the first page, you become mildly interested and decide to finish reading it.

Further Reading

The Loch Ness Monster— Fact or Fiction?

Martin Walsh

Northern Scotland is a land of beauty. Mountain ranges covered with trees, evergreen shrubs, and purple heather give the region a beauty that is known throughout the world. The beautiful lakes, or lochs as they are called by the Highland people, lie among the rugged mountains. They add to the spectacular scenery of the area.

But despite the beauty, the Scottish Highlands are strange and lonely. Empty farmhouses dot the area. Crumbling medieval castles stand in silent tribute to a romantic past. Often the mountains are covered with a cold mist. In the early morning, a thick fog sometimes blankets the area, seeming to settle on the many beautiful lakes.

In the midst of the Highlands lies Loch (Lake) Ness, the largest and deepest lake in Great Britain. Loch Ness has become the center of a raging controversy. Reports have been coming from Loch Ness that tell of a large animal that supposedly lives in the loch. The reports describe an animal with a small head, long neck, and very large body. Many sightings from reliable eyewitnesses have been reported. Disbelievers scoff at the mention of a monster living in the loch. But the evidence can no longer be ignored. A look at some of the strange events that have occurred at Loch Ness will make even the most stubborn doubter question.

In 1952, at Loch Ness, John Cobb, the famous English speedboat enthusiast, stepped into his jet propelled boat, the *Crusader*. He wanted to better the world speedboat record. The waters of the loch were perfectly calm. There was absolutely no wind blowing as the *Cru-sader* raced across the waters of Loch Ness. The *Crusader* reached the incredible speed of 207 miles per hour. Suddenly, in front of the speedboat, rose a path of large ripples. The boat struck one of the ripples with great force. The impact turned the *Crusader* sideways, causing it to strike the next wave. Suddenly the stillness of Loch Ness was broken by a loud explosion as the *Crusader* blew apart, scattering parts everywhere. John Cobb was dead.

What had caused the death of John Cobb? How could waves suddenly appear on a calm, cloudless day? People who lived in the area shook their heads. They knew that John Cobb's death had been caused by the Loch Ness monster. For some reason the monster rose from the loch, causing the waves and the death of Cobb.

There never has been any explanation. Indeed, there has been little scientific explanation, until recently, for the many mysterious sightings of whatever lives in Loch Ness.

The legend of the Loch Ness monster goes back to very early times. St. Columba, an Irish missionary who was sent to Scotland to spread Christianity, notes seeing the monster in his writings as early as A.D. 565. Throughout the centuries since then, local people have known of the monster, and have seen the creature.

But it wasn't until 1934 that a remarkable photograph was taken by a London surgeon. It clearly showed the neck and head of a large aquatic creature, emerging from the waters of the loch.

Dr. Wilson's photograph was greeted with mixed reactions. Some said it was proof that the Loch Ness monster was real. Others cried fraud, saying that the photograph was either a trick or a tree stump which looked a lot like a living creature.

Since 1934, sightings of the monster have been reported more often in the newspapers. Several other photographs have appeared which are said to be of the monster. Expeditions were organized which attempted to prove or disprove the existence of the monster. None of them was able to prove the existence of the creature.

In 1963, however, two British naturalists, Richard Fitter and Peter Scott, thought that Loch Ness should be investigated scientifically. They asked the British Parliament in London for money. Then the men took their idea to David James, a Member of Parliament. At first, Mr. James laughed when Fitter and Scott told him what they wanted. At last the two men convinced James that they were serious. They showed him written accounts and photographs of actual sightings made of the monster. James became

WARNING!
ACHTUNG!   ATTENTION!
PERSONS WHO LEAVE THEIR VEHICLES IN THIS VICINITY
DURING THE BREEDING SEASON OF THE LOCH NESS
MONSTER, DO SO ENTIRELY AT THEIR OWN RISK
BATHING IS STRICTLY PROHIBITED
SAFETY MEASURES
MOTOR-HORNS SHOULD BE SOUNDED AT 5MIN. INTERVALS
ALL CASULTIES MUST BE
REPORTED IMMEDIATELY

BY ORDER   TOWN AND COUNTRY PLANNING ACT
                            (1939) SUB-SECT 'B' PARA 2(C)

convinced when he read the accounts made by reliable people.

Mr. James finally decided to visit Loch Ness himself. He talked to many fishermen, farmers, policemen, and other local people, many of whom claimed to have seen the monster. There was no doubt in Mr. James's mind now. Together with Richard Fitter, Peter Scott, and others, Mr. James helped found the Loch Ness Phenomena Investigation Bureau in 1963.

Twenty-four volunteers, led by Mr. James, then traveled to Loch Ness with mixed feelings about their mission. They faced a disbelieving public, and even their own faith in ever achieving success was not very strong.

However, soon after arriving at Loch Ness, seven members of the expedition noticed a disturbance in the waters of the loch in Urquhart Bay. It was one of the deepest parts of the loch and a frequent spot of monster sightings. The disturbance was caused by the splashing of a large number of salmon. They seemed to be trying to escape some underwater object. Then, before the eyes of the seven, the object began to rise from the water. The men could see two distinct humps, three feet high and ten to twelve feet long. Luckily, they were carrying their cameras and took several clear photographs.

This was all that the members of the Investigation Bureau needed. It convinced them of the importance of their task. Before long, there were eighty volunteers at the loch. Gifts were received from several sources. Soon the Bureau was busy manning seven observation stations at various strategic places around the loch. Each station was fully equipped with powerful cameras mounted with telephoto lenses which covered ninety percent of the loch's surface.

For some men like David James and Clem Skelton, the search for the monster has now become a way of life. Skelton is the resident technician of the Loch Ness Phenomena Investigation Bureau. He claims to have seen the monster more times than any other person. He will not be satisfied until he has proved the monster's existence.

Shortly after arriving at Loch Ness, Skelton was ferrying some people across the loch. The loch was clear and calm. Somehow Skelton's outboard motor gave out. There was nothing for him to do but row.

Suddenly there was a noise behind him. Later, he said that the noise sounded like a panting horse. Skelton stopped rowing and wheeled about. What he saw made him freeze in terror. Clearly visible, with its head and neck coming up from the water, was the monster. There could be no doubt in Skelton's mind.

What Skelton said matched the description of others who have sighted the monster. The creature had a small head and a long, slim neck which gradually thickened as it reached the water. Skelton could see little of the monster's body. Judging by the length and thickness of the neck, he estimated that it must have been at least forty feet long.

For several minutes, Clem Skelton stopped rowing and sat spellbound. The monster just seemed to sit there staring at him. Then Skelton's instinct for survival overcame his fear. He began to row quickly away.

What had Clem Skelton seen in the middle of Loch Ness? Are we to disregard the reports of eyewitnesses such as

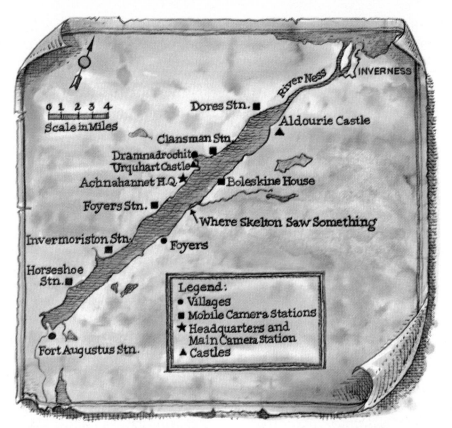

Legend:
- Villages
- Mobile Camera Stations
- ★ Headquarters and Main Camera Station
- ▲ Castles

Skelton and others? Are we to pass off the sightings as mass hallucination? Many scientists now believe that a large creature or, more likely, a group of creatures, live in the deepest waters of Loch Ness. In fact, reports have also been received from Canada, Alaska, and Russia of monsters living in the deepest lakes in these places. Although there still is no definite proof, scientists have examined every possible theory and can come to no other conclusion.

Scientists point first of all to the depth of Loch Ness. At its deepest point, the loch is 754 feet deep. This makes it much deeper than the ocean waters of the nearby North Sea and English Channel. A lake of this type would be deep enough for such a creature, or a large school of such creatures.

The great depth of Loch Ness was probably formed at the close of the ice age when the polar ice cap retreated from northern Scotland. At this time, Loch Ness was probably connected to the sea. An earthquake or the retreating ice caused a shifting of the earth's surface. This formed the deep lake, and trapped large aquatic animals in the loch. The Loch Ness monster, then, may be a survivor of this prehistoric event.

Loch Ness is well-protected from cold winds and storms by the large mountain ranges which rise on all sides. Such protection as this would make it possible for an animal to survive from prehistoric times. In fact, the loch is so well protected, that its surface has never been known to freeze, even in the coldest weather.

Scientists also point out that the loch is separated from the sea. This means that no predatory animals such as sharks would be able to prey on animals living in the loch.

Loch Ness is filled with fish. It has trout and salmon weighing as much as thirty pounds. It also contains eels as long as ten feet. It is fed by many smaller lakes and streams. These also supply fish. With such a large amount of fish, survival would be possible for an animal even as large as the Loch Ness monster.

Several animals, once thought extinct, have been found. The coelacanth, a large fish thought to be extinct, was discovered in 1939 off the coast of Africa. The Komodo Dragon, the largest living lizard, also thought to be extinct, was recently discovered still living on some small islands in Indonesia. Other animals completely unknown to human beings have been discovered in this century, as explorers enter into the last remaining wilderness areas, and go deeper and deeper into the unknown depths of the sea.

Advanced scientific investigation seems to be the only answer to the mystery. In 1968, a research team from Birmingham University, using the newest in sonar equipment, noted a large object moving along the bottom of the loch. The sonar screen showed the object to be over sixty-five feet long and moving at the speed of approximately 450 feet per minute.

Looking at all of the evidence then, there is little doubt that a creature, or creatures, of great size and speed lives in Loch Ness. As a well-known scientist said recently, "There's something in Loch Ness. What it is we can't be exactly sure at this time. But there's no doubt that an animal of immense size inhabits the loch, and one of these days we're going to find it."

EXPERIENCE

The Fun They Had

Isaac Asimov

Margie even wrote about it that night in her diary. On the page headed *May 17, 2155,* she wrote, "Today Tommy found a real book!"

It was a very old book. Margie's grandfather once said that, when he was a little boy, *his* grandfather told him there was a time when all stories were printed on paper.

They turned the pages, which were yellow and crinkly, and it was awfully funny to read words that stood still instead of moving the way they were supposed to—on a screen, you know. And then, when they turned back to the page before, it had the same words on it that it had had when they read it the first time.

"Gee," said Tommy, "what a waste. When you're through with the book, you just throw it away, I guess. Our television screen must have had a million books on it, and it's good for plenty more. I wouldn't throw *it* away."

"Same with mine," said Margie. She was eleven and hadn't seen so many tele-books as Tommy had. He was thirteen.

She said, "Where did you find it?"

"In my house." He pointed without looking because he was busy reading. "In the attic."

"What's it about?"

"School."

Margie was scornful. "School? What's there to write about school? I hate school." Margie always hated school, but now she hated it more than ever. The mechanical teacher had been giving her test after test in geography, and she had been doing worse and worse until her mother had shaken her head sorrowfully and sent for the County Inspector.

He was a round little man with a red face and a whole box of tools with dials and wires. He smiled at her and gave her an apple, then took the teacher apart. Margie had hoped he wouldn't know how to put it together again, but he knew how all right. And after an hour or so, there it was again, large and black and ugly, with a big screen on which all the lessons were shown and the questions were asked. That wasn't so bad. The part she hated most was the slot where she had to put homework and test papers. She had to write them always in a punch

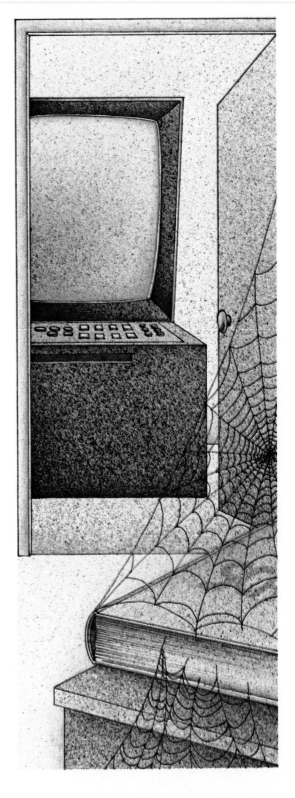

code they made her learn when she was six years old. The mechanical teacher calculated the mark in no time.

The Inspector had smiled after he was finished, and patted her head. He said to her mother, "It's not the little girl's fault, Mrs. Jones, I think the geography sector was geared a little too quick. Those things happen sometimes. I've slowed it up to an average ten-year level. Actually, the overall pattern of her progress is quite satisfactory." And he patted Margie's head again.

Margie was disappointed. She had been hoping they would take the teacher away altogether. They had once taken Tommy's teacher away for nearly a month because the history sector had blanked out completely.

So she said to Tommy, "Why would anyone write about school?"

Tommy looked at her with very superior eyes. "Because it's not our kind of school, stupid. This is the old kind of school that they had hundreds and hundreds of years ago." He added loftily, pronouncing the word carefully, "*Centuries* ago."

Margie was hurt. "Well, I don't know what kind of school they had all that time ago." She read the book over his shoulder for a while, then said, "Anyway, they had a teacher."

"Sure they had a teacher, but it wasn't a *regular* teacher. It was a man."

"A man? How could a man be a teacher?"

"Well, he just told the boys and girls things and gave them homework and asked them questions."

"A man isn't smart enough."

"Sure he is. My father knows as much as my teacher."

"He can't. A man can't know as much as a teacher."

"He knows almost as much, I betcha."

Margie wasn't prepared to argue that. She said, "I wouldn't want a strange man in my house to teach me."

Tommy screamed with laughter. "You don't know much, Margie. The teachers didn't live in the house. They had a special building and all the kids went there."

"And all the kids learned the same thing?"

"Sure, if they were the same age."

"But my mother says a teacher has to be adjusted to fit the mind of each boy and girl it teaches, and that each kid has to be taught differently."

"Just the same, they didn't do it that way then. If you don't like it, you don't have to read the book."

"I didn't say I didn't like it," Margie said quickly. She wanted to read about those funny schools.

They weren't even half finished when Margie's mother called, "Margie! School!"

Margie looked up. "Not yet, Mama."

"Now," said Mrs. Jones. "And it's probably time for Tommy, too."

Margie said to Tommy, "Can I read the book some more with you after school?"

"Maybe," he said. He walked away whistling, the dusty old book tucked beneath his arm.

Margie went into the schoolroom. It was right next to her bedroom. The mechanical teacher was on and waiting for her. It was always on at the same time every day except Saturday and Sunday, because her mother said little girls learned better if they learned at regular hours.

The screen was lit up, and it said: "Today's arithmetic lesson is on the addition of proper fractions. Please insert yesterday's homework in the proper slot."

Margie did so with a sigh. She was thinking about the old schools they had when her grandfather's grandfather was a little boy. All the kids from the whole neighborhood came, laughing and shouting in the schoolyard, sitting together in the schoolroom, going home together at the end of the day. They learned the same things so they could help one another on the homework and talk about it.

And the teachers were people. . . .

The mechanical teacher was flashing on the screen: "When we add the fractions 1/2 and 1/4——"

Margie was thinking about how the kids must have loved it in the old days. She was thinking about the fun they had.

1. This story takes place in the future. (a) What date does Margie write in her diary? (b) What happens on this date?

2. Margie and Tommy turn the pages of the book. It seems strange to read words that stand still. How is this book different from their telebooks?

3. Margie is scornful when she finds out the book is about a school. (a) Why does she hate school? (b) How is the school in the book different from Margie's school?

4. Margie thinks "the kids must have loved it in the old days." What does Margie like about the old schools?

Plot

The plot is the pattern of events in a story. When you tell the plot, you tell how each event is connected to other events in the story. These events are ordered in such a way as to bring about change.

1. Tommy's finding a book is the first event in this story. Why is it unusual to find a book?

2. At first, Tommy and Margie think a book is "a waste." Why?

3. How does finding the book make Margie change her feelings about school?

Activities

1. Imagine that Margie and Tommy have traveled through time to your school. What questions do you think they would ask? What would you most like to show them? What would you most like to ask them?

2. Sketch the mechanical "teacher" in this story. Label the different parts you think the "teacher" would have. For example, it would have a homework slot.

RELATIONSHIPS

Understanding Time Order

Time order tells you when each event happened in relation to other events. For example, if you were building a model airplane, you would be careful to do each step in the correct time order. Remember: Time order answers the question "When?"

1. Read the three events below. On a separate piece of paper, put 1 by the event that happened first, 2 by the event that happened next, and 3 by the event that happened third.
   a. Tommy showed Margie the book he found.
   b. Margie wrote in her diary that Tommy found a book.
   c. Tommy found a book.

2. Read the three events below. Put 1 by the event that happened first, 2 by the event that happened next, and 3 by the event that happened last.
   a. The mechanical teacher named the arithmetic lesson.
   b. Mrs. Jones called Margie in for school.
   c. Margie thought about the fun kids must have had in the old days.

3. (a) What was the last event in the story? (b) Do you think this event would have happened if Tommy had not found the book?

WORD ATTACK

Understanding Compound Words

Compound words are made by joining two words. You can understand a compound word if you break it into two parts. For example, the word *supermarket* is a combination of the words *super* and *market*. These are stores where people buy a whole week's or a whole month's groceries at one time. Did you ever think of these stores as *super* markets?

1. Below are some compound words from the story. Break each word into the two words that were joined.
   a. grandfather
   b. homework
   c. overall
   d. anyone
   e. schoolroom
   f. bedroom
   g. schoolyard

2. Play a game with your classmates. Think of your own compound word. Then draw a picture of each of the two words used to make your compound word. See if your classmates can add the two pictures together and guess what the new word is.

First Jump

James M. Ware

Fear gripped Michael as he looked down at the white canvas X that marked the target.

When Michael found himself sitting next to the pilot, on the floor where the right seat of the Cessna had been, his legs strapped to the floor, he had to overcome sensations, not images, of fear. His stomach felt oily, and his knees really were weak. His Uncle Dan and the jumpmaster sat behind him, and he tried to look normal.

The door on Michael's right had been removed, but at first he had felt comfortably enclosed. His eyes were level with the instrument panel, making the doorway his window.

Then the plane banked to the right, and the sensations of fear started. Michael was pitched toward the doorway. Clutching the sides of the opening, he looked down at the miniature landscape and felt its pull. Now he wasn't so sure that his mother's fears were misplaced.

Both Michael's father and uncle had enjoyed their paratrooper training so much, that they had taken up sport parachuting when they left the Army.

Michael's father had even managed to find a job that gave him a chance to do some jumping. He had been a forest ranger who jumped into remote areas to fight fires while they were small. Even when conditions were good, it was dangerous work. He had been killed when the updraft of a canyon fire swept him and his parachute into an outcropping of rocks.

For several years, Michael's mother had refused to let him go along with his Uncle Dan on weekends, when he jumped with a club at a small airport out in the farm country. Finally, Uncle Dan had persuaded Michael's mother to let him go—*just to watch.* A year passed and, wonder of wonders, Uncle Dan actually got her to agree that Michael could, on his fifteenth birthday, take the lessons that led to a first jump.

Michael was beside himself with happiness when his mother signed the permission form. Then she avoided any discussion of the whole subject. She was trying hard to let him grow up, and he understood that. He didn't talk about the upcoming event around his mother.

As the time approached, it was Michael himself who became his enemy. Images of his father's funeral would flash through his mind, and he dreamed about hanging in a parachute above enemy soldiers and forest fires. He would have to remind himself that sport parachuting—unlike the jumping done by firefighters and soldiers—had so many safeguards, that it was one of the safest sports around.

Earlier today, Uncle Dan had paid for Michael's instructions and equipment rental. It was his birthday present. In a locker room, he and two other beginners had put on their black boots, white coveralls, and orange football helmets. All afternoon, they listened to instructions and practiced on the ground the things they were to do in the air. They sat in a plane and moved to the standby position. On the ground, where there was no wind, it had seemed silly to pivot gingerly and to lean out carefully.

Then they jumped from the parked plane to the ground where they stood, spread-eagled, backs arched, counting aloud to six. This posture anticipated free-fall parachuting,[1] which would come after a series of static-line jumps.[2]

Later, they jumped backwards from a shoulder-high platform onto sand and rolled into landing falls.

Now and again during practice, they stopped and squinted at the sky to watch others jump. The jumpers came out, so tiny against the sky that, at first, it seemed that a small part of the plane had fallen off. Then, in free fall, they slashed across the sky and suddenly braked. Their chutes trailed out, then puffed open to let them drift down like dandelion seeds. Sometimes, those on the ground could hear the wind whistle over the bodies of the free fallers.

Michael was proud to see his uncle in a bright red and white jumpsuit flash across the sky like a superman. He would turn to the right and left, then open his chute and maneuver himself to within

---

1. free-fall parachuting: The part of the parachute jump that takes place before the parachute opens.
2. static-line jumps: jumps made with a static line, a cord attached at one end to the parachute pack and at the other end to the airplane.

ten feet of the center of the target. Starting his jump a mile up, he could usually get that close to the target.

When Michael watched, the plane seemed to be very low. He had wished for a higher jump than the 1,500 feet he would be allowed for his first time.

Now, braced against the edges of the exit, he thought the plane was very high. The other beginners had jumped. There was just enough light left for Michael's jump.

Michael had felt no fear when the plane took off. He had sat calmly watching the fast blur of ground slowly focus and recede. He had been surprised that his heart beat normally. He was careful not to think of accidents. Nevertheless, a picture of his father, chuted-up and ready to jump, came to mind repeatedly. But the picture was not accompanied by fear.

Then, when the plane suddenly banked, pitching him toward the opening, something clicked deep within his body. A chill crept over his skin. Before, when he had been facing the close dials, with gravity comfortably beneath him, his body had been ignorant of its situation.

Now it knew. His heart beat faster while Michael looked down at the area they were circling. Beneath what seemed miles of emptiness, was a strip of concrete, several hangars,[3] and a dozen private airplanes. The target, a white canvas X, was spread in the middle of a circularly plowed field. Two men and a station wagon were near the target.

The plane leveled, and Michael looked up at the pilot, who grinned

---

3. hangars (hăng'ərz) n.: Sheds housing airplanes.

mischievously. Then Michael studied the toes of his boots. His muscles were weak, but he still did not doubt himself. He knew he would jump, especially with his uncle sitting right behind him. And yet. . . .

Michael looked over his shoulder at the jumpmaster's smooth, tanned face. When he dropped a wind indicator and leaned out slightly to watch its drift, his cheek rippled eerily like a flag in the wind.

"It landed by the first hangar," shouted the jumpmaster. "We're almost ready."

It occurred to Michael that the jumpmaster was wearing a parachute. "Are you going to jump, too?"

"No."

"Then why the chute? The pilot doesn't have one."

The jumpmaster smiled, and he leaned close to Michael's ear so that he would not have to shout. "Two years ago, an instructor in France was pulled out of the plane by a panicky beginner. He wasn't wearing a chute." The jumpmaster paused, then leaned over to add, "All the way down, he did rolls and figure eights." Michael gave him a sickly grin, and the jumpmaster shouted over the engine noise, "Don't worry. This isn't the Army. If you don't jump five seconds after 'go,' I'll help you back in."

Michael thought of the humiliation of being pulled in, of landing in the plane, of facing his uncle, who doubtless would still be very kind.

For the fifth or sixth time since leaving the ground, Michael reviewed the procedure to himself: At "stand by," unstrap legs, pivot slowly into place on the threshold; at "go," stand up, pause, then jump backward (spread-eagle and head up); count six, no chute, go for the reserve; after opening, check the canopy[4] for damage; turn toward the target.

When the plane approached the jump site, the jumpmaster checked the static line that connected the rip cord[5] of Michael's parachute to the plane. He shouted, "Stand by!"

Michael unstrapped his legs. Placing his hands on the sides of the doorway, he began to pivot toward the opening. The wind snatched at his feet. He braced them against the two-by-four bolted above the wheel. He inched forward until he was perched on the edge of the doorway. He leaned out and turned to face the wind. He looked, as he had been taught, at the horizon, not down at the earth.

Then the pilot cut the motor to reduce prop wash, and the husky engine racket was replaced by the metallic whistle of the wind over the wings.

"Have a good jump and go." On the last word, the jumpmaster gave Michael a light slap on the shoulder. Michael felt the signal. He got out, sliding his hands along the strut that connects the wing with the bottom of the fuselage. For one second, he stood on the two-by-four outside the cabin. Then he jumped backward.

He saw only the plane shrinking in the sky. His body felt the fall in a strange, electric way. Every fiber seemed to shriek, but his throat made no sound. "I'm not counting," he realized. He raced to catch up, "onetwothreefour. . . ."

Then he found himself supported by a wonderful swing. Confident with the feel of support, he grinned as he pulled down on the handle attached to the cords on the right side of the chute. That half collapsed and Michael turned toward the target. Then he made a left turn, followed by a full corkscrew. It was wonderful fun to maneuver over the growing target, swinging with and against the wind.

Near the ground, he made his final turn into the wind to reduce ground speed. Then he drew his legs together and bent his knees and hips. He looked off at the horizon to overcome the urge to spread his legs at impact. He hit the dirt, rolled all in one motion to his feet, and ran downwind to collapse the parachute.

His cold fingers were fumbling helplessly with the release snaps of the harness, when the two men on the ground reached him. One released his harness for him, while the other began to fold up the canopy.

The sun rolled over the horizon as the three trudged toward the station wagon, and their coveralls faded from orange to gray. Far across the field, the plane was landing.

Michael didn't have to see his uncle to know that he was smiling.

---

4. canopy (kăn′ə-pē) n.: The dome-shaped surface of a parachute.
5. rip cord: The cord that opens the parachute.

Close Up

1. (a) Why doesn't Michael's mother want him to take up sport parachuting? (b) Who persuades her to change her mind?

2. As the time for his first jump approaches, Michael begins to feel fear. (a) What event does he remember? (b) Why does he really have no need to fear?

3. When Michael stands on the ground watching the jumpers, he wishes his first jump could be higher than 1,500 feet. (a) What happens to make Michael change his mind? (b) What does the jumpmaster say that shows he knows that Michael is afraid?

4. After Michael jumps, he realizes he is not counting. (a) Why is it important that Michael count? (b) Do you think Michael feels confident, or does he still feel afraid when he starts to maneuver toward the target? How do you know this?

5. At the end of the story, why does Michael think his uncle is smiling?

Flashbacks

A flashback is a look into the past. It breaks the order of events and tells you about something that happened earlier in the story. Usually, it gives you background information that helps you to understand the story.

1. At the beginning of "First Jump," Michael is sitting in the plane, awaiting his turn. Then there is a flashback, or look into Michael's past. What does this flashback describe?

2. (a) Did the first events in the flashback occur a year ago, several years ago, or more than fifty years ago? (b) How do you know?

3. The events in the flashback help to explain why Michael's mother refuses to let him jump. (a) How do the events explain this? (b) How do the events explain Michael's fear?

Activities

1. **Composition.** Create several lines of dialogue that Michael and his uncle may have spoken at the end of the story.

2. Make a list of local regulations for sport parachuting. Report your findings to the class.

RELATIONSHIPS

Understanding Connectors That Show Time Order

Connectors are little words that join two ideas or events. Sometimes, these little words signal the time relationship between the events. This means that they tell you whether one event happened earlier than the other, at the same time as the other, or later than the other. Connectors showing time relationships are *after, as, before, earlier, finally, later, meanwhile, now, since, then, until, when,* and *where.*

▶ Each item below contains two events. One event is printed in *italics.* The connector showing the time relationship between the two events is printed in **boldface.** On a separate piece of paper, mark each item *B, S,* or *L.* Mark *B* if the event in italics happened *before* the other event. Mark *S* if the event in italics happened *at the same time* as the other event. Mark *L* if the event in italics happened *later* than the other event.

a. "His eyes were level with the instrument panel, making the doorway his window. **Then** *the plane banked to the right, and the sensations of fear started.*"

b. "Both Michael's father and uncle had enjoyed their paratrooper training so much, that they had taken up sport parachuting **when** *they left the Army.*"

c. "His heart beat faster **while** *Michael looked down at the area they were circling.*"

d. "Michael had felt no fear **when** *the plane took off.*"

e. "A chill crept over his skin. **Before,** . . . *his body had been ignorant of its situation.*"

f. "Confident with the feel of support, he grinned **as** *he pulled down on the handle attached to the cords on the right side of the chute.*"

g. "One released his harness for him, **while** *the other began to fold up the canopy.*"

h. "The plane leveled, and Michael looked up at the pilot, who grinned mischievously. **Then** *Michael studied the toes of his boots.*"

i. "He had wished for a higher jump than the 1,500 feet he would be allowed for his first time. **Now,** . . . *he thought the plane was very high.*"

j. "He had been killed **when** *the updraft of a canyon fire swept him and his parachute into an outcropping of rocks.*"

WORD ATTACK

Understanding Compound Words

A compound word is made by joining two words. Two ideas combine to form a new word. For example, the ideas of *week* and *end* combine to form the word *weekend*. Breaking compound words into their parts may help you to better understand their meanings.

1. Match each word in column (a) with a word in column (b) to form a new word. You can check your work by looking in the story to find the words you have formed.

(a)	(b)
out	port
air	draft
fire	noon
safe	fighters
after	cropping
up	guards
super	man
door	planes
	way
	come

2. Try again. Match each word in column (a) with a word from column (b) to form a new word.

(a)	(b)
stand	ball
jump	all
cork	by
cover	master
foot	screw

The Cremation of Sam McGee

Robert Service

There are strange things done in the midnight sun
By the men who moil for gold;
The Arctic trails have their secret tales
That would make your blood run cold;
5   The Northern Lights have seen queer sights,
But the queerest they ever did see
Was that night on the marge of Lake Lebarge
I cremated Sam McGee.

Now Sam McGee was from Tennessee, where the cotton blooms and blows.
10 Why he left his home in the South to roam 'round the Pole, God only knows.
He was always cold, but the land of gold seemed to hold him like a spell;
Though he'd often say in his homely way that "he'd sooner live in hell."

On a Christmas Day we were mushing our way over the Dawson trail.
Talk of your cold! through the parka's fold it stabbed like a driven nail.
15 If our eyes we'd close, then the lashes froze till sometimes we couldn't see;
It wasn't much fun, but the only one to whimper was Sam McGee.

And that very night, as we lay packed tight in our robes beneath the snow,
And the dogs were fed, and the stars o'erhead were dancing heel and toe,
He turned to me, and "Cap," says he, "I'll cash in this trip, I guess;
20 And if I do, I'm asking that you won't refuse my last request."

Well, he seemed so low that I couldn't say no; then he says with a sort of
    moan:
"It's the cursèd cold, and it's got right hold till I'm chilled clean through to the
    bone.
Yet 'tain't being dead—it's my awful dread of the icy grave that pains;
So I want you to swear that, foul or fair, you'll cremate my last remains."

25   A pal's last need is a thing to heed, so I swore I would not fail;
    And we started on at the streak of dawn; but God! he looked ghastly pale.
    He crouched on the sleigh, and he raved all day of his home in Tennessee;
    And before nightfall a corpse was all that was left of Sam McGee.

    There wasn't a breath in that land of death, and I hurried, horror-driven,
30   With a corpse half hid that I couldn't get rid, because of a promise given;
    It was lashed to the sleigh, and it seemed to say: "You may tax your brawn and
        brains,
    But you promised true, and it's up to you to cremate those last remains."

    Now a promise made is a debt unpaid, and the trail has its own stern code.
    In the days to come, though my lips were dumb, in my heart how I cursed that
        load.
35   In the long, long night, by the lone firelight, while the huskies, round in a ring,
    Howled out their woes to the homeless snows—O God! how I loathed the
        thing.

And every day that quiet clay seemed to heavy and heavier grow;
And on I went, though the dogs were spent and the grub was getting low;
The trail was bad, and I felt half mad, but I swore I would not give in;
40   And I'd often sing to the hateful thing, and it hearkened with a grin.

Till I came to the marge of Lake Lebarge, and a derelict there lay;
It was jammed in the ice, but I saw in a trice it was called the "Alice May."
And I looked at it, and I thought a bit, and I looked at my frozen chum;
Then "Here," said I, with a sudden cry, "is my cre-ma-tor-ium."

45   Some planks I tore from the cabin floor, and I lit the boiler fire;
Some coal I found that was lying around, and I heaped the fuel higher;
The flames just soared, and the furnace roared—such a blaze you seldom see;
And I burrowed a hole in the glowing coal, and I stuffed in Sam McGee.

Then I made a hike, for I didn't like to hear him sizzle so;
50   And the heavens scowled, and the huskies howled, and the wind began to
    blow.
It was icy cold, but the hot sweat rolled down my cheeks, and I don't know
    why;
And the greasy smoke in an inky cloak went streaking down the sky.

I do not know how long in the snow I wrestled with grisly fear;
But the stars came out and they danced about ere again I ventured near;
55   I was sick with dread, but I bravely said: "I'll just take a peep inside.
I guess he's cooked, and it's time I looked"; . . . then the door I opened wide.

And there sat Sam, looking cool and calm, in the heart of the furnace roar;
And he wore a smile you could see a mile, and he said: "Please close that door.
It's fine in here, but I greatly fear you'll let in the cold and storm—
60   Since I left Plumtree, down in Tennessee, it's the first time I've been warm."

There are strange things done in the midnight sun
By the men who moil for gold;
The Arctic trails have their secret tales
That would make your blood run cold;
65   *The Northern Lights have seen queer sights,*
But the queerest they ever did see
Was that night on the marge of Lake Lebarge
I cremated Sam McGee.

Close Up

1. Cap says that many blood-chilling events have happened in the Arctic. What event does he find the strangest of all?

2. (a) What does Sam hate about the Arctic? (b) What does he fear will happen to him?

3. (a) Why does Cap agree to cremate Sam? (b) Why does Sam ask to be cremated?

4. Cap says that "a promise made is a debt unpaid." What does he do that shows he really believes this?

5. At last, on Lake Lebarge, Cap finds the perfect crematorium. After he thinks Sam is cooked, he takes a peek inside. What does he find?

6. Support your answers. (a) Do you think Cap really saw Sam McGee or was he "half-mad"? (b) Do you think Sam McGee might have been playing a practical joke?

Plot

A poem may have a plot just as a short story does. The plot is the pattern of events that leads to some kind of change.

1. The plot of this poem is the pattern of events leading to Sam McGee's cremation. What happens on the Dawson Trail that makes Sam think he will die?

2. When Cap sees that Sam is dead, he tries to find a crematorium. (a) What does he do with the corpse first? (b) What does he do with the corpse when he reaches Lake Lebarge?

3. How is Sam different, or changed, at the end of the poem?

Activities

1. **Composition.** Imagine that you are Sam McGee. Write a short note to a friend back in Tennessee. Tell your friend your impressions of the Arctic.

2. Imagine you are about to begin a journey to the Arctic. List ten items you would bring along. Explain why each item would be necessary.

RELATIONSHIPS

Seeing Cause and Effect

A cause makes something happen. An effect is what happens. For example, the extreme cold makes Sam whimper. When you read what a character does in a story, ask "Why?" or "What is the cause?"

1. Why did Sam leave his home in Tennessee?
   a. He wanted to find gold.
   b. He liked cold weather.
   c. He wanted to be cremated in a derelict ship.

2. Why did Cap keep his promise even when it became harder and harder to keep?
   a. There was nothing else he could do with the body.
   b. He really enjoyed carrying Sam's corpse with him.
   c. He believed that a promise made to a dying person should be kept.

3. Why did Cap have a hard time finding a crematorium?
   a. Wood is scarce in the Arctic.
   b. Cap's sled was broken.
   c. The food was getting low.

4. Why was Sam smiling at the end of the story?
   a. His face was frozen into a smile.
   b. He liked being warm.
   c. He was back in Tennessee.

WORD ATTACK

Understanding Contractions

As people use language, they tend to take shortcuts. Instead of using two words, they sometimes blend two words into one. **Contractions are words that have been blended.** The left-out letters are replaced, in writing, by an apostrophe. For example, you must have (must've) noticed many contractions when you read "The Cremation of Sam McGee."

1. Read each item below and look at the contraction in *italics*. Write the two words that were blended to form each contraction.
   a. "*I'll* cash in this trip, I guess;"
   b. "Though *he'd* often say in his homely way that '*he'd* sooner live in hell.' "
   c. "It *wasn't* much fun, but the only one to whimper was Sam McGee."
   d. "*I'm* chilled clean through to the bone."
   e. "Well, he seemed so low that I *couldn't* say no;"
   f. "So I want you to swear that, foul or fair, *you'll* cremate my last remains."
   g. "But you promised true, and *it's* up to you to cremate those last remains."
   h. "And *I'd* often sing to the hateful thing, and it harkened with a grin."
   i. "Then I made a hike, for I *didn't* like to hear him sizzle so;"
   j. "Since I left Plumtree, down in Tennessee, it's the first time *I've* been warm."

2. Why do you think the two words "will not" became "won't" rather than "willn't"?

The Dinner Party

Mona Gardner

The country is India. A colonial official and his wife are giving a large dinner party. They are seated with their guests—army officers and government attachés and their wives, and a visiting American naturalist—in their spacious dining room, which has a bare marble floor, open rafters, and wide glass doors opening onto a veranda.

A spirited discussion springs up between a young girl who insists that women have outgrown the jumping-on-a-chair-at-the-sight-of-a-mouse era and a colonel who says that they haven't.

"A woman's unfailing reaction in any crisis," the colonel says, "is to scream. And while a man may feel like it, he has that ounce more of nerve control than a woman has. And that last ounce is what counts."

The American does not join in the argument but watches the other guests. As he looks, he sees a strange expression come over the face of the hostess. She is staring straight ahead, her muscles contracting slightly. With a slight gesture, she summons the native boy standing

behind her chair and whispers to him. The boy's eyes widen, and he quickly leaves the room.

Of the guests, none except the American notices this or sees the boy place a bowl of milk on the veranda just outside the open doors.

The American comes to with a start. In India, milk in a bowl means only one thing—bait for a snake. He realizes there must be a cobra in the room. He looks up at the rafters—the likeliest place—but they are bare. Three corners of the room are empty, and in the fourth the servants are waiting to serve the next course. There is only one place left—under the table.

His first impulse is to jump back and warn the others, but he knows the commotion would frighten the cobra into striking. He speaks quickly, the tone of his voice so arresting that it sobers everyone.

"I want to know just what control everyone at this table has. I will count to three hundred—that's five minutes— and not one of you is to move a muscle. Those who move will forfeit fifty rupees. Ready!"

The twenty people sit like stone images while he counts. He is saying " . . . two hundred and eighty . . ." when, out of the corner of his eye, he sees the cobra emerge and make for the bowl of milk. Screams ring out as he jumps to slam the veranda doors safely shut.

"You were right, Colonel!" the host exclaims. "A man has just shown us an example of perfect control."

"Just a minute," the American says, turning to his hostess. "Mrs. Wynnes, how did you know the cobra was in the room?"

A faint smile lights up the woman's face as she replies, "Because it was crawling across my foot."

Close Up

1. At the dinner party, the Colonel says that men have more self-control than women. What takes the American's attention away from the lively discussion?

2. The American realizes that a bowl of milk on the veranda means a cobra is in the room. How does he know that the snake must be under the table?

3. The American is afraid that the snake will strike if anyone moves. What does he do to stop everyone from moving?

4. When the snake has gone, the host points out the American's example of perfect control. But this still does not prove that men have more self-control than women. Why not?

Suspense

Suspense is the quality of a story that makes you wonder what will happen next. In a story full of suspense, you worry about the fate of the characters. You feel uncertain about how the story will end.

1. Suspense begins when the American sees a strange expression come over the face of the hostess. What does the servant do that heightens the suspense?

2. Suspense increases when you begin to worry about the fate of the characters. What do you think may happen to this story's characters?

3. Would the story be as suspenseful if the American could see the snake? Why or why not?

4. The suspense is greatest when the American begins to count. What do you fear at this point?

5. When does the suspense end?

Activities

1. **Composition.** Write the comment you think the host might have made when the hostess said, "Because it was crawling across my foot." Then write the comment you think the colonel might have made.

2. What paragraph in this story gives you the best picture of what is happening in the dining room? Compare your choice with the choices of other students.

3. Which character in this story do you admire most? Tell why.

RELATIONSHIPS

Understanding Cause and Effect

Many ideas and events are connected in a cause and effect relationship. The *cause* is what makes something happen. The *effect* is what happens. For example, in "The Dinner Party," the colonel says that any crisis makes a woman scream. The *cause* is any crisis. The *effect* is a woman screams.

---

1. Each pair of sentences below shows a cause and effect relationship. Draw one line under the sentence that is the cause. Draw two lines under the sentence that is the effect.
    a. The native boy puts a bowl of milk on the veranda. Mrs. Wynnes whispers to the native boy.
    b. Mrs. Wynnes asks the boy to put milk on the veranda. She realizes there is a cobra in the room.
    c. The American knows that a disturbance would frighten the cobra and make it strike. He does not jump back from the table.
    d. The American asks everyone to test self-control. He knows there is a cobra under the table.
    e. Mrs. Wynnes knows the cobra is in the room. It has been crawling across her foot.

2. **Composition.** Write two sentences showing a cause and effect relationship.

WORD ATTACK

Understanding the Sounds of S

The letter s stands for two different sounds. One sound is /s/ as in seal. The other sound is /z/ as in please. For example, notice the two sounds of s in the following sentence. "With a slight gesture, she summons the native boy standing behind her chair and whispers to him."

---

1. The following words are from "The Dinner Party." Look up each word in the dictionary. Check to see if the letter s stands for /s/ or /z/. Write /s/ or /z/ by each word.

   a. leaves   **f.** spirited
   b. naturalist   **g.** last
   c. glass   **h.** visiting
   d. wives   **i.** rafters
   e. has   **j.** gesture

2. The author repeats these two sounds of s throughout "The Dinner Party" to make you sense the presence of the lurking snake. Read the fourth paragraph aloud. Emphasize the sounds spelled by s.

Harriet Tubman

Ann Petry

The road to freedom was long and dangerous. But Harriet Tubman believed, "We got to go free or die. And freedom's not bought with dust."

Along the Eastern Shore of Maryland, in Dorchester County, in Caroline County, the masters kept hearing whispers about the man named Moses, who was running off slaves. At first they did not believe in his existence. The stories about him were fantastic, unbelievable. Yet they watched for him. They offered rewards for his capture.

They never saw him. Now and then they heard whispered rumors to the effect that he was in the neighborhood. The woods were searched. The roads were watched. There was never anything to indicate his whereabouts. But a few days afterward, a goodly number of slaves would be gone from the plantation. Neither the master nor the overseer had heard or seen anything unusual in the quarter. Sometimes one or the other would vaguely remember having heard a whippoorwill call somewhere in the woods, close by, late at night. Though it was the wrong season for whippoorwills.

Sometimes the masters thought they had heard the cry of a hoot owl, repeated, and would remember having thought that the intervals between the low moaning cry were wrong, that it had been repeated four times in succession instead of three. There was never anything more than that to suggest that all was not well in the quarter. Yet when morning came, they invariably discovered that a group of the finest slaves had taken to their heels.

Unfortunately, the discovery was almost always made on a Sunday. Thus a whole day was lost before the machinery of pursuit could be set in motion. The posters offering rewards for the fugitives could not be printed until Monday. The men who made a living hunting for runaway slaves were out of reach, off in the woods with their dogs and their guns, in pursuit of four-footed game, or they were in camp meetings saying their prayers with their wives and families beside them.

Harriet Tubman could have told them that there was far more involved in this matter of running off slaves than signaling the would-be runaways by imitating the call of a whippoorwill, or a hoot owl. There was far more involved than a matter of waiting for a clear night when the North Star was visible.

In December, 1851, when she started out with the band of fugitives that she planned to take to Canada, she had been in the vicinity[1] of the plantation for days, planning the trip, carefully selecting the slaves that she would take with her.

She had announced her arrival in the quarter by singing the forbidden spiritual—"Go down, Moses, 'way down to Egypt Land"—singing it softly outside the door of a slave cabin, late at night. The husky voice was beautiful even when it was barely more than a murmur borne on the wind.

Once she had made her presence known, word of her coming spread from cabin to cabin. The slaves whispered to each other, ear to mouth, mouth to ear, "Moses is here." "Moses has come." "Get ready. Moses is back again." The ones who had agreed to go North with her put ashcake[2] and salt herring in an old bandanna, hastily tied it into a bundle, and then waited patiently for the signal that meant it was time to start.

There were eleven in this party, including one of her brothers and his wife. It was the largest group that she had

ever conducted, but she was determined that more and more slaves should know what freedom was like.

She had to take them all the way to Canada. The Fugitive Slave Law[3] was no longer a great many incomprehensible words written down on the country's lawbooks. The new law had become a reality. It was Thomas Sims, a boy, picked up on the streets of Boston at night and shipped back to Georgia. It was Jerry and Shadrach, arrested and jailed with no warning.

She had never been in Canada. The route beyond Philadelphia was strange to her. But she could not let the runaways who accompanied her know this. As they walked along, she told them stories of her own first flight. She kept painting vivid word pictures of what it would be like to be free.

But there were so many of them this time. She knew moments of doubt when she was half-afraid, and kept looking back over her shoulder, imagining that she heard the sound of pursuit. They would certainly be pursued. Eleven of them. Eleven thousand dollars' worth of flesh and bone and muscle that belonged to Maryland planters. If they were caught, the eleven runaways would be whipped and sold South, but she—she would probably be hanged.

They tried to sleep during the day, but they never could wholly relax into sleep. She could tell by the positions they assumed, by their restless movements. And they walked at night. Their progress was slow. It took them three nights of walking to reach the first stop. She had told them about the place where

---

1. vicinity (vĭ-sĭn′ə-tē) n.: Nearby area
2. ashcake (ăsh′kāk) n.: A cornmeal cake baked in hot ashes.

3. Fugitive Slave Law: A series of laws providing for the return of escaped slaves to their masters.

Harriet Tubman

Black Heritage USA 13c

ishment and fear at the eleven disheveled runaways who were standing near her. Then he shouted, "Too many, too many. It's not safe. My place was searched last week. It's not safe!" and slammed the door in her face.

She turned away from the house, frowning. She had promised her passengers food and rest and warmth, and instead of that, there would be hunger and cold and more walking over the frozen ground. Somehow she would have to instill courage into these eleven people, most of them strangers, would have to feed them on hope and bright dreams of freedom instead of the fried pork and corn bread and milk she had promised them.

They stumbled along behind her, half-dead for sleep, and she urged them on, though she was as tired and as discouraged as they were. She had never been in Canada but she kept painting wondrous word pictures of what it would be like. She managed to dispel their fear of pursuit, so that they would not become hysterical, panic-stricken. Then she had to bring some of the fear back, so that they would stay awake and keep walking, though they drooped with sleep.

Yet during the day, when they lay down deep in a thicket, they never really slept, because if a twig snapped or the wind sighed in the branches of a pine tree, they jumped to their feet, afraid of their own shadows, shivering and shaking. It was very cold, but they dared not make fires because someone would see the smoke and wonder about it.

She kept thinking, eleven of them. Eleven thousand dollars' worth of slaves. And she had to take them all the way to Canada. Sometimes she told them about

they would stay, promising warmth and good food, holding these things out to them as an incentive to keep going.

When she knocked on the door of a farmhouse, a place where she and her parties of runaways had always been welcome, always been given shelter and plenty to eat, there was no answer. She knocked again, softly. A voice from within said, "Who is it?" There was fear in the voice.

She knew instantly from the sound of the voice that there was something wrong. She said, "A friend with friends," the password on the Underground Railroad.

The door opened, slowly. The man who stood in the doorway looked at her coldly, looked with unconcealed aston-

Thomas Garrett, in Wilmington. She said he was their friend, even though he did not know them. He was the friend of all fugitives. He called them God's poor. He was a Quaker and his speech was a little different from that of other people. His clothing was different, too. He wore the wide-brimmed hat that the Quakers wear.

She said that he had thick white hair, soft, almost like a baby's, and the kindest eyes she had ever seen. He was a big man and strong, but he had never used his strength to harm anyone, always to help people. He would give all of them a new pair of shoes. Everybody. He always did. Once they reached his house in Wilmington, they would be safe. He would see to it that they were.

She described the house where he lived, told them about the store where he sold shoes. She said he kept a pail of milk and a loaf of bread in the drawer of his desk so that he would have food ready at hand for any of God's poor who should suddenly appear before him, fainting with hunger. There was a hidden room in the store. A whole wall swung open, and behind it was a room where he could hide fugitives. On the

wall there were shelves filled with small boxes—boxes of shoes—so that you would never guess that the wall actually opened.

While she talked, she kept watching them. They did not believe her. She could tell by their expressions. They were thinking. New shoes, Thomas Garrett, Quaker, Wilmington—what foolishness was this? Who knew if she told the truth? Where was she taking them anyway?

That night they reached the next stop—a farm that belonged to a German. She made the runaways take shelter behind trees at the edge of the fields before she knocked at the door. She hesitated before she approached the door, thinking, suppose that he, too, should refuse shelter, suppose——Then she thought, Lord, I'm going to hold steady on to You and You've got to see me through—and knocked softly.

She heard the familiar guttural voice say, "Who's there?"

She answered quickly, "A friend with friends."

He opened the door and greeted her warmly. "How many this time?" he asked.

"Eleven," she said and waited, doubting, wondering.

He said, "Good. Bring them in."

He and his wife fed them in the lamplit kitchen, their faces glowing, as they offered food and more food, urging them to eat, saying there was plenty for everybody, have more milk, have more bread, have more meat.

They spent the night in the warm kitchen. They really slept, all that night and until dusk the next day. When they left, it was with reluctance. They had all been warm and safe and well-fed. It was hard to exchange the security offered by that clean warm kitchen for the darkness and the cold of a December night.

Harriet had found it hard to leave the warmth and friendliness, too. But she urged them on. For a while, as they walked, they seemed to carry in them a measure of contentment; some of the serenity and the cleanliness of that big warm kitchen lingered on inside them. But as they walked farther and farther away from the warmth and the light, the cold and the darkness entered into them. They fell silent, sullen, suspicious. She waited for the moment when some one of them would turn mutinous.[4] It did not happen that night.

Two nights later she was aware that the feet behind her were moving slower and slower. She heard the irritability in their voices, knew that soon someone would refuse to go on.

She started talking about William Still and the Philadelphia Vigilance Committee.[5] No one commented. No one asked any questions. She told them the story of William and Ellen Craft and how they escaped from Georgia. Ellen was so fair that she looked as though she were white, and so she dressed up in a man's clothing and she looked like a wealthy young planter. Her husband, William, who was dark, played the role of her slave. Thus they traveled from Macon, Georgia, to Philadelphia, riding on the trains, staying at the finest hotels. Ellen pretended to be very ill—her right arm was in a sling, and her right hand was bandaged, because she was supposed to

---

4. mutinous (my$\overline{oo}$t'n-əs) *adj.*: Rebellious.
5. Philadelphia Vigilance Committee: A group that helped slaves escape to Canada.

have rheumatism. Thus she avoided having to sign the register at the hotels for she could not read or write. They finally arrived safely in Philadelphia, and then went on to Boston.

No one said anything. Not one of them seemed to have heard her.

She told them about Frederick Douglass, the most famous of the escaped slaves, of his eloquence, of his magnificent appearance. Then she told them of her own first vain effort at running away, evoking the memory of that miserable life she had led as a child, reliving it for a moment in the telling.

But they had been tired too long, hungry too long, afraid too long, footsore too long. One of them suddenly cried out in despair, "Let me go back. It is better to be a slave than to suffer like this in order to be free."

She carried a gun with her on these trips. She had never used it—except as a threat. Now as she aimed it, she experienced a feeling of guilt, remembering that time, years ago, when she had prayed for the death of Edward Brodas, the Master, and then not too long afterward had heard that great wailing cry that came from the throats of the field hands, and knew from the sound that the Master was dead.

One of the runaways said, again, "Let me go back. Let me go back," and stood still, and then turned around and said, over his shoulder, "I am going back."

She lifted the gun, aimed it at the despairing slave. She said, "Go on with us or die." The husky low-pitched voice was grim.

He hesitated for a moment and then he joined the others. They started walking again. She tried to explain to them why none of them could go back to the plantation. If a runaway returned, he would turn traitor. The master and the overseer would force him to turn traitor. The returned slave would disclose the stopping places, the hiding places, the cornstacks they had used with the full knowledge of the owner of the farm, the name of the German farmer who had fed them and sheltered them. These people who had risked their own security to help runaways would be ruined, fined, imprisoned.

She said, "We got to go free or die. And freedom's not bought with dust."

This time she told them about the long agony of the Middle Passage[6] on the old slave ships, about the black horror of the holds, about the chains and the whips. They too knew these stories. But she wanted to remind them of the long hard way they had come, about the long hard way they had yet to go. She told them about Thomas Sims, the boy picked up on the streets of Boston and sent back to Georgia. She said when they got him back to Savannah, got him in prison there, they whipped him until a doctor who was standing by watching said, "You will kill him if you strike him again!" His master said, "Let him die!"

Thus she forced them to go on. Sometimes she thought she had become nothing but a voice speaking in the darkness, cajoling, urging, threatening. Sometimes she told them things to make them laugh, sometimes she sang to them, and heard the eleven voices behind her blending softly with hers, and then she knew that for the moment all was well with them.

---

6. the Middle Passage: The journey from Africa to America on the slave ships.

She gave the impression of being a short, muscular, indomitable woman who could never be defeated. Yet at any moment she was liable to be seized by one of those curious fits of sleep, which might last for a few minutes or for hours.

Even on this trip, she suddenly fell asleep in the woods. The runaways, ragged, dirty, hungry, cold, did not steal the gun as they might have, and set off by themselves, or turn back. They sat on the ground near her and waited patiently until she awakened. They had come to trust her implicitly, totally. They, too, had come to believe her repeated statement, "We got to go free or die." She was leading them into freedom, and so they waited until she was ready to go on.

Finally, they reached Thomas Garrett's house in Wilmington, Delaware. Just as Harriet had promised, Garrett gave them all new shoes, and provided carriages to take them on to the next stop.

By slow stages they reached Philadelphia, where William Still hastily recorded their names, and the plantations whence they had come, and something of the life they had led in slavery. Then he carefully hid what he had written, for fear it might be discovered. In 1872 he published this record in book form and called it *The Underground Railroad.* In the foreword to his book he said: "While I knew the danger of keeping strict records, and while I did not then dream that in my day slavery would be blotted out, or that the time would come when I could publish these records, it used to afford me great satisfaction to take them down, fresh from the lips of fugitives on the way to freedom, and to preserve them as they had given them."

William Still, who was familiar with all the station stops on the Underground Railroad, supplied Harriet with money and sent her and her eleven fugitives on to Burlington, New Jersey.

Harriet felt safer now, though there were danger spots ahead. But the biggest part of her job was over. As they went farther and farther north, it grew colder; she was aware of the wind on the Jersey ferry and aware of the cold damp in New York. From New York they went on to Syracuse, where the temperature was even lower.

In Syracuse she met the Reverend J. W. Loguen, known as "Jarm" Loguen. This was the beginning of a lifelong friendship. Both Harriet and Jarm Loguen were to become friends and supporters of Old John Brown.[7]

From Syracuse they went north again, into a colder, snowier city—Rochester. Here they almost certainly stayed with Frederick Douglass, for he wrote in his autobiography:

"On one occasion I had eleven fugitives at the same time under my roof, and it was necessary for them to remain with me until I could collect sufficient money to get them to Canada. It was the largest number I ever had at any one time, and I had some difficulty in providing so many with food and shelter, but, as may well be imagined, they were not very fastidious in either direction, and were well content with very plain food, and a strip of carpet on the floor for a bed, or a place on the straw in the barnloft."

Late in December, 1851, Harriet arrived in St. Catharines, Canada West (now Ontario), with the eleven fugitives.

---

7. John Brown (1800–1859): A leader in the fight against slavery.

It had taken almost a month to complete this journey; most of the time had been spent getting out of Maryland.

That first winter in St. Catharines was a terrible one. Canada was a strange frozen land, snow everywhere, ice everywhere, and a bone-biting cold the like of which none of them had experienced before. Harriet rented a small frame house in the town and set to work to make a home. The fugitives boarded with her. They worked in the forests, felling trees, and so did she. Sometimes she took other jobs, cooking or cleaning house for people in the town. She cheered on these newly arrived fugitives, working herself, finding work for them, finding food for them, praying for them, sometimes begging for them.

Often she found herself thinking of the beauty of Maryland, the mellowness of the soil, the richness of the plant life there. The climate itself made for an ease

of living that could never be duplicated in this bleak, barren countryside.

In spite of the severe cold, the hard work, she came to love St. Catharines, and the other towns and cities in Canada where black men lived. She discovered that freedom meant more than the right to change jobs at will, more than the right to keep the money that one earned. It was the right to vote and to sit on juries. It was the right to be elected to office. In Canada there were black men who were county officials and members of school boards. St. Catharines had a large colony of ex-slaves, and they owned their own homes, kept them neat and clean and in good repair. They lived in whatever part of town they chose and sent their children to the schools.

When spring came she decided that she would make this small Canadian city her home—as much as any place could be said to be home to a woman who traveled from Canada to the Eastern Shore of Maryland as often as she did.

In the spring of 1852, she went back to Cape May, New Jersey. She spent the summer there, cooking in a hotel. That fall she returned, as usual, to Dorchester County, and brought out nine more slaves, conducting them all the way to St. Catharines, in Canada West, to the bone-biting cold, the snow-covered forests—and freedom.

She continued to live in this fashion, spending the winter in Canada, and the spring and summer working in Cape May, New Jersey, or in Philadelphia. She made two trips a year into slave territory, one in the fall and another in the spring. She now had a definite crystallized purpose, and in carrying it out, her life fell into a pattern which remained unchanged for the next six years.

Close Up

1. During biblical times, Moses led the Israelites from slavery in Egypt. Although he himself was free, he risked his life to lead his people to freedom. (a) Why was "Moses" a good name for Harriet Tubman? (b) Why did she need a code name?

2. (a) Why did Harriet Tubman plan the escape so that the slaves would not be missed until Sunday? (b) What else did she do that shows Harriet was a clever and careful planner?

3. Harriet was capable of quick action when the moment demanded. (a) How did she stop the mutiny? (b) Why couldn't she allow a runaway to return?

4. Good leaders must inspire respect and trust. Why didn't the fugitives steal the gun when Harriet fell asleep?

5. Do you think that a person can be afraid and still be heroic? Why or why not?

Character

An author can tell you about a character in a story in five ways. First, the author can comment directly on the character: She was a courageous and brave woman. Second, the author can tell you what the character looks like. Third, the author can reveal the character's thoughts and feelings. Fourth, the author can tell you what other characters say about or think about this character. Fifth, the author can show you the character's actions and let you draw conclusions about the character from these actions.

1. The author tells you that Harriet Tubman sang with a husky voice. What else does she tell you about Harriet's voice?

2. Write a complete sentence describing what Harriet Tubman looked like.

3. (a) How does Harriet feel when she and the runaways are turned away from the first house? (b) Why doesn't she show her feelings to the runaways?

4. The masters hear whispers about a person named Moses. (a) What do the whispers say that Moses does? (b) Do the masters think Moses is clever? Why or why not?

5. Harriet's actions show you that she thinks freedom is worth many hardships. List two things she does at St. Catharines that show freedom is important to her.

RELATIONSHIPS

Understanding Comparison and Contrast

One way in which details are connected in a story is called a comparison and contrast relationship, which shows how things are alike and how they are different. For example, look at the following sentence. "She had promised her passengers food and rest and warmth, and instead of that, there would be hunger and cold and more walking over the frozen ground." This sentence shows how what Harriet Tubman promised the slaves is different from what she could give them.

---

1. Read passages **(1)** through **(5).** Then answer questions *a* through *e*.

(1)
"If they were caught, the eleven runaways would be whipped and sold South, but she—she would probably be hanged."

(2)
"They stumbled along behind her, half-dead for sleep, and she urged them on, though she was as tired and discouraged as they were."

(3)
"It was hard to exchange the security offered by that clean warm kitchen for the darkness and the cold of a December night."

(4)
"She gave the impression of being a short, muscular, indomitable woman who could never be defeated. Yet at any moment she was liable to be seized by one of those curious fits of sleep, which might last for a few minutes or for hours."

(5)
"He (Thomas Garrett) was a Quaker and his speech was a little different from that of other people. His clothing was different, too."

a. Which passage shows how Harriet Tubman is different from the picture she creates? How is she different?

b. Which passage shows how Thomas Garrett is different from other people? In what two ways is he different?

c. Which passage shows how Harriet's fate would be different from the runaways' if they were caught? What would happen to Harriet?

d. Which passage shows that Harriet's feelings are the same as the runaways' feelings? How do they feel?

e. Which passage shows how the night the runaways spend in the kitchen is different from the night they spend outside? The words *security, clean,* and *warm* describe the night in the kitchen. Which two words describe the night outside?

2. List two words that describe each of the following:
   a. The lives of slaves in slavery.
   b. The lives of slaves on the road.
   c. The lives of slaves in Canada.

WORD ATTACK

Understanding Negative Prefixes

A prefix is a letter or combination of letters attached to the front of a word. A prefix gives a new meaning to that word. Certain prefixes give a negative sense to a word. This means that the prefixes stand for the word *not.* Prefixes that give a negative sense are *a-, un-, de-* or *dis-,* and *il-, im-,* or *in-.* For example, the word *illegal* means "not legal."

1. Complete the following sentences.
   a. Something that is unbelievable is not _____.
   b. Someone who is discouraged no longer has _____.
   c. Something which has been displaced is no longer in

   _____.

   d. Something which is indescribable cannot be _____.
   e. Someone who is unusual is not _____.

2. Add the proper negative prefix to each of the words in *italics.* Check your work in a dictionary.
   a. "She now had a definite crystallized purpose, and in carrying it out, her life fell into a pattern which remained __*changed* for the next six years."
   b. "The Fugitive Slave Law was no longer a great many __*comprehensible* words written down on the country's lawbooks."
   c. "__*fortunately,* the discovery was almost always made on a Sunday."
   d. "The man . . . looked with __*concealed* astonishment and fear at the eleven disheveled runaways who were standing near her."

Mama Is a Sunrise

Evelyn Tooley Hunt

When she comes slip-footing through the door,
        she kindles us
        like lump coal lighted,
        and we wake up glowing.
5   She puts a spark even in Papa's eyes
    and turns out all our darkness.

When she comes sweet-talking in the room,
        she warms us
        like grits and gravy,
10   and we rise up shining.
    Even at night-time Mama is a sunrise
    that promises tomorrow and tomorrow.

Close Up ▶ People often connect fear and darkness. (a) What does Mama do to remove the family's fears? (b) What does her courage promise?

Ghost Town

Jack Schaefer

"When a pink-cheeked young tenderfoot with maybe some fuzz on his chin that hasn't even begun to be real whiskers comes your way, just watch your step."

I owned a whole town once. What was left of it anyway. A ghost town. One of the mining camps back in the hills that must have been quite a place when the gold rush was on. Then the diggings there petered out, and people began moving on, and the flimsy houses started collapsing after everyone was gone.

You can find traces of plenty of those old towns scattered up the back creeks. But this one was better than most. Some of the men there knew how to build a kiln and fire it and there was a clay bank nearby. A half dozen buildings were made of brick and these stood solid enough through the years. The roofs had fallen in, and the windows and doors were missing, but the walls were still standing. You could even figure out what they had been: a general store; a post office and stage station; a black-smith shop; a two-room jail; a small saloon; another saloon with space for dancing or gambling tables and some rooms on a second floor.

This old town of mine was up a narrow gulch that wasn't good for a thing once the gold was gone. But it was only about a half mile from a modern main highway and the old dirt road leading to it was still passable. I drove in there one day and was poking around when another car loaded with tourists pulled up and the people piled out and wandered around with the women oh-ing and ah-ing as if they were seeing something wonderful.

That's when I had my idea.

It took time but I ran that town down on the tax books and found out all about it. The county had taken title to the whole place for back taxes maybe fifty years before—so long before, it had been written off the accounts as a dead loss and just about forgotten. When I offered to buy it, the county officials thought I was crazy and jumped to make a deal. They hadn't expected ever to get another nickel out of the place. I paid $800 and I owned a town.

I cleaned out the old buildings enough so you could walk around inside them. I painted names on them telling what they had been. I fixed a few bad spots in the dirt road. I plastered signs along the highway, for maybe five miles in each direction, and a big one where the dirt road turned off. I roofed over one room of the old jail for my own quarters. I charged fifty cents a head for a look-see through the old place—and I was in business.

It was a good business. Not in the winter, of course, and slow in the spring and fall, but good all summer—enough to carry me comfortably all year. During the rough months, I'd stay at a rooming house in the live town that was the county seat and, as soon as the weather was right, I'd move out and start collecting my half dollars.

Sometimes, I'd have four or five cars at a time parked by the entrance and a dozen or more people listening to my talk. I'd check the license plates and temper the talk accordingly. If they were from the home state or one nearby, I'd go easy on the fancy trimmings. Those people might know too much real history. But if they were from far states, maybe eastern ones, I'd let loose and make it strong. I'd tell about fights in the saloons—shootings and knifings and big brawls with bottles flying. I'd tell about road agents stopping stages carrying gold and getting caught and being locked up in the jail and maybe a daring escape or two. I'd make it good and the eastern

tourists lapped it up. What if all of it happened only in my head? Such things could have happened and maybe did. What if I did get a couple of complaints from the state historical society? There wasn't anything anyone could do so long as I made up the names too. The town belonged to me.

It was a good business. For three years. Then it collapsed just the way the old town itself did way back when. The state started straightening the highway and knocked off the loop that came near my ghost town. That put the main route about seven miles away. I slapped up more signs but not many people would bother to turn off onto the old route and try to find the place. My business started skidding. I tried to unload it on the historical society, and they just laughed at me. They'd bought a ghost town of their own and were fixing it up. Soon as they had it open, they'd finish the job of killing my business.

I was stuck with that town. I'd put hard money into it and now I was stuck with it. The summer season started, and I was lucky to average a single car a day. I was figuring I'd have to swallow the loss and move on, when this pink-cheeked young fellow came along. It was late one afternoon, and he was pink-cheeked like a boy with maybe a little fuzz on his chin that hadn't begun to be whiskers yet. He drove up in an old car that had lost its color in dust, and he paid fifty cents and started poking around. I was so lonesome for customers, or just anyone to talk to, that I stuck close and kept words bouncing back and forth with him. He looked so young and innocent, I figured he was a college kid seeing some of the country on vacation time. But no. He said he'd had all the college he could absorb. He was a mining engineer by profession, but there wasn't much professing to be done in that field about then, so he was knocking around looking over the old camps. He liked to see how they did things in the old days. Maybe he'd write a book on it some time.

"Mighty interesting town you have here," he said. "Those buildings. Brick. Don't see much brick in the old camps. They haul them in here?"

"Why no," I said. "They had a kiln right here—you can see where it was behind the blacksmith shop. They dug the clay out of the bank over there." And right away, this young fellow had to see that too.

"Mighty interesting," he said. "Found the clay right here. Don't often come on good brick clay in these parts. But you can see they cleaned out this streak in the bank. They sure liked bricks. If they hadn't run out of the clay they might still be making them."

"That'd be a fool stunt," I said. "Who'd be wanting bricks around here now?"

"Yes," he said. "Yes, it would. A fool stunt." And he wandered on, me with him and him talking more about what sturdy buildings these bricks had made and other things like that.

"Mighty interesting business you're in," he said. "Playing nursemaid to an old town like this and having people pay to look it over. Must be kind of a nice life."

That's when I had another idea.

I took that pink-cheeked young fellow into my jail-room and persuaded him to stay for supper. I began coughing at strategic intervals during the meal and I told him my health was bad and the climate bothered me, otherwise I wouldn't even be thinking of maybe leaving such a nice life in such an interesting business. I played it clever with indirect questions and got out of him the fact he had a bit of cash to invest. Then I really went to work on him.

"Stay here tonight," I said, "and stick around tomorrow. You'll see what a good business this really is." He said he would, and I worked on him some more, and, after a while, I asked him to keep an eye on the place while I drove over to the county seat to tend to a few things.

I tended to the things all right but not at the county seat. I burned up the roads getting to various men I knew around about. Each stop I put the same proposition. "There's ten dollars in it for you," I said, "if you'll take time tomorrow to put the missus and anyone else handy in the car, and drive over to the old town, and make like a tourist gawking around some." I covered a lot of miles and I was turned down at a few stops. But, at last, I had eleven cars promised and, with the extras, that would run to about forty people.

When I got back, my pink-cheeked baby was sleeping like one on the cot I'd fixed up for him. He woke long enough to grunt a greeting, then rolled over and went to sleep again. But I could tell he'd been snooping in the last summer's tally-book I'd left out on purpose where he would see it. The highway change hadn't been finished then and that had been a good summer.

Come morning, everything clicked just right. My home-grown tourists started coming, and kept coming, at about the times I'd suggested all the way through the morning and early afternoon. I was worried that my young visitor might get to talking with them and sniff some suspicions, but he didn't bother with them at all. He just watched what was going on and wandered around by himself and spent some time poking in what was left of the old kiln. I worked on him a bit during lunch and about the middle of the afternoon, when the last of the cars had left, I figured it was time to hook him.

"Not bad," I said. "Eleven cars and forty-one people. Twenty dollars and a fifty-cent piece over. And all I did was just sit here and let them come."

"Mighty interesting," he said. "That's more people than I expected."

"That?" I said. "Just a low average. Good enough for a weekday but you should see the weekends. Saturdays double it. And Sundays? Why, Sundays triple it."

"You don't say?" he said. "Too bad about your health. Didn't you mention something about wanting to sell out?"

And right then I knew I had him.

It was just a matter of price after that and on price I always was a tough one. When I chucked my things in my car so I could turn the place over to him that same day, and led the way to the county seat with him following so we could find a notary and sign the papers, I'd pushed him up to a thousand bucks. He looked so young and innocent tagging after me into the notary's that I was almost ashamed of myself . . . .

Brother, let me tell you something. When a pink-cheeked young tenderfoot with maybe some fuzz on his chin that hasn't even begun to be real whiskers comes your way, just watch your step. Watch it close. That's the kind will take you for anything you've got worth taking—while you're still wondering whether he's been weaned. It wasn't a

week later I saw this baby-faced sucker I thought I'd trimmed coming toward me along a street, and I ducked quick into a bar. He followed me in and cornered me.

"How's business?" I said, hoping to get any unpleasantness over with fast.

"Business?" he said. "Now that's mighty interesting. Do you really think you fooled me with those fake tourists? The license plates tipped me right away. All from this state. All from this county." He grinned—the same innocent grin he had the first time I saw him. "Let me buy you a drink. No hard feelings. Your so-called business didn't interest me at all. It was the buildings. I've a crew out there now tearing them down."

"Tearing them down?" I said.

"Certainly," he said. "Those bricks. That clay was the best pocket of pay dirt in the whole gulch—only those old-time miners didn't know it. There was gold dust in that clay and it's right there in the bricks. I'm having them crushed and washing the gold out. There's close to a hundred tons of those bricks and they're panning about eight hundred dollars to the ton."

Close Up

1. At first, the ghost town seems useless. When a group of tourists start "oh-ing and ah-ing," the storyteller gets an idea. What is his idea?

2. He fixes up the town and gives historical tours to tourists, but he is not very truthful. (a) What does he do if the tourists are from eastern states? (b) Why does he change his story if the tourists are local people?

3. When a new road takes his customers away, he wants to get rid of the town. Why does he think the mining engineer can be easily fooled into buying the worthless town?

4. What does the storyteller do to convince the engineer that the town is valuable?

5. This story is really about a double swindle. (a) Why does the mining engineer buy the town? (b) Who really tricks whom?

Motives

A motive is the reason behind a certain action. When you understand the characters' motives, the reasons for their actions become clearer.

1. What is the storyteller's motive for each action?
   a. He buys a ghost town.
   b. He coughs and tells the mining engineer about his poor health.
   c. He offers the engineer a bed for the night.
   d. He leaves his tally-book on the table.

2. What is the engineer's motive for each action?
   a. He asks the man if the bricks were hauled in or dug out of the bank.
   b. He tells the man the business looks "mighty interesting."

3. The man thinks he is tricking the engineer. But the engineer wants him to think this. What is the engineer's motive?

Activities

1. Draw one or two signs the man who owned the town might have made. Remember, he put these signs up to attract tourists to his ghost town.

2. **Composition.** Write a paragraph describing some tourist attraction you have visited.

RELATIONSHIPS

Understanding Comparison and Contrast

Comparing and contrasting characters can help you better understand them. When you compare characters, you show how they are alike. When you contrast characters, you show how they are different.

1. The two characters in "Ghost Town" are alike in some respects, but they are different in others. Read the descriptions below. On a separate piece of paper, put an *A* by any description that shows how the two characters are alike. Put a *D* by any description that shows how they are different. If the description shows how they are different, tell whether the description fits the storyteller or the engineer.
   a. interested in making money
   b. young
   c. makes up stories
   d. crafty
   e. looks innocent
   f. observant

2. The engineer is different because he knows something about the town's value that the storyteller doesn't know. What does the engineer know?

3. Both men are clever. Who is more clever? Why?

WORD ATTACK

Understanding Figurative Expressions

In figurative expressions most of the words do not have their usual meanings. They work together to create a totally new meaning. A figurative expression is usually colorful and descriptive. Here is an example: "I *burned up the roads* getting to various men I knew around about." The expression *burned up the roads* has nothing to do with setting roads on fire. It is a colorful way of saying, "I *drove my car fast along the road* getting to various men I knew around about."

▶ Each sentence below contains a figurative expression. In your own words, write the meaning of each expression in *italics*. Try to let the other words in the sentence help you.

a. "When I offered to buy it, the county officials thought I was crazy and *jumped to make a deal.*"

b. "I'd make it good and the eastern tourists *lapped it up.*"

c. "I was so lonesome for customers, or just anyone to talk to, that I stuck close and *kept words bouncing back and forth* with him."

d. "... after a while I asked him *to keep an eye on the place* while I drove over to the county seat to tend to a few things."

e. "Then I really *went to work on him.*"

f. "I was worried that my young visitor might get to talking with them and *sniff some suspicions,* but he didn't bother with them at all."

g. "I figured it was time *to hook him.*"

h. "He was a mining engineer by profession, but there wasn't much professing to be done in that field about then, so *he was knocking around* looking over the old camps."

Thank You, M'am

Langston Hughes

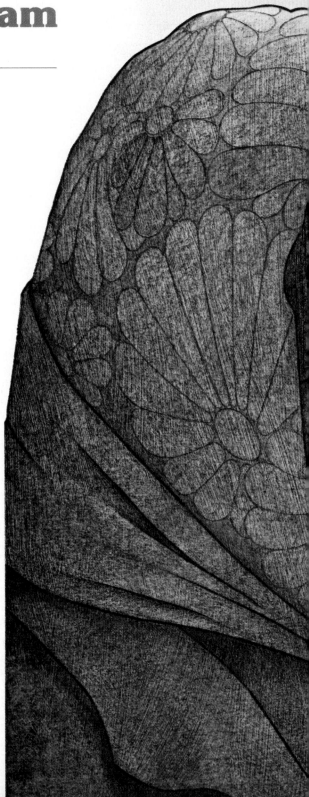

She was a large woman with a large purse that had everything in it but hammer and nails. It had a long strap and she carried it slung across her shoulder. It was about eleven o'clock at night, and she was walking alone, when a boy ran up behind her and tried to snatch her purse. The strap broke with the single tug the boy gave it from behind. But the boy's weight, and the weight of the purse combined caused him to lose his balance so, instead of taking off full blast as he had hoped, the boy fell on his back on the sidewalk, and his legs flew up. The large woman simply turned around and kicked him right square in his blue-jeaned sitter. Then she reached down, picked the boy up by his shirt front, and shook him until his teeth rattled.

After that the woman said, "Pick up my pocketbook, and give it here."

She still held him. But she bent down enough to permit him to stoop and pick up her purse. Then she said, "Now ain't you ashamed of yourself?"

Firmly gripped by his shirt front, the boy said, "Yes'm."

The woman said, "What did you want to do it for?"

The boy said, "I didn't aim to."

She said, "You a lie!"

By that time two or three people passed, stopped, turned to look, and some stood watching.

"If I turn you loose, will you run?" asked the woman.

"Yes'm," said the boy.

"Then I won't turn you loose," said the woman. She did not release him.

"I'm very sorry, lady, I'm sorry," whispered the boy.

"Um-hum! And your face is dirty. I got a great mind to wash your face for you. Ain't you got nobody home to tell you to wash your face?"

"No'm," said the boy.

"Then it will get washed this evening," said the large woman starting up the street, dragging the frightened boy behind her.

He looked as if he were fourteen or fifteen, frail and willow-wild, in tennis shoes and blue jeans.

The woman said, "You ought to be my son. I would teach you right from wrong. Least I can do right now is to wash your face. Are you hungry?"

"No'm," said the being-dragged boy. "I just want you to turn me loose."

"Was I bothering *you* when I turned that corner?" asked the woman.

"No'm."

"But you put yourself in contact with *me*," said the woman. "If you think that that contact is not going to last awhile, you got another thought coming. When I get through with you, sir, you are going to remember Mrs. Luella Bates Washington Jones."

Sweat popped out on the boy's face and he began to struggle. Mrs. Jones stopped, jerked him around in front of her, put a half nelson about his neck, and continued to drag him up the street. When she got to her door, she dragged the boy inside, down a hall, and into a large kitchenette-furnished room at the rear of the house. She switched on the light and left the door open. The boy could hear other roomers laughing and talking in the large house. Some of their doors were open, too, so he knew he and the woman were not alone. The woman still had him by the neck in the middle of her room.

She said, "What is your name?"

"Roger," answered the boy.

"Then, Roger, you go to that sink and wash your face," said the woman, whereupon she turned him loose—at last. Roger looked at the door—looked at the woman—looked at the door—*and went to the sink.*

"Let the water run until it gets warm," she said. "Here's a clean towel."

"You gonna take me to jail?" asked the boy, bending over the sink.

"Not with that face, I would not take you nowhere," said the woman. "Here I am trying to get home to cook me a bite to eat and you snatch my pocketbook! Maybe you ain't been to your supper either, late as it be. Have you?"

"There's nobody home at my house," said the boy.

"Then we'll eat," said the woman. "I believe you're hungry—or been hungry—to try to snatch my pocketbook."

"I wanted a pair of blue suede shoes," said the boy.

"Well, you didn't have to snatch my pocketbook to get some suede shoes," said Mrs. Luella Bates Washington Jones. "You could of asked me."

"M'am?"

The water dripping from his face, the boy looked at her. There was a long pause. A very long pause. After he had dried his face and not knowing what else to do dried it again, the boy turned around, wondering what next. The door was open. He could make a dash for it down the hall. He could run, run, run, run, *run!*

The woman was sitting on the day-bed. After a while she said, "I were young once and I wanted things I could not get."

There was another long pause. The boy's mouth opened. Then he frowned, but not knowing he frowned.

The woman said, "Um-hum! You thought I was going to say *but,* didn't you? You thought I was going to say, *but I didn't snatch people's pocketbooks.* Well, I wasn't going to say that." Pause.

Silence. "I have done things, too, which I would not tell you, son—neither tell God, if he didn't already know. So you set down while I fix us something to eat. You might run that comb through your hair so you will look presentable."

In another corner of the room behind a screen was a gas plate and an icebox. Mrs. Jones got up and went behind the screen. The woman did not watch the boy to see if he was going to run now, nor did she watch her purse which she left behind her on the day-bed. But the boy took care to sit on the far side of the room where he thought she could easily see him out of the corner of her eye, if she wanted to. He did not trust the woman *not* to trust him. And he did not want to be mistrusted now.

"Do you need somebody to go to the store," asked the boy, "Maybe to get some milk or something?"

"Don't believe I do," said the woman, "unless you just want sweet milk yourself. I was going to make cocoa out of this canned milk I got here."

"That will be fine," said the boy.

She heated some lima beans and ham she had in the icebox, made the cocoa, and set the table. The woman did not ask the boy anything about where he lived, or his folks, or anything else that would embarrass him. Instead, as they ate, she told him about her job in a hotel beauty shop that stayed open late, what the work was like, and how all kinds of women came in and out, blonds, red-heads, and brunettes. Then she cut him a half of her ten-cent cake.

"Eat some more, son," she said.

When they were finished eating, she got up and said, "Now, here, take this ten dollars and buy yourself some blue suede shoes. And next time, do not make the mistake of latching onto *my* pocket-book *nor nobody else's*—because shoes come by devilish like that will burn your feet. I got to get my rest now. But I wish you would behave yourself, son, from here on in."

She led him down the hall to the front door and opened it. "Goodnight! Behave yourself!" she said, looking out into the street.

The boy wanted to say something else other than, "Thank you, m'am," to Mrs. Luella Bates Washington Jones, but he couldn't do so as he turned at the barren stoop and looked back at the large woman in the door. He barely managed to say, "Thank you," before she shut the door. And he never saw her again.

Close Up

1. After Roger tries to steal Mrs. Jones' pocketbook, she does not call the police. (a) How does she get Roger to come home with her? (b) What would she teach Roger if he were her son?

2. At first, Roger obeys Mrs. Jones because he is small and frightened, and she is big and strong. (a) What does he think Mrs. Jones will do with him? (b) Why do you think he stays when Mrs. Jones goes behind the screen?

3. Mrs. Jones reveals that she did things when she was young that she is ashamed of now. (a) Do you think her experiences have helped her to understand Roger? (b) Why does she leave her pocketbook on the daybed when she goes into the kitchen?

4. Because Mrs. Jones considers Roger's future more important than the ten dollars, she gives him money for shoes. What details show that Roger has learned something worthwhile from her example?

Conflict

The plot of a story usually centers around a conflict. One type of conflict is a struggle between two characters.

1. This story centers around a struggle between Roger and Mrs. Luella Bates Washington Jones. What does Roger do that starts that conflict?

2. At first, Roger wants money from Mrs. Jones so he can buy blue suede shoes. What does he want from Mrs. Jones at the end of the story?

3. At first, Mrs. Jones uses force to make Roger do what she wants. Later, she uses kindness and generosity to make Roger learn self-respect. (a) How does she show kindness? (b) How does she show generosity?

4. The struggle ends when Mrs. Jones gives Roger the ten dollars he wants so badly. (a) When he gets the money, do you think he wants it as much? Why or why not? (b) What lesson has Mrs. Jones taught him?

Activities

1. Debate or discuss the following statement: Sometimes kindness does more to prevent crime than punishment does.

2. **Composition.** Have you ever known a person who believed in you and made you believe in yourself? Write a paragraph describing this person.

RELATIONSHIPS

Understanding Contrast Words

Certain words or groups of words tell you that two things are being contrasted. They are being examined to see how they are different from each other. Among the words or word groups that show contrast are *although*, *but*, *however*, *instead*, *nevertheless*, *on the other hand*, and *yet*.

---

1. In each of the following items, find the word or words showing that two things are being contrasted.
   a. Roger wanted to run fast, but he lost his balance and fell.
   b. Roger expected Mrs. Jones to bring him to the police station. Instead, she brought him home.
   c. Although Roger wanted to run out the door, he went to the bathroom and washed his face.
   d. Mrs. Jones understood why Roger wanted the money. Nevertheless, she didn't want him to steal.
   e. Instead of lecturing him, Mrs. Jones told Roger she had been young once and had done things she was ashamed of.
   f. Mrs. Jones only had one ten-cent cake. However, she cut it in two and gave half of it to Roger.
   g. Mrs. Jones did not ask Roger about anything that would embarrass him. Instead, she told him about her job.
   h. Mrs. Jones showed she trusted Roger. She left her purse where Roger could take it and run. Yet Roger did not trust her *not* to trust him.
   i. Mrs. Jones did not want Roger to steal to buy shoes. On the other hand, she wanted him to have those shoes, so she gave him ten dollars.
   j. Roger wanted to say something special to Mrs. Jones, yet all he could say was "Thank you, M'am."

2. Mrs. Jones says, "I was young once and I wanted things I could not get." (a) What else does Roger expect Mrs. Jones to say to him? (b) How would this show she was different from Roger? (c) How does she make him think that, in some ways, they are the same?

WORD ATTACK

Understanding Modifiers

Authors often use words or groups of words to add details to objects, characters, or actions in a story. These words or groups of words are called modifiers. They tell how, which one, when, or where, and help readers form a better picture of details in the story.

---

1. Join the words in column **(a)** with the modifiers in column **(b)**.

    (a)
    (1) large purse
    (2) shook him
    (3) started up the street
    (4) had him
    (5) let the water run
    (6) her job in a hotel beauty salon
    (7) "Goodnight! Behave yourself, boy!" she said

    (b)
    (a) that stayed open late
    (b) looking out into the street
    (c) until it gets warm
    (d) by the neck
    (e) until his teeth rattled
    (f) that had everything in it but a hammer and nails
    (g) dragging the frightened boy behind her

2. Select the pairs above that give you the best pictures of what is being described.

My Hero

Zoltan Malocsay

They were running from a bear—a large, angry, determined grizzly.

Jackson heard his dog yelping off in the pines and he sighed. First a flat tire and now what? He hoped she wasn't learning about skunks or porcupines.

Tossing the tire iron and jack into the trunk of his subcompact, he slammed down the trunk lid and called her. "Here, Detta. Come on, girl. Ready to go now." He shaded his eyes, tried to peer deeper into the Montana woods.

Her yelping got closer; then she dashed into view, her eyes white-rimmed with fright. "Come here——" Jackson started, then he flinched. She was running from a bear, a huge, angry, determined bear. A grizzly!

"H-hey, don't come . . ." Jackson muttered, backing up. He jumped into the car. Reaching for the ignition switch, he remembered that the keys were still in the trunk lid. *No time now.* Detta howled a DON'T LEAVE ME! and the grizzly gained fast behind her, all claws and teeth and great roaring rage. Jackson rolled up the windows and slapped down door locks, holding his own door open until Detta could bound in. Then he slammed it shut.

The grizzly reached out with one paw, punched at the glass. Jackson saw the window spider-web, break inward with a dull crunch that sent little cubes of safety glass spraying. Gasping, he ducked to avoid the clawing paw that swept inside. Then the grizzly caught the panel and yanked, tearing away the locked door.

Jackson hit the door on the other side and rolled out, with his retriever howling and climbing all over him. He scrambled a few feet on his hands and knees, then got to his feet and ran for the tree-covered slope that fell away beside the road.

Too big to make it through the car, the grizzly had to back out and come around—a tiny head start for Jackson. Yet he couldn't help remembering what he'd read somewhere: *For a short distance, a grizzly can outrun a horse!*

Detta raced ahead, easily outrunning Jackson. *Am I the slowest one here?* he asked himself. *I'm—I'm the slowest one here!*

With the claws cutting ground behind him, he angled down the hillside, catching trees first with one hand and then the other, using his speed to swing him in wide zigzags. It worked. The grizzly's bulk wouldn't let him run his fastest downhill or along the hillside. He had to slow down to keep his balance.

Jackson could see a grassy meadow below. *Musn't go down there and run out of slope,* so he turned to run straight along the mountainside. *Got to wear him down,* he told himself. *Bears are sprinters, not distance runners.*

Yet neither was Jackson. Just another tourist from the lowlands, not used to this thin air. Soon the altitude had him puffing; the soft ground wore out his ankles.

Detta ran just ahead, every once in a while stopping to bark at the grizzly. *What'd you do to get him so mad?* Jackson wondered.

Suddenly they came to a place where an old rock slide cut across their path, a spill of black flaky stuff that reached all the way down the mountain. Still running, Jackson tried to scramble across it, but that rock was slate, dull little brittle bits that slipped and slid over each other. With a whoosh, he rocketed away down the slope. Rolling, sliding, he tried for a hold, but then he heard

another swooshing noise above and looked up to see the grizzly sliding down after him, madder than ever.

When he reached the bottom, he didn't have the strength to try running uphill, so he struck out across the flat meadow, elbows and legs churning.

The grizzly kept after him, eating up the distance between them. Jackson didn't have to look back. He could hear the paws falling closer and closer behind him.

Suddenly, he caught one foot in the grass, tripped, and went down. Halfway to the ground he knew he was a goner, so when he hit, he froze. He tried to tell himself that some animals depend on playing dead; but it was pretty hard to pretend with his chest heaving.

Then he heard the dry grass crunching near him, felt the grizzly's hot breath move over him, and he died a little. Jackson held his breath and kept his eyes shut hard, waiting . . . .

Detta barked, came suddenly. *That wonderful dog!* The bear roared and dashed out in pursuit again. *Saved! Oh, that marvelous dog!*

With the bear drawn away, Jackson leaped to his feet; but as soon as he was up and running, Detta joined him again. "Go away!" he yelled at her. "Go away!"

So she did, running out ahead of him again, and that put the grizzly back on his heels. *Pick a tree!*

Running to the first big tree at the edge of the woods, Jackson leaped for the

lowest branch. Both fists closed on it and he pulled himself up, grabbed the tree trunk high with his legs, and started up, using his knees, chin, elbows, anything.

He didn't get far before the grizzly galloped up to the tree and stood up, reaching. That bear would've had him right there, but Detta charged up behind and took a nip at his tail.

Whirling, the bear went after Detta again and Jackson got his chance to climb high out of reach. *Oh that dog! If she hadn't nipped that grizzly——*He watched her, yelping, scared, running with her tail between her legs; but he knew that she was a hero just the same. He promised her special goodies for the rest of her life.

Then a rifle cracked, once, twice. The bear stopped, looked toward the sound, and started running away. A jeep drove up, a jeep with a ranch brand painted on the side. The rancher got out to pet Detta.

Jackson hurried down to thank him.

"Don't mention it," said the old man. "Maybe you won't believe this, but most folks around here don't have much trouble with bears. Even grizzlies. You've just got to make enough noise. If they know you're coming, they're glad to get out of your way. You'll never even see one, if they can help it. But if I were you, young fella, I'd get myself another dog."

"What?" Jackson flared. "Another— why she's the best dog! She saved my life. Twice."

"Hold on." The old man grinned. "I just meant you need two dogs in this country—that's all. Two or none."

"What?"

"Sure. You know how dogs are. They'll go sniff out a bear and bark at him and antagonize him. Grizzlies won't put up with that. They hate that."

"But you said two dogs."

"Yeah. Two dogs protect each other. You know, they get on each side. The bear can't go for one without the other jumping in. But that's with two dogs. One dog can't do that. One dog can't do anything but make a grizzly real mad and then RUN! Understand?"

Jackson nodded slowly. Then he saw his golden retriever slinking away sheepishly, and his eyes sharpened. *My hero!* he simmered.

The rancher's voice was amused. "That's why folks around here won't go near the woods with just one dog, son. You never know when she might turn out to be a retriever!"

Close Up

1. Jackson might have saved himself easily from other animals by climbing into his car and locking the doors. (a) Why isn't Jackson's car a good protection against the grizzly? (b) What does the grizzly do?

2. Jackson tries several plans to escape from the grizzly. (a) Why does he zigzag down the mountain? (b) Why does the bear have to slow down when running downhill?

3. Starting across the meadow with the bear close behind him, Jackson trips. (a) Why does he decide to freeze and pretend he is dead? (b) Why is it difficult for him to pretend he is dead?

4. (a) How does Detta help Jackson when the bear reaches up to grab him in the tree? (b) What finally drives the bear away?

5. (a) Why isn't a golden retriever a good dog to have in bear country? (b) Why does the old man suggest that Jackson get another dog?

6. Sometimes people say one thing when they mean just the opposite. (a) At the end of the story, do you think Jackson really considers Detta his "hero"? (b) What does he really mean?

Conflict

One type of conflict involves a person struggling against nature. Nature can take such forms as a bear, a shark, or a violent snowstorm.

1. "My Hero" is about a conflict between Jackson and a grizzly. When does the conflict begin?

2. In this conflict, the grizzly has certain advantages. It has enormous strength, sharp claws and teeth, and great speed. (a) List its two disadvantages. (b) What advantage does Jackson have over the grizzly?

3. (a) At what two points in the story do you think the grizzly will win the conflict? (b) Who saves Jackson each time?

4. How does Jackson finally win the conflict?

Activity

► **Composition.** Write one or two sentences Jackson might have whispered in Detta's ear when they got back in the car together.

RELATIONSHIPS

Understanding Spatial Order

Spatial order tells where objects are in relation to one another (for example, *in front of, in back of*). In this sentence from the story, "Jackson could see a *grassy meadow below*," Jackson is above and the meadow is below.

1. Find the words showing spatial order in the sentences below. Remember: These words answer the question "Where?" Here is an example: "Jackson heard his dog yelping *off in the pines* and he sighed."
   a. "Detta howled a DON'T LEAVE ME! and the grizzly gained fast behind her, all claws and teeth and great roaring rage."
   b. "Detta raced ahead, easily outrunning Jackson."
   c. "He could hear the paws falling closer and closer behind him."
   d. "(He) felt the grizzly's hot breath move over him, and he died a little."
   e. "That's why folks around here won't go near the woods with just one dog, son."

2. Reread paragraphs 6 and 7. Draw a picture showing where Jackson, Detta, and the bear are in that scene.

WORD ATTACK

Understanding Colorful Verbs

Verbs are the action words in sentences. They tell what characters or objects do. Colorful verbs are used to make descriptions more vivid. For example, ". . . *slapped* down the door locks" gives a vivid picture of the way Jackson locked his car doors.

▶ Find the colorful verbs in the following descriptions. Look up their meanings in a dictionary.

   a. ". . . he slammed down the trunk lid. . . ."
   b. "He scrambled a few feet on his hands and knees. . . ."
   c. ". . . he rocketed away down the slope."
   d. ". . . when he hit, he froze."
   e. ". . . the dry grass crunching near him. . . ."
   f. "Jackson flared."
   g. ". . . his golden retriever slinking away. . . ."
   h. " 'My hero!' he simmered."

100 Handkerchiefs

Christine Miskovits

Marsha is sixteen years old—with a bright and exciting life ahead of her. She has no use for the past.

It's not that I didn't love my grandmother. It's just that there was something vaguely unsettling about the prospect of her coming to live with us. Maybe the uncertainty came from seeing how it was with some of my friends whose grandmothers lived with them. It seemed they were constantly being reminded, "Don't slam the door. Don't turn up the stereo too loud. Don't make so much noise, your grandmother is resting." Or maybe it was Peggy, my best friend, who planted the seeds of uneasiness. "Oh, you poor kid!" she had exclaimed when I told her. "Having your grandmother around will be just like having an extra parent. And who needs that?"

Whatever the reasons, the doubts were there and growing larger as we neared the farmhouse. If I had known then why Grandma was coming to live with us, I would have acted very differently.

"We're here," my mother called excitedly from the front seat, as we turned onto the gravel road leading off the highway.

The small plumpish figure on the front porch of the sprawling, ramshackle house made my doubts melt into waves of love. It was so good to see her again.

After hugs and kisses of hello, the grown-ups got into a discussion about furniture, land titles, and all sorts of dull things. I went inside, where it was cool and quiet.

Wandering around the empty rooms, I couldn't help thinking of the many happy days I'd spent here—the holidays, family picnics, and especially the summer vacations.

As a little girl, I'd always loved spending a week or two at Grandma's farm. I knew there'd always be a tin box of freshly baked cookies in the pantry; a tub of homemade ice cream in the freezer; and every night, when the breeze turned cool, a fire in the huge stone fireplace. And best of all, there'd be Grandma, sitting beside me on her wooden rocker, a box of handkerchiefs carefully balanced on her generous lap.

The handkerchiefs—I smiled at remembering them. My grandmother must have had at least a hundred handkerchiefs. She collected them the way some people collect coins or stamps or dainty teacups. And each one—each square of linen, lace, or voile—had its own particular story connected with a person or event from the past. How I'd loved hearing Grandma tell those stories. And how she'd loved telling them!

But now the fireplace was cold and dusty; Grandma's rocking chair was gone. Stripped of all that had made it homey and comfortable, the house looked old and shabby. The paint was chipped, the wallpaper faded—with squares and circles marking the places where pictures had hung.

I could feel my uneasiness returning. Half of me was stirred by the little bits of warm memories; the other half was apprehensive. Would Grandma still expect me to sit and listen to stories of the past?

I hoped not. That girl was gone, just as the furniture, the pictures, and soon the house itself would be. I was sixteen years old now, with a bright and exciting life. I had no use for the past.

During the drive home, everyone was quiet—lost, I guess, in their own thoughts. I know I was. "It's really happening," I kept thinking. "The house has been sold, and Grandma's here for good—suitcases, handkerchiefs, and all. And what of it?" another part of me argued. "What possible changes can she make in your life?" It was as though I were two separate people—one for Grandma, one against her—and the constant inner struggle made my head throb.

The only solution to the problem, I decided, was simply not to let Grandma interfere with my life. Then and there, while we were still gliding along the highway back to Henderson, I resolved to be polite but firm if she tried to take over in any way.

But she didn't. Not really. Oh, she did mumble about the "racket" I blared on the radio; she did raise an eyebrow and frown when I left the house wearing jeans and sandals and a sweat shirt; and she did comment on why the boys I knew didn't look more like boys instead of being "all fancied up" with bright shirts and striped pants and hair "practically long enough to braid."

And she did try to corner me with her "handkerchief" stories. Whenever she'd catch me sitting and staring at the

ceiling or flipping through a magazine, she'd settle herself in the nearest chair and pull a handkerchief out of the pocket of her apron. "Remember this one?" she might say. "You were just eight years old when you gave me this. It was on my sixtieth birthday, and your mom and dad had that wonderful surprise party for me. Remember what an exciting day that was?"

"Yes, I remember, Grandma," I'd answer politely. "But I don't know why you bothered saving it. It's only a piece of cotton. It's not even worth anything." Then I'd get up and maybe look at my watch or the clock on the mantle. "Gee, I didn't realize what time it was," I'd say.

"I've got to go, Grandma. We'll talk some other time, OK?" After all, I was sixteen years old, with a bright and exciting life. I had no use for old handkerchiefs.

Every Tuesday afternoon, my mother drove Grandma to the nursing home just outside town. Maude Holloway, Grandma's oldest and dearest friend, was a patient there. Mom would spend the afternoon shopping or browsing through the stores while Grandma and her friend visited.

This particular Tuesday was an important one for me. There was a new boy at school who had shown an interest in me; and Peggy had found out that he'd be doing some work at the library when baseball practice ended at 4:30. I planned to be there too. With the spring dance only weeks away, it wouldn't hurt to be within asking distance.

"How did you manage to find out he'd be at the library?" I giggled as we got through the last of our homework.

"Don't ask for trade secrets," Peggy answered mysteriously. "Just be there."

Then the telephone rang. It was my mother.

"Marsha, I'm supposed to pick Grandma up at the nursing home, but I've had car trouble and I can't get back there. Call a cab and go for her, will you, dear?"

I almost dropped the phone. "Mom, I can't. I've got something important to do at the library."

"You can do it tonight," Mom answered.

"I can't do it tonight!" I half screamed. "Why can't Grandma come home in a cab by herself? Why do I have to go there and get her?"

Mom's voice was firm. "Because your grandmother is still a little strange in town and not used to riding around in cabs, and because I'd feel better knowing you were with her."

I could see it was useless to argue. Angrily, I called the cab.

At 4:30, instead of walking into the public library, I was crossing the softly carpeted, blue-walled solarium[1] of the Henderson Home for the Aged. I spotted Grandma and her friend sitting near the window, so busy talking they didn't even notice me walking toward them.

"Well, isn't it wonderful that you have a granddaughter thoughtful enough to come all the way over here for you," Maude remarked. When I told Grandma about Mom and the car, Maude Holloway said, "Young people are so wrapped up with themselves these days, they don't want to be bothered with us old folks. But I can see Marsha is different."

Grandma said something gushy about how I was, indeed, very thoughtful and understanding. When I blushed, they thought it was from the compliments.

The ladies were in the middle of tea, so I curled up in a chair to wait for them to finish their visit. On the table between them, I noticed, were several of Grandma's old handkerchiefs.

"Do you know who this one belonged to, Maude?" I heard Grandma say, picking up a plain white cotton square. "This is from Roberta Dickson."

"The tomboy!" Miss Holloway blurted. Then they both burst into laughter and went on reminiscing about tomboy Roberta Dickson and how she'd played baseball with the eighth-grade boys!

Watching them, I felt my anger slipping away, being slowly replaced by a new feeling. It was a strange mixture of warmth and sadness—a recognition of their loneliness.

Watching them, I finally understood why my grandmother liked to spend so much time talking about the past. It was because she missed those days. Those were her bright and exciting days, just as these were mine. And the happiness of recalling them meant so much more when it was shared by someone she loved.

---

1. solarium (sō-lar'ē-əm) n.: a glass-enclosed room or porch where people can sun themselves.

I put aside my old resolution, which I had to admit was unnecessary in the first place, and made a new one. I vowed to listen whenever Grandma pulled out a handkerchief and latched onto a memory—even if it was a story I'd heard a hundred times before.

That was Tuesday. On Thursday, Grandma died.

"You don't look shocked," I said to my mother. "Did you know Grandma was sick?"

She nodded wordlessly.

"Is that why you brought her here to live?" I asked.

Another nod. "The doctor called us months ago and said her heart was very

bad, that it was only a matter of time. We didn't want her to be alone."

"But she was alone," I thought. "At least as far as I was concerned."

I went into Grandma's room and sat there alone for a long time—touching, thinking, feeling, regretting.

When my mother came in, I was sitting on the bed, looking through her handkerchief collection. "Sometimes you know all along that you care for a person, but you don't realize how much till they're gone." I said flatly.

Mom didn't answer.

"These handkerchiefs," I went on, more to myself than to my mother, "they weren't handkerchiefs at all. They were a hundred faces out of the past. A hundred beautiful memories that Grandma wanted to share with me. Only I didn't have the time. I was always too busy."

"Busy making your own memories," Mom said gently. "It's a very human thing to do."

"But selfish," I answered, cutting away the very excuse I'd hid behind these past weeks. "Did I really do anything so great, so unforgettable in the few afternoons I could have spent with Grandma?"

At last the tears spilled over and ran down my face—hot and wet, yet comforting. "Mom, I did love her! I only wish I'd have acted differently so that she'd have known how much. I only wish—"

"Wishing is for children," Mom cut in. "And somehow I don't think you're a child anymore."

Mom was right. I wasn't a child anymore. Grandma had changed that. She'd done the very thing I feared most. She'd changed my life, but in a way I'd never imagined.

Still, there was a guilt and regret about the way I'd treated her. "How do I live with guilt feelings, Mom?" I asked.

"Maybe by doing for someone else what you regret not doing for her. The world is full of lonely people, Marsha. Just reach out. Someone will take your hand."

The following Tuesday, I walked again into the solarium of the Henderson Home for the Aged. Near the window, in the same chair she'd occupied the week before, was Maude Holloway. Her empty eyes brightened when she saw me. "It's so nice of you to come, Marsha," she said. "I have no family, you know, and your grandmother was my only visitor."

Her loneliness reached out and touched me, but this time I didn't turn away from it. "I'll come every week, Miss Holloway," I said softly. "Just like my grandmother did."

Maybe I was still being selfish, trying to ease my own conscience by giving my time to this lonely old woman; but at least Maude Holloway wouldn't be alone because of my selfishness. I reached into my purse and pulled out a lavender handkerchief, edged with white lace. "Do you know the story behind this one?" I said. "It was Grandma's favorite." And so I pushed back the loneliness from Miss Holloway for a little while.

Close Up

1. (a) At the beginning of the story, what good things does Marsha remember about her grandmother? (b) What does she fear will happen if Grandma comes to live with her family?

2. When Marsha picks up her grandmother at the Henderson Home for the Aged, the two women think she is being thoughtful and understanding. What are Marsha's real reasons for picking up Grandma?

3. Marsha realizes that her grandmother spent so much time talking about her handkerchiefs because she missed the past. (a) What did each handkerchief represent? (b) What does Marsha vow to do on Tuesdays?

4. (a) Why did Grandmother really come to live with Marsha's family? (b) Do you think Marsha would have acted as she did, if she had known this reason? Why or why not?

5. What does Marsha do that shows she is no longer a child?

Conflict

Internal conflict takes place inside a character. One part of a character's personality seems to be warring with another part. For example, a character sees a child drowning. The person wants to save the child, but is afraid of water. The conflict ends when the person decides what to do.

1. Marsha feels as though she is two separate people—"One for Grandma, one against her." (a) What does the side that is "for Grandma" want to happen? (b) What does the side that is "against Grandma" want to happen?

2. How does Marsha solve her conflict?

3. The side for Grandma wins when Marsha recognizes her grandmother's loneliness. When Grandmother dies, Marsha feels guilty. How does she solve this problem?

Activities

1. Make a list of things you could do, or that you already do, to make life easier and happier for an older person.

2. The grandmother in this story collected handkerchiefs. What are some other things people collect to help them recall happy memories? Do you have such a collection? If so, you might want to share it with your classmates.

RELATIONSHIPS

Identifying Relationships

Stories are made up of many different kinds of relationships. These are time order, cause and effect, comparison and contrast, and spatial order. A time order relationship answers the question "When?" A cause and effect relationship answers the question "Why?" or "How?" A comparison and contrast relationship answers the question "Are they alike?" or "Are they different?" A spatial relationship answers the question "Where?"

1. Identify the relationship in each passage below. On a separate piece of paper write T for time order, CE for cause and effect, CC for comparison and contrast, and S for spatial order.
   a. "Maybe the uncertainty came from seeing how it was with some of my friends whose grandmothers lived with them."
   b. "I went inside, where it was cool and quiet."
   c. " . . . there'd be Grandma, sitting beside me on her wooden rocker. . . ."
   d. "That girl was gone, just as the furniture, the pictures, and soon the house itself would be."
   e. "It was on my sixtieth birthday, and your mom and dad had that wonderful surprise party for me."
   f. "Mom's voice was firm. 'Because your grandmother is still a little strange in town and not used to riding around in cabs, and because I'd feel better knowing you were with her.' "
   g. "I spotted Grandma and her friend sitting near the window. . . ."
   h. "Young people are so wrapped up with themselves these days, they don't want to be bothered with us old folks. But I can see Marsha is different."
   i. "Watching them, I finally understood why my grandmother liked to spend so much time talking about the past. It was because she missed those days."
   j. "That was Tuesday. On Thursday, Grandma died."
   k. " 'Wishing is for children,' Mom cut in. 'And somehow I don't think you're a child anymore.' "

2. Complete each of the following sentences with an example of the relationship described in parenthesis.
   a. Grandma sat down (spatial relationship).
   b. First Marsha saw the house, and (time relationship).

    c. Marsha felt guilty (cause and effect relationship).

    d. Marsha had changed. Her selfishness was replaced by (comparison and contrast relationship).

WORD ATTACK

Using Prefixes and Suffixes to Make Antonyms

Antonyms are words which have opposite meanings. Many antonyms are formed by adding a prefix or a suffix to a word, or by changing the prefix or suffix of a word. For example, *happy* is the opposite of *unhappy*, and *careful* is the opposite of *careless*. The entire meaning of a sentence can be changed by misreading a prefix or a suffix.

---

1. Write the antonym for each of the following words by adding or changing a prefix or suffix. Check the story to see if you made the correct addition or change.
   - **a.** settling
   - **b.** certainty
   - **c.** easiness
   - **d.** useful
   - **e.** thoughtless
   - **f.** necessary
   - **g.** forgettable

2. Which of the following words contain a prefix that creates an antonym from the base word?
   - **a.** unforgettable
   - **b.** unselfish
   - **c.** regret
   - **d.** disloyal
   - **e.** apprehensive
   - **f.** nonfatal
   - **g.** unfaithful
   - **h.** ungrateful
   - **i.** resolve

REVIEW QUIZ

On the Selections

1. In "The Fun They Had," the County Inspector comes to fix the mechanical teacher. He smiles at Margie and gives her an apple. How is his giving Margie an apple different from what was done in "the old days"?

2. In "First Jump," Michael stands on the ground watching the parachute jumpers. They slash through the sky in free fall and then use their chutes as brakes. What is *free fall*?

3. In "The Cremation of Sam McGee," Cap lashes the corpse to the sleigh and tries to find a crematorium. What does he do with the corpse that shows he is mad?

4. In "The Dinner Party," the American looks at the woman's face and sees that something is wrong. What happens to her face?

5. The main idea in "Harriet Tubman" is that freedom is worth many hardships. List two hardships Harriet endured to obtain freedom for her people.

6. In "Ghost Town," the man says, "When I got back, my pink-cheeked baby was sleeping like *one* on the cot I'd fixed up for him." *One* refers to which words?

7. In "Thank You, M'am," why does Roger try to steal the pocketbook?

8. In "My Hero," why couldn't Jackson start the car and drive away from the grizzly?

9. In "100 Handkerchiefs," what does Marsha want to do instead of picking up her grandmother at the nursing home?

10. How does Grandmother change Marsha's life?

On Relationships

1. Put the following events in correct time order. Number the event that happened first 1, the event that happened second 2, and the event that happened last 3.
   a. Michael's father became a forest ranger.
   b. Michael's mother refused to let him take up sport parachuting.
   c. Michael's father joined the paratroopers.

2. In "The Dinner Party," the American's first impulse is to jump back and warn the others of the cobra. If he had done this, what might have happened?

3. Compare and contrast Harriet Tubman and Thomas Garrett. List two ways they are alike. List two ways they are different.

4. Underline the word in the following sentence that shows you two things are being contrasted. "It was a good business, although in the winter things fell off." Write your answer on a separate piece of paper.

5. Underline the words showing spatial order in the following sentences. Write your answers on a separate piece of paper.
   a. "With a whoosh, he rocketed away down the slope."
   b. "In another corner of the room behind a screen was a gas plate and an icebox."
   c. "This old town of mine was up a narrow gulch that wasn't good for a thing once the gold was gone."
   d. "There is only one place left—under the table."

COMPOSITION

Sentence Combining

You can write a clear and precise sentence by removing repeated words and combining sentences. Use the first sentence as your base. Remove the repeated words in the second and third sentence. Then combine the three sentences using the commas and connecting word that appear in parentheses. For example, notice that the words "attended the dinner party" appear in each of the following three sentences.

> Army officers attended the dinner party.
> Government attachés attended the dinner party. (,)
> An American naturalist attended the dinner party. (, and)
> *becomes*
> Army officers, government attachés, and an American naturalist attended the dinner party.

Notice which words were removed in the next example:

> Michael turned to the right.
> Michael opened his chute. (,)
> Michael maneuvered himself over the target. (, and)
> *becomes*
> Michael turned to the right, opened his chute, and maneuvered himself over the target.

▶ Combine each group of three sentences into one sentence. Remember to use the first sentence as your base. Then remove the repeated word or words from the second and third sentences and use the commas and connecting word that appear in parentheses.

   a. Michael put on black boots.
   Michael put on white coveralls. (,)
   Michael put on an orange football helmet. (, and)

   b. She was a short woman.
   She was a muscular woman. (,)
   She was an indomitable woman. (, and)

   c. The roofs of the buildings were missing.
   The windows of the buildings were missing. (,)
   The doors of the buildings were missing. (, and)

   d. Jackson used his knees to climb the tree.
   Jackson used his chin to climb the tree. (,)
   Jackson used his elbows to climb the tree. (, and)

BEFORE GOING ON

Scanning for Facts

Many times, you read to find specific facts or information. For example, you may be interested only in finding out where the jacks tournaments is held, or how old Diane Rodriguez is, or how marbles is different from jacks. Scanning is a reading skill that helps you search quickly through a reading selection to find specific information fast.

Here are some tips for scanning:

1. Before you start scanning, know all of the pieces of information you will be searching for.
2. Select the piece of information your common sense tells you is likely to be near the beginning of the selection. (Experience will help you become increasingly expert at this.)
3. Run your finger quickly across and down the page. Search for key words for the information you want; for example, place names or numbers.
4. When you find the information you're searching for, stop the scanning process and write down the information you found. If you happen to see some information you will need later, write it down. That's why you study all of the pieces of information you want *before* you scan for individual pieces.

▶ Scan "Jacks," to find answers to the questions below.
   a. What grade is Diane Rodriguez in?
   b. How does Diane feel during a competition?
   c. How many people judge a jacks state tournament?
   d. How much money does the winner of the jacks state tournament get?
   e. What equipment do you need to play jacks?
   f. What is doubleups?
   g. Who taught Debbie to play jacks?
   h. At what age is a contestant too old to enter a jacks state tournament?

Further Reading

Jacks

Karen Folger Jacobs

**An Interview with Diane Rodriguez/12
Lafayette Middle School
Lafayette, Colorado**

I saw an article about Colorado's jacks champion Diane Rodriguez, in a Mexican-American magazine, *La Luz.*

The Ladies Auxillary of the Colorado Veterans of Foreign War sponsors local jacks tournaments in April and a state championship in May. These competitions provide a sport that every girl can afford. Famous for skiing, golf, and mountain climbing, Colorado generally offers little in the way of sporting opportunity for anyone without cash for equipment and transportation. Jacks are played with gear that costs about half a dollar.

After calling most of the Rodriguez listings in Lafayette, I located Diane.

She told me, "Yes, I was the jacks champion last year, and I hope to be again this year. In fact, I'm practicing with my mom right now; she helps me. Almost all of the girls in my class [seventh grade] play jacks. It's the funnest thing to do! It's a challenge. And you can win trophies from the VFW."

At the Rodriguez home I talk to Diane.

How did the state tournament go this year?

"This year my family wasn't sure how I'd do. I hadn't practiced nearly as much as last year. My family makes me nervous, so I don't let them come with me to the tournaments. They waited for me to phone. Last year I called them when I won. By six o'clock in the evening they realized that the tournament must be over. They were getting ready to tell me it was okay that I didn't win again, that going to state was good enough.

"I didn't call because I was too tired, too out of it. I was so determined and so nervous that I didn't know what was happening. In competition my stomach

gets upset, and my hands get jittery. I'm shaky. After the first game I'm all right. But even now I still can't remember anything that happened before the final game.

"For the final game there are six judges—six VFW ladies standing over you to watch for misses. After I won the match, the other girl's parents protested the judging. The officials made us replay the match. My right hand was tired; it felt like it was going to fall off. I'd started playing jacks early in the morning and played all day, and now it was dark outside. When I won the rematch the other girl's parents protested again! This time my sponsor, the lady from the Lafayette VFW, protested back."

Was your family suprised?

"When I got home it was late. When

my sponsor rang the bell, dad opened the door. He didn't say anything; he just looked straight through me. Inside the house, my whole family looked like they were going to cry. So I said, 'Hey, dad, I won again. I got another TV.' Then they all jumped up and hugged me.

"My sponsor told them that the Lafayette VFW was proud of me. They wanted to take my picture again—with all the VFW officers. Only one other girl from Lafayette ever won the jacks tournament, and she's twenty-four now! Three Lafayette boys won the marbles tournament twice—Mark Valenzuela, Ronnie Ramirez, and Henry Quesada. This year a nine-year-old boy from Denver won the marbles."

Is the marbles contest at the same time as the jacks?

"While we're inside playing jacks, the boys are outside having the marbles tournament. But you know what? The boy winner gets more prizes than the girl winner. Both winners get a trophy and a TV, but the boy gets a hundred dollars, and the girl only gets twenty-five. And the boy gets a wristwatch and a ten-speed, but the girl doesn't."

Perhaps you're playing the wrong game.

"I never played marbles; I never even used a shooter. One time a ten-year-old girl wanted to play marbles. The VFW wouldn't let her; they told her to play jacks. But she wanted to play marbles. She was *good* at marbles! She didn't play in the marbles tournament or the jacks tournament, either—she didn't play at all. There are some boys who want to play jacks, too. But they're not allowed."

(Later I phoned Marie Williams of the Denver VFW Ladies Auxiliary. She told me, "The sex restriction has been removed. Next year the thirty-first annual jacks and marbles tournaments will be open to players of both sexes. We adopted this new policy in order to comply with the equal rights regulations of Title VII.")

Diane, how do you play jacks?

"You need eight jacks and a ball, but for competition we don't use the little red ball that you get when you buy a set of jacks. The VFW has special competition balls made. They're bigger, $1\frac{1}{2}$ inches in diameter, and they're gray. At tournaments they give you one to use, and then you can keep it.

"To the competitions I only take my jacks and powder; the powder is for my hands and the floor, to keep the jacks from sticking. And I wear a sleeveless top and comfortable pants.

"Now the jacks games most people play are called 'babies' or 'taps.' In babies, you pick up one jack at a time and put it in your hand and then grab the ball after it bounces. Then you pick up pairs, then threes. Taps is the same, but you tap the jacks on the floor before you put them into your other hand.

"At tournaments they draw names out of a hat to see who plays who. To see who goes first, each player tosses her jacks onto the back of one hand. The one who catches the most jacks begins the five stunts. When she misses or fouls, the other player goes and continues until she misses or fouls. The first to complete the five stunts wins the game. The first to win two games wins the match."

What's a stunt? Do you sit in a split while you play jacks?

Diane laughs and then replies, "No, but that might be fun! Let me get you the official rules."

The blue card lists five stunts: (1) pigs in the pen—jacks are placed inside one hand, the outside edge of which is held curved on the floor; (2) pigs over the fence—jacks are placed within five inches of the back of the hand without touching it; (3) around the world—the hand with the jacks must circle the ball after it bounces; (4) sweep the floor—jacks are swept along the floor to the body; (5) doubleups (no bounce)—catch the ball before it bounces.

"That last one, 'no bounces,' is the hardest! Be sure to see the rules, too. There are lots of rules!"

There are ten fouls or misses and sixteen Supplementary Rules, such as No. 12: "player may not rest arm on knee or leg while playing" and No. 14: "contestants arguing with other player or judge may be automatically disqualified."

Have you been playing jacks for years and years?

"I first played with my sister Traci. She's eighteen now, and she's married, and she has two babies, and she's having another one this week! I don't look so big for an aunt do I?

"Traci showed me how to play, and we used to play a lot before she got married. Traci is really good at sports! In school she got the top fitness patch; she was the only one who got it. I got the patch below it."

Mrs. Rodriguez smiles at her daughter and then says, "Di, tell her about your competitions."

"I went to my first jacks tournament when I was eight. I didn't win anything, but the VFW gave me a ball to take home! My own ball!

"Then, when I was nine I won a flag pin for fourth place in Lafayette. The girls who came in first, second, and third got trophies and went to the state tournament. I missed going by only one place. I decided to work on jacks.

"The next year I took first in Lafayette. And I got splinters, too. The VFW was in a new building, and they hadn't sanded the floors yet, so I kept getting pieces of wood under my fingernails—especially on sweepsies. When I brought my trophy home, Mom had to use a tweezers to take the splinters out from under my nails. It hurt!

"The next month I got to go to the state tournament. I had to sit in an uncomfortable position—with one leg stretched straight out. It was hard to reach over; and if you lift your butt it's a miss! My leg had to be straight because it was full of stitches. The week before the tournament, a boy on a ten-speed ran into me while I was walking. Every time I bent over for the jacks I felt every single stitch. I didn't do so well in that meet, but I made up my mind!"

About what?

"After that tournament I walked into our house and said, 'I don't care what it takes. I'm gonna practice and practice until I win state. I'm like you, dad; if I do something, I want to do it right. I'm going to take state next year.'

"If you want to win enough, you will. If you want to win more than anybody else does, you try harder, practice more than everybody. I like seeing trophies! I know that if I practice enough they'll keep coming."

How much is enough?

"Oh, I only play jacks from January to May. I practice in the school yard if it's nice out. I play every recess, and I skip lunch to practice. My girl friend Sharon and I used to play in the auditorium before school, but after the season gets going they don't let us because it's too small to hold all the girls who want to play jacks."

Do you play with anybody besides Sharon?

"Most girls in school don't want to play with me because I'm too good.

"After school I practice on the cement porch outside our front door. I practice better if I play somebody, so everybody in my family gets drafted! My mom, my dad, my sister Traci, and my brother Tony take turns playing with me. After dinner somebody always plays me. We play on a wooden floor, like in tournaments. We play until ten o'clock, when I go to bed."

Diane's mother adds, "Even though I don't like jacks much, I play with Di just to help her. She really wants to win. Diane loves those trophies, and she has always had a lot of determination!

"If her math average drops below B, which it does during the jacks season, she works hard to bring it back up. After the tournaments she still misses lunch, staying in her classroom doing extra math problems to bring up her grade!"

Diane interrupts, "Oh, mom, please! You know, mom's really good at jacks. She got good practicing with me, but she thinks jacks is dull. Mom used to bowl. See those trophies of hers next to my jacks trophies? Mom bowled when I was a baby. She had to give it up, though; it was too expensive to pay baby-sitters for enough hours to keep her game up."

What does it take to be good at jacks?

"To be a good jacks player, you need good coordination. You've got to coordinate both your hands. Your eyes have to see it, and your muscles have to do the perfect thing with perfect timing! You need to throw the jacks the right distance—not so far that you can't reach them and not so close that you'll touch one when picking up another (that's a miss). You have to be able to toss the ball so that it doesn't bounce on a jack. You have to be able to pick up the jacks in a hurry and put them in the other hand without dropping them or any of the jacks already in the other hand. And you can't miss! That's the most important thing."

Do you do any other sports?

"Sure, I do other sports. I play intramurals at school, and at my 4-H club we do sit-ups and chin-ups and running. All summer long I ride Debbie's skateboard with her; and I do gymnastics."

What will happen when you're too old to enter the jacks tournament?

"Once you're fifteen, there's no place to go with jacks—no place to win trophies. I'll retire. I might want to judge jacks tournaments for the VFW. But the very best thing about playing jacks is that it helps me with gymnastics."

Jacks helps gymnastics?

"If you play a lot of jacks your eyes get good at telling your body what to do. For jacks and for gymnastics, you need timing and coordination. The main difference between the two sports is that in gymnastics you coordinate more than your hands."

By phone Diane adds, "I'm not doing any more jacks until I have to get ready for the spring tournament. My gymnastics teacher is *so* good! I *love* gymnastics. I'm taking ballet now in order to get form for competition. We go over to Boulder three times a week now; my mom drives me, but if gas prices get any higher, we might have to quit."

VISIONS

One Day at the Griffith Park Zoo

Dr. Wesley A. Young
written with Gloria D. Miklowitz

The day could not begin without Arturo. I would walk to the zoo office before eight each morning, greeting keepers, listening for the familiar sounds: the macaws gossiping, the lions yawning, the elephants testing their early-morning voices, but it was Arturo who began the day.

As soon as I approached the path leading up to the old administration building, Arturo's excited voice would greet me: "Hello, Doc. Nice day, *Awk, awk*," and I was truly back in my special world.

Arturo, the zoo mascot, was a beautiful blue and gold macaw with a most impressive vocabulary that sometimes got him into trouble. His wolf whistles and "Hello, Baby!" to passing females, his "Go to the devil" to visiting city councilmen, brought many inquiries as to who was prompting him. Periodically, Arturo's curses got so out of hand that he was removed from public contact to undergo retraining in zoo etiquette.

Then, after leaving Arturo, there was always the drama of the night before to greet me at my desk in the morning, often in cryptic notes scribbled by hurried keepers. Today's read "Three snakes stolen" . . . "Ivan swatted Bournevan" . . . "Coyote pups look seedy."

This morning, even before I had reached my desk, a zookeeper rushed up the path behind me, arms tenderly cradling a small body. "I think it's dead," he said anxiously. "Got out of the barn during the night, and it's been pretty cold."

It was the two-day-old tapir, the first to be born at the zoo since my arrival. I had seen it only the evening before, healthy and demanding as it nursed at its mother. Now it was stiff and cold, unwilling even to suck on my finger. The inside of its mouth was like ice water. Its heartbeat was so faint only my stethoscope could find it.

What had caused the infant tapir to leave the warmth of the barn we would

never know. The mother must have tried to bring her young back, nudging and pushing it, but was unable to carry it, as a dog or cat might. Out in the cold night, the baby would have first stopped nursing, and then become drowsy from the cold. Growing weaker with each hour, it could not have found the strength to return to the barn.

To give it immediate warmth, I placed the tiny, stiff body near heat lamps, then injected milk from its mother through a small tube pushed down its esophagus,[1] into its stomach. Warm mother's milk was put into a bottle with a special lamb's nipple; but

the tapir, exhausted and weak, found sucking just too much effort.

When news went around that the newborn tapir was barely hanging on to life, keepers hurried through their chores elsewhere so as to be able to take a few minutes with those nursing the spark of life. "Let me massage it," a burly elephant keeper pleaded. "I'll be gentle." And, watching the anxiety on his face, I was sure he would be.

Before the zoo opened, nearly every one of the keepers found a moment to look in, "willing" the tapir to life when he could not help it in a physical way. By 10:00 A.M., opening hour to the public, the same men were silently heading back to their duties. The tapir's lack of response to treatment was disheartening. If it would not take the bottled milk, by

---

1. esophagus (ĭ-sŏf'ə-gəs) n.: The tube through which food passes to the stomach.

evening it would die. For the moment, there was nothing more I could do for it except prescribe warmth, massage, and periodic injections of milk.

Already the cars of visitors and busloads of schoolchildren were arriving. Even the blind children came to "see" through their fingers what a duck or lamb "looked" like. By the thousands the visitors appeared each day, and if there was time, I was there to share my world with them.

But today there was no time. The tapir required constant checking, and there were the usual demands of the rest of the zoo. As I made my rounds of the cages, compounds, and corrals, my eyes swiftly sought out the abnormal: the peculiar growth on the flank of the wild horse, the limp of the zebra, the elephant whose nails needed clipping, the mangy look of the coyote pups.

The coyote pups, like the tapir, were recent births, offspring of a pair donated by Walt Disney after being used in one of his films. True to nature, the parents had dug a den under the house in their corral. There the pups were born and were kept while very young. The hole was a dustbin, a perfect breeding place for fleas. And that was exactly why the pups looked "seedy." Covered with fleas, they were literally being chewed up. And until we could get them out and deflea them and the hole in which they lived, they could continue to look like motheaten balls for fur.

And what of the stolen snakes? But before I reached the reptile exhibit, a commotion at the chimpanzee cages drew my attention. I knew immediately what caused the screams and laughter and cries of dismay. It would be Skippy. Skippy was a "spitter." Though the fifteen feet from his cage to the guard rail was a formidable distance to spit, he had discovered that if he first filled his mouth with water, then ran to the front of the cage, his aim sometimes found a mark. And if he climbed to the top of the cage with the water still in his mouth, he could do much better, often spraying more than one individual. Visitors were either delighted or disgusted, depending upon whether they were the observers or the victims. Eventually, we would have to curb the rambunctious animal by putting glass against his bars.

The reptile exhibit, I discovered, had suffered a severe loss. Whoever had broken into the zoo during the night had taken three of the finest snakes. It must have been someone who knew reptiles, because the glass display cases were side by side, poisonous snake next to nonpoisonous, and the cages that had been broken into were only those of the nonpoisonous. There was always a guard on duty, but one guard for twenty acres was not enough.

Usually, the night belonged to the animals. Bobcat, deer, coyote, raccoon, skunk, and opossum from the Griffith Park hills and woods visited the zoo inhabitants then, attracted by the smells of food and the scent of animals. These were the thieves we normally had to guard against, for, if there was a way to get at a small animal or bird, the park wildlife would find it.

Before the day was over, we were fortunate in acquiring a replacement for at least one of the stolen snakes. It was an anaconda, and the manner in which we received the reptile provided some additional drama.

Behind in my schedule, I had chosen to eat a sandwich lunch in my office while answering the many letters that arrived from all over the world each day. From animal dealers, zoo directors, mothers asking about ideal pets for their five-year-olds, offers of donations, requests for information on feeding exotic animals—the letters were as varied as the senders. When the telephone interrupted my work, I thought it might be the news of the tapir. I had left it only a short while before, after finding it still too weak to take the bottle and giving it another milk injection.

"Dr. Young here," I said expectantly, but it was the guard at the front gate calling.

"Got a lady with a snake wants to see you, Dr. Young," the guard informed. "Shall I send her up?"

Permission granted, I returned to my lunch and correspondence. About an hour passed and the lady had not arrived. Had she changed her mind, as so often happened with people donating pets? Probably so, I decided, when the phone rang again.

"This is Yrineo, at the elephant house. There's a gal here with an anaconda draped around her neck. She's scaring the visitors and stirring up Geeta and Bojo. What'll I do?"

When I arrived at the elephant compound, I glanced automatically at Geeta, noting that the baby elephant had a more than usually smooth, shiny hide. I smiled, for it was well known that Yrineo, the keeper, had been buying gallons of baby oil with his own money in an effort to keep the young elephant's hide soft. Many years later, it would be possible to identify Geeta in any group of elephants, for her hide was always the least wrinkled.

I made my way to the center of the knot of people, and discovered the source of the trouble. A young woman with an anaconda curled around her neck and shoulders like a fur stole was thoroughly enjoying a leisurely stroll through the zoo, oblivious to the commotion she was causing. When I finally ushered her into my office, she undraped her unusual pet, and regretfully handed him over to me.

"You realize you can never have him back?" I asked, passing a release to her to sign.

"Yes," she sighed. "And he has been such a good companion."

"Then why are you giving him up?" I asked. Too many people donated pets to the zoo one day, and then wanted them back the next. I had felt sorry for the distraught donors in the beginning, but time had hardened me. Now I rarely agreed to return a donated animal.

"I'm giving him up," the girl said, "because of my boyfriend."

I listened politely.

"He's jealous. He says he won't come to see me unless I get rid of George." She smiled shyly. "He says he won't kiss me again if George is hanging around my neck."

George was a fine specimen, obviously well fed and cared for. I thanked the young woman, and assured her that she could see her pet any time she wished to visit the zoo. Then I gave him over to the reptile keeper.

There was one more problem before I could leave for the day, and that was Ivan. Ivan was a polar bear who had lived with Lena, his mate, for eleven years at the zoo. Only recently, we had brought in two young bears, male and female, and moved the family of four to the grizzly grotto where there was more room. The keeper's note that Ivan was fighting Bournevan (a Scandinavian name for "children's friend") was worth checking, because adult male polar bears can be vicious if they are crossed.

This day, when I looked in on the family in the bear grotto,[2] Lena was happily splashing in the pool, while the two young ones were exploring the rocks. And Ivan, huge and powerful though he was, lay drowsing contentedly in the shade. In the months to come, Ivan was to jump on and kill Bournevan, the young male, in a jealous fit over food, splash the young female to death because she playfully stomped him in the face, and put a tooth through Lena's skull when she spurned his attentions. Ivan was a killer, but there was no way of knowing it then.

Despite an occasional tragedy caused by a vicious animal, creatures in zoos live more than twice as long as they would had they remained in the wilds, thanks largely to their isolation from natural enemies, to well-balanced diets, and to constant medical care.

Late in the day, when the last tired visitors had made their way back down the hilly zoo paths to the front gate, and the maintenance men were at work hosing the hot littered walks, I stopped again to examine the tapir. Curled up in a little ball, its body looked pitifully small under the large heat lamps, but the heartbeat was stronger, and the warmth of its body was not the warmth of fever or that of heat lamps.

Cradling the small animal in my arms, I put my finger to its lips. The lips

---

2. grotto (grŏt'ō) n.: a cave or cave-like structure.

parted, and the mouth moved in a weak sucking movement. Encouraged, I lifted the bottle of warm mother's milk to the tapir's lips and teased it with a few drops. Suddenly, the infant took the nipple, letting it rest idly in its mouth for a moment, until the muscles began the gentle sucking reflex that is automatic with all newborn babies. When I finally gave the tapir over to an attendant who would care for it through the night, the baby had taken an ounce of milk.

Whenever it was time to leave each day, I liked to stand outside my office for a moment, and listen. If the sounds were normal, those, say, of the male peacock announcing his beauty in an almost human cry, the flutter of a hundred birds rushing upward at the fearful thud of a sonic boom, the excited argument of orangutans at play, then I knew my special world was settling down for the night.

There was one last ritual to perform. "Good evening, Arturo," I would say as I headed down the zoo path for home. And invariably Arturo would answer, "Nice day, Doc. *Awk, awk,*" after trying a variety of less appropriate phrases first.

That day, I answered the zoo mascot without hesitation. "It was indeed, Arturo," I said warmly, "a very nice day."

Close Up

1. Dr. Young's day begins when he hears Arturo, a macaw, say, "Hello, Doc." How does Arturo's vocabulary sometimes get him into trouble?

2. Dr. Young's first task is to take care of the problems that happened the night before. (a) What three problems does the note on his desk tell him about? (b) How does Dr. Young receive a replacement for one of the stolen snakes?

3. Dr. Young shows you that the staff at the zoo give the animals loving care. (a) How do they show their affection for the tapir? (b) How does Yrineo, the elephant keeper, show affection for the baby elephant?

4. When Dr. Young leaves the zoo in the evening, Arturo says, "Nice day, Doc." What happened to the tapir that made Dr. Young's day "very nice"?

Who Tells the Story

The *narrator* is the character who tells the story. In a true story, the narrator is usually the author. Sometimes the narrator tells about an experience in the *first person*. This means that the narrator uses the first-person pronoun "I" when telling about himself or herself. For example, Dr. Wesley Young says, "I was truly back in my special world."

Reading a true story written in the first person is like reading a diary. You learn *only* the narrator's private thoughts and feelings. You learn about events from the narrator's *point of view*, or angle of vision.

1. Which of the following sentences are written in the first person?
   a. Back at his office, Dr. Young found a note.
   b. I knew I would have to deflea the coyotes.
   c. The zookeepers were worried about the tapir, and so was I.
   d. He said "Good morning" to Arturo.

2. (a) How does Dr. Young feel when the tapir does not respond to treatment? (b) How does he feel about donors who want their pets back?

Activity

▶ Imagine you are going to interview Dr. Young for your school newspaper. What three questions would you most like to ask him?

JUDGMENTS

Judging a Reliable Source

Can you trust the information the author gives you? Is the author a reliable source? Ask yourself these questions:
1. Is the author qualified?
2. Is the author presenting information fairly?
3. Is the information accurate?

Is the author qualified? Usually you can trust an author with training and experience in one field to give you accurate information about *this* field.

Is the author presenting information fairly? Some authors try to be fair and present the information truthfully. However, other authors may falsify the information in order to persuade you to do something that will benefit them.

Is the information accurate? If you disagree with information in an article, then check another source to see who is right. You might check an encyclopedia, another book on the subject, or another expert in the field.

---

1. Judge whether or not Dr. Young is a reliable source. First, is he qualified to give you information about running a zoo? Why or why not?

2. Next, do you think Dr. Young tries to be fair and presents the information truthfully? What evidence can you find in this story that supports your judgment?

3. Third, judge whether the information is accurate. (a) Do you agree with Dr. Young's statement that animals in zoos live more than twice as long as they would have in the wild? (b) If you don't agree, what other sources could you check?

WORD ATTACK

Using Context

What can you do when you read an unfamiliar word in a sentence? Sometimes you can use the context to help you find the meaning.

The context is the group of words surrounding the unfamiliar word. For example, notice how the context helps you find the meaning of *abnormal* in the following sentences. "As I made my rounds of the cages, compounds, and corrals, my eyes swiftly sought out the *abnormal*: the peculiar growth on the flank of the wild horse, the limp of the zebra, the elephant whose nails needed clipping, the mangy look of the coyote pups."

▶ Use context to discover the meaning of the words in *italics* in the following sentences. Then find these words in the glossary and see how close you came to discovering their meaning.
  a. "The coyote pups, like the tapir, were recent births, *offspring* of a pair donated by Walt Disney after being used in one of his films."
  b. "Though the fifteen feet from his cage to the guard rail was a *formidable* distance to spit, he had discovered that if he first filled his mouth with water, then ran to the front of the cage, his aim sometimes found a mark."
  c. "Too many people *donated* pets to the zoo one day, and then wanted them back the next."
  d. "Suddenly, the infant took the nipple, letting it rest idly in its mouth for a moment, until the muscles began the gentle sucking *reflex* that is automatic with all newborn babies."
  e. "Periodically, Arturo's curses got so out of hand that he was removed from public contact to undergo retraining in zoo *etiquette*."

One Day at the Griffith Park Zoo   **155**

The Cherub and My Sainted Grandmother

Barbara Corcoran

Maggie said she would break the pony, and she didn't want to go back on her word—even if the pony was murder.

When I was thirteen, I took on the job of breaking a pony for the Hagens up the road. They had sent to Colorado for this pony for their ten-year-old daughter, and after it came, nobody could do a thing with it. The pony cost a hundred and fifty dollars, and Mr. Hagen offered me a hundred to break it. That made a pretty expensive pony, it seemed to me, but I was glad of the chance to earn the money. There was a beautiful Mexican saddle at the Merc that I had my heart set on, and it cost ninety-eight dollars and fifty cents.

My father always bragged about the way I could break horses. "My daughter," he told people. "has got a way with horses."

What he didn't know was that I had found a book in the library about horse training. The author believed in getting the horse to trust you, gentling it instead of "showing the horse who's boss." I tried the idea on some of the range colts that my dad brought in and it worked like a charm. Using the longeing rein[1] and a tail rope instead of the old snubbing post, and patience instead of force, turned out better horses, it seemed to me. Horses aren't as dumb as people sometimes think. They can learn a lot if you get them to trust you. Look at the Arabians or the Lippizans, for instance.

Anyway, my father hitched up the horse trailer, and we drove over to Hagens' one early September afternoon.

I saw the pony at the other side of the fenced pasture. He was a three-year-old Shetland, a pinto with a pretty face but too much fat. I looked him over. I had

---

1. longeing (lŭnj'ing) rein: A long rope fastened to a horse's head. It is used to lead or guide a horse in training.

never worked with a horse that someone else had tried to break. But a little pony shouldn't be too bad.

"What's his problem, Aaron?" my father asked.

"Nobody can stay on him, that's his problem," Mr. Hagen said. "He's fired off everybody that got on him. And they call him Cherub![2] Can you beat it?"

"He's not very big," I said. I have never understood why anyone wants to ride a pony anyway. I was riding horses when I was four.

"He's murder!" Mr. Hagen said. "Big or not big. And I paid a hundred fifty cash for him!"

My father leaned on the rail fence and narrowed his eyes the way he does when he's sizing up stock. "Maybe he's just plain mean," he said. "Animals are like people: some are bad clear through and some are good clear through. Take my sainted mother. Not a bad bone in her body."

He always spoke of Grandma as "my sainted mother," although I knew for a fact that sometimes he got furious with her. She lived in a cabin up the river, and she wouldn't let him or anyone else "do" for her. She was as independent as you can get.

Besides, I have never believed that about some being all good, some all bad. I knew, though, that Dad was giving me an out with the pony. He didn't want me to get hurt or take on a job I couldn't finish.

"Well, Maggie, what do you think?" he asked me.

"I'll give 'er a try," I said. It made me feel important to have grown-ups want-ing my opinion of a horse. I climbed the fence and I started to walk slowly toward the pony. I expected him to shy off to the far end of the corral. Instead he ran straight at me.

I was too surprised to move. A horse will almost never run at a person, unprovoked. I kept waiting for him to stop but he didn't. He charged at me and bit my arm. I had on a heavy jacket, so it wasn't too bad, but it made me mad. I didn't have a rope, so I grabbed his mane and jerked his head down. He slewed[3] around, kicking like mad, but I had a good grip and he couldn't get his head up. After a minute he quieted down; but I got a look at his eyes, and I knew he was figuring what to do next.

My father and Mr. Hagen came running. I thought I could use a tail rope to get him to the trailer; but when my father saw the blood on my jacket, he jerked the pony around and tied him up like a side of beef. Then he and Mr. Hagen half dragged and half shoved him to the trailer, with the pony heaving and fighting all the way.

I felt sick. This was no way to begin. But Dad was too upset to reason with. All the way home he sputtered. He wasn't going to let me work with a monster like that one. He would take a hand at breaking the pony himself, since we had made a bargain with Hagen.

It wasn't until the pony was turned out in our corral, and Dad had taken me to the doctor for a tetanus shot, that I got to talk to him. I told him I'd said I would break the pony and I didn't want to go back on my word. My father was always impressed by that kind of statement. He

---

2. Cherub (chĕr′əb) n.: An angel usually pictured as a winged child with a chubby face.

---

3. slewed (slōōd) v.: Turned around, pivoted.

was a great one for not going back on your word. Finally he agreed to let me try if I promised to be careful, and if I would go and stay with my grandmother for a couple of days until my arm healed. He knew me well enough to know that if I stayed around where the pony was, I'd be out there with him.

I liked to visit my grandmother. And I think she enjoyed me because she could talk to me, and I wouldn't try to boss her around.

Grandma's cabin was on the edge of the forest, ten miles from the nearest house. There were only three rooms, but it was comfortable and gracious.

She was unloading her jeep when we got there. She had just been to town, and when Grandmother went to town, she bought almost a boxcar load of stuff so she wouldn't have to go again in a hurry. Dad and I helped her unpack, and Dad gave her lots of advice about taking care of herself and getting in plenty of stovewood before snow, and things like that. She smiled and thanked him and patted him as if he were a little boy, and he went away happy.

"Now," she said, settling down in the rocker in the sunny living room, "to what do I owe the honor of this visit?"

I told her about the pony. When I came to the part about Dad saying he had a sainted mother, she laughed hard, and her rocker squeaked back and forth, and her sneakers made little patting sounds on the floorboards.

"You and I know how sainted I am, don't we?" she said. I knew she meant about Great Uncle James. I knew the story by heart but I loved to hear it.

So she told me again about Grandfather's brother, James. "A good man, James was, but he was never wrong in his life, and that can be a trying thing. He came out here to the cabin after your grandfather died, and he told me I could not live here alone. It wasn't fitting, he said, and people would criticize him if he let me.

"When he was all through, I said, 'James, you mean well, but I intend to live as I choose.' Well, he was stunned. He said he was going to force me out of here. And then he said your grandfather was shiftless, which was not true. And——" Her eyes sparkled wickedly as she remembered. "It just so happened that I had taken a key lime pie out of the icebox, intending to offer him a piece. But when he said that about your grandfather——"

Her pupils got very black, and I could almost see her, glaring at Uncle James.

She gave me a contented sigh. "I just let the pie fly." Every time she told me, I practically rolled on the floor laughing. Great Uncle James died before I was born, but I had seen pictures of him, with a moustache and a cold face. In my mind's eye I saw that lovely fluffy pie spread all over that face.

"And that," Grandma said, "is your sainted grandmother." She went to get some oatmeal cookies, the kind with millions of raisins and nuts in them. "I ought never to have told you. It really makes me sort of ashamed when I think of it."

"Why?" I asked. "He deserved it."

She only shook her head. "One shouldn't throw pie in the face of a person's dignity."

"But he was bossy. And mean about Grandfather."

"James was a stubborn and a self-righteous man; but still, I shouldn't have done it," sighed Grandma.

I was truly sorry when my visit was over, and I heard Dad's pickup down on the county road. But I was anxious, too, to start working with the Cherub.

When Grandma heard Dad coming, she said, "Margaret, you're growing up now, so I'll tell you a little secret."

I didn't feel grown up at all but I was curious. "Fire away, Grandma," I said.

"You can succeed through love. Not force or power or always being right, just love. Use love with your pony," she said. "I think he needs it." She put a package of pralines in my pocket and kissed me.

As soon as I got home, I went to work on the Cherub problem. I was out in the corral every morning right after sun-up. I tried every trick in the book. The trouble was, whoever had begun to train him had done everything wrong. Cherub was determined not to be broken.

For the first few days, he tried to charge at me again, but I tried a trick I had read about. I held up a stick, just an ordinary stick, in front of his face. It worked.

I used a soft-web longeing rein at first, looped around under his tail. It didn't work too well, so I changed to a

lariat.[4] That has a little more bite but not enough to injure him. Pretty soon I could guide him with light pulls on the hackamore.[5] There were setbacks, of course. Some days he wouldn't do a thing I wanted him to, and one day he jerked suddenly and I found myself sitting on the ground. He thought that was pretty funny. You let a horse think he's outsmarted you once, and it takes a long time to get him over it. Cherub has intelligent eyes in that pretty little face of his, and I was sure he was laughing at me.

Day by day, though, he got a little better. He got so he'd let me lead him around the ring I had marked out for him. I usually use a whip to flick a horse on the hocks,[6] to direct him, but I couldn't use a whip with Cherub. The minute he saw it, he froze. Somebody must have tried to whip-break him.

One morning when things were going well, Dad came out to look us over. Suddenly Cherub tore the line out of my hands and raced around the ring like a maniac.

"He's no good," Dad said. "I told you all along. We'll take him back to Hagen before you break your neck."

But it was more than earning the money now. I wanted to train Cherub and I knew I could. The next day, when

---

4. lariat (lăr′ē-ət) n.: A long rope having a loop with a slipknot at one end.
5. hackamore (hăk′ə-môr′) n.: A rope or rawhide halter with a wide band that can be tightened around the horse's nose.

6. hocks (hŏkz) n.: The part of a horse corresponding to the human ankle.

The Cherub and My Sainted Grandmother **161**

the sun was spreading pink light all over the ground, I took the stock saddle I'd used when I was little, and I went out to the corral. A child's saddle is light-weight. I had tied the stirrups to the horn so they wouldn't bang against him. I walked up to him slow and easy, talking all the time. He let me put the halter on, but he craned his neck around suspiciously while I put on the saddle.

The minute he felt its weight, he reared. He plunged and danced like a wild bronc. The saddle went sailing through the air and hit me in the head. It knocked me out for a minute. When I came to, Cherub was at the other end of the corral, still kicking up those wicked little heels. I had a thundering head-ache.

I took the saddle to the barn and went to the house to lie down. Dad hit the roof when he saw me. My head was a little bloody. So he went through the whole thing again of taking me to the doctor, vowing to take the pony back, and so on. This time, I couldn't talk him out of it; but luckily Grandmother happened to come by.

"Let her handle the pony her own way, Victor," she said to my father. She seldom spoke to him in that stern way; but when she did, he just said, "Yes,

ma'am." And when she saw Cherub, she said, "He's too fat. No wonder he won't take a saddle. Put him on a diet."

So Cherub went on a diet. It worked two ways; he lost weight, and he got so hungry that he was glad to see me when I came with his dinner. Once a week, to boost his morale, I gave him a candy bar. And when he got better about letting me touch him, I decided to try the saddle again.

One morning I waited till he had his nose in a bucket of oats. He shied a little, but he let me put the saddle on. As soon as he started to pull away, I took it off. I did this about a dozen times, and by the time Dad whistled me up for lunch, Cherub was taking the saddle with no fuss.

After that, I kept a saddle on him while I longed him and while he was eating. When I tightened the cinch,[7] he just peered at me to see what I was up to.

I put him on long reins then, and taught him commands. He was a smart little pony, and once he decided it was fun, he learned fast.

On a Sunday morning, I decided to ride him for the first time. When I got up, I found it was raining, a slow, cold drizzle. But I had told Cherub I was going to ride him, and I'd begun to get crazy notions that he knew what I said to him.

In case he didn't take to the idea of somebody on his back, I took along a pair of D hobbles[8] and a rope. If I had to, I would use the "running W" trip rope. I

---

7. cinch (sĭnch) n.: The strap holding the saddle on the horse.
8. hobbles (hŏb′əlz) n.: A rope or strap used to tie the legs of a horse together.

had never seen it used but I had read about it. The way it works is, if the horse gets out of hand, you pull on the rope that is attached to the hobbles. This trips him and brings him to his knees.

I led him out to the north pasture. He was acting sweet as honey, but the minute I swung my leg over the saddle, he bucked. I tried to control him with my hands and my voice, but he didn't pay any attention. The rain was dripping down my neck, and I was cold, and Cherub was jarring me in every bone. I pulled on the rope.

Quickly and easily, I slid right up onto his neck, and before I got the rope taut, he had nearly fought his way back on his feet. I got off. He was down on his knees looking foolish and hurt in his feelings. He gave me a look that said, "I thought we were friends."

"Well," I said, "you have to learn that crime doesn't pay."

To complete the "running W," I was supposed to push him over on his side and pull his head around and tie the rope to the cinch. This doesn't really hurt the horse, but it is uncomfortable, and it makes him feel helpless. If there is one thing a horse is terrified of, it's losing his footing.

I put my hand on Cherub's neck to push him over. But I couldn't do it. He was looking at me with those black eyes rolled back a little, scared and pleading. All of a sudden I knew what Grandma meant about the key lime pie. It just doesn't feel right to destroy somebody's dignity.

I let up on the rope. Cherub struggled to his feet and stood still, his sides heaving. I patted him and gave him half a candy bar. He didn't even try to bite my hand. I got up on him again. I touched him lightly with my heels, and he broke into a nice trot. I rode him for over an hour, and he acted proud.

When my father saw us ride up to the barn, he stood still, afraid of spooking Cherub, and also surprised, I guess.

At the end of the week my father said, "Hagen was asking after the pony. I told him you were about ready."

Cherub was ready but I wasn't. I made excuses to keep him another week. It was ridiculous; he was riding perfectly. And Firefly, my own horse, was getting fat and lazy from lack of exercise.

The day came when I couldn't put it off any longer. I rode Cherub to the Hagens' and my father came along in the pickup. I felt like crying. I talked to Cherub all the way and gave him an extra candy bar.

Mr. Hagen gave me a check for a hundred dollars, and I led Cherub out to the pasture. Mr. Hagen's little daughter was dancing up and down, eager to get on her pony. She was carrying a fancy little whip.

"You'd better not carry the whip," I told her. "Cherub doesn't like a whip."

"I got it for my birthday," she said. As if that settled it.

Her father boosted her up, and she plunked down in the saddle. I held my breath. Cherub did a little sideways dance, and Mr. Hagen jerked hard on the reins. The girl dug her heels into Cherub's side, and at the same moment she moved the whip, and Cherub caught sight of it. He bucked, and the girl slid out of the saddle. Her father grabbed her, and Cherub headed for me.

Mr. Hagen and his daughter glared at Cherub and me. The girl wasn't hurt but she was crying, and Mr. Hagen was furious.

"I thought you said that pony was broke," he said.

"He is broke," my father said. He was furious too. "You saw Maggie ride him up here."

I handed Mr. Hagen his check. "I'll pay for the pony," I said. "One hundred dollars and fifty dollars. Fifty dollars a month."

"Take him!" Mr. Hagen said. "He's an outlaw!"

So that's how I happen to have a pony. For about a year, until I got too big, I rode him once or twice a week. After that I took him on a lead rein when I rode Firefly. They got to be good friends.

Cherub is old and plump now; but he wanders around the pasture enjoying himself, usually sticking close to Firefly. And once a week, my sainted grandmother brings him some cookies.

Close Up

1. Why doesn't Maggie expect Cherub to charge at her when she first meets him?

2. Maggie's grandmother tells her the Key Lime Pie story. What did Grandmother actually hurt when she hit James with the pie?

3. (a) How is Maggie's pushing Cherub over on his side like Grandmother's throwing the pie? (b) How does Cherub act when Maggie lets him up?

Who Tells the Story

The narrator of a story may be a character created by the author. The narrator may tell the story in the first person from his or her point of view. When you read a story told this way, you feel that the narrator is talking directly to you. You learn about most of the events of the story directly from the narrator who experienced them. At times, you may learn more about the narrator than other characters in the story ever do.

1. (a) Who is the narrator of this story? (b) Who is the author?

2. Maggie gives you first-hand, or direct, information about most of the events that occur. Which event can Maggie not give you first-hand information about?

3. (a) Maggie's father doesn't know how she learned to handle horses differently. How did she learn this? (b) Name one thing you know about Maggie that other characters in the story do not know.

Activities

1. Imagine that this story is being made into a movie. (a) What actors would you cast in each of the roles? (Try to choose actors who seem like the characters in the story.) (b) Who would have the largest role? (c) Who would have the smallest?

2. **Composition.** Write a paragraph telling this story from Cherub's point of view.

JUDGMENTS

Identifying Statements of Fact and Statements of Opinion

A statement of fact contains information that can be proved true or false. It contains information about things that happened in the past or are happening in the present. "Maggie trained horses," "Cherub came from Colorado," and "The Merc was a store that sold saddles" are all statements of fact. Each contains information that can be proved true or false.

A statement of opinion expresses a personal belief or attitude. It does not contain information that can be proved true or false. "I think Cherub is cute" and "Pralines taste better than any other cookie" are all statements of opinion. Each expresses a personal belief or attitude.

A statement of opinion may express beliefs about the past, the present, or the future. All statements about the future are statements of opinion, since information about the future cannot be proved true or false. "Maggie will grow up to be an animal trainer" is a statement of opinion since it expresses a prediction about the future.

1. On a separate piece of paper, write *Fact* by each statement of fact.
   a. The saddle cost ninety-eight dollars and fifty cents.
   b. I think that one hundred and fifty dollars is too much money to spend on a pony.
   c. In my opinion, girls are better animal trainers than boys.
   d. Lippizans and Arabians are special breeds of horses.
   e. Maggie used patience instead of force to train Cherub.

2. On a separate piece of paper, write *Opinion* by each statement of opinion.
   a. Cherub was the prettiest horse alive.
   b. Mr. Hagen offered Maggie $100.00 to break Cherub.
   c. Gentling a horse is the best way to train a horse.
   d. The author of the book Maggie read believed you should get a horse to trust you.
   e. The best way to train a horse is to get it to trust you.

3. On a separate piece of paper, write *Fact* by each statement of fact. Write *Opinion* by each statement of opinion.
   a. Maggie had never worked with a horse that someone else had tried to break.

b. Mr. Hagen's daughter will never ride Cherub.
c. Maggie's father doesn't want Maggie to train Cherub.
d. Grandmother will bring Cherub cookies every week.
e. James was Maggie's great uncle.

WORD ATTACK

Understanding Idioms

An idiom is a group of words that has a special meaning all its own. You cannot find the meaning of an idiom by looking at each word in the group. Common idioms are *it beats me*, *go take a walk*, and *put up with*. Do you know what each of these idioms means?

▶ Think about the meaning of each idiom in *italics* below. Then choose the group of words that expresses the same idea as each idiom.

a. "There was a beautiful Mexican saddle at the Merc that I *had my heart set on*, and it cost ninety-eight dollars and fifty cents."
(1) put a deposit on
(2) put my heart on top of
(3) wanted badly

b. "I didn't want *to go back on my word*."
(1) to fail to keep my promise
(2) to repeat my words
(3) to talk too much

c. "He's *fired off* everybody that got on him."
(1) burned
(2) dismissed from employment
(3) thrown off

d. "Take my sainted grandmother. *Not a bad bone in her body*."
(1) None of her bones is broken.
(2) She is all good.
(3) She is all bad.

It's Not a Game for Girls

William Heuman

"He needed pitchers the way a drowning man needs a life preserver, but this was a girl pitcher."

Part 1

I mean, who ever heard of such a thing? There are games for boys, and there are games for girls, and they're altogether different, and that's the way it's supposed to be. If there's no law about it, there should be.

Give a girl a beanbag, or a badminton racket, or a doll, and forget about it. But not baseball.

"She's going to try out for the team," Flip Andrews told me the night before the opening of baseball practice at Wilson High.

"She'll never make it," I scowled. "She'll never make it in a million years. The worst substitute on the Wilson squad has to be about nine times better than any girl you ever saw."

"I know," Flip nodded, "but this Hepzibah Sloane is still trying out for the team, and there's nobody can stop her."

We'd all been hearing about Hepzibah Sloane who'd just transferred from an upstate school. She had started the rumor that she was a ballplayer.

"With a girl's softball team," I'd said when I first heard about it. "A volleyball team. Imagine a girl powdering her nose and putting on lipstick and things like that before going out on the field?"

"I know," Flip had said.

He is a little fellow with red hair and snapping blue eyes, and a mighty good shortstop.

"She pitches," Flip had told me.

"My Aunt Tillie can probably pitch," I told him, "but not for Wilson High."

From what I'd heard, this Hepzibah Sloane had been going up to her father's camp every summer since she was knee-high to a grasshopper, and they were always short of ballplayers to make up two teams. That was how she'd gotten started. I'd heard somebody who was very gullible say that she could throw as hard as a boy.

"Some boys don't play baseball," I'd said. "They're marble players."

"Anyway," Flip was telling me now, "she's trying out for the team, Willis. I even asked Mr. Daugherty about it. He said that there was nothing he could do."

Mr. Daugherty is our baseball coach, and we all liked him. He's a chubby little man with steel-rimmed eyeglasses and he's always mopping his face with a handkerchief even when it's not warm.

"She can try out for the team," I said, "and she can be dropped after the first practice session. Imagine, batteries[1] for today's game—Hepzibah Sloane, pitching, Fat Phelps, catching. It's ridiculous!"

"I know," Flip agreed.

This didn't prevent Hepzibah from coming out for that opening session. I was wondering what she'd wear and I was also wondering where she'd change, because when girls get mixed up in something like this they complicate everything.

She lived near the school, so I guess she ran home after her last class and got into this rather seedy-looking baseball uniform that she'd probably worn up at this camp where she'd learned to play.

From a distance you could hardly tell that she was a girl. She's kind of scrawny and she has this short, curled red hair and brown eyes to go with it. I mean, the eyes and the hair aren't so bad. She has a pretty nice face with a few freckles around the nose, and her mouth isn't so bad. I mean, it's all there—the eyes and the nose and the chin and so forth. She doesn't look like a tomboy or somebody like that.

I mean, if she wasn't a ballplayer, you could even say that she wasn't bad-looking. But when you see her walk out on the field with a baseball glove under her arm, and her hair tucked in under her cap, you forget all these things. It's unnatural—like a chicken trying to swim or something like that.

I saw her talking with Mr. Daugherty in the dugout,[2] and Mr. Daugherty was wiping his face with a handkerchief, looking around helplessly. Mr. Daugherty has been coaching at Wilson High for about fifteen years, but he's never had a problem like this before, and there's nothing in the rule book about it.

After a while, I saw him walk over to where I was standing with Fat Phelps. He said, after taking a deep breath, "Fat, warm her up, will you."

I saw Fat gulp, too. "Who, me?" he asked.

"You're the catcher," I told him after Mr. Daugherty walked on. "Better put an extra sponge in your mitt. Ha-ha."

"Ha-ha," Fat muttered, and he waddled toward the dugout to get a baseball.

We were all kind of watching Hepzibah out of the corners of our eyes, as she started warming up with Fat Phelps along the third-base sideline. We were supposed to be loosening up, ourselves, after a winter of inactivity, but when this

---

1. battery (băt'ə-rē) n., pl. -ies: In baseball, the pitcher and the catcher.

2. dugout (dŭg'out') n.: A shelter at the side of a baseball diamond where the players sit when they are not playing.

girl started to throw a baseball, everything stopped.

Anyway, she could throw a baseball, and she didn't throw it like a girl. She took a long easy windup and then let the ball go.

Fat caught it and threw it back to her, real easy, so it wouldn't hurt her hand, for crying out loud. Hepzibah was only throwing it slow, of course, as this was the first day of practice. It would have been foolish to start bearing down and risk a sore arm the rest of the season. I mean, she wasn't showing off or anything like that. I'll give her credit for that.

The way she threw the ball, you could tell that she could probably throw it fairly fast, maybe as fast even as Wingy Doberman, one of our utility pitchers who'd never been any good.

"Not so bad," Flip said to me.

"Wait'll you see her with men on the bases," I said. "And two away and we have a one-run lead to protect. Wait'll you see her then."

Mr. Daugherty was watching her, too, even though he pretended that he wasn't. I think he was hoping that it was all a mistake, that she couldn't play ball at all, and that all he had to do was tell her at the end of the session that she shouldn't come back tomorrow.

The rest of us were having batting practice while Hepzibah warmed up on the sideline. It was kind of a crazy practice session because everybody knew there was a girl on the ball field, and there hadn't been one there before. I mean, with a girl around you do things differently. You're kind of thinking about it all the time.

She threw pretty good once she was warmed up. I mean, you could see she'd played a lot of baseball before. We did notice this right away about Hepzibah Sloane. She got the ball over the plate, which was something our best pitchers were having trouble with even last year. I mean, you fill the bases and start walking people, and the old ball game is over the hill and gone.

To make a long story short, Mr. Daugherty asked this girl to go in and pitch batting practice after a while. The first man to face her was Link Bannerman, who has shoulders a yard wide and who is our best batter.

Link swallowed, looked at me, grinned, got serious, and then grinned again, before stepping up to the plate. Link had hit about .498 last year in regular-season play; but he was nervous now, as who wouldn't be.

Heck Hoppinger, our first baseman, called down to Link, "Better pull it out to left, Link. Don't hit it straight down the middle. You might hurt——"

"Just hit it," Hepzibah said quietly.

"Sure," Link muttered, *"ma'am."*

Ma'am, I was thinking. *For crying out loud!*

This Hepzibah was loosened up now and throwing real easy, and the first ball she threw to Link was a curve. She hadn't been throwing any curves while she'd been warming up with Fat Phelps, and this curve ball caught Link way off balance. He cut and he missed the ball by a foot.

"Oops," he said.

"Shut up, you dope," I told him from behind the batting cage, "and whack a few."

I mean, we had to discourage this girl pitcher right away. That curve ball hadn't been so bad, though. I mean, it broke right over the outside corner.

It's Not a Game for Girls **171**

Link fouled off one pitch and then this Hepzibah came in with a change-up,[3] of all things. Link was way ahead of the pitch, catching it on the tip of his bat, rolling it foul.

He looked back at me apologetically. I'm the captain of the Wilson High team.

"She's throwing *stuff*, Willis," he told me.

"You never saw a change-up before?" I asked him sourly.

"Not from a girl," Link said, which was true. It could make a difference.

Link hit a few, but not solid. Of course, this was the opening session and

he didn't have his batting eye as yet. In the beginning, the pitchers are always ahead of the batters.

Mr. Daugherty was watching from the dugout, pretending that he wasn't. Other guys got up there, took their hits, and stepped away again, and none of them were getting any real wood on the ball. I mean, this girl was throwing a nice breaking pitch, mixing it in with a change-up and, now and then, a rather sneaky fast ball, which you didn't expect.

I saw Mr. Daugherty wiping his face. I guess there wasn't too much doubt about it now that what our baseball coach had here was a girl pitcher who probably was going to make the squad. I couldn't tell whether he was disap-

---

3. change-up, n.: A ball that changes pace or speed.

pointed or pleased. He needed pitchers the way a drowning man needs a life preserver, but this was a *girl* pitcher.

Flip Andrews said to me reflectively, "She can really pitch, Willis. Why don't you take a few shots, yourself."

"Never mind," I said, and I walked toward the dugout and sat down.

I could see this Hepzibah Sloane watching me as I walked away from the cage. I mean the whole thing was kind of crazy, this skinny girl, or maybe she was just slender, throwing pretty fast balls and change-ups and things like that, and our guys not hitting them.

Mr. Daugherty said to me, "Well, she throws all right, Willis."

I wasn't going to argue the point. I said, "For a girl."

Mr. Daugherty wiped his face with the handkerchief. "I don't know what the other teams are going to say," he told me, "but there's no rule."

I was getting a little tired about this business of no rule. You can make up rules, can't you?

She came into the dugout after a while and she sat a few feet away from me on the bench. I was working some oil into the pocket of my glove and I didn't look at her.

She said to me, "If I can make the team, why shouldn't I try out for it?"

"You're trying out for it," I said.

I guess she kind of sensed that I wasn't too happy to have her around.

"As captain of the team," she said, "you should be happy if I make good."

"I'm so happy," I said, "I could drop dead."

"What an attitude," she told me.

I mean, even *talking* like that. You just don't hear this kind of talk on a dugout bench.

She sat there, scraping her spikes on the dugout step, and she didn't say any more. I almost wished I hadn't made that nasty remark, but I was kind of upset and all.

I noticed she was a little pale as she picked out a bat from the rack and got ready to go up to the plate. Wingy Doberman was not pitching batting practice.

I couldn't help saying, "I suppose you're a homerun hitter, too, ma'am."

She didn't say anything, but she tossed her head as she walked up to the plate, swinging two bats. I mean, *tossing her head.* You know?

She wasn't a good hitter. She could hit a baseball, maybe as good as Louie Bowman, our utility shortstop,[4] who generally hit about .150 or less. She didn't have any power with the bat, and you could get her on a curve ball without too much trouble.

I think if she'd been a .400 hitter or something like that, I'd have given up baseball. When she came back to the dugout, she said to me, "You satisfied?"

I didn't have much to say.

Of course she made the squad. I mean, even a kangaroo who could pitch would have made our pitching squad this year. We were that weak on the mound. Mr. Daugherty would have kept an orangutan on the squad if he could throw curve balls over the plate.

Hepzibah Sloane wasn't an orangutan or a kangaroo by any means. I mean, dressed up and in class, she didn't look too bad at all. She just looked kind of skinny in a baseball uniform, as what girl wouldn't.

---

4. shortstop (shôrt′stŏp′) n.: The player whose position is between second and third base.

Part 2

Mr. Daugherty used her for the first time in relief when Lefty Henderson lost his control and started winging the ball up against the screen behind home plate. Hepzibah had been warming up out in the bullpen[5], and when Mr. Daugherty came out to the box and waved for her to come in, this Whitman High team we were playing stopped and stared. By now, of course, everybody in creation knew that Wilson High had a girl pitcher on the squad. News like that got around quicker than anything Paul Revere could ever say.

---

5. bullpen (bo͞ol'pĕn') n.: An area on the field where relief pitchers warm up during a game.

The Whitman players were sitting out on the edge of the dugout steps as Hepzibah came across the grass toward the pitcher's mound. She had to pass by me at second base. I guess I was supposed to say something like, "We're all behind you, kid," but I just looked down at the ground as she went by.

I could see, though, that she was kind of pale and nervous, especially when the Whitman crowd in the dugout began to shout, "Oh, Miss Hepzibah, don't throw it too hard," and other cute things like that, which you might expect from Whitman players.

The first pitch she threw, though, was a beautiful curve that broke across the outside corner for a called strike, and they stopped yelling.

We had a 2–1 lead in the eighth, one away, runners on first and second, a pretty tight spot any way you looked at it. I thought she might be nervous, and start walking more batters, and hand them the game.

She didn't choke up, though, and I'll give her credit for that. She got the ball in there and she kept it low, like Mr. Daugherty had told her.

The Whitman batter knocked it on the ground over toward second. I came up with the ball and tossed it to Flip covering second. Flip whipped it over to first base for the double play, and we were out of the hole.

As I trotted past Hepzibah on my way to the dugout, she said softly, "Thanks, Mr. McGinnis."

"My job," I said gruffly.

I mean, Lefty Henderson and people like that wouldn't give you the skin off their teeth, even if you pulled an unassisted triple play with a circus catch.

Fat Phelps said to me in the dugout, "She stayed in there, Willis."

"She threw two pitches," I told him, "for crying out loud."

"They could have been home-run pitches," he observed, which was true also.

"Would you like it," I asked him sourly, "if we had a girl catcher, too?"

"What are you sore about, Willis?" Fat asked.

"Who's sore," I told him. "Go soak your head, Fat."

Anyway, the next inning Hepzibah gave these Whitman fellows one hit, and then set them down in order. I think it was the change-up more than anything else that got them. They were swinging away, and the ball wasn't coming in as fast as they thought it was.

When the last Whitman batter had popped up to Flip at short, we trotted off the field. Hepzibah walked toward the dugout, head down, slapping her glove gently.

Heck Hoppinger said to her as he went by, "Nice game, Hep."

Hep, I was thinking.

In the dugout I figured I had to say something because, after all, I'm the captain of the team, and we had won the game. I said, "Well, you got them out."

"I did the best I could," she told me. I mean, she wasn't bragging about it or anything like that.

Of course, all the crazy girls at Wilson High were gloating about Hepzibah making it with the boys' baseball team. I mean, you couldn't hear the last of it on the campus or in the corridors. You'd think she'd pitched a no-hitter or something, instead of throwing to five batters.

"Those dim-witted girls," I said to Flip, "would probably burn the school down if she pitched and won a full game."

"I know," Flip nodded. Then he added, "Did you know that Heck Hoppinger is making goo-goo eyes at her? And the same with Link Bannerman?"

"Link Bannerman!" I said. "For crying out loud! He should go to the zoo if he's looking for a girlfriend."

I wasn't too happy about Heck being interested in Hepzibah, not that it meant anything to me, of course. He could date a duck for all I cared. But the way I look at it, a ballplayer should concentrate upon his ballplaying and not upon the other sex, especially when the other sex is on the ball field with him.

Our next game was with Milbrook Prep. Again Mr. Daugherty brought Hepzibah into the game in the late innings to save a two-run lead. It was 6-4 in the ninth, and Whitey Maddox, our pitcher, had just started off the bottom of the inning by walking two in a row.[6]

When Hepzibah came in from the bullpen, I noticed Heck was waiting there on the mound, all smiles. He was holding the baseball out to her the way a small boy gives his teacher an apple. He looked just as dumb, too.

"We're all behind you, Hep," he said. "We know you can do it."

I was on the edge of the infield grass, listening to this hogwash. I said, sarcastically, as Heck trotted back to his position, "I know you can do it, Mr. Hoppinger."

He looked at me queerly, but I was already moving out toward second.

You might have known that Heck would make a beautiful catch of a line drive the first batter hit down the first-base line. He caught the ball, stepped on the bag, doubling the runner on first, and then fired to Flip, covering second, for the triple play.

I mean, if the guy had planned it, it couldn't have worked out any better.

Hepzibah gave him a big smile as he trotted toward the dugout, pounding his glove happily.

"Pin a rose on him," I said as I walked by.

Hepzibah looked at me with those brown eyes.

In the dugout Heck right away ran and got Hepzibah's jacket and helped her on with it. I mean, a ballplayer should be able to put on his own jacket.

Flip said to me in the dressing room, "She's going to do all right, Willis."

"She's going to help us win the county championship," Heck said proudly. "She's terrific."

"Why don't you go soak your head," I told him, and I walked toward the shower room.

"What's the matter with him?" Heck asked.

This was the way it went most of the season, with Hepzibah coming in now and then to save a ball game for us and bringing us right up to the county championship game against a tough Madison High nine.

On the away games, when we were traveling by school bus to another school, I noticed that Heck usually managed to be in the seat next to Hepzibah, and in the dugout, when she was pitching, he was always there with the jacket. I said to him one afternoon, "Can't she put her own jacket on, Hoppinger?"

He looked at me. "What's the difference, Willis?" he asked.

"It just doesn't look right," I told him. "For crying out loud."

I heard Heck say to Fat Phelps later on, "You know, Willis is getting awful grouchy lately."

I didn't have much to say to Hepzibah, myself. After all, a baseball dugout is not a place for romance and things like that. You're out there to play ball.

Anyway, in this championship game, we jumped to a quick two-run lead. Madison picked up one in the seventh, and it was 2–1 for us going into the ninth with Lefty Henderson doing real well.

He was throwing too hard, though, because in the ninth he weakened. The first batter hit safely, and then Lefty walked the next man on four straight pitches. When he threw two more balls

---

6. by walking two in a row: In baseball, if the pitcher throws four balls, the batter is allowed to walk to first base.

busloads of Wilson people with us, mostly girls, because of Hepzibah. They were making a lot of noise, as girls usually do.

Heck was waiting for Hepzibah to come in, ready to lay down his baseball shirt across any puddles in her way. I stood near the mound with the others as Hepzibah took the ball from Heck.

I saw her swallow and look over at me.

"We're all behind you," Heck was saying excitedly. "Just wing it in there."

I didn't say anything. I just stood there, slapping my glove. After a while I turned and trotted toward second, leaving Heck there, running off at the mouth.

So what happened on the first pitch, Heck bobbled a ground ball that could have been an easy double-play ball. The bases are now filled with still nobody out, and, with Madison batting last, a base hit can win them the championship.

I guess this was the worst hole Hepzibah had ever been in. With nobody out, Mr. Daugherty called the infield in to make the play at home and choke off that tying run.

I was in close on the grass now, and I said, "Just keep it low. We'll make the play."

I mean, I had to say something, as captain of the team.

Anyway, I did make the play. This next Madison batter whacked one straight toward me, a pretty hard shot, low. I scooped it up off the grass, fired to home, and Fat Phelps stepped on the plate, then shot the ball down to first for the double play.

I trotted back to my regular position. It was two away, but with runners still

to the following batter, Mr. Daugherty came out of the dugout. It wasn't hard to tell when Lefty Henderson was finished for an afternoon, and he was finished now.

Mr. Daugherty looked toward the bullpen and patted his right arm. Hepzibah was a right-hander, and she came in.

We had a big crowd for this championship game, which was being played on a neutral field. We had a half-dozen on second and third, and a base hit would still give Madison the ball game. Mr. Daugherty ordered Hepzibah to walk the next batter, filling the bases and setting up a play all around.

Everybody was yelling. Everybody was excited. Everybody was standing up.

Hepzibah stayed in there. She kept the ball low, trying to make the batter hit it into the dirt. This Madison batter hit from the left side and, with a two-and-two count, he rapped one on the ground to the right of Heck Hoppinger.

I started moving with the crack of the bat. It looked to me as if that ball was going through to the outfield for the big hit.

Heck lunged at it desperately, but missed and sprawled on the ground. I was moving fast now on the deep grass as the ball was going out toward right. I knew I had to cut it off some way.

I took a long dive, got a glove on the ball and rolled over, winging the ball toward first even as I was rolling. Hepzibah knew enough about baseball to cover the sack when the first baseman was out of position.

She was there, taking the throw on the run and touching the sack with her spikes a fraction of a second before the runner. It was the ball game. I came off the field sweating, myself, because I hadn't thought I'd reach that one.

We had to drive back to school late that afternoon, and when I got into the bus behind Heck Hoppinger, I noticed that Hepzibah was already in her seat halfway down where she usually sat. But this time, she was out on the aisle seat instead of by the window.

Heck was hurrying to get down to her; but when he reached the seat, Hepzibah looked up at him, smiled, and said, "It's taken, Heck."

Heck just looked at her, a little flustered, and then passed on down to the other end of the bus. As I was going by, Hepzibah slid across toward the window and said, "Won't you sit down, Willis."

I sat down because most of the seats were already taken, and she *was* on the team. I said, "Well, we won it."

I mean, it wasn't a very brilliant remark.

You'd think Hepzibah Sloane would be bubbling over about the ball game, but she didn't even say anything about it. What she said was, "The Homecoming Dance is on tonight, Willis. I thought you might like to go. I don't have a date."

I mean, who ever heard of a second baseman dating a relief pitcher; but she didn't have a date, and I'm the captain of the team. I mean, what else could I do? You know?

1. (a) When the story starts, has either Willis or Flip seen Hepzibah play baseball? (b) Why do they think she will be a terrible player?

2. Even when Willis sees that Hepzibah is a good pitcher, he doesn't want her on his team. What else does Willis do that shows he is stubborn?

3. Throughout the season, Willis says that he ignores Hepzibah. (a) Has he really ignored her? (b) Why do you think he says he has?

4. What happens at the end of the story that shows how Willis really feels about Hepzibah?

Who Tells the Story

When you read a story told in the first person, you depend on a character, the narrator, for information about other characters and events. You have to judge whether the narrator is being fair and telling the whole story. You may find the story would be quite different if another character had the chance to tell his or her side.

1. Suppose Hepzibah told the story. Which of Willis's statements do you think Hepzibah would disagree with?
   a. Hepzibah had transferred from an upstate school.
   b. Hepzibah had started a rumor that she was a ballplayer.
   c. Hepzibah had played baseball at her father's camp.
   d. Hepzibah looked "unnatural—like a chicken trying to swim," when she walked out on the field.

2. You may have been surprised by the ending of this story. (a) Why couldn't Willis tell you that Hepzibah planned to ask him to the dance? (b) Suppose Hepzibah had told the story. Could she have given you this information?

Activities

1. Debate whether or not girls and boys should play on the same athletic teams.

2. "We had a 2–1 lead in the eighth, one away, runners on first and second, a pretty tight spot any way you looked at it." Sketch the scoreboard and baseball diamond at this point in the game.

3. Take an interest survey. Have your classmates list five of their interests. Compare the girls' and the boys' interests.

JUDGMENTS

Recognizing Stereotypes

A stereotype is an opinion about a group of people that does not allow for individual differences. A stereotype is not based on proof. Two common stereotypes are "All nurses are women" and "All librarians wear glasses." A stereotype can cloud your judgment and prevent you from seeing the worth of an individual.

▶ Which of Willis's opinions are stereotypes?

   a. "Give a girl a beanbag, or a badminton racket, or a doll, and forget about it. But not baseball."

   b. "The worst substitute on the Wilson squad has to be about nine times better than any girl you ever saw."

   c. "The way she threw the ball, you could tell that she could probably throw it fairly fast . . . ."

   d. "Anyway, she could throw a baseball, and she didn't throw it like a girl."

   e. "There are games for boys, and there are games for girls, and they're altogether different, and that's the way it's supposed to be."

WORD ATTACK

Understanding Idioms

Some idioms are made up of two words. Together, these two words have a special meaning that has little to do with the real meaning of each word. For example, when you *back up* a story, you *support* a story, when you *look out* for danger, you *watch* for danger, and when you *keep up* with the Joneses, you *live in the same style as* the Joneses.

▶ Look at the following sentences from the story. What do you think is the meaning of each idiom?

  a. "The rest of us were having batting practice while Hepzibah *warmed up* on the sideline."

  b. "She's going to *try out* for the team."

  c. " '*Shut up*, you dope,' I told him from behind the batting cage, 'and whack a few.' "

  d. "I mean, she wasn't *showing off* or anything like that."

  e. "I think if she'd been a .400 hitter or something like that, I'd have *given up* baseball."

To Satch

Samuel Allen

Sometimes I feel like I will *never* stop
Just go on forever
Till one fine mornin'
I'm gonna reach up and grab me a handfulla stars
5　Throw out my long lean leg
And whip three hot strikes burnin' down the heavens
And look over at God and say
How about that!

Close Up ▶ The speaker of this poem is Satchel Paige, an amazing baseball player who once pitched sixty-four scoreless innings in a row. His remarkable career lasted over thirty years. (a) Will Satch go on playing even after he dies "one fine mornin' "? (b) Satch knows how good he is. How does he let you know this?

A Man of His Own

Corey Ford

The Boss was all right, but he wanted someone closer to his own age.

He had always wanted a man of his own. His father had a man that he hunted with and slept on the floor beside at night. His father always called this man the Boss. His father's man, however, was a good bit older than he personally had in mind. Plainly, his father didn't think his man was so old, but then they had belonged to each other ever since his father was a puppy. Probably his father didn't realize that there was a little gray in the man's hair now, and that he didn't jump over stone walls or run up a steep hill as fast as he used to. The Boss was all right for his father, but what he wanted was somebody more his own age. He wanted somebody he could grow with and have all his life.

He used to plan what he'd do with this man when he found him. He would take him wherever he went, of course, and let him sleep in the same room with him. In the fall they would go hunting

together. He was not quite sure what hunting was, because he was only six months old and his father had never let him come along. He had seen his father and the Boss getting into the car. The Boss would have a gun, and they would both be grinning. His father would be making a funny little whining sound in his throat as if he were about to burst with excitement. Oh, he was sure that hunting would be fun.

He used to dream at night how it would be when he owned somebody he could take hunting with him. He would dream about it so hard that his paws would twitch in his sleep and scratch on the kennel floor. Then his brother, the big one with the black patch, would growl at him and wake him up.

He knew this man the moment he saw him. You can always tell about a thing like that. It was a warm afternoon, and he was standing in the kennel yard in the sun. He was watching a big orange-and-black butterfly moving in lazy circles through the air. Now and then the butterfly would fly close to him. Then, for some reason he did not understand, he would begin to tremble a little. The butterfly landed at last on the grass just outside the wire, and he began to move toward it carefully. He lifted his paws one by one and set them down again, feeling that strange trembling inside him. At that moment, somebody moved between him and the butterfly. He looked up, and a boy was standing on the other side of the wire.

The boy was young and gangling, just like himself. His cheeks were smooth and his forearms had not begun to feather out yet with shaggy hair like the Boss's. But his hands were big enough to handle a gun. His back was

long and he carried himself very straight, with his head high. Something about him made you know that he was used to being in the woods, maybe just the easy way he moved. This was his man, he knew at a glance. He did not have to look any further.

The boy was with an older man, about the same age as the Boss. The older man and the Boss knew each other, because the Boss came hurrying out of the house and shook the older man's hand. He shook hands with the boy, too. "I heard you had this new litter, Earl," the older man said to the Boss, "so I

brought the youngster over. I want him to have a good hunting dog."

"They're all good," the Boss smiled. "They're by old Duke, that I've hunted with for over six years."

The boy was standing so near that he could almost touch him. He braced his paws against the wire and tried to catch the boy's eye. If he could catch the boy's eye and tell him, then the boy would know, too. Once the boy almost looked at him. But just then the older man spoke to him, and he turned.

"Which one do you like, son?" the older man asked.

The boy's eyes moved slowly over the other pups in the yard, and finally came to him, and stopped. He looked up at the boy. He thought of all the things they were going to do together. He could see them reflected clearly in his eyes, like looking at himself in a pan of water. He saw them getting into a car together. The boy had a gun, and they were both grinning. He began to make a funny whining sound in his throat. Then, because he could not hold himself back any longer, he barked out loud.

His father had told him never to bark. Men didn't like dogs that barked

and made pests of themselves, but this was his man and he had to tell him. Of course it was wrong, because the Boss yelled "Hey!" at him. The older man said, "He's noisy, isn't he, that little white one?"

He knew he had done the wrong thing. The boy wasn't even looking at him now. "I don't know," he said slowly. "I like them all."

"That big one with the black patch looks like the pick of the litter to me," the older man said. "How about him?"

He was trying to catch the boy's eye, but the boy was looking at his brother instead. "Yes," he said at last, "I like him."

"Well, then," the Boss smiled, "that settles it, I guess."

He could not even bark because it was wrong to bark. He stood with his paws braced against the wire, wagging his tail a little to keep his courage up. He saw the Boss lift his brother over the wire. The Boss carried his brother toward the car, the older man and the boy following. He waited, but the boy did not look back. His ears drooped, and his paws dropped heavily to the ground. The other pups had begun to play again. The sun was shining, and overhead the orange-and-black butterfly was still flying in circles, nearer and nearer. . . .

The butterfly lighted on the dirt inside the yard, a few feet in front of him. Suddenly everything inside him seemed to go tight. He began to tremble all over. His eyes were fixed on the butterfly, and slowly his neck stretched out toward it. His tail stiffened, and his right forepaw drew up beneath him. He stood there motionless, frozen by some instinct he did not understand. He felt the most delicious excitement he had ever known.

He heard the boy call sharply, "Hey, Dad! Look!"

"Say, Earl, you've been holding out on us," the older man exclaimed. "There's a hunting dog!"

He could not take his eyes from the butterfly; but somewhere far off he heard the boy ask, "Is it all right if I change my mind?"

"It's your dog," the Boss said.

He heard the boy's feet pounding across the grass toward him. A shadow fell across the dirt, and the butterfly darted away. He would have to teach the boy not to run up on a point like that. There was a lot to learn about hunting, but they would learn it together. He had his man, and that was all that mattered now.

Close Up

1. Why does the puppy want a young man for an owner?

2. The puppy knows his man the moment he sees him. (a) What does the puppy do when he gets excited? (b) Why is this the wrong thing to do?

3. (a) What happens to the puppy when he focuses on the butterfly? (b) Why does the boy change his mind about him?

Who Tells the Story

Sometimes the narrator does not appear as a character in the story. The narrator tells one character's story for him or her in the *third person*. This means that the narrator uses third-person pronouns (he, she, it) to refer to this character and all others. In "A Man of His Own," the narrator tells the story from the puppy's point of view and shows you what the puppy thinks and feels.

1. Find the verbs in the following sentences that show the narrator is telling what the puppy is thinking or feeling. (Example: "He *wanted* someone he could grow with. . . .")
   a. "He knew this man the moment he saw him."
   b. "He thought of all the things they were going to do together."
   c. "He felt the most delicious excitement he had ever known."
   d. "He wanted somebody he could grow with and have all his life."

2. The narrator can tell only things the puppy knows. Which of the following does the puppy know?
   a. How he feels when the boy decides to take him.
   b. How successful they will be on their first hunt.
   c. What the boy is thinking when he sees the puppy for the first time.
   d. Why he wants a man younger than the Boss.

3. Sometimes it's fun to view things from odd angles. (a) Did you enjoy viewing the world through a puppy's eyes? (b) What amused you about the way the puppy sees the world?

Activity

▶ Tell a story from an odd angle. Choose one of the following topics or make up your own. Be sure to tell your story in the third person.
   a. A bird watching a cat trying to break into its birdcage
   b. A fish seeing a worm on a hook

JUDGMENTS

Forming Valid Opinions

A valid opinion is a judgment or belief supported by facts. You form valid opinions every day. For example, you judge if you will have enough money left at the end of the week to go to the movies. You base your opinion on facts: how much money you have now and how much money you normally spend during the week.

1. The boy and his father form certain opinions about the puppy. These opinions are lettered **a.**, **b.**, and **c.** Find the facts that support each opinion. Choose between (1) and (2).
   a. The boy and his father judge that one of these puppies will make a good hunting dog.
      (1) Hunting dogs often pass on their traits to their puppies. These puppies were fathered by old Duke.
      (2) The puppies belong to the Boss. He takes good care of them.
   b. At first, the father judges that the puppy will not make a good hunting dog.
      (1) The puppy has never been on a hunt.
      (2) The puppy barks, and good hunting dogs never bark on the hunt.
   c. The boy and his father decide the puppy will make a good hunting dog after all.
      (1) The puppy points when he sees a butterfly. Good hunting dogs know how to point by instinct.
      (2) The puppy's ears droop when his brother is chosen. Puppies with drooping ears look cute.

2. Which item best supports the opinion: *The puppy will make a good hunting dog.*
   a. The puppy notices the gray in the Boss's hair. He likes butterflies.
   b. The puppy knows how to point by instinct. He was fathered by a good hunting dog and he is young and healthy.
   c. The puppy is noisy. A noisy dog is useful on the hunt because it can tell the hunter where the bird is.

WORD ATTACK

Finding the Meaning That Fits the Context

The English language contains many words that have more than one meaning. Look at these two sentences: (1) She *bores* a hole through the wood. (2) He *bores* his friends. In the first sentence, *bore* means "to drill." In the second sentence, *bore* means "to weary or tire by being dull." The meaning of *bore* in the second sentence would not fit the first sentence.

▶ Two correct meanings are given for each of the *italicized* words below. Choose the one meaning that fits the context.

a. "Men didn't like dogs that barked and made *pests* of themselves. . . ."
   (1) nuisances   (2) troublesome insects

b. "His eyes were *fixed* on the butterfly, and slowly his neck stretched out toward it."
   (1) repaired   (2) concentrated

c. "He heard the boy's feet *pounding* across the grass toward him."
   (1) beating into a pulp   (2) moving with heavy steps

d. "Then, for some *reason* he did not understand, he would begin to tremble a little."
   (1) sanity   (2) cause or motive

e. "He looked up, and the boy was standing on the other side of the *wire*."
   (1) metal barrier   (2) telegram

f. "His cheeks were *smooth* and his forearms had not begun to feather out yet with shaggy hair like the Boss's."
   (1) calm   (2) free from rough hair

g. "Something about him made you know that he was used to being in the woods, maybe just the *easy* way he moved."
   (1) relaxed   (2) not strict, lenient

h. "Then his brother, the big one with the black *patch*, would growl at him and wake him up."
   (1) spot   (2) small plot of land

i. "But his hands were big enough to *handle* a gun."
   (1) control   (2) sell

j. "He *braced* his paws against the wire and tried to catch the boy's eye."
   (1) supported   (2) refreshed

Young Ladies Don't Slay Dragons

Joyce Hovelsrud

When an exceedingly evil dragon plagues the Palace of Hexagon, it's up to Princess Penelope to slay it.

A dragon with exceedingly evil intentions was plaguing the Palace of Hexagon. Night and day he lurked about the courtyard walls, belching fire and smoke, and roaring in a most terrible fashion. Things looked bad for the royal household.

"Mercy," said the queen.

"Dear me," said the king. "One of these days he'll get a royal blaze going, and when he does—poof! That'll be it."

"Well, what are you going to do about it?" asked the queen sharply. "I mean, you can't just sit there counting out your money and ignoring the problem."

"I have asked every brave man in the kingdom to slay the dragon," said the king. "They all said they had more important things to do."

"Nonsense," said the queen with a breathy sigh. "What could be more important than saving the palace from a monstrous dragon? Perhaps you should offer a reward."

"I *have* offered a reward," said the king. "No one seems interested."

"Well then, offer something of value to go with it," said the queen. And with that, she slammed the honey jar on the table and stomped out of the room.

"I'll slay the dragon," said the Princess Penelope, jumping from behind an antique suit of armor. There, she had just

happened to be listening to the conversation while oiling a rusty joint.

The king blinked his eyes twice—once with shock because he was taken by surprise, and once with pride because he was taken by his daughter's dazzling beauty. "You can't slay a dragon," he said. "Why don't you go knit a vest for the palace poodle or something?"

The princess flexed the arm of the ancient armor. "See? No more clink." She smiled.

"No more clink," said the king vacantly.

"And I just fixed the drawbridge, too," said the princess. "You won't have to worry about the clank anymore."

"Clink, clank, clunk," said the king. "I have more important worries anyway."

"I know," said Penelope. "The dragon. I *said* I'd slay him for you."

"Nonsense," said the king. "Young ladies don't slay dragons."

"They don't oil armor or fix drawbridges, either," said the princess matter-of-factly.

The king scratched his head and thought about that for a while. Princess Penelope was always giving him something to think about. For one thing, he thought her rare beauty was unsurpassed by that of any princess on earth. For another, it seemed she never behaved as beautiful princesses should.

"Slaying dragons is men's work," he said finally, "and that's that."

The princess didn't really think that was that. But she knew her father did. So she said no more about it—to him, anyway.

It seemed to her that a young lady could do anything she wanted, if she set her mind to it. And in her tender years she had set her mind to many things the king and queen had said only men could do.

She once whittled a whistle from a green willow stick when she was supposed to be sewing a fine seam.

She once built a birdhouse for the palace puffin when she was supposed to be practicing her lute lesson.

And once she even killed a mouse. She had come into the bedchamber to find her mother standing on a chair and screaming—as queens do in the presence of mice. "Don't worry, Mother, I'll get him," Penelope said.

"Young ladies don't kill mice," the queen said. "For heaven's sake, stand on a chair and scream along with me."

But Penelope didn't stand on a chair and scream. She caught the mouse and disposed of it tidily.

Well, she would dispose of the dragon, too. And she would get some ideas on how to go about it.

She went to speak to the royal cook. "How would you slay a dragon?" she asked.

"I would cut off his head with a carving knife," said the cook. "But of course you couldn't do that."

"Why not?" asked the princess.

"Young ladies don't slay dragons," the cook said.

"My father said that, too," said Penelope, and she went to speak to the royal tailor. "How would you slay a dragon?" she asked.

"I would stab him through the heart with a long needle," the tailor said.

"Would you lend me a long needle?" asked the princess.

"Young ladies don't slay dragons," the tailor said. "Besides, I don't have a needle long enough or strong enough."

So Princess Penelope went to the royal court jester. "How would you slay a dragon?" she asked.

"I would tell him such a funny story he would die laughing," said the jester.

"Do you have such a funny story?" asked Penelope.

"There aren't any stories *that* funny," said the jester. "Besides, young ladies don't slay dragons."

"You may be in for a surprise," said the princess, and she went to speak to the royal wizard. "How would you slay a dragon?" she asked.

The royal wizard thought a long time. Then he said, "Why do you want to know?"

"Because I want to slay the dragon," Penelope said matter-of-factly.

"Well, if you really want the truth," the wizard said, "the fact is, young ladies don't slay dragons."

"How do you know they don't?" Penelope asked.

"Everybody knows that," the wizard said. "Don't ask me how I know—it's just a fact."

"Well, then," the princess said, "if a brave young man wanted to save the palace from a smoke-blowing, flame-throwing, fierce and wicked dragon, what advice would you give him?"

The royal wizard wrinkled his forehead, squinted his eyes, and made arches with his fingers while he thought. Then he said, "I would advise him to fight fire with fire."

"I see," said Penelope.

"My feet are cold," said the wizard. "Do me a favor and slide that hot bucket over here. I want to warm my toes on it."

Penelope did as he bade. "How does the bucket stay hot?" she asked.

"It's filled with a magic liquid that burns without fire," said the wizard. "I conjured it up myself."

"A good bit of magic," said Penelope admiringly. "Can you get the liquid to flame up?"

"If I want flames, I just drop a hot coal into the bucket," said the wizard. And then he fell asleep. He always fell asleep after talking three minutes, and now his three minutes were up. Besides, it was nap time for everybody in the palace.

But how anybody could sleep through the dragon's terrible roaring was a mystery to Penelope. And how anybody could sleep while evil threatened the palace was another mystery to her.

The wizard had given the princess an idea, though, and she tiptoed out of the room.

She found a pipe in her collection of iron and sealed it at one end. She tiptoed back to the wizard's room and filled the pipe with liquid from the magic bucket. With a pair of tongs, she took a hot coal from the fire and tiptoed away. She paused in the great hall long enough to don a suit of armor—minus the helmet that hurt her ears and hung low over her eyes. Finally she found a shield she could lift.

Then, clanking, she made her way through the courtyard to the gates. Though she was not strong enough to open them, she managed to push herself sideways through the iron bars. And she wasn't the least bit afraid.

Now, the dragon was the biggest, the most ferocious dragon that ever lived. Princess Penelope didn't know that, but she rather suspected it, for why else wouldn't the brave men in the kingdom come to slay him?

And the dragon, who was also the wisest dragon that ever lived, had a hunch someone was after him. So he crept slowly around the walls to see who it was—roaring terrible roars and belching the sky full of fire and smoke as he went.

"I wish he wouldn't smoke so much," Penelope muttered as she crept after him. Rounding the corner, she could just make out the monstrous tip of the dragon's tail disappearing around the corner ahead.

"This will never do," she said after the third corner. Turning, she crept the other way—and she met the dragon face to face!

Now, it isn't easy to describe the ferocious battle that ensued, but it went something like this.

"Stop or I'll shoot," said Penelope calmly.

"What's a nice girl like you doing out slaying dragons?" sneered the dragon as he crept toward her, blinking several times because of her dazzling beauty.

"I said, stop or I'll shoot."

"You don't *shoot* dragons," the dragon said, coming closer. "Everybody I ever heard of slays them with swords."

"I'm not like everybody you ever heard of," Penelope said.

"I wonder why that is," the dragon said. And though he didn't know it at the time, the dragon had spoken his last words.

Princess Penelope raised her lead pipe, ignited the liquid with her hot coal, and dealt the deadly dragon a deadly blow.

Now, nobody would believe the terrible fire that followed, so it isn't necessary to describe it. But it was like the end of the world.

At last the smoke cleared away. And there, standing among the charred remains of the world's most ferocious dragon was—the world's most handsome prince. Penelope couldn't believe her eyes.

"I've been waiting for something like that to happen," said the prince, smiling a handsome smile and blinking a winsome blink. "You'll marry me, of course."

But—Penelope was the world's most beautiful princess. Having her for a wife was more than the prince had dared dream, especially while bouncing about in the body of a dragon.

"I have a kingdom ten times the size of this pea patch," he added, "and it's all yours if you'll say yes."

Penelope gazed into his eyes a long time. Thoughtfully, she said, "I've been waiting for someone like you to ask me something like that. But there's something you should know about me first. I wouldn't be happy just being a queen and doing queen-things. I like to fix drawbridges, build birdhouses, slay dragons—that sort of thing."

"It so happens I have bridges, birds, and dragons to spare," said the prince hopefully.

"Then my answer is yes," said Penelope.

And with that they saddled up a white horse and rode off into the sunset.

Now, even though this is the end of the story, you realize, of course, they are still living happily ever after.

Close Up

1. Name three things Penelope does that princesses in fairy tales aren't expected to do.

2. When Penelope decides to slay the dragon, she asks for advice. (a) How does she get advice from the wizard? (b) What is his advice?

3. (a) How does Penelope slay the dragon? (b) Why did you expect her to slay the dragon in a way no one else would?

4. (a) Why does Penelope agree to marry the prince? (b) Did you expect Penelope to marry the prince at the end of the story? Why or why not?

Who Tells the Story

Sometimes the narrator takes you inside the minds of several characters. The narrator lets you know what each character thinks and feels. The narrator stands outside the story and tells it in the third person. At times, the narrator comments on the story. For example, the narrator says, "Now it isn't easy to describe the ferocious battle that ensued, but it went something like this."

1. In which of the following sentences does the narrator take you inside the minds of the characters?
   a. "She had come into the bedchamber to find her mother standing on a chair and screaming. . . ."
   b. "For one thing, he thought her rare beauty was unsurpassed by any princess on earth."
   c. "It seemed to her that a young lady could do anything she wanted, if she set her mind to it."
   d. "Penelope gazed into his eyes a long time."
   e. "And the dragon, who was the wisest dragon that ever lived, had a hunch someone was after him."

2. In which of the following sentences does the narrator comment on the story? In which does the narrator just tell what happens?
   a. "The king scratched his head and thought about that for a while."
   b. "Now, nobody would believe the terrible fire that followed, so it isn't necessary to describe it. But it was like the end of the world."
   c. "She caught the mouse and disposed of it tidily."
   d. "Now, even though this is the end of the story, you realize, of course, they live happily ever after."

3. (a) List two ways this tale is like a traditional fairy tale. (b) List two ways it is different.

JUDGMENTS

Recognizing Opinions Labeled as Facts

A statement of fact contains information that can be proved true or false. A statement of opinion expresses a personal belief or attitude. Sometimes people believe something so strongly that they state it as a fact, when really it is an opinion. For example, someone might say, "*It's a fact* that Brand X cookies taste better than Brand Y." Someone else might say, "*Everyone knows that* our team will win the game." These are really statements of opinion that contain information that *cannot* be proved true or false. The first statement is a matter of taste or personal judgment. The second predicts the future. Statements containing phrases like "it's a fact that" or "everyone knows that" may hide opinions.

1. When Penelope asks the wizard for advice, he tells her:

    "Well, if you really want to know the truth, . . . the fact is, young ladies don't slay dragons."

    (a) Which two phrases might fool you into thinking this is a statement of fact? (b) How do you know it is really a statement of opinion?

2. When Penelope asks the wizard how he knows that young ladies don't slay dragons, he answers:

    "Everybody knows that . . . Don't ask me how I know—it's just a fact."

    (a) Which two groups of words might fool you into thinking this is really a statement of fact? (b) Can the wizard give any evidence to support his opinion? Why or why not?

WORD ATTACK

Using Context Clues

Context can help you find the meaning of a word you do not know. Context is the group of words surrounding an unknown word. Sometimes the context of a word is the sentence it is in. Sometimes the context is a whole group of sentences. If you read closely, you will find that the context often contains general clues that help you to make an intelligent guess about the meaning of the unknown word.

1. You probably never heard of a palace "puffin" before you read this story. Look again at the sentence *puffin* is in: "She once built a birdhouse for the palace *puffin* when she was supposed to be practicing her lute lesson." Since Penelope built the puffin a *birdhouse*, what type of creature do you think it is? Check the glossary to see if your guess is right.

2. You may be unfamiliar with the word "ignited." Look at the following sentence: "Princess Penelope raised her lead pipe, *ignited* the liquid with her hot coal, and dealt the dragon a deadly blow." Since Penelope used a *hot coal* to ignite the liquid before it exploded, what do you think the word *ignite* means? Check the glossary to see if your answer is right.

3. Sometimes the context of a word is a whole group of sentences. Read the passage below and see if you can figure out what a jester does for a living. Then check the glossary to see if your answer is right.

   "So Princess Penelope went to the royal court jester. 'How would you slay a dragon?' she asked.
   'I would tell him such a funny story he would die laughing,' said the jester.
   'Do you have such a funny story?' asked Penelope.
   'There aren't any stories that funny,' said the jester."

4. You may be unfamiliar with the word *plaguing* in the following passage:

   "A dragon with exceedingly evil intentions was *plaguing* the Palace of Hexagon. Night and day he lurked about the courtyard walls, belching fire and smoke and roaring in a most terrible fashion."

   After you read the word *plaguing*, you read examples of things the dragon did. Study these examples and then decide what you think *plaguing* means. Then check the glossary.

REVIEW QUIZ

On the Selections

1. In "One Day at the Griffith Park Zoo," Dr. Young is worried because the coyote pups look seedy. Why are their coats seedy?

2. How does Dr. Young receive a replacement for one of the lost snakes?

3. In "The Cherub and My Sainted Grandmother," Maggie's father says, "Animals are like people: some are bad clear through and some are good clear through." (a) What person does he think is all good? (b) What animal does he think is all bad?

4. In your opinion, does Maggie really have "a way with horses"? What facts can you give to support your opinion?

5. In "It's Not a Game for Girls," Willis gets angry when he sees Heck help Hepzibah on with her jacket. Do you think Willis is feeling stubborn, lonely, or jealous?

6. Which one of these two statements do you think the author wants you to believe?
   a. Baseball really isn't a game for girls.
   b. Some girls make good baseball players.

7. In "To Satch," what does the pitcher plan to use instead of a ball to throw three "hot" strikes?

8. In "A Man of His Own," the puppy responds to instinct and points at the butterfly. What is an *instinct*?

9. What does the puppy do at night that shows he is dreaming of hunting?

10. In "Young Ladies Don't Slay Dragons," why doesn't the dragon expect Penelope to shoot him?

On Judgments

1. Look at each pair below. Which source would probably give you the *more* reliable information?
   a. An athlete giving you information about the best toothpaste to use, or a dentist giving you information about the best toothpaste.
   b. An astronaut describing the loneliness of outer space, or a reporter describing the loneliness of outer space.
   c. Your doctor telling you about your need for vitamin tablets or the manufacturer of vitamin tablets writing about your need for them.

2. Which of the following statements is a statement of fact and which is a statement of opinion?
   a. "Annie" is the best musical you will ever see.
   b. Hank Aaron broke Babe Ruth's long-standing record.

3. Which of the following statements are stereotypes?
   a. "All people with long fingers are excellent piano players."
   b. "All motorcycle drivers in this state need a special license."
   c. "All sports car drivers are reckless."

4. From the following group of statements, choose the one opinion that is valid.
   a. Aretha will win the race. She won her last four races. She has trained every day this month. Her health is excellent.
   b. Aretha will win the race. She is my best friend. I don't know any of the other contestants. We will have a big party after Aretha wins.
   c. Aretha will win the race. She has new racing sneakers and an expensive jogging suit. She even has a sweatband with the school colors on it.

5. Which of the following are statements of fact and which are statements of opinion?
   a. Everyone knows that all basketball players are tall.
   b. It's a fact that the runner with the longest legs always wins.
   c. The truth is that a stuntwoman performs many of the star's daring deeds.

COMPOSITION

Narration When you write narration, you tell a story. Your story has a beginning, a middle, and an end. In the beginning, you introduce your readers to the main character. In the middle, you tell what happens to this character and explain the conflict. In the end, you tell how the character resolves the conflict. Also, you may tell how the main character feels about the way the conflict has turned out.

You tell a story in logical order. Many stories are told in chronological order, which is the order in which events occurred.

▶ Write a narrative paragraph using one of the ideas below.
   a. Write a paragraph describing one event that happened to you at a zoo or with an unusual animal. Try to begin your paragraph with a sentence that will capture the attention of your readers. At the end of the paragraph, let your readers know how you feel about the way the event turned out.
   b. Imagine you are Mr. Hagen's daughter. Write a paragraph telling what happened the first time you rode Cherub.
   c. Imagine you are Hepzibah Sloane. Write a paragraph explaining what happened when you pitched to Link Bannerman. You might start your paragraph with this sentence: *I was scared; I was up against Link Bannerman, who has shoulders a mile wide and who is the team's best batter.*
   d. Imagine you are the boy in "A Man of His Own." Write a paragraph telling about the first time you take your dog hunting.
   e. Write a paragraph telling how the prince became a dragon in the first place. Be sure to use the third-person pronoun *he* when talking about the prince or dragon.
   f. Make up your own fairy tale. Begin with the words: *Once upon a time, there lived a most unusual prince (or princess).* Try to give the ending of your fairy tale a modern twist.

BEFORE GOING ON

Making a Reading Survey

A good technique for reading a selection rapidly is to make a reading survey. First, read the title to get an idea of what the selection is about. Then read the first one or two paragraphs. Then read the final paragraph. Then, determine what questions you have about the selection, based on these steps. Finally, keep your questions in mind and skim the entire selection, noting key words and ideas.

▶ Make a reading survey of this selection. Then decide whether the following statements are true or false.

    a. In ancient times, people thought comets meant good times were ahead.

    b. Some people believe that ancient sculpture was created by space creatures.

    c. Allied fliers reported seeing UFOs during World War II.

    d. The word "flying saucer" was made up by a reporter in 1947.

    e. Mantell mistook the planet Venus for a flying saucer.

    f. The United States Navy has the job of investigating UFO sightings.

    g. The Air Force considered Project Blue Book of vital importance.

    h. An IFO is an informational flying object.

    i. All UFOs are saucer shaped.

    j. Nearly all UFO observers have made their sightings at night.

Further Reading

Those Mysterious UFOs

David C. Knight

The Story of Unidentified Flying Objects

For hundreds of years people have reported seeing strange objects in the sky. In ancient times, for example, a comet was a frightening sight. People who saw one often thought it meant that bad times were coming.

Throughout history, too, many people have thought that these strange objects bring visitors from other worlds. Tales of queer sights in the heavens have caused some persons to think that our earth may have been visited many times in the past. For instance, the story in the Bible of the wheel of fire seen by the prophet Ezekiel seems to some people like a description of a modern flying saucer. And some ancient sculpture found in South America seems to look like space-uniformed men in saucer-like vehicles.

A few years before our own century began, dozens of strange objects were reported in the skies over America. One, called "The Airship," was seen in many states. It could move swiftly, had powerful lights, and was seen to land several times in different places. Whether or not it was the same object each time is not known.

"The Airship" may have been what a Kansas farmer saw just a few feet above his cow pasture on the night of April 21, 1897. The farmer later wrote that it had a large, cigar-shaped section about 300 feet long, with a carriage underneath made of glass or something else you could see

through. It was brightly lighted inside and everything could be plainly seen. The farmer went on to say: "It was occupied by six of the strangest beings I ever saw. They were jabbering together but we could not understand a word they said."

The frightened farmer and his two companions saw a great "turbine wheel" begin to turn underneath the craft. Then it rose "as lightly as a bird." As it did so, the farmer saw that a cable from the ship had been tied around one of his cows. Then the craft, cow and all, rapidly gained altitude and soon vanished in the western sky.

What this farmer saw in 1897 is very much like flying saucer reports of today. The craft was silent. It was a glowing red color. It used some revolving wheel-like thing to fly. It was cigar-shaped and brightly lit. And it was plainly under the control of human-like creatures.

There was not much news after that about mysterious objects seen in the skies until the 1940s, during World War II. Then the objects showed up again. Allied fliers on bombing missions over Germany often reported strange balls of light flying alongside their planes— sometimes three or more in formation. The fliers named them "foo fighters" after a comic-strip word of the time. A "foo" would suddenly appear, stay with the plane for an hour or so, and then vanish. Nobody could explain what the "foos" were, just as no one could explain the appearance of strange craft over Sweden right after the war. Night after night, thousands of persons watched these faintly shining objects zipping about the skies, sometimes hovering silently, and then zipping away again at odd angles.

The modern history of flying saucers began on a clear June day in 1947 when an Idaho businessman, Kenneth Arnold, was flying his private plane near Mount Rainier, Washington. Suddenly he saw a group of odd-looking craft flying in formation. Arnold counted nine of the disk-like things; they were making amazing maneuvers.

When Arnold landed, he reported what he had seen: "They flew very close to the mountain tops . . . as if they were linked together . . . I watched them for about three minutes—a chain of saucer-like things at least five miles long . . . . They were flat, like a piepan, and so shiny they reflected the sun . . . I never saw anything so fast."

Arnold's story was printed in many newspapers and in a few days the whole country was talking excitedly about it. Arnold had told one reporter that the objects skimmed along "as a saucer would if you skipped it across water." When the reporter wrote his story, he made up the term "flying saucer."

Within a month, disk-like flying craft had been seen in every state in the country, and the flying saucer scare of 1947 was in full swing. It reached its peak during late summer with well over one hundred sightings reported. Toward Christmas, people's interest in flying saucers seemed to die down. But a tragedy that took place on January 7, 1948 brought it back to life.

Early that afternoon, observers at an Air Force base in Kentucky saw a mysterious flying object overhead. Four Air National Guard pilots in F-51 fighters were ordered aloft to investigate. The flight leader, Captain Thomas F. Mantell, radioed back that he was closing in "to take a good look." A few minutes later

Mantell reported that the object appeared to be metallic and very large. "It's going up now and forward as fast as I am," he barked over his radio. "That's 360 miles an hour. I'm going up to 20,000 feet and if I'm no closer, I'll abandon chase."

There was no further contact with Mantell that day—or ever. Late that afternoon his body was found in the wreckage of his plane. The offical Air Force explanation was that he had blacked out from lack of oxygen and died of suffocation before crashing. The object he had pursued was at first identified as the planet Venus, but further investigation showed that Venus had not appeared on that day in the sky where the object had been sighted. The thing Mantell lost his life chasing is still unidentified, although it may have been a research balloon flying in the area at the time.

The Mantell incident touched off a new wave of flying saucer sightings in 1948. Some of the mysterious objects were spotted by planes, others by observers on the ground. A number were also picked up on radar screens. These reports were all the more believable because many were being turned in by people trained as good observers: airline pilots, Weather Bureau observers, radar operators, and Air Force and Navy fliers.

At first, people outside the United States looked on the flying saucer excitement as just another American fad. It would quickly pass. But this craze did not go away. Year after year reports kept coming in from practically every country. People all over the world began to discover that the things they saw looked the same. Observers were seeing solid, metallic objects whose strange movements and super speeds could not be explained. Sometimes they even appeared in photographs.

Often these objects interfered with TV and radio reception, caused car engines to stall, and animals to panic. When they were seen to land and depart again, they left scorched bushes and grass and marks of their landing gear in fields.

People's interest in flying saucers came and went, but as early as 1947 the United States government had become alarmed at the growing number of reports of strange objects in the skies. Too many had been made by reliable people to be ignored. Officials in Washington demanded that something be done.

So in January 1948, the United States Air Force, whose job it was to defend the country from the air, was given the task of investigating the mysterious objects. At this time many people feared that a foreign country had a secret new aircraft that threatened America's national safety. Perhaps the saucers being reported were such aircraft. The Air Force investigation was later called Project Blue Book.

Today, writers looking back at what the Air Force did seem to agree that the job wasn't handled very well. Those who find fault with the work of the Air Force at the time say that the men of Project Blue Book didn't pay enough attention to the scientific parts of the reports as they came in from private citizens. Yet in all fairness to the Air Force, it must be said that their main responsibility was the defense of the nation, not science. So, when the Air Force received an observer's report that seemed to be no threat to

America's safety, it was seldom followed up for such scientific information, as to the unknown object's exact speed, direction, and size.

However, the men of Project Blue Book did consult scientists about some sightings. For many years, one astronomer checked whether some of the strange objects could be explained as stars, comets, or other heavenly bodies. But all too often the Air Force sent these reports to the scientists weeks or months after the objects were seen. Observers, when questioned, no longer were sure what they had seen. Also, Blue Book questionnaires given observers to fill out did not contain some questions that should have been included to cover all the details of a sighting. Finally, the staff of Project Blue Book was small, their work considered unimportant compared with other Air Force work, and their commanding officers were often of low rank and had little authority. (For many months, a sergeant with little technical training was given the job of checking the reports.)

Project Blue Book changed little during the twenty-two years it lasted. Many reports were handled in a routine way and not carefully investigated. This was especially true of puzzling, unusual cases. These were often just labeled "Unidentified" and filed away. That is how the term "Unidentified Flying Object," or UFO for short, came into use.

But the men of Blue Book did try in one way or another to label the sighting an IFO—*Identified* Flying Object. This meant, for example, that the object could have been a balloon, or what the observer might have mistaken for a planet, and wasn't any threat to America's safety. Blue Book's files are still filled with hundreds of cases stamped "Unidentified" or "Insufficient Information."

By far the largest number of UFOs being reported were flying saucer, or disk, types. There were large ones of one hundred feet or more across, medium-sized disks, and very small ones of only a few feet. As the years passed, these seemed to change in design. Early types appeared to have tall domes on top that gave them a faintly bell-shaped look. Later disk UFOs had lower, smaller domes.

People were also reporting UFOs shaped like balls, doughnuts, and cigars. There were also rocket-shaped craft ranging in length from 100 to 1,000 feet. In some cases, these seemed to serve as mother ships for disk types. Some people reported that UFOs grew larger or smaller. Almost every color UFO was reported, and many observers swore that they glowed, throbbed, or changed their color.

Nearly all UFO observers seemed to agree that they could perform fantastic maneuvers. They were seen to move every which way and at nearly any speed. Sometimes they hung motionless in the air, then shot skyward, zigzagged, made 90-degree turns, and then reversed their courses with unbelievable suddenness. Some made low humming noises, but most were reported to be completely silent.

Many UFO watchers around the world reported they saw their objects around sunrise or sunset. But they have been seen at all hours of the day and night. Some UFOs are seen to travel in bunches, others alone. One UFO may suddenly divide into smaller ones, or a group may join and become a single saucer.

Every observer who reports a UFO has seen something. But *what?* As American investigators—together with those of other countries looking into UFOs—checked case after case, they found that many sightings made some kind of sense. Some of the "somethings" turned out not to be flying craft at all. Observers often mistook meteors, especially those called fireballs, for UFOs. Or they caught glimpses of the planet Venus which, as the evening star, is low and brilliant on the horizon.

Or many of these people may have seen some kind of flying craft, but not necessarily spaceships from other worlds. Some may have been catching the sun's reflection from planes flying at high altitudes. Dozens of other sightings turned out to be nothing more than kites, flocks of birds, jet plane trails, or balloons. In the early 1950s, one scientist said that many of the UFOs reported were probably Skyhook balloons—large plastic, unmanned craft used to carry weather instruments to great heights. Seen against the background of the sky, they sometimes look quite disk-like.

People also mistook weather signs for UFOs. Queer cloud formations called "a stack of plates" or "grindstone" clouds look very much like saucer-type UFOs. So do effects called "sun dogs," which are images of the sun reflected through ice crystals high in the atmosphere. At night, a similar effect can produce "moon dogs." One noted scientist, who was often consulted by the Air Force, is sure that many UFOs are due to reflections produced by air layers of different temperature near the earth. If such conditions are right, images of things on the earth can be flashed up against the sky; city lights, street lamps, or car headlights may seem to float in the air or, if the air is disturbed, seem to dart about like UFOs.

One scientist put together a list of over seventy-five explanations of what UFOs *are not;* it included insect swarms, lightning, fireworks, overactive imaginations, and failure to wear glasses by observers who needed them.

Certainly man-made satellites have been responsible for many mis-sightings since the 1957 launching of Sputnik I by the Soviet Union. And, even though photographs have been made of UFOs, some have proved to be fakes and hoaxes; others were caused by faulty cameras.

Finally, scores of UFO "sightings" were due to downright trickery; for instance, pranksters have tossed disk-shaped objects like pie tins out of buildings at night to fool onlookers. One man was suspected of fooling people for years by taking realistic pictures of a chicken-hatching machine and passing them off as a genuine UFO.

Flight into Danger

Arthur Hailey

Characters

ABOARD FLIGHT 714:

The Passengers:

George Spencer

Dr. Frank Baird

Seven Male Passengers

Two Women Passengers

The Crew:

Captain

First Officer

Stewardess

AT VANCOUVER AIRPORT:

Captain Martin Treleaven

Airport Controller

Harry Burdick

Switchboard Operator

Radio Operator

Tower Controller

Teletype Operator

AT WINNIPEG AIRPORT:

First Passenger Agent

Second Passenger Agent

Act I

Fade in: The passenger lobby of Winnipeg Air Terminal at night. At the departure counter of Cross-Canada Airlines, a male passenger agent in uniform (First Agent) is checking a manifest. He reaches for P.A. mike.

First Agent: Flight 98, direct fleet-liner service to Vancouver, with connections for Victoria, Seattle, and Honolulu, leaving immediately through gate four. No smoking. All aboard, please.

(During the announcement George Spencer enters through the main lobby doorway. About thirty-five, he is a senior factory salesman for a motortruck manufacturer. Spencer pauses to look for the Cross-Canada counter, then hastens toward it, arriving as the announcement concludes.)

Spencer: Is there space on Flight 98 for Vancouver?

First Agent: Sorry, sir, that flight is full. Did you check with reservations?

Spencer: Didn't have time. I came straight out on the chance you might have a "no show" seat.

First Agent: With the big football game on tomorrow in Vancouver, I don't think you'll have much chance of getting out before tomorrow afternoon.

Spencer: That's no good. I've got to be in Vancouver tomorrow by midday.

First Agent (hesitates): Look, I'm not supposed to tell you this, but there's a charter flight in from Toronto. They're going out to the coast for the game. I did hear they were a few seats light.

Spencer: Who's in charge? Where do I find him?

First Agent. Ask at the desk over there. They call themselves Maple Leaf Air Charter. But mind, I didn't send you.

Spencer (smiles): Okay, thanks. (Spencer crosses to another departure counter, which has a cardboard sign hanging behind it—Maple Leaf Air Charter. Behind the desk is an agent in a lounge suit. He is checking a manifest.)

Spencer: Excuse me.

Second Agent: Yes?

Spencer: I was told you might have space on a flight to Vancouver.

Second Agent: Yes, there's one seat left. The flight's leaving right away, though.

Spencer: That's what I want.

Second Agent: Very well, sir. Your name, please?

Spencer: Spencer—George Spencer.

Second Agent: That'll be fifty-five dollars for the one-way trip.

Spencer: Will you take my air travel card?

Second Agent: No, sir. Just old-fashioned cash.

Spencer: All right. (Produces wallet and counts out bills.)

Second Agent (handing over ticket): Do you have any bags?

Spencer: One. Right here.

Second Agent: All the baggage is aboard. Would you mind keeping that with you?

Spencer: Be glad to.

Second Agent: Okay, Mr. Spencer. Your ticket is your boarding pass. Go through gate three and ask the commissionaire for Flight 714. Better hurry.

Spencer: Thanks a lot. Good night.

Second Agent: Good night.

(Exit Spencer. Enter Stewardess.)

Second Agent: Hi, Janet. Did the meals get aboard?

Stewardess: Yes, they've just put them on. What was the trouble?

Second Agent: Couldn't get service from the regular caterers here. We had to go to some outfit the other side of town. That's what held us up.

Stewardess: Are we all clear now?

Second Agent: Yes. Here's everything you'll need. (*Hands over papers.*) There's one more passenger. He's just gone aboard. So that's fifty-six souls in your lovely little hands.

Stewardess: I'll try not to drop any.

Second Agent (*reaching for coat*): Well, I'm off home.

Stewardess (*as she leaves*): 'Night.

Second Agent (*pulling on coat*): 'Night, Janet. (*Calls after her.*) Don't forget to cheer for the Blue Bombers tomorrow.

(*The Stewardess waves and smiles.*)

(*Dissolve to: The passenger cabin of a DC-4 airliner. There is one empty aisle seat. Seated next to it is Dr. Frank Baird, 55. George Spencer enters, sees the unoccupied seat, and comes toward it.*)

Spencer: Pardon me, is this anyone's seat?

Baird: No.

Spencer: Thanks.

(*Spencer sheds his topcoat and puts it on the rack above the seats. Meanwhile the plane's motors can be heard starting.*)

(*Cut to: Film insert of four-engined airplane exterior. Night, the motors starting.*)

(*Cut to: The passenger cabin.*)

Baird: I presume you're going to the big game like the rest of us.

Spencer: I'm ashamed to admit it, but I'd forgotten about the game.

Baird: I wouldn't say that too loudly if I were you. Some of the more exuberant fans might tear you limb from limb.

Spencer: I'll keep my voice down. (*Pleasantly*) Matter of fact, I'm making a sales trip to the coast.

Baird: What do you sell?

Spencer: Trucks.

Baird: Trucks?

Spencer: That's right. I'm what the local salesmen call the son-of-a-gun from head office with the special prices. . . . Need any trucks? How about forty? Give you a real good discount today.

Baird (*laughs*): I couldn't use that many, I'm afraid. Not in my line of country.

Spencer: Which is?

Baird: Medicine.

Spencer: You mean you're a doctor?

Baird: That's right. Can't buy one truck, leave alone forty. Football is the one extravagance I allow myself.

Spencer: Delighted to hear it, Doctor. Now I can relax.

(*As he speaks, the run-up of the aircraft engines begins, increasing to a heavy roar.*)

Baird (*raising his voice*): Do you think you can in this racket? I never can figure out why they make all this noise before take-off.

Spencer (*shouting, as noise increases*): It's the normal run-up of the engines. Airplane engines don't use battery ignition like you have in your car. They run on magneto ignition, and each of the magnetos is tested separately. If they're okay and the motors are giving all the power they should—away you go!

Baird: You sound as if you know something about it.

Spencer: I'm pretty rusty now. I used to fly fighters in the Air Force. But that was ten years ago. Reckon I've forgotten most of it. . . . Well, there we go.

(*The tempo of the motors increases. Baird and Spencer lean toward the window to watch the take-off, although it is dark outside.*)

(*Cut to: Film insert of airplane taking off, night.*)

(*Cut to: The passenger cabin. The noise of the motors is reduced slightly, and the two men relax in their seats. Spencer reaches for cigarettes.*)

Spencer: Smoke?

Baird: Thank you.

(*They light up. The Stewardess enters from aft of airplane and reaches for two pillows from the rack above.*)

Stewardess: We were held up at Winnipeg, sir, and we haven't served dinner yet. Would you care for some?

Spencer: Yes, please.

(*The Stewardess puts a pillow on his lap.*)

Stewardess (*to Baird*): And you sir?

Baird: Thank you, yes. (*To Spencer*) It's a bit late for dinner, but it'll pass the time away.

Stewardess: There's lamb chop or grilled halibut.

Baird: I'll take the lamb.

Spencer: Yes, I'll have that, too.

Stewardess: Thank you, sir.

Baird (*to Spencer*): Tell me. . . By the way, my name is Baird.

Spencer: Spencer, George Spencer. (*They shake hands.*)

Baird: How'd 'do. Tell me, when you make a sales trip like this, do you . . .

(*Fade voices and pan with the Stewardess, returning aft. Entering the airplane's tiny galley, she picks up a telephone and presses a call button.*)

Voice of First Officer: Flight deck.

Stewardess: I'm finally serving the dinners. What'll "you all" have—lamb chops or grilled halibut?

Voice of First Officer: Just a minute. (*Pause*) Skipper says he'll have the lamb . . . Oh, hold it!. . . No, he's changed his mind. Says he'll take the halibut. Make it two fish, Janet.

Stewardess: Okay. *(The Stewardess hangs up the phone and begins to arrange meal trays.)*

(Cut to: Spencer and Baird.)

Spencer: No, I hadn't expected to go west again this quickly.

Baird: You have my sympathy. I prescribe my travel in small doses.

(The Stewardess enters and puts meal tray on pillow.)

Baird: Oh, thank you.

Stewardess: Will you have coffee, tea, or milk, sir?

Baird: Coffee, please.

Stewardess: I'll bring it later.

Baird: That'll be fine. *(To Spencer)* Tell me, do you follow football at all?

Spencer: A little. Hockey's my game, though. Who are you for tomorrow?

Baird: The Argos, naturally. *(As the Stewardess brings second tray)* Thank you, dear.

Stewardess: Will you have coffee, tea, or——

Spencer: I'll have coffee, too. No cream.

(The Stewardess nods and exits.)

Spencer *(to Baird)*: Must be a calm night outside. No trouble in keeping the dinner steady.

Baird *(looking out of window)*: It is calm. Not a cloud in sight. Must be a monotonous business flying these things, once they're off the ground.

Spencer: It varies, I guess.

(Audio: Fade up the roar of motors.)

(Dissolve to: Film insert of airplane in level flight, night.)

(Dissolve to: The aircraft flight deck. The Captain is seated on left, the First Officer on right. Neither is touching the controls.)

First Officer *(into radio mike)*: Height 16,000 feet. Course 285 true. ETA[1] Vancouver 0505 Pacific Standard. Over.

Voice on Radio: Flight 714. This is Winnipeg Control. Roger. Out.

(The First Officer reaches for a log sheet and makes a notation, then relaxes in his seat.)

First Officer: Got any plans for Vancouver?

Captain: Yes, I'm going to sleep for two whole days.

(The Stewardess enters with a meal tray.)

Stewardess: Who's first?

Captain: You take yours, Harry.

(The Stewardess produces a pillow and the First Officer slides back his seat, well clear of the control column. He places the pillow on his knees and accepts the tray.)

First Officer: Thanks.

Captain: Everything all right at the back, Janet? How are the football fans?

Stewardess: They tired themselves out on the way from Toronto. Looks like a peaceful, placid night.

First Officer *(with mouth full of food, raising fork for emphasis)*: Aha! Those are the sort of nights to beware of. It's in the quiet times that trouble brews. I'll bet you right now that somebody's getting ready to be sick.

Stewardess: That'll be when you're doing the flying. Or have you finally learned how to hold this thing steady? *(To Captain)* How's the weather?

Captain: General fog east of the mountains, extending pretty well as far

---

1. ETA: Estimated time of arrival.

as Manitoba. But it's clear to the west. Should be rockably smooth the whole way.

Stewardess: Good. Well, keep junior here off the controls while I serve coffee. *(Exits.)*

Captain: How's the fish?

First Officer *(hungrily):* Not bad. Not bad at all. If there were about three times as much it might be a square meal.

(Audio: Fade voices into roar of motors.)

(Dissolve to: The passenger cabin. Spencer and Baird are concluding their meal. Baird puts down a coffee cup and wipes his mouth with a napkin. Then he reaches up and presses a call button above his head. There is a soft "ping," and the Stewardess enters.)

Stewardess: Yes, sir?

Baird: That was very enjoyable. Now, if you'll take the tray I think I'll try to sleep.

Stewardess: Surely. *(To Spencer)* Will you have more coffee, sir?

Spencer: No, thanks.

(The Stewardess picks up the second tray and goes aft. Spencer yawns.)

Spencer: Let me know if the noise keeps you awake. If it does, I'll have the engines stopped.

Baird *(chuckles):* Well, at least there won't by any night calls—I hope.

(Baird reaches up and switches off the overhead reading lights so that both seats are in semidarkness. The two men prepare to sleep.)

(Dissolve to: Film insert of airplane in level flight, night.)

(Dissolve to: The passenger cabin. The Captain emerges from the flight deck and strolls aft, saying "Good evening" to one or two people who glance up as he goes by. He passes Spencer and Baird, who are sleeping. As the Captain progresses, the Stewardess can be seen at the rear of the cabin. She is bending solicitously over a woman passenger, her hand on the woman's forehead. The Captain approaches.)

Captain: Something wrong, Miss Burns?

Stewardess: This lady is feeling a little unwell. I was going to get her some aspirin. *(To the Woman Passenger)* I'll be back in a moment.

Captain: Sorry to hear that. What seems to be the trouble?

(The Woman Passenger has her head back and her mouth open. A strand of hair has fallen across her face, and she is obviously in pain.)

First Woman Passenger *(speaking with effort):* I'm sorry to be such a nui-

sance, but it hit me all of a sudden . . . just a few minutes ago . . . dizziness and nausea and a sharp pain . . . *(indicating abdomen)* down here.

Captain: Well, I think the Stewardess will be able to help you.

(Stewardess returns.)

Stewardess: Now, here you are; try these. *(She hands over two aspirin and a cup of water. The passenger takes them, then puts her head back on the seat rest.)*

First Woman Passenger: Thank you very much. *(She smiles faintly at the Captain.)*

Captain *(quietly, taking the Stewardess aside)*: If she gets any worse you'd better let me know and I'll radio ahead. But we've still five hours' flying to the coast. Is there a doctor on board, do you know?

Stewardess: There was no one listed as a doctor on the manifest. But I can go round and ask.

Captain *(looks around)*: Well, most everybody's sleeping now. We'd better not disturb them unless we have to. See how she is in the next half hour or so. *(He bends down and puts a hand on the woman's shoulder.)* Try to rest, madam, if you can. Miss Burns will take good care of you.

(The Captain nods to the Stewardess and begins his return to the flight deck. The Stewardess arranges a blanket around the Woman Passenger. Spencer and Baird are still sleeping as the Captain passes.)

(Dissolve to: Film insert of airplane in level flight, night.)

(Dissolve to: The passenger cabin. Spencer stirs and wakes. Then he

glances forward to where the stewardess is leaning over another section of seats, and her voice can be heard softly.)

Stewardess: I'm sorry to disturb you, but we're trying to find out if there's a doctor on board.

First Male Passenger: Not me, I'm afraid. Is something wrong?

Stewardess: One of the passengers is feeling unwell. It's nothing too serious. (Moving on to the next pair of seats) I'm sorry to disturb you, but we're trying to find out if there's a doctor on board.

(There is an indistinct answer from the two people just questioned, then Spencer sits forward and calls the Stewardess.)

Spencer: Stewardess! (Indicating Baird, who is still sleeping) This gentleman is a doctor.

Stewardess: Thank you. I think we'd better wake him. I have two passengers who are quite sick.

Spencer: All right. (Shaking Baird's arm) Doctor! Doctor! Wake up!

Baird: Um . . . Um . . . What is it?

Stewardess: Doctor, I'm sorry to disturb you. But we have two passengers who seem quite sick. I wonder if you'd take a look at them.

Baird (sleepily): Yes . . . yes . . . of course.

(Spencer moves out of seat to permit Baird to reach the aisle. Baird then follows the Stewardess aft to the First Woman Passenger. Although a blanket is around her, the woman is shivering and gasping, with her head back and eyes closed. The doctor places a hand on her forehead, and she opens her eyes.)

Stewardess: This gentleman is a doctor. He's going to help us.

First Woman Passenger: Oh, Doctor . . . !

Baird: Now, just relax.

(He makes a quick external examination, first checking pulse, then taking a small pen-type flashlight from his pocket and looking into her eyes. He then loosens the blanket and the woman's coat beneath the blanket. As he places a hand on her abdomen, she gasps with pain.)

Baird: Hurt you there? (With an effort she nods.) There?

First Woman Passenger: Oh, yes! Yes!

(Baird replaces the coat and blanket, then turns to the stewardess.)

Baird (with authority): Please tell the Captain we must land at once. This woman has to be gotten to a hospital immediately.

Stewardess: Do you know what's wrong, Doctor?

Baird. I can't tell. I've no means of making a proper diagnosis. But it's serious enough to land at the nearest city with hospital facilities. You can tell your captain that.

Stewardess: Very well, Doctor. (Moving across the aisle and forward) While I'm gone will you take a look at this gentleman here? He's also complained of sickness and stomach pains.

(Baird goes to a male passenger indicated by the Stewardess. The man is sitting forward and resting his head on the back of the seat ahead of him. He is retching.)

Baird: I'm a doctor. Will you put your head back, please?

(The man groans, but follows the doctor's instruction. He is obviously weak. Baird makes another quick examination, then pauses thoughtfully.)

Baird: What have you had to eat in the last twenty-four hours?

Second Male Passenger (with effort): Just the usual meals . . . breakfast . . . bacon and eggs . . . salad for lunch . . . couple of sandwiches at the airport . . . then dinner here.

(The Stewardess enters, followed by the Captain.)

Baird (to the Stewardess): Keep him warm. Get blankets around him. (To the Captain) How quickly can we land, Captain?

Captain: That's the trouble. I've just been talking to Calgary. There was light fog over the prairies earlier, but now it's thickened and everything is closed in this side of the mountains. It's clear at the coast, and we'll have to go through.

Baird: Is that faster than turning back?

Captain: It would take us longer to go back now than to go on.

Baird: Then, how soon do you expect to land?

Captain: At about 5 A.M. Pacific time. (As Baird glances at his watch) You need to put your watch on two hours because of the change of time. We'll be landing in three hours forty-five minutes from now.

Baird: Then I'll have to do what I can for these people. Can my bag be reached? I checked it at Toronto.

Captain: We can get it. Let me have your tags, Doctor.

(Baird takes out a wallet and selects two baggage tags, which he hands to the Captain.)

Baird: There are two bags. It's the small overnight case I want.

(As he finishes speaking, the airplane lurches violently. Baird and the Stewardess and the Captain are thrown sharply to one side. Simultaneously the telephone in the galley buzzes several times. As the three recover their balance, the Stewardess answers the phone. Quickly)

Stewardess: Yes?

First Officer's Voice (under strain): Come forward quickly. I'm sick!

Stewardess: The First Officer is sick. He says come quickly.

Captain (to Baird): You'd better come too.

(The Captain and Baird move quickly forward, passing through the flight deck door.)

(Cut to: The flight deck. The First Officer is at the controls on the right-hand side. He is retching and shuddering, flying the airplane by will power and nothing else. The Captain promptly slides into the left-hand seat and takes the controls.)

Captain: Get him out of there!

(Together Baird and the Stewardess lift the First Officer from his seat, and, as they do, he collapses. They lower him to the floor, and the Stewardess reaches for a pillow and blankets. Baird makes the same quick examination he used in the two previous cases. Meanwhile the Captain has steadied the aircraft, and now he snaps over a button to engage the automatic pilot. He releases the controls and turns to the others, though without leaving his seat.)

Captain: He must have been changing course when it happened. We're back on auto pilot now. Now, Doctor; what is it? What's happening?

Baird: There's a common denominator in these attacks. There has to be. And the most likely thing is food. (To the Stewardess) How long is it since we had dinner?

Stewardess: Two and a half to three hours.

Baird: Now, then, what did you serve?

Stewardess: Well, the main course was a choice of fish or meat.

Baird: I remember that. I ate meat. (*Indicating the First Officer*) What did he have?

Stewardess (*faintly, with dawning alarm*): Fish.

Baird: Do you remember what the other two passengers had?

Stewardess: No.

Baird: Then, go back quickly and find out, please.

(*As the Stewardess exits, Baird kneels beside the First Officer, who is moaning.*)

Baird: Try to relax. I'll give you something in a few minutes to help the pain. You'll feel better if you stay warm.

(*Baird arranges the blanket around the First Officer. Now the Stewardess reappears.*)

Stewardess (*alarmed*): Doctor, both those passengers had fish. And there are three more cases now. And they ate fish too. Can you come?

Baird: Yes, but I need that bag of mine.

Captain: Janet, take these tags and get one of the passengers to help you. (*Hands over Baird's luggage tags.*) Doctor, I'm going to get on the radio and report what's happening to Vancouver. Is there anything you want to add?

Baird: Yes. Tell them we have three serious cases of suspected food poisoning, and there appear to be others. When we land we'll want ambulances and medical help waiting, and the hospitals should be warned. Tell them we're not sure, but we suspect the poisoning may have been caused by fish served on board. You'd better suggest they put a ban on serving all food which originated wherever ours came from until we've established the source for sure.

Captain: Right. (*He reaches for the radio mike, and Baird turns to go aft. But suddenly a thought strikes the Captain.*) Doctor, I've just remembered. . .

Baird. Yes.

Captain (*quietly*): I ate fish.

Baird: When?

Captain. I'd say about half an hour after he did. (*Pointing to the First Officer*) Maybe a little longer. Is there anything I can do?

Baird: It doesn't follow that everyone will be affected. There's often no logic to these things. You feel all right now?

Captain: Yes.

Baird: You'd better not take any chances. Your food can't be completely digested yet. As soon as I get my bag I'll give you something to help you get rid of it.

Captain: Then, hurry, Doctor. For God's sake, hurry! (*Into mike*) Vancouver control. This is Maple Leaf Charter Flight 714. I have an emergency message. Do you read? Over.

Voice on Radio (Vancouver Operator): Go ahead, 714.

Captain: We have serious food poisoning on board. Several passengers and the First Officer are seriously ill. . . .

(*Dissolve to: The luggage compartment below the flight deck. A passenger is hurriedly passing up bags to the Stewardess. Baird is looking down from above.*)

Baird: That's it! That's it down there! Let me have it!

(*Fade out.*)

Close Up

1. Why does George Spencer decide to take the charter flight to Vancouver?

2. What does Spencer tell Dr. Baird about himself that may be important later in the play?

3. The charter flight has been delayed because the airline cannot get service from their regular caterer. How does this fact explain what happens to several people on board?

4. Several characters make statements that hint at things to come. For example, when the Stewardess says, "Looks like a peaceful, placid night," the First Officer replies, "Those are the sort of nights to beware of. It's in the quiet times that trouble brews." Find two other statements that hint at things to come.

5. Sometimes a character makes a statement that turns out to be truer than the character really meant. For example, the doctor is only kidding when he says, "Well, at least there won't be any night calls——" or calls to the doctor for aid. But it turns out that there really are night calls—many night calls. We call this kind of statement ironic. Find one other ironic statement.

Act II

Fade In: The control room, Vancouver Airport. At a radio panel an Operator, wearing headphones, is transcribing a message on a typewriter. Partway through the message he presses a button on the panel and a bell rings stridently, signaling an emergency. At once an Airport Controller appears behind the operator and reads the message as it continues to come in. Nearby is a telephone switchboard manned by an Operator, and a battery of teletypes clattering noisily.

Controller (over his shoulder, to the Switchboard Operator): Get me Area Traffic Control, then clear the teletype circuit to Winnipeg. Priority message. (Stepping back to take phone) Vancouver Controller here. I've an emergency report from Maple Leaf Charter Flight 714, ex-Winnipeg for Vancouver. There's serious food poisoning among the passengers, and the First Officer is down too. They're asking for all levels below them to be cleared, and priority approach and landing. ETA is 0505. . . Roger. We'll keep you posted. (To a Teletype Operator who has appeared) Got Winnipeg? (As the Teletype Operator nods) Send this message. Controller Winnipeg. Urgent. Maple Leaf Charter Flight 714 reports serious food poisoning among passengers believed due to fish dinner served on flight. Imperative check source and suspend all other food service originating same place. That's all. (To the Switchboard Operator) Get me the local agent for Maple Leaf Charter. Burdick's his name—call his home. And after that, I want the city police— the senior officer on duty. (Controller crosses to radio control panel and reads message which is just being completed. To the Radio Operator) Acknowledge.

Say that all altitudes below them are being cleared, and they'll be advised of landing instructions here. Ask them to keep us posted on condition of the passengers.

Switchboard Operator: Mr. Burdick is here at the airport. I have him on the line now.

Controller: Good. Controller here. Burdick, we've got an emergency on one of your flights—714, ex-Toronto and Winnipeg. *(Pause)* No, the aircraft is all right. There's food poisoning among the passengers, and the First Officer has it too. You'd better come over. *(Replaces phone. Then to the Switchboard Operator)* Have you got the police yet?*(As the Operator nods)* Right, put it on this line. Hullo, this is the Controller, Vancouver Airport. Who am I speaking to, please? *(Pause)* Inspector, we have an emergency on an incoming flight. Several of the passengers are seriously ill, and we need ambulances and doctors out here at the airport. *(Pause)* Six people for sure, maybe more. The flight will be landing at five minutes past five local time—that's about three and a half hours. Now, will you get the ambulances, set up traffic control, and alert the hospitals? Right. We'll call you again as soon as there's anything definite.

(During the above, Harry Burdick, local manager of Maple Leaf Air Charter, has entered.)

Burdick: Where's the message?

(The Radio Operator hands him a copy which Burdick reads.)

Burdick *(to Radio Operator)*: How's the weather at Calgary? It might be quicker to go in there.

Controller: No dice! There's fog down to the deck everywhere east of the Rockies. They'll have to come through.

Burdick: Let me see the last position report. *(As Controller passes a clipboard)* You say you've got medical help coming?

Controller: The city police are working on it now.

Burdick: That message! They say the First Officer is down. What about the Captain? Ask if he's affected, and ask if there's a doctor on board. Tell them we're getting medical advice here in case they need it.

Controller: I'll take care of that.

Burdick *(to the Switchboard Operator)*: Will you get me Doctor Knudsen, please? You'll find his home number on the emergency list.

Controller *(into radio mike)*: Flight 714, this is Vancouver.

(Dissolve to: The airplane passenger cabin. Baird is leaning over another prostrate passenger. The main lighting is on in the cabin, and the other passengers, so far not affected, are watching, with varying degrees of concern and anxiety. Some have remained in their seats; others have clustered in the aisle. The doctor has obtained his bag and it is open beside him. The Stewardess is attending to another passenger nearby.)

Baird *(to the Stewardess)*: I think I'd better talk to everyone and tell them the story. *(Moving to center of cabin, he raises his voice.)* Ladies and gentlemen, may I have your attention, please? If you can't hear me, perhaps you would come a little closer. *(Pause, as passengers move in)* My name is Baird, and I am a doctor. I think it's time that everyone knows what is happening. So far as I can tell, we have several cases of food poisoning, and we believe that the cause of it was the fish which was served for dinner.

Second Woman Passenger (*with alarm, to man beside her*): Hector! We both had fish!

Baird: Now, there is no immediate cause for alarm or panic, and even if you did eat fish for dinner, it doesn't follow that you are going to be affected too. There's seldom any logic to these things. However, we are going to take some precautions, and the Stewardess and I are coming around to everyone, and I want you to tell us if you ate fish. If you did we'll tell you what to do to help yourselves. Now, if you'll go back to your seats we'll begin right away. (*To the Stewardess, as passengers move back to their seats*) All we can do now is to give immediate first aid.

Stewardess: What should that be, Doctor?

Baird: Two things. First, everyone who ate fish must drink several glasses of water. That will help dilute the poison. After that we'll give an emetic.[2] I have some emetic pills in my bag, and if there aren't enough we'll have to rely on salt. Do you have salt in the galley?

Stewardess: A few small packets which go with the lunches, but we can break them open.

Baird: All right. We'll see how far the pills will go first. I'll start at the back here. Meanwhile you begin giving drinking water to the passengers already affected and get some to the First Officer too. I'll ask someone to help you.

First Male Passenger: Can I help, Doctor?

Baird: What did you eat for dinner—fish or meat?

---

2. emetic [ĭ-mĕt′ĭk] n.: A medicine that causes vomiting.

First Male Passenger: Meat.

Baird: All right. Will you help the Stewardess bring glasses of water to the people who are sick? I want them to drink at least three glasses each—more if they can.

Stewardess (going to galley): We'll use these cups. There's drinking water here and at the rear.

First Male Passenger: All right, let's get started.

Baird (to the Stewardess): The Captain! Before you do anything else you'd better get him on to drinking water, and give him two emetic pills. Here. (Takes bottle from his bag and shakes out the pills.) Tell him they'll make him feel sick, and the sooner he is, the better.

Stewardess: Very well, Doctor.

Second Woman Passenger (frightened): Doctor! Doctor! I heard you say the pilots are ill. What will happen to us if they can't fly the plane? (To husband) Hector, I'm frightened.

Third Male Passenger: Take it easy, my dear. Nothing has happened so far, and the doctor is doing all he can.

Baird: I don't think you'll have any reason to worry, madam. It's quite true that both of the pilots had the fish, which we believe may have caused the trouble. But only the First Officer is affected. Now, did you and your husband eat fish or meat?

Third Male Passenger: Fish. We both ate fish.

Baird: Then, will you both drink at least three—better make it four—of those cups of water which the other gentleman is bringing around. After that, take one of these pills each. (Smiling) I think you'll find there are little containers under your seat. Use those. (Goes to rear of plane.)

Fourth Male Passenger (in broad English Yorkshire accent): How's it commin', Doc? Everything under control?

Baird: I think we're holding our own. What did you have for dinner?

Fourth Male Passenger: Ah had the bloomin' fish. Didn't like it neither. Fine how d'you do this is. Coom all this way t'see our team win, and now it looks like ah'm headed for a mortuary slab.

Baird: It really isn't as bad as that, you know. But just as a precaution, drink four cups of water—it's being brought around now—and after that take this pill. It'll make you feel sick.

Fourth Male Passenger (pulls carton from under seat and holds it up): It's the last time I ride on a bloomin' airplane! What a service! They give you your dinner and then coom round and ask for it back.

Baird: What did you have for dinner, please—meat or fish?

Second Male Passenger: Meat, Doctor.

Fifth Male Passenger: Yes, I had meat too.

Baird: All right, we won't worry about you.

Sixth Male Passenger: I had meat, Doctor.

Seventh Male Passenger: I had fish.

Doctor: Very well, will you drink at least four cups of water, please? It'll be brought round to you. Then take this pill.

Sixth Male Passenger (slow speaking, a little dull-witted). What's caused this food poisoning, Doctor?

Baird: Well, it can either be caused through spoilage of the food, or some

kind of bacteria—the medical word is staphylococcus[3] poisoning.

Sixth Male Passenger *(nodding knowledgeably):* Oh yes. . . staphylo. . . I see.

Baird: Either that, or some toxic substance may have gotten into the food during its preparation.

Seventh Male Passenger: Which kind do you think this is, Doctor?

Baird: From the effect I suspect a toxic substance.

Seventh Male Passenger: And you don't know what it is?

Baird: We won't know until we make laboratory tests. Actually, with modern food-handling methods—the chances of this happening are probably a million to one against.

Stewardess *(entering):* I couldn't get the First Officer to take more than a little water, Doctor. He seems pretty bad.

---

3. staphylococcus (stăf′ə-lō-kŏk′əs).

Baird: I'll go to him now. Have you checked all the passengers in the front portion?

Stewardess: Yes, and there are two more new cases—the same symptoms as the others.

Baird: I'll attend to them—after I've looked at the First Officer.

Stewardess: Do you think. . .

(Before the sentence is completed, the galley telephone buzzes insistently. Baird and the Stewardess exchange glances quickly, then, without waiting to answer the phone, race to the flight deck door.)

(Cut to: The flight deck. The Captain is in the left-hand seat. Sweat pouring down his face, he is racked by retching, and his right hand is on his stomach. Yet he is fighting against the pain and attempting to reach the radio transmitter mike. But he doesn't make it, and as Baird and the Stewardess reach him, he falls back in his seat.)

Captain (*weakly*): I did what you said. . . guess it was too late. . . . You've got to give me something, Doctor. . . so I can hold out. . . till I get this airplane on the ground. . . . You understand?. . . It'll fly itself on this course. . . but I've got to take it in. . . . Get on the radio. . . . Tell control. . .

(*During the above Baird and the Stewardess have been helping the Captain from his seat. Now he collapses into unconsciousness, and Baird goes down beside him. The Doctor has a stethoscope now and uses it.*)

Baird: Get blankets over him. Keep him warm. There's probably a reaction because he tried to fight it off so long.

Stewardess (*alarmed*): Can you do what he said? Can you bring him round long enough to land?

Baird (*bluntly*): You're part of this crew, so I'll tell you how things are. Unless I can get him to a hospital quickly, I'm not even sure I can save his life. And that goes for the others too.

Stewardess: But—

Baird: I know what you're thinking, and I've thought of it too. How many passengers are there on board?

Stewardess: Fifty-six.

Baird: And how many fish dinners did you serve?

Stewardess (*composing herself*): Probably about fifteen. More people ate meat than fish, and some didn't eat at all because it was so late.

Baird: And you?

Stewardess: I had meat.

Baird (*quietly*): My dear, did you ever hear the term "long odds"?

Stewardess: Yes, but I'm not sure what it means.

Baird: I'll give you an example. Out of a total field of fifty-five, our chance of

safety depends on there being one person back there who not only is qualified to land this airplane, but who didn't choose fish for dinner tonight.

(*After her initial alarm the Stewardess is calm now, and competent. She looks Baird in the eye and even manages a slight smile.*)

Stewardess: Then, I suppose I should begin asking.

Baird (*thoughtfully*): Yes, but there's no sense in starting a panic. (*Decisively*) You'd better do it this way. Say that the First Officer is sick and the Captain wondered if there's someone with flying experience who could help him with the radio.

Stewardess: Very well, Doctor. (*She turns to go.*)

Baird: Wait! The man who was sitting beside me! He said something about flying in the war. And we both ate meat. Get him first! But still go round to the others. There may be someone else with more experience.

(*The Stewardess exits and Baird busies himself with the First Officer and the Captain. After a moment, George Spencer enters.*)

Spencer: The Stewardess said—— (*Then, as he sees the two pilots. . .*) No! Not both pilots!

Baird: Can you fly this airplane—and land it?

Spencer: No! No! Not a chance! Of course not!

Baird: But you told me you flew in the war.

Spencer: So I did. But that was fighters—little combat airplanes, not a great ship like this. I flew airplanes which had one engine. This has four. Flying characteristics are different. Controls don't react the same way. It's another kind of flying altogether. And besides that, I haven't touched an airplane for over ten years.

Baird *(grimly)*: Then, let's hope there's someone else on board who can do the job. . . because neither of these men can.

(The Stewardess enters and pauses.)

Stewardess *(quietly)*: There's no one else.

Baird: Mr. Spencer, I know nothing of flying. I have no means of evaluating what you tell me. All I know is this: that among the people on this airplane who are physically able to fly it, you are the only one with any kind of qualification to do so. What do you suggest?

Spencer *(desperately)*: Isn't there a chance—of either pilot recovering?

Baird: I'll tell you what I just told the Stewardess here. Unless I can get them to a hospital quickly, I can't even be sure of saving their lives.

(There is a pause.)

Spencer: Well—I guess I just got drafted. If either of you are any good at praying, you can start any time. *(He slips into the left-hand seat.)* Let's take a look. Altitude 16,000. Course 290. The ship's on automatic pilot—we can be thankful for that. Air speed 210 knots. *(Touching the various controls)* Throttles, pitch, mixture, landing gear, flaps, and the flap indicator. We'll need a check list for landing, but we'll get that on the radio . . . . Well, maybe we'd better tell the world about our problems. *(To the Stewardess)* Do you know how to work this radio? They've added a lot of gismos since my flying days.

Stewardess *(pointing)*: It's this panel up here they use to talk to the ground, but I'm not sure which switches you have to set.

Spencer: Ah, yes, here's the channel selector. Maybe we'd better leave it where it is. Oh, and here we are—"transmit." *(He flicks a switch, and a small light glows on the radio control panel.)* Now we're in business. *(He picks up the mike and headset beside him, then turns to the other two.)* Look, whatever happens I'm going to need another pair of hands here. Doc, I guess you'll be needed back with the others, so I think the best choice is the Stewardess here. How about it?

Stewardess: But I know nothing about all this!

Spencer: Then, that'll make us a real good pair. But I'll tell you what to do ahead of time. Better get in that other seat and strap yourself in. That all right with you, Doc?

Baird: Yes, do that. I'll take care of things in the back. And I'd better go there now. Good luck!

Spencer: Good luck to you. We're all going to need it.

(Baird exits.)

Spencer: What's your first name?

Stewardess: Janet.

Spencer: Okay, Janet. Let's see if I can remember how to send out a distress message. . . . Better put on that headset beside you. *(Into mike)* May Day! May Day! May Day! *(To the Stewardess)* What's our flight number?

Stewardess: 714.

Spencer *(into mike)*: This is Flight 714, Maple Leaf Air Charter, in distress. Come in anyone. Over.

Voice on Radio *(immediately, crisply)*: This is Calgary, 714. Go ahead!

Voice on Radio (Vancouver Operator): Vancouver here, 714. All other aircraft stay off the air. Over.

Spencer: Thank you, Calgary and Vancouver. This message is for Vancouver. This aircraft is in distress. Both pilots and some passengers——*(To the Stewardess)* How many passengers?

Stewardess: It was seven a few minutes ago. It may be more now.

Spencer: Correction. At least seven passengers are suffering from food poisoning. Both pilots are unconscious and in serious condition. We have a doctor on board who says that neither pilot can be revived. Did you get that, Vancouver? *(Pause)* Now we come to the interesting bit. My name is Spencer, George Spencer. I am a passenger on this airplane. Correction: I was a passenger. I have about a thousand hours' total flying time, but all of it was on single-engine fighters. And also, I haven't flown an airplane for ten years. Now, then, Vancouver, you'd better get someone on this radio who can give me some instructions about flying this machine. Our altitude is 16,000, course 290 magnetic, air speed 210 knots. We are on automatic pilot. Your move, Vancouver. Over. *(To the Stewardess)* You want to take a bet that that stirred up a little flurry down below?

(The Stewardess shakes her head, but does not reply.)

(Dissolve to: The control room, Vancouver. The Controller is putting down a phone as the Radio Operator brings a message to him. He reads the message.)

Controller: Oh, no! *(To the Radio Operator)* Ask if—No, let me talk to them.

(The Controller goes to panel and takes the transmitter mike. The Radio Operator turns a switch and nods.)

Controller *(tensely):* Flight 714. This is Vancouver control. Please check with your doctor on board for any possibility of either pilot recovering. Ask him to do everything possible to revive one of the pilots, even if it means neglecting other people. Over.

Spencer's Voice on Radio: Vancouver, this is 714, Spencer speaking. I understand your message. But the doctor says there is no possibility whatever of either pilot recovering to make the landing. He says they are critically ill and may die unless they get hospital treatment soon. Over.

Controller: All right, 714. Stand by, please. *(He pauses momentarily to consider the next course of action. Then briskly to the Switchboard Operator)* Get me Area Traffic Control—fast. *(Into phone)* Vancouver controller. The emergency we had! . . . Right now it looks like it's shaping up for a disaster.

(Fade out.)

Close Up

1. It will take three and a half hours for the plane to reach Vancouver. Why can't it land somewhere closer?

2. (a) Why does the doctor give water to everyone who ate the fish? (b) Why does he give everyone an emetic?

3. How do Baird, the Stewardess, and the Captain show courage in the face of the emergency?

4. (a) Although Spencer has flying experience, it is unlikely that he will be able to land the plane successfully. Why? (b) What does his decision to try tell you about him?

5. At the end of the second act, the Vancouver controller says that the emergency "looks like it's shaping up for a disaster." Why do you think the playwright chose to end the act with this statement?

Act III

Fade in: The control room, Vancouver. The atmosphere is one of restrained pandemonium. The Radio Operator is typing a message. The teletypes are busy. The Controller is on one telephone, and Harry Burdick on another. During what follows, cut back and forth from one to the other.

Controller *(into phone)*: As of right now, hold everything taking off for the East. You've got forty-five minutes to clear any traffic for South, West, or North. After that, hold everything that's scheduled outward. On incoming traffic, accept anything you can get on the deck within the next forty-five minutes. Anything you can't get down by then for sure, divert away from this area. Hold it. *(A messenger hands him a message which he scans. Then to messenger)* Tell the security officer. *(Into phone)* If you've any flights coming in from the Pacific, divert them to Seattle. And any traffic inland is to stay well away from the east-west land between Calgary and Vancouver. Got that? Right.

Burdick *(into phone)*: Is that Cross-Canada Airlines?. . . Who's on duty in operations?. . . Let me talk to him. *(Pause)* Mr. Gardner, it's Harry Burdick of Maple Leaf Charter. We have an incoming flight that's in bad trouble, and we need an experienced pilot to talk on the radio. Someone who's flown DC-4s. Can you help us? *(Pause)* Captain Treleaven? Yes, I know him well. *(Pause)* Can he come over to control right away? *(Pause)* Thank you. Thank you very much. *(To the Switchboard Operator)* Get me Montreal. I want to talk with Mr.

Barney Whitmore. You may have to try Maple Leaf Air Charter office first, and someone there'll have his home number. Tell them the call is urgent.

Switchboard Operator: Right. *(To the Controller)* I've got the Fire Chief.

Controller *(into phone)*: Chief, we have an emergency. It's Flight 714, due here at 0505. It may be a crash landing. Have everything you've got stand by. If you have men off duty, call them in. Take your instructions from the tower. They'll tell you which runway we're using. And notify the city fire department. They may want to move equipment into this area. Right. *(To the Switchboard Operator)* Now get me the city police again—Inspector Moyse.

Switchboard Operator: I have Seattle and Calgary waiting. They both received the message from Flight 714 and want to know if we got it clearly.

Controller: Tell them thank you, yes, and we're working the aircraft direct. But ask them to keep a listening watch in case we run into any reception trouble. *(Another message is handed him. After reading, he passes it to Burdick.)* There's bad weather moving in. That's all we need. *(To the Switchboard Operator)* Have you got the police? Right! *(Into phone)* It's the Airport Controller again, Inspector. We're in bad trouble, and we may have a crash landing. We'll need every spare ambulance in the city out here—and doctors and nurses too. Will you arrange it? *(Pause)* Yes, we do—fifty-six passengers and a crew of three. *(Pause)* Yes, the same time—0505. That's less than three hours.

Burdick *(to the Switchboard Operator)*. Is Montreal on the line yet?. . . Yes, give it to me. . . Hullo. Hullo. Is that you,

Barney? . . . It's Harry Burdick in Vancouver. I'll give you this fast, Barney. Our flight from Toronto is in bad trouble. They have food poisoning on board, and both pilots and a lot of the passengers have passed out. There's a doctor on board, and he says there's no chance of recovery before they get to a hospital. *(Pause)* It's a passenger doing the flying. He's just been on the radio. *(Pause)* No, he isn't qualified. He flew single-engine fighters in the war, nothing since. *(Pause)* I've asked him that. This doctor on board says there isn't a chance. *(Pause)* What else can we do? We've got to talk him down. Cross-Canada is lending us a pilot. It's Captain Treleaven, one of their senior men. He's here now, just arrived. We'll get on the radio with a check list and try to bring him in. *(Pause)* We'll do the best we can. *(Pause. Then impatiently.)* Of course it's a terrible risk, but can you think of something better? *(Pause)* No, the papers aren't on to it yet, but don't worry, they will be soon. We can't help that now. *(Pause. Anxious to get off phone.)* That's all we know, Barney. It only just happened. I called you right away. ETA is 0505 Pacific time; that's just under three hours. I've got a lot to do, Barney. I'll have to get on with it. *(Pause. Nodding impatiently.)* I'll call you. I'll call you as soon as I know anything more. . . . G'by.

(During the foregoing Captain Martin Treleaven, forty-five, has entered. He is wearing an airline uniform. As Burdick sees Treleaven, he beckons him, indicating that he should listen.)

Burdick *(to Treleaven)*: Did you get that?

Treleaven *(calmly)*: Is that the whole story?

Burdick: That's everything we know. Now, what I want you to do is get on the horn and talk this pilot down. You'll have to help him get the feel of the airplane on the way. You'll have to talk him round the circuit. You'll have to give him the cockpit check for landing, and—so help me—you'll have to talk him onto the ground.

(Captain Treleaven is a calm man, not easily perturbed. While Burdick has been talking, the Captain has been filling his pipe. Now, with methodical movements, he puts away his tobacco pouch and begins to light the pipe.)

Treleaven *(quietly)*: You realize, of course, that the chances of a man who has only flown fighter airplanes, landing a four-engine passenger ship safely are about nine to one against.

Burdick *(rattled)*: Of course I know it! You heard what I told Whitmore. But do you have any other ideas?

Treleaven: No. I just wanted to be sure you knew what we were getting into, Harry. . . . All right. Let's get started. Where do I go?

Controller: Over here.

(They cross to the radio panel, and the Operator hands him the last message from the aircraft. When he has read it, he takes the transmitter mike.)

Treleaven: How does this thing work?

Radio Operator *(turning a switch)*: You're on the air now.

Treleaven *(calmly)*: Hullo, Flight 714. This is Vancouver, and my name is Martin Treleaven. I am a Cross-Canada Airlines captain, and my job right now is to help fly this airplane in. First of all, are you hearing me okay? Over.

Voice of Spencer: Yes, Captain, loud and clear. Go ahead, please.

Treleaven: Where's that message? *(As Operator passes it, into mike)* I see that I'm talking to George Spencer. Well, George, I don't think you're going to have much trouble. These DC-4s handle easily, and we'll give you the drill for landing. But first of all, please tell me what your flying experience is. The message says you have flown single-engine fighters. What kind of airplanes were these, and did you fly multi-engine airplanes at all? Let's hear from you, George. Over.

(Cut to: The flight deck.)

Spencer *(into mike)*: Hullo, Vancouver, this is 714. Glad to have you along, Captain. But let's not kid each other, please. We both know we need a lot of luck. About my flying. It was mostly on Spitfires and Mustangs. And I have around a thousand hours' total. And all of that was ten years ago. Over.

(Cut to: The control room.)

Treleaven *(into mike)*: Don't worry about that, George. It's like riding a bicycle. You never forget it. Stand by.

Controller *(to Treleaven)*: The Air Force has picked up the airplane on radar, and they'll be giving us courses to bring him in. Here's the first one. See if you can get him on that heading.

Treleaven *(nods. Then into mike)*: 714, are you still on automatic pilot? If so, look for the auto pilot release switch. It's a push button on the control yoke and is plainly marked. Over.

(Cut to: The flight deck.)

Spencer *(into mike)*: Yes, Vancouver. I see the auto pilot switch. Over.

(Cut to: The control room.)

Treleaven *(into mike)*: Now, George, in a minute you can unlock the automatic pilot and get the feel of the controls, and we're going to change your course a little. But first, listen carefully.

When you use the controls they will seem very heavy and sluggish compared with a fighter airplane. But don't worry, that's quite normal. You must take care, though, to watch your air speed carefully, and do not let it fall below 120 knots while your wheels and flaps are up. Otherwise you will stall. Now, do you have someone up there who can work the radio to leave you free for flying? Over.

(Cut to: The flight deck.)

Spencer *(into mike)*: Yes, Vancouver. I have the Stewardess here with me, and she will take over the radio now. I am now going to unlock the automatic pilot. Over. *(To the Stewardess as he depresses the auto pilot release)* Well, here we go. *(Feeling the controls, Spencer eases into a left turn. Then, straightening out, he eases the control column slightly forward and back.)*

(Cut to: The control room.)

Treleaven's Voice: Hullo, 714. How are you making out, George? Have you got the feel of her yet?

(Cut to: The flight deck.)

Spencer: Tell him I'm on manual now and trying out some gentle turns.

Stewardess *(into mike)*: Hullo, Vancouver. We are on manual now and trying out some gentle turns.

(Cut to: The control room.)

Treleaven *(into mike)*: Hullo, George Spencer. Try the effect of fore-and-aft control on your air speed. To begin with, close your throttles slightly and bring your air speed back to 160. Adjust the trim as you go along. But watch that air speed closely. Remember to keep it well above 120. Over.

(Cut to: The flight deck.)

Spencer: *(tensely. Still feeling out the controls)*: Tell him okay.

Stewardess (*into mike*): Okay, Vancouver. We are doing as you say.

Treleaven's Voice (*after a pause*): Hullo, 714. How does she handle, George?

Spencer (*disgustedly*): Tell him sluggish like a wet sponge.

Stewardess: Sluggish like a wet sponge, Vancouver.

(*Cut to: The control room. There is a momentary relaxing of tension as Captain Treleaven and the group around him exchange grins.*)

Treleaven (*into mike*): Hullo, George Spencer. That would be a natural feeling, because you were used to handling smaller airplanes. The thing you have got to remember is that there is a bigger lag in the effect of control movements on air speed, compared with what you were used to before. Do you understand that? Over.

(*Cut to: The flight deck.*)

Spencer: Tell him I understand.

Stewardess (*into mike*): Hullo, Vancouver. Yes, he understands. Over.

(*Cut to: The control room.*)

Treleaven (*into mike*): Hullo, George Spencer. Because of that lag in air speed you must avoid any violent movements of the controls, such as you used to make in your fighter airplanes. If you do move the controls violently, you will overcorrect and be in trouble. Is that understood?

(*Cut to: The flight deck.*)

Spencer (*nodding, beginning to perspire*): Tell him—yes, I understand.

Stewardess (*into mike*): Yes, Vancouver. Your message is understood. Over.

(*Cut to: The control room.*)

Treleaven (*into mike*): Hullo, George Spencer. Now I want you to feel

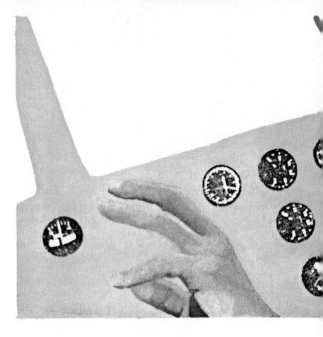

how the ship handles at lower speeds when the flaps and wheels are down. But don't do anything until I give you the instructions. Is that clear? Over.

(*Cut to: The flight deck.*)

Spencer: Tell him okay; let's have the instructions.

Stewardess (*into mike*): Hullo, Vancouver. Yes, we understand. Go ahead with the instructions. Over.

Treleaven's Voice: First of all, throttle back slightly, get your air speed steady at 160 knots, and adjust your trim to maintain level flight. Then tell me when you're ready. Over.

Spencer: Watch that air speed, Janet. You'll have to call it off to me when we land, so you may as well start practicing.

Stewardess: It's 200 now. . . 190. . . 185. . . 180. . . 175. . . 175. . . 165. . . 155. . . 150. . . (*Alarmed*) That's too low! He said 160!

Spencer (*tensely*): I know. I know. Watch it! It's that lag on the air speed I can't get used to.

Stewardess: 150. . . 150. . . 155. . . 160. . . 160. . . . It's steady on 160.

Spencer: Tell them.

Stewardess *(into mike)*: Hullo, Vancouver. This is 714. Our speed is steady at 160. Over.

(Cut to: The control room.)

Treleaven *(into mike)*: Okay, 714. Now, George, I want you to put down twenty degrees of flap. But be careful not to make it any more. The flap lever is at the base of the control pedestal and is plainly marked. Twenty degrees will mean moving the lever down to the second notch. Over.

(Cut to: The flight deck.)

Spencer: Janet, you'll have to put the flaps down. *(Pointing)* There's the lever.

Treleaven's Voice: Can you see the flap indicator, George? It's near the center of the main panel.

Spencer: Here's the indicator he's talking about. When I tell you, push the lever down to the second notch and watch the dial. Okay?

Stewardess: Okay. *(Then with alarm)* Oh, look at the air speed! It's down to 125!

(Spencer grimaces and pushes the control column forward.)

Spencer *(urgently)*: Call off the speed! Call off the speed!

Stewardess: 140. . . 150. . . 160. . . 170. . . 175. . . Can't you get it back to 160?

Spencer *(straining)*: I'm trying! I'm trying! *(Pause)* There it is.

(Cut to: The passenger cabin.)

Second Woman Passenger *(frightened)*: Hector! We're going to crash! I know it! Oh, do something! Do something!

Baird *(appears at her elbow)*: Have her take this. It'll help calm her down. *(Gives pill and cup to the Third Male Passenger.)* Try not to worry. That young man at the front is a very experienced pilot. He's just what they call "getting the feel" of the airplane. *(He moves aft in the cabin.)*

First Male Passenger: Doctor!

Baird: Yes.

First Male Passenger: Tell us the truth, Doctor. Have we got a chance? Does this fellow know how to fly this thing?

Baird: We've got all kinds of chances. He's a very experienced pilot, but it's just that he's not used to flying this particular type and he's getting the feel of it.

Fourth Male Passenger: You didn't need none of them pills to make me sick. Never mind me dinner. Now ah'm workin' on yesterday's breakfast.

(Cut to: The flight deck.)

Stewardess *(into mike)*: Hullo, Vancouver. Air speed is 160, and we are ready to put down the flaps. Over.

(Cut to: The control room.)

Treleaven *(into mike)*: Okay, 714. Go ahead with your flaps. But be careful—only twenty degrees. Then, when you have twenty degrees down, bring back the air speed to 140, adjust your trim, and call me again. Over.

(Cut to: The flight deck.)

Spencer: Okay, Janet—flaps down! Twenty degrees.

(The Stewardess pushes down the flap lever to its second notch.)

Spencer: Tell them we've got the flaps down, and the air speed's coming to 140.

Stewardess *(into mike)*: Hullo, Vancouver. This is 714. The flaps are down, and our air speed is 140.

(Cut to: The control room.)

Treleaven: All right, 714. Now, the next thing is to put the wheels down. Are you still maintaining level flight?

(Cut to: The flight deck.)

Spencer: Tell him—more or less.

Stewardess *(into mike)*: Hullo, Vancouver. More or less.

(Cut to: The control room.)

Radio Operator: This guy's got a sense of humor.

Burdick: That's a real help.

Treleaven *(into mike)*: Okay, 714. Try to keep your altitude steady and your speed at 140. Then, when you are ready, put down the landing gear and let your speed come back to 120. You will have to advance your throttle setting to maintain that air speed, and also adjust your trim. Is that understood? Over.

(Cut to: The flight deck.)

Spencer: Ask him—what about the propeller controls and mixture?

Stewardess *(into mike)*: Hullo, Vancouver. What about the propeller controls and mixture? Over.

(Cut to: The control room.)

Controller: He's thinking anyway.

Treleaven *(into mike)*: Leave them alone for the time being. Just concentrate on holding that air speed steady with the wheels and flaps down. Over.

(Cut to: The flight deck.)

Spencer: Wheels down, Janet, and call off the air speed.

Stewardess *(selects landing gear down)*: 140. . . 145. . . 140. . . 135. . . 130. . . 125. . . 120. . . 115. . . The speed's too low!

Spencer: Keep calling it!

Stewardess: 115. . . 120. . . 120. . . Steady on 120.

(Cut to: The control room.)

Treleaven *(into mike)*: Hullo, George Spencer. Your wheels should be down by now, and look for three green lights to show that they're locked. Over.

(Cut to: The flight deck.)

Spencer: Are they on?

Stewardess: Yes—all three lights are green.

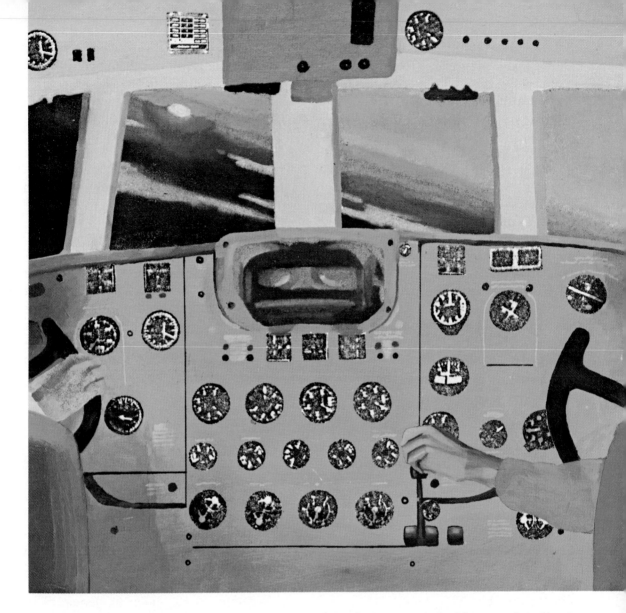

Spencer: Tell them.

Stewardess *(into mike):* Hullo, Vancouver. Yes, there are three green lights.

(Cut to: The control room.)

Treleaven: Okay, 714, now let's put down full flap so that you can feel how the airplane will handle when you're landing. As soon as full flap is down, bring your air speed back to 110 knots and trim to hold it steady. Adjust your throttle setting to hold your altitude. Is that understood? Over.

(Cut to: The flight deck.)

Spencer: Tell him yes.

Stewardess *(into mike):* Yes, Vancouver. That is understood.

Spencer: Full flap, Janet! Push the lever all the way down, and call off the air speed.

Stewardess: 120. . . 115. . . 115. . . 110. . . 110. . .

Spencer: Okay, tell 'em we've got full flap and air speed 110, and she still handles like a sponge, only more so.

Stewardess (*into mike*): Hullo, Vancouver. We have full flap, and air speed is 110. And the pilot says she still handles like a sponge, only more so.

(*Cut to: The control room. Again there is a momentary sense of relief.*)

Treleaven (*into mike*): That's nice going, George. Now I'm going to give you instructions for holding your height and air speed while you raise the flaps and landing gear. Then we'll run through the whole procedure again.

(*Cut to: The flight deck.*)

Spencer: Again! I don't know if my nerves'll stand it. (*Pause*) All right. Tell him okay.

(*Dissolve to: Control room clock showing 2:55.*)

(*Dissolve to: Control room clock showing 5:20.*)

(*Dissolve to: The control room. Captain Treleaven is still seated in front of the transmitter, but has obviously been under strain. He now has his coat off and his tie loosened, and there is an empty carton of coffee beside him. Burdick and the Controller are in the background, watching tensely. A phone rings and the Controller answers it. He makes a note and passes it to Treleaven.*)

Treleaven (*into mike*): Hullo, Flight 714. Our flying practice has slowed you down, and you are later than we expected. You are now twelve minutes flying time from Vancouver Airport, but it's getting light, so your landing will be in daylight. You should be able to see us at any minute. Do you see the airport beacon? Over.

Stewardess' Voice: Yes, we see the airport beacon. Over.

Treleaven: Okay, George, now you've practiced everything we need for a landing. You've flown the ship with wheels and flaps down, and you know how she handles. Your fuel feeds are checked, and you're all set to come in. You won't hear from me again for a few minutes because I'm moving to the control tower so I'll be able to see you on the circuit and approach. Is that clear? Over.

Stewardess' Voice: Yes, Vancouver, that is understood. Over.

Treleaven: All right, George. Continue to approach at two thousand feet on your present heading and wait for instructions. We'll let you know the runway to use at the last minute, because the wind is shifting. Don't forget, we want you to do at least one dummy run, and then go round again so you'll have practice in making the landing approach. Over. (*He mops his forehead with a crumpled handkerchief.*)

(*Cut to: The flight deck. Spencer, too, has his coat off and tie loosened. His hair is ruffled, and the strain is plainly beginning to tell on him. The Stewardess is still in the copilot's seat, and Baird is standing behind them both. The Stewardess is about to acknowledge the last radio message, but Spencer stops her.*)

Spencer: I'll take it, Janet. (*Into mike*) No dice, Vancouver. We're coming straight in and the first time is "it." Dr. Baird is here beside me. He reports two of the passengers and the First Officer are in critical condition, and we must land in the next few minutes. The doctor asks that you have stomach pumps and oxygen equipment ready. Over.

(*Cut to: The control room.*)

Burdick: He mustn't! We need time!

Treleaven: It's his decision. By all the rules he's in command of the airplane. *(Into mike)* 714, your message is understood. Good luck to us all. Listening out. *(To Burdick and the Controller)* Let's go!

(Dissolve to: The flight deck.)

Spencer: This is it, Doctor. You'd better go back now and make sure everybody's strapped in tight. Are both the pilots in seats?

Baird: Yes.

Spencer: How about the passengers who aren't sick? Are they worried?

Baird: A little, but there's no panic. I exaggerated your qualifications. I'd better go. Good luck.

Spencer *(with ironic grin):* Thanks.

(Dissolve to: The control tower, Vancouver Airport. It is a glass-enclosed area, with radio panels and other equipment, and access is by a stairway from below. It is now daylight, and the Tower Controller is looking skyward, using binoculars. There is the sound of hurried feet on the stairway and Treleaven, the Controller, and Burdick emerge in that order.)

Tower Controller: There he is!

(Treleaven picks up a second pair of binoculars, looks through them quickly, then puts them down.)

Treleaven: All right—let's make our decision on the runway. What's it to be?

Tower Controller: Zero eight. It's pretty well into wind now, though there'll be a slight crosswind from the left. It's also the longest.

Treleaven *(into mike):* Hullo, Flight 714. This is Martin Treleaven in Vancouver tower. Do you read me? Over.

(Cut to: The flight deck.)

Stewardess *(into mike):* Yes, Vancouver Tower. Loud and clear. Over.

(Cut to: The tower.)

Treleaven *(crisply, authoritatively, yet calmly):* From here on, do not acknowledge any further transmissions unless you wish to ask a question. You are now ready to join the airport circuit. The runway for landing is zero eight. That

means you are now crosswind and will shortly make a left turn on to the down-wind leg. Begin now to lose height to one thousand feet. Throttle back slightly and make your descent at 400 feet a minute. Let your air speed come back to 160 knots and hold it steady there. . . . Air speed 160.

Controller (reaching for phone): Runway is zero eight. All vehicles stand by near the extreme south end. Do not, repeat not, go down the runway until the aircraft has passed by you because it may swing off. Is that clear? (Pause) Right.

(Cut to: Film insert of fire trucks and ambulances. They are manned and move away with sirens wailing.)

(Cut to: The flight deck. Spencer is pushing the throttles forward, and the tempo of the motors increases.)

Spencer: Tell them we're at one thousand feet and leveling off.

Stewardess (into mike): Vancouver Tower. We are now at one thousand feet and leveling off. Over.

Treleaven's Voice: Now let's have twenty degrees of flap. Do not acknowledge this message.

Spencer: Twenty degrees of flap, Janet.

(The Stewardess reaches for flap lever and pushes it down while she watches the flap indicator.)

Treleaven's Voice: When you have your flaps down, bring your air speed back slowly to 140 knots, adjust your trim, and begin to make a left turn onto the downwind leg. When you have turned, fly parallel with the runway you see on your left. I repeat—air speed 140 and begin a left turn.

(Cut to: Close-up of an instrument panel showing artificial horizon and air-speed indicator. The air speed first comes back to 140, goes slightly below it, then returns to 140. The artificial horizon tilts so that the airplane symbol is banked to the left.)

(Cut to: The flight deck. Spencer has control yoke turned to the left and is adjusting the throttles.)

(Cut to: The tower.)

Treleaven: Watch your height! Don't make that turn so steep! Watch your height! More throttle! Keep the air speed on 140 and the nose up! Get back that height! You need a thousand feet!

(Cut to: The flight deck. Spencer eases the throttles open, and the tempo of the motors increases. He eases the control column forward, then pulls back again.)

(Cut to: Close-up of climb and descent indicator. The instrument first shows a descent of 500 feet per minute, then a climb of 600 feet, and then gradually begins to level off.)

(Cut to: The control tower. Captain Treleaven is looking out through binoculars, the others anxiously behind him.)

Treleaven (angrily): He can't fly the bloody thing! Of course he can't fly it! You're watching fifty people going to their deaths!

Burdick (shouting): Keep talking to him! Keep talking! Tell him what to do!

Treleaven (urgently, into mike): Spencer, you can't come straight in! You've got to do some circuits, and practice that approach. You've enough fuel left for three hours' flying. Stay up, man! Stay up!

(Cut to: The flight deck.)

Spencer: Give it to me! (Taking the mike. Then tensely) Listen, down there! I'm coming in! Do you hear me? . . . I'm coming in. There are people up here who'll die in less than an hour, never mind three. I may bend your precious airplane a bit, but I'll get it down. Now, get on with the landing check. I'm putting the gear down now. *(To the Stewardess)* Wheels down, Janet!

(The Stewardess selects landing gear "down," and Spencer reaches for the throttles.)

(Cut to: Film insert of airplane in flight, day. Its landing wheels come down.)

(Cut to: The flight deck.)

Stewardess *(looks out of window, then back to Spencer)*: Wheels down and three green lights.

(Cut to: The tower.)

Burdick: He may not be able to fly, but he's sure got guts.

Treleaven *(into mike)*: Increase your throttle slightly to hold your air speed now that the wheels are down. Adjust your trim and keep that height at a thousand feet. Now check your propeller setting and your mixture—propellers to fully fine; mixture to full rich. I'll repeat that. Propellers to fully fine; mixture to full rich.

(Cut to: The flight deck.)

Spencer *(to himself, as he moves controls)*: Propellers fully fine. Mixture full rich. *(To the Stewardess)* Janet, let me hear the air speed.

Stewardess: 130. . . 125. . . 120. . . 125. . . 130. . .

(Cut to: The tower.)

Treleaven *(into mike)*: You are well downwind now. You can begin to make a left turn on the crosswind leg. As you turn, begin losing height to 800 feet and let your air speed come back to 120. I'll repeat that. Start a left turn. Lose height to 800. Air speed 120. *(He picks up binoculars, then puts them down hurriedly, and takes mike again.)* You are losing

height too fast! You are losing height too fast! Open up! Open! Hold your height, now! Keep your air speed at 120.

(Cut to: The flight deck.)

Stewardess: 110. . . 110. . . 105. . . 110. . . 110. . . 120. . . 120. . . Steady at 120.

Spencer: What a blasted insensitive wagon this is! It doesn't respond! It doesn't respond at all!

Stewardess: 125. . . 130. . . 130. . . Steady on 130.

(Cut to: The tower.)

Treleaven: Start your turn into wind now to line up with the runway. Make it a gentle turn—you've plenty of time. As you turn, begin losing height, about 400 feet a minute. But be ready to correct if you lose height too fast. Adjust your trim as you go. . . That's right!. . . Keep turning! As soon as you've completed the turn, put down full flap and bring your air speed to 115. I'll repeat that. Let down 400 feet a minute. Full flap. Then air speed 115. *(To the others)* Is everything ready on the field?

Controller: As ready as we'll ever be.

Treleaven: Then, this is it. In sixty seconds we'll know.

(Cut to: The flight deck.)

Spencer *(muttering)*: Not quite yet . . . a little more. . . that should do it. *(As he straightens out of the turn)* Janet, give me full flap!

(The Stewardess reaches for the flap control, pushes it down, and leaves it down.)

Spencer: Height and air speed!

Stewardess: 700 feet, speed 130. . . 600 feet, speed 120. . . 500 feet, speed 105. . . . We're going down too quickly!

Spencer: I know! I know! *(He pushes throttles forward, and the tempo* of the motors increases.) Keep watching it!

Stewardess: 450 feet, speed 100. . . 400 feet, speed 100. . .

(Cut to: Film insert of airplane DC-4 with wheels and flaps down, on a landing approach.)

(Cut to: The tower.)

Treleaven *(urgently into mike):* Open up! Open up! You're losing height too fast! *(Pause)* Watch the air speed! Your nose is too high! Open up quickly or she'll stall! Open up, man! Open up!

Burdick: He heard you. He's recovering.

Treleaven *(into mike):* Maintain that height until you get closer into the runway. But be ready to ease off gently. . . You can start now. . . Let down again. . . That looks about right. . . But watch the air speed. Your nose is creeping up. . . *(More steadily)* Now, listen carefully, George. There's a slight crosswind on the runway, and your drift is to the right. Straighten up just before you touch down, and be ready with your right rudder as soon as you are down. And remember to cut the switches if you land too fast. *(Pause)* All right, your approach is good. . . Get ready to round out—now! *(Pause. Then urgently)* You're coming in too fast! Lift the nose up!

(Cut to: The flight deck.)

Treleaven's Voice: Lift the nose up! Back on the throttles! Throttles right back! Hold her off! Not too much! Not too much! Be ready for that crosswind! Ease her down, now! Ease her down!

(Cut to: Film insert of a landing wheel skimming over a runway and about to touch down. As it makes contact, rock picture to show instability.)

(Cut to: The flight deck. There is a heavy thud, and Spencer and the Stew-ardess are jolted in their seats. There is another, another, and another. Everything shakes.)

Spencer *(shouting):* Cut the switches! Cut the switches!

(The Stewardess reaches upward and pulls down the cage of the master switches. Instantly the heavy roar of motors stops, but there is still a whistling because the airplane is traveling fast. Spencer stretches out his legs as he puts his full strength into applying the airplane toe brakes, at the same time pulling back on the control column. There is a screaming of rubber on pavement, and Spencer and the Stewardess are thrown violently to the left. Then, except for the hum of the radio and gyros, there is a silence as the airplane stops.)

Spencer *(disgustedly):* I ground looped! I did a lousy stinking ground loop! We're turned right around the way we came!

Stewardess: But we're all right! We're all right! You did it! You did it!

(She leans over and kisses him. Spencer pulls off his radio headset. Outside there is a rising note of approaching sirens. Then, from the headset we hear Captain Treleaven's voice.)

Treleaven's Voice *(exuberantly):* Hullo, George Spencer. That was probably the lousiest landing in the history of this airport. So don't ever ask us for a job as a pilot. But there are some people here who'd like to shake you by the hand, and later on we'll buy you a drink. Stay right where you are, George! We're coming over.

(Fade out.)

Close Up

1. Captain Treleaven believes that Spencer's chances of landing the plane safely are extremely slim. Yet Treleaven tells Spencer that he doesn't think Spencer will have much trouble. Why does he say this?

2. Why does Spencer ask the stewardess to operate the radio for him?

3. (a) The stewardess must repeat all the messages between Spencer and Treleaven. Do you think this increases tension? Why or why not? (b) How does Spencer try to break the tension?

4. At which point in the third act do you think the tension is greatest? Why?

5. Spencer tells Treleaven that he will land the plane on his first try. (a) What reasons does he give for his decision? (b) What other reasons do you think he may have?

6. Burdick tells Treleaven that Spencer "may not be able to fly, but he's sure got guts." Do you agree with this judgment? Why or why not?

LANDSCAPES

The Great Cross-Tunisia Raccoon Chase

Richard Wolkomir

With Peter Pappas' record for mishaps, he was lucky the raccoon hadn't hijacked the airplane.

When our airliner finally landed in Tunisia, I was in a scramble to get out and look. In fact, I tripped over Uncle Baxter. And I nearly forgot Rex, the Raccoon, scratching around in his travel box under my seat.

Don't think I'm not a man of the world. After all, I'm from New York City, which is a big town. I'd traveled before, too. Last year, for instance, when the construction company where my dad works gave out bonuses, our whole family drove to Florida. I've also been on field trips with Uncle Baxter—that's Dr. Baxter Hoople, my mother's younger brother, who's a biologist.

But flying to North Africa was zingier. We'd left home the night before, in a March blizzard; and it was also snowing in Paris, France, where we changed planes for the flight south, over the Mediterranean. But when I finally walked off the plane in Tunisia, toting Rex in his box, the sun was bright and

warm, with flowers blooming everywhere.

And what a crowd,—people in ordinary business suits and dresses, men in hooded robes, others wearing the red, brimless hat called a *fez*, and women completely cocooned in layers of gauzy white fabric. The airport hummed with conversations in French and Arabic.

Beyond the terminal building, I could see the palm-lined highway into Tunisia's capital city, Tunis. It was jammed with cars and trucks. There were also wagons drawn by horses. Robed and bearded men trotted by on donkeys, like a scene from Biblical times.

"Wow, Uncle Bax," I said. "Thanks for bringing me."

"With your record, Peter Pappas, we're lucky that raccoon didn't escape and hijack the plane," he said, peering down at me over his horn-rimmed glasses.

Uncle Baxter's university had selected him to give an exchange lecture at the University of Tunis. Aunt Jean, his wife, was supposed to go along, but she's also a biologist and couldn't leave some important experiments. Naturally, I nominated myself to use her ticket.

"Nothing doing!" Uncle Bax had said. "Remember how you fell into that tidal pool I was studying in Maine? Remember my box of rare Amazonian insects you opened to see why it buzzed?"

Sometimes I get a bit carried away, is what he meant. Secretly, though, Uncle Bax is proud that I'm planning to be a biologist like him, and so I pointed out that the trip would be educational. I also reminded him I was the one who'd suggested that the best North American animal to bring as a present for the Tunisians would be a raccoon, because they're small, smart, and don't make much noise. Besides, I said, I could work as raccoon-sitter. And so there we were—Uncle Baxter, Rex the Raccoon, and me—walking out of the Tunis-Carthage Airport building.

Waiting for us at the curb was our host, Dr. Abdel Kahia, a biology professor at the University of Tunis. He was tall, like Uncle Bax, with a black mustache and a high-voltage smile. With him was a thin kid about my age, who turned out to be his son, Anwar.

Anwar looked friendly, and he had alert brown eyes that took in everything. But I have to admit that I was sort of cool towards him. It was because of Rex.

I'd been taking care of Rex for a month, watching him caper around our apartment like a mischievous masked bandit—smearing himself with my older sister's cosmetics, leaping from the hall hatrack onto unwary visitors. He'd even learned to work the bathtub taps, so that he could help himself to a swim.

I wasn't keen on giving him up. Especially to a guy I didn't know. Would he appreciate Rex and watch out for him?

"A New York, avez-vous une bicyclette?"[1] Anwar asked me in French. "Je ne parle pas français,"[2] I stammered. That means "I don't speak French," and it's the sad truth, since it's my worst subject in school.

"Excuse me, please," Anwar said, switching smoothly to English. "I was wondering if at home in New York you have a bicycle?"

---

1. "A New York, avez-vous une bicyclette?" (ä New York, ä′vä-vōō ōōn bĭsĭ-klet′).
2. "Je ne parle pas français." (jə nə pärl pä frä-sä).

Show-off! I thought, figuring that Anwar was demonstrating how superior he was at languages. That was bone-headed of me, especially since Uncle Bax had already told me that Tunisia was a French protectorate[3] until it became independent in 1956, and that most Tunisians speak French almost as naturally as Arabic. Why I expected Anwar to speak my language automatically I don't know—I was lucky he spoke English at all.

But I decided he was showing off. And so I did some showing off myself.

"Sure, I have a bicycle," I said. "But mostly I get around the city on the subways. Do you have subway trains in Tunis?"

When Anwar shook his head, I smugly added: "Of course, Tunis only has about 700,000 people, doesn't it? Pretty small compared to New York's eight million."

Anwar looked at me, thoughtfully sucking his lower lip. I congratulated myself on taking him down a peg.

"Ah, yes, an immense city, New York," he said finally. "And is it an old city—mature, shall we say?"

"Sure is," I said. "Goes back more than 360 years!"

"I see," said Anwar with a sly smile. "Tunis, as you perhaps know, is 3,000 years old."

My eyes must have popped. And Dr. Kahia gave me one of his electric smiles. "Yes, indeed, my friends," he said. "Three thousand years ago, when the Phoenicians founded the great city of Carthage—now a suburb of Tunis—Tunis was already a thriving town of Berbers, who were the first Tunisians."

"Later it was a Roman province, wasn't it?" said Uncle Baxter.

"Indeed yes," said Dr. Kahia. "My own ancestors, the Arabs, came in the Middle Ages, and we've been an Arabic-speaking land ever since."

"Also," said Anwar, "Tunis was a capital of the Barbary pirates,[4] and we could see their weapons in the museum. But perhaps you are uninterested, coming from so large a metropolis as New York?"

I just mumbled something. Meanwhile, Anwar was eyeing Rex's box. "And what is this?" he asked finally.

"It's a raccoon, named Rex," I said.

"Indeed?" said Anwar. "I am eager to view this creature. May one pet him?"

"Sure," I said. "Of course, I trained him and he does what I say. Let's take him out for a quick look."

Of course, being a raccoon, Rex never obeyed anything but his own curiosity and appetite. If only Uncle Bax had been watching as I opened that cage door!

"What a handsome little gentleman!" Anwar said. "Such a twitchy nose. Such a droll mask. And such eyes—what is it that he observes so alertly?"

Rex was observing a truck creeping down the airport driveway. It was piled high with red peppers.

"No, Rex!" I shouted, as he wiggled out of my hands, scampered between Anwar's legs, and cannonballed into

---

3. protectorate (prə-tĕk'tər-ĭt) n.: A country under the political control of another country that has greater power.

4. Barbary pirates: Tunisia, Tripoli, Algeria, and Morocco were known as the Barbary States. Until the early 1800s, piracy was active off their coasts.

Uncle Baxter, just behind his knees. "Yowch!" Uncle Baxter snorted, sitting on the sidewalk with a thump.

Meanwhile, Rex had galloped across Dr. Kahia's feet and was beelining after the pepper truck. I ran after him, yelling, "Come back!" Anwar—whom I hadn't figured for an athlete—raced right past me, crying something in Arabic. Like most young Tunisians, he was an ardent soccer player, I later learned. But now I was mostly interested in retrieving my raccoon.

We were gaining on Rex, but he was gaining on the truck. And as it slowed at the airport's exit, Rex hopped aboard. We watched him roar down the highway toward Tunis, triumphantly perched on the pile of peppers, munching on the first course.

"Peter Pappas, you've done it again!" Uncle Baxter sighed when we got back. "Tarnished the glory of your Greek ancestors."

I couldn't have agreed more. Rex was in deep trouble, and on the drive through Tunis to the Kahias' house, I didn't say much. Neither did Anwar.

The Kahias lived on a hill, and from their rooftop patio you could see Tunis tumbling down to the blue Mediterranean in a jumble of cubes, domes, and spiky minarets.[5] At its center was the old medieval section called the *medina*, where the streets were twisty and narrow. Stretching out from the *medina* were the modern city's sleek office buildings and broad avenues. Tunisian houses, like the Kahias', were hollow squares, with a garden at the center.

But I was too miserable to pay much attention. I hardly touched the supper that Mrs. Kahia prepared, a North African stew called "couscous."[6] And, that night, when everyone was asleep, I lay open-eyed. Finally, I tiptoed up to the roof. And there I found Anwar.

"You are troubled, too, yes?" he asked. "About Rex?"

"What'll happen to him, alone in a strange country?" I said. "It's all my fault for opening his box."

"And mine, for asking you to do it," Anwar said. "But we will find him. I have a plan."

"What is it?" I asked.

"In the morning, we'll go to the *medina* and find the market where the truck was delivering its peppers," he said. "And there, perhaps, we will find Rex."

But it didn't turn out to be so simple. The *medina* is a maze of tangled streets. It teems with people, especially in the market sections—the *souqs*[7]—where the streets are roofed over with more buildings, turning them into great echoing tunnels, crammed with shops. And there are scores of vegetable markets. It wasn't until noon that I saw we'd found the right one—for when Anwar spoke to the workers, they answered excitedly.

"Rex was here," Anwar reported. "He arrived on the pepper truck, they say, a strange masked beast, too crafty to catch. Very fond of cabbages."

"But isn't he here now?" I asked.

"He jumped on a melon truck going south—its first stop will be a Berber village, Takrouna, about twenty miles below Tunis," Anwar said.

---

5. minarets [mĭn′ə-rĕtz′] n.: The tall towers on top of the mosques from which the criers call the people to prayers.

---

6. couscous (ko͞os′ko͞os′).
7. souqs (so͞okz).

I looked at Anwar. He looked at me. "We must go to Takrouna," he said firmly.

An hour later, we were exiting from a bus at Takrouna. The village was far above us, perched like a stone eagle's aerie atop a hill that pokes up from the plain. And after we'd hiked up a donkey trail to the town, we knew we'd come to the right place. Children were swarming through the streets, masking their eyes with their fingers and telling one another in perfect raccoonese: "Chrrr, chrrr."

The adults, in their bright red-and-black robes, spoke only Berber. But the children, who'd learned French in school, told Anwar that the truckdriver had hauled Rex up the hill in a bag of melons. He'd scampered around the village for an hour—no one could catch him—and then escaped on another truck loaded with honey.

"He is going to Sousse," Anwar said. "That's a big city farther south."

I sat down on a stone wall with a sigh, glumly resting my chin on my hands. I could see Rex lost in a big city, chased by cats and dogs, starving. I wanted to cry. I might have, except for Anwar.

"Hurry, Peter," he said. "We must catch the bus for Sousse."

And a few hours later, after rolling through tiny white seaside fishing villages and miles and miles of olive orchards, we were getting off a bus in Sousse. Anwar had learned that the honey truck was headed for a certain market in Sousse's old walled-in *medina* section. After threading our way through the narrow streets, we found it.

The market was a shambles. Vegetables were strewn across the floor, and three large crocks, overturned and cracked, were oozing honey over the paving stones. A sad-eyed man with a drooping mustache was mournfully surveying the mess while he helped a driver load boxes of olives into a truck. Obviously, Rex had left his mark.

Just when they'd cornered him in an orange bin, the grocer told Anwar, a fish truck had rumbled by, heading inland for the little towns bordering the Sahara Desert. Magnetized by the smell of the fish, Rex had hopped aboard. And now he was bouncing southwest, toward the Sahara.

"What'll we do, Anwar?" I asked desperately.

"I don't know," he answered. "I have only a few coins left, not enough for another bus."

It looked hopeless. Night was coming and Rex was far ahead of us. I didn't want to think about what would happen to him when he reached the desert. We both sat down on the curb, feeling awful. But then the truckdriver said something and Anwar brightened. They talked for a few minutes more, and he jumped up.

"Come on, Peter," he said. "This man is also driving to the Sahara towns, and he says we can ride in back."

Soon we were lying atop the olive crates, watching the countryside sweep by in the moonlight. Now the landscape changed from sandy olive groves to a vast, stony plain. Here and there I spotted the low, black tents of nomadic[8] Bedouins, and their little herds of goats and camels. I wondered if Uncle Bax and Dr. Kahia were worried about us; but the thought seemed to drift sleepily away. When I opened my eyes, it was dawn.

We were driving through the strangest landscape I'd ever seen. Mountains billowed all around us, like petrified ocean waves. But they were all bare and brown, from horizon to horizon.

"These mountains rim the Sahara Desert," Anwar told me, sitting up and rubbing his eyes. "Here the people live in cave villages."

Soon the truck creaked to a stop. The driver got out and announced: "Matmata."

I saw no town at all, just the brown hills. Smiling, Anwar pointed to a pit in the ground.

Peering over the edge, I saw that it was a room-sized, one-story-deep shaft. At the bottom was a courtyard, where a woman was baking bread at a clay oven. Opening off the courtyard were whitewashed wooden doors, which Anwar said led to the various rooms of the family's cave house. Now I saw that the hilltop was pocked with similar shafts, an underground community.

While the driver delivered his olives, we scoured Matmata for word of Rex. Finally we found an old woman who'd seen him. She gave us fresh bread for breakfast, while she explained that when the fish truck drove through town at dawn, she'd spied a strange masked animal with a fish in its paws. But the

---

8. nomadic (nō-măd'ĭk) *adj.*: Wandering.

truck had jounced through Matmata without stopping.

Anwar asked her something in Arabic. And when she answered, "Douz," I saw him frown.

"Rex is going to Douz," he said. "It's a market village built on the sand, right at the Sahara's edge. If he should run off into the desert. . . ."

While the truckdriver ate breakfast, Anwar found a telegraph office. Using our last few coins, he wired home that we were going to Douz, after Rex.

Soon we were back in the truck, bouncing down from the brown mountains. Overhead, the sun was like a furnace. Slowly, the land flattened. Then, abruptly, it turned to sand. Here and there grew clumps of palms, like islets in a sandy sea, but these tiny oases disappeared near the horizon. Beyond was only miles of sand.

"The Sahara," Anwar said.

Douz resembled a handful of sugar cubes scattered on the sand. Its center was a large square, the market where desert dwellers came to sell their dates, figs, carpets, and textiles. Camels were tethered everywhere. At the square's center we spotted the fish truck, with an excited crowd milling around it. Anwar asked a man what had happened.

"He was here," Anwar told me. "Everybody in the market came to see the strange animal on the fish truck, including the dogs. . . ."

I felt my face go white. The dogs I could see prowling the streets looked ferocious.

"The dogs and children chased him," Anwar said, translating the man's words.

"What happened?" I stammered out.

"First he ran up a palm tree—there," Anwar said, pointing. "Then he jumped to the roof of that house. From there, he leaped down on that camel, making it rear up."

"And then?" I asked.

"Nobody knows—that was the last they saw of him," Anwar said sadly.

We ran to where the camel was tethered. *Would we find him trampled?* I wondered. But we couldn't find him at all, not a hair. Desperately, we searched the sand for a clue. Then Anwar pointed. Leading out of the village was a trail of small, handlike prints. He'd run off into the Sahara.

"Rex!" I yelled. And the next thing I knew, I was running after the prints, out into the desert.

"Stop!" Anwar called behind me. "You mustn't do this."

The sand sucked hotly at my feet. Gradually, my knees turned to rubber, and I felt dizzy. Unexpectedly, I found myself lying prone on the sand, too tired to move. Anwar floundered up behind me and fell down panting.

"It's no use, Peter," he gasped. "We just can't go on foot into the Sahara."

Neither of us said anything more. I don't know how long we lay there on the sand. Over and over, I saw myself opening that cage door at the Tunis airport, and it made me groan.

Suddenly a shadow fell over us. I looked up into fiery eyes. Staring down on us from atop enormous camels were two fierce-looking men, robed and hooded, with inky beards.

"Tuaregs!" whispered Anwar. "Desert nomads."

It seemed like hours before they spoke. When they finally did, Anwar answered, pointing back to the north from which we'd come, then pointing to the raccoon tracks leading out across the dunes.

Again the two riders silently gazed at us. Then they broke into tremendous peals of laughter. Suddenly, one man scooped up Anwar and placed him behind him on the camel. The other Tuareg hauled me up, so high I was giddy.

Off across the sand we shot. I held tightly to the Tuareg's waist as the camel rocked under us and the dry desert air seared my face. Up ahead, Anwar's Tuareg pointed. I squinted into the distance, where the sun shimmering on the sand looked like pools of water. And then I saw it: Limping resolutely across the dunes was a ball of gray fur.

"Rex!" Anwar and I yelled simultaneously.

Later, on the camel ride back to Douz, I gave Rex to Anwar to hold. After all, Rex was his raccoon now.

We arrived just in time to see Uncle Bax and Dr. Kahia drive in. Needless to say, a lot of explanations were due. But they were overjoyed to see us safe, and Rex, too.

After that our week in Tunisia flew by. Anwar took me and Rex—on a leash—all around Tunis, and to Carthage, too. Dr. Kahia drove us into the countryside to see Roman ruins. Then, before I knew it, the Tunis-Carthage Airport was dwindling away under our airliner, as we headed home.

Before we'd taken off, Dr. Kahia had promised us that Anwar could visit me in New York. And scratching around in a travel box under my seat was Ali the fennec—a North African desert fox with huge ears and enormous eyes. As Anwar had put it: "Peter, I was reluctant to give Ali to you until I was sure you'd be a good friend to him. Now I'm sure."

And I had said to Anwar, "I know just what you mean."

Close Up

1. Peter brings Rex the Raccoon as a gift for the Tunisians. Why is Peter uncomfortable about giving Rex to someone Peter doesn't know?

2. (a) Why does Peter think Anwar is showing off? (b) How does Peter's desire to show off allow Rex to escape?

3. To track Rex, Peter and Anwar travel across part of Tunisia. (a) Where do they finally find Rex? (b) When they find Rex, what does Peter do that shows he now trusts Anwar?

4. Peter wants to be a biologist, just like his Uncle Bax. What traits does he show in this story that would make him a good scientist?

Setting

Setting is the place and time in which the events in a story occur. Authors help you visualize, or picture in your mind, the setting by including many details that appeal to your five senses. For example, Richard Wolkomir helps you visualize the setting by including details that let you *feel* the hot Tunisian sun and *smell* the blooming flowers.

1. Knowing the history of a place gives you a better picture of what it is like. List three details Anwar tells Peter about Tunis' history.

2. Find three details in the description below that help you visualize Tunis.

   "The Kahias lived on a hill, and from their rooftop patio you could see Tunis tumbling down to the blue Mediterranean in a jumble of cubes, domes, and spiky minarets. At its center was the old medieval section called the *medina*, where the streets were twisty and narrow. Stretching out from the *medina* were the modern city's sleek office buildings and broad avenues. Tunisian houses, like the Kahias', were hollow squares, with a garden at the center."

3. The five senses are sight, smell, hearing, touch, and taste. To which senses does each lettered detail below appeal?
   a. "Mountains billowed all around us, like petrified ocean waves."
   b. "The airport hummed with conversations in French and Arabic."
   c. "Overhead, the sun was like a furnace."
   d. "Just when they'd cornered him in an orange bin, the grocer told Anwar, a fish truck had rumbled by, heading inland for the little towns bordering the Sahara Desert."

INFERENCES

An inference is an intelligent guess you make based upon the evidence in the story. When you read a story, you do not learn everything directly. Sometimes you have to figure out information that has only been suggested. This means that you have to read between the lines and make inferences, or intelligent guesses, based on the evidence. For example, you do not learn directly what the climate is like in Tunisia. By reading between the lines, you can infer that it is very warm.

▶ The excerpts below contain evidence from which you can make inferences. Match each of the excerpts with one of the inferences.

Evidence

a. "And I nearly forgot Rex, the Raccoon, scratching around in his travel box under my seat."
b. "We'd left home the night before, in a March blizzard. . . ."
c. " 'With your record, Peter Pappas, we're lucky that raccoon didn't escape and hijack the plane.' "
d. "Of course, being a raccoon, Rex never obeyed anything but his own curiosity and appetite."
e. "The market was a shambles. Vegetables were strewn across the floor, and three large crocks, overturned and cracked, were oozing honey over the paving stones."
f. "Magnetized by the smell of fish, Rex had hopped aboard (the fish truck)."
g. "Children were swarming through the streets, masking their eyes with their fingers and telling one another in perfect raccoonese: 'Chrrr, chrrr.' "

Inferences

(1) Raccoons like to eat fish.
(2) Peter is known for causing mishaps or unfortunate accidents.
(3) Rex had been at the market.
(4) Peter had been living in a cold climate.
(5) Some airlines allow animals to travel in planes if they are in special containers.
(6) The children had seen Rex.
(7) Raccoons are curious animals always in search of food.

WORD ATTACK

Understanding Vivid Verbs

An author may want you to get a very strong and intense picture of what is happening in a story. To give you this picture, the author may use vivid, or strong, verbs to describe the action. For example, notice the vivid verbs in the following sentence. "We watched him *roar* down the highway toward Tunis, triumphantly *perched* on the pile of peppers, *munching* on the first course."

▶ Look up the meaning of each *italicized* word below. Then use each word in an original sentence.

a. ". . . when I finally walked off the plane in Tunisia, *toting* Rex in his box. . . ."

b. " . . . women completely *cocooned* in layers of gauzy white fabric."

c. "But the truck had *jounced* through Matmata without stopping."

d. " 'No, Rex!' I shouted as he *wiggled* out of my hands, *scampered* between Anwar's legs, and *cannonballed* into Uncle Baxter . . . ."

e. "Meanwhile, Rex had *galloped* across Dr. Kahia's feet and was *beelining* after the pepper truck."

f. "Now I saw that the hilltop was *pocked* with similar shafts . . . ."

g. "Mountains *billowed* all around us . . . ."

The Word

Mildred Clingerman

Cleel, Lodi, and Mun are stranded on a strange planet. They must leave the safety of their spaceship and search for food.

I can tell you we were frightened when that woman opened the door. God-dess-tall, she was, like all those people. It is only when they are children their size does not frighten one . . . much. Even hunger, I think, could not have driven us forth from our hiding place to mingle with those giants in their crowded streets, but on that night, Lodi had slipped back to report that the streets were thronged only with the little ones. We decided to chance it. Dorion would yet be three days repairing the ship, he said, and his fingers had slowed and grown clumsy because of his hunger.

Lodi blamed himself bitterly for the hunger that gnawed at the four of us. Lodi is a good leader, and I, for one, would follow him anywhere, but Mun and I sometimes have to sit on Lodi. Literally, I mean. For instance, while

Dorion grumbled over his repairs and paid no attention at all to anything else, Mun and I had been forced to listen to Lodi explaining over and over just how it happened that he forgot to fill the emergency food bins. At last Mun nodded wearily at me. So Mun sat on Lodi's head and I sat on his feet, and we took turns feeding back his own sad story, with variations.

"Old Yaud called you in to explain an entry in our ship's log. How could you explain it when you couldn't even read it?" said Mun.

"There we were," I took up the refrain, "just ready to take off from Big Ship with a million details to attend to, and you off in old Yaud's office buttering up the old idiot instead of checking the loading!"

But we couldn't keep Lodi down.

That's why I'd rather be on his observer ship than any of the twenty-three others attached to Big Ship. What if his crew is always being called to scuff the green carpet in the council chamber? With Lodi as our leader (and he tromping all over rules and regulations), we bring back the clearest, closest viewing of all. Tiu, who never leaves the Big Ship, but sits before the viewscreens day after day, blesses Lodi for his daring and pleads for us in the council chamber.

Now Lodi squirmed out from under us and got to his feet. "Shut up a minute," he said, and looked at Dorion who was driving himself at the repairs despite his slowing fingers. Then Lodi beckoned for Mun and me. We left the comparative safety of the ship and stumbled after him. I almost envied Dorion left groaning over his work. It was very dark outside the ship, but Lodi knew the way. Every night since the forced landing, Lodi had sneaked into the nearby town with the small, portable viewtaker he'd persuaded Dorion to make for him. Tiu, we knew, would be delighted with these views. While we walked, we imagined among ourselves how his round belly would shake with his whoops of joy, and of how he would speak up in the council chamber, slowly and powerfully in our defense. It was comforting to remember Tiu at this moment, because we were breaking the strictest rule of all. Lodi was ignoring it, and my empty belly and I saw no reason to remind him of the fact that crews are supposed, under all circumstances, to *stay inside the ship.*

It was a long walk. But at last Lodi halted us and made us lie down in some deep shadows, while he crawled ahead to assess our position. Mun and I communicated our nervousness silently and lifted our heads to peer at the lights ahead. I remembered the giants who lived there, and I shuddered. I had never seen one any closer than ship's length away, staring goggle-eyed at us through the window of his aircraft.

Suddenly, I felt something rubbing against my hand. My heart almost stopped before I saw it was a small, mewing animal that meant no harm. I scratched its neck as I would have scratched the neck of a *pprrr* at home. It liked it.

Lodi sounded the clear-ahead whistle. Mun and I stood up and walked forward into the lights. I saw, from afar, Lodi standing calmly on a walk jostled by a crowd of children. All along the street the light standards showed dozens of strolling children, but none of the frightening big ones. Not one of the children paid much attention to Lodi, I saw, other than to point at him and stare a moment, smiling, before they moved on.

"It's all right, Cleel," Lodi reassured me, although he did not speak aloud. Lodi, too, was nervous. "They all have food. All of them. Smell it?" He waved his arm encompassingly. "Do you see they are all carrying sacks full of food? Watch them. They go up to a house, knock, say a certain word, and more food is put in their sacks. It's a curious procedure, and I am even now recording it with the viewtaker." As he talked silently, coaxingly, we edged nearer to him. Lodi grabbed Mun impatiently and pulled him along by the hand. I was shaking with fright all the way to my toenails, but I plodded beside them.

"And are we, God forbid, to rob these children of their full sacks?" I have followed Lodi into many a trouble-making, council-shaking act, but I would not rob even a giant's child.

"No, no!" Lodi glared at me. "Have I yet led you into the unlawful?"

Mun and I clutched each other and snickered. Lodi dropped Mun's hand and stalked ahead. Another kind of animal, much larger than the mewing one (or we), came running up to Lodi, wagging its tail and licking Lodi on the chin. Lodi kept pushing it away and patting it timidly all at the same time. The animal then ran around and around Lodi, keeping him a prisoner and almost knocking him off his feet. Ahead of us a child turned and whistled. The animal went bounding away.

"Thank God," Lodi muttered. "I thought I had been chosen for Only-Love. Think how Dorion would have cursed if I'd been forced to return to the ship with that great beast. Now watch and extend your hearing." We all paused before a lighted house, and sheltered by the hedge, watched a group of children who waited before the open door. The light poured out on their upturned faces, and I gasped at the sight. One of the children bore the face of a man aged in wickedness. Another that of a polished skull. One child straddled a broom and wore a high, peaked hat and had the face of a toothless crone.

"Oh, pity their parents!" I cried out. Lodi hushed me so that we might hear the secret word. A man giant came to the open door. The children all screeched together, so that it was difficult to sort out the syllables.

"How sad that they have the voices of children with such faces!"

Lodi shushed me again while we watched. The man put a piece of food into each sack. The children pushed and shoved each other in their eagerness. One child spilled all the contents of his sack and, wailing, stooped to retrieve them. And, oh then! His face fell off. I myself wailed at the horror of it. Lodi stuffed his hand against my mouth, and then I saw that underneath the face-that-fell dwelt another gentler face, like any child's.

"Did you hear the word?" Lodi hissed.

"No, did you?" Mun reached out and dragged Lodi into the shadow.

"Clang-heads!" Lodi whispered heatedly. "I will give you the word, but where oh where are *your* ears? Cleel must needs make the night ghastly with howling. Oh, yes, your lungs are ever-present, your mouth is ever-moving, your belly ever-calling, but who, *who* is it that does the head work, always and forever? *Who,* I say, makes it possible for you two honk-heads to stay in Observation? *Who?*"

"Tiu," I answered him. Lodi stopped raving and started giggling. We all sat down in the midst of the hedge and giggled. When we could stop, we got up and walked to the last house with a light. Lodi whispered the word to us, but we pushed him into the leading position, so that it was he who knocked on the door.

A light came on over our heads. The door opened. Goddess-tall was that woman standing in the doorway. Mun grabbed my hand, and my heart almost stopped again. But she was beautiful, that giant woman. She smiled down at us, and Lodi, who is susceptible to all the nuances of love, flapped his antennae in shy acknowledgment.

"Triggertree?" His thin, sweet voice gave him away. Lodi was in love again and, as usual, it was mutual. He lifted his eyes to the woman and she knelt before him. Just like that. That's Lodi for you. I poked Mun in the ribs. Mun started to giggle again.

"Oh, you darlings!" the woman's mind said. And I'd swear it was the same thing she said aloud. She kept murmuring at us, and we caught the no-sack concept, and you should have seen Lodi pulling his face into a no-sack-poor-little-thing to match her mind-talk. She loved it, that one. And Lodi wasn't half trying. Just then, in the middle of all that exclamatory murmuring of hers, I caught a concept that froze me to the marrow. Translated into words it was enough to set us all trembling again. Do you know what that woman's mind was saying to us, not about us, but right to us?

"Oh, the darling little men from Mars! See their cunning little cos-

tumes. . . . Your mother must have worked hours. . . . And did you come in a lit-tle space ship all that way just to say 'trick or treat' at my house? And did you think I wouldn't give you anything just because you forgot your sacks? Wait, just wait. I've got just the things little Martians like!"

She stood up suddenly. Mun and I fell back in fright. But she didn't seem to notice. She went darting deeper into the house, while we stood there frantically communicating, all mind-talking at once, with Lodi louder and stronger than Mun or I, trying to keep us from bolting and running shipwards. We stayed, but you can't always trust Lodi's judgment when he's newly in love. He was stamping his foot and silently cursing us when the woman came back. She had three enormous sacks stuffed with food. We staggered as she placed them in our arms. I could smell the food, and some of my panic stilled. Food does that, you know.

"Now go home, darlings," the woman said in effect. "It's getting late, and your mother will worry." I thought of Dorion sweating back in the ship with never a thought for us. But I was too scared to giggle. I ran with the heavy sack. Out on the street I stopped to look back. Mun was right behind me, but that Lodi! He had his arms around the woman's neck. She was kneeling before him and kissing him right between the antennae! I heard her call as he broke away from her at last. "Be sure to come back next year. Don't forget!"

And do you know, we may do that, if Tiu ever gets us out of disciplinary confinement. He's working at it. We had some of the food left when we got back to Big Ship. Tiu says any civilization that can cook like that can't be all bad . . . or mad. Lodi, who was too full of love to be afraid, kept his ears open, and says the woman mind-named the things as she placed them in the sacks. Every day now, while he plucks glucklings for Morden, he names them over like a love song.

"Popcorn, peanuts, apples, candy, doughnuts, cookies, cupcakes, *dandy!*" I don't know which was which. Neither does Lodi. But I'm going to remember the word Triggertree. Nobody has ever kissed me right between the antennae. Lodi says it's wonderful.

"I'm sorry, sonny. We've run out of candy."

Drawing by Chas. Addams; © 1952
The New Yorker Magazine, Inc.

1. A group of Martians are stranded in the United States. Why are their food bins empty?

2. Why do the Martians think it might be safe to leave the ship on this particular night?

3. The Martians are horrified to see ugly faces on children who have such sweet voices. When one child loses its ugly face, Cleel wails in horror. (a) What does Cleel think has happened? (b) What really has happened?

4. Why isn't the woman surprised to see "darling little men from Mars" on her doorstep?

5. The Martians think the word is "triggertree." What is the real word?

Setting

Sometimes the *place* where a story occurs is very important. The author describes the place in detail to help you picture it clearly in your mind.

1. The place where "The Word" occurs is very important to the story. Why would the story have been different if the Martians had landed in China?

2. Which details below help explain why the Martians could pass through the streets unrecognized on this particular night?
   a. The streets were crowded with children.
   b. The streets were well lighted.
   c. The children were carrying sacks of food.
   d. The children were wearing masks and costumes.
   e. There were dogs and cats in the streets.

3. Why could the Martians fill their empty food bins on this special night?

Activities

1. Imagine that the Martians have landed in the United States on the Fourth of July. Write a paragraph describing what they see from their viewscreen.

2. Make a mobile to illustrate this story. You might include various Halloween masks and pieces of costumes.

INFERENCES

Making Inferences About Place

An author may not tell you directly where a story takes place. Instead, the author may provide clues that help you make inferences about certain details of the place. By adding these details together, you can determine the place.

▶ Match each clue with the discovery you infer from it.

Clues

a. "Goddess-tall she was, like all those people. It is only when they are children their size does not frighten one . . . much."

b. "Do you see they are all carrying sacks full of food? Watch them. They go up to a house, knock, say a certain word, and more food is put in their sacks. It's a curious procedure, and I am even now recording it with the view-taker."

c. "One of the children bore the face of a man aged in wickedness. Another that of a polished skull. One child straddled a broom and wore a high, peaked hat and had the face of a toothless crone."

d. "Another kind of animal, much larger than the mewing one (or we), came running up to Lodi, wagging its tail and licking Lodi on the chin. Lodi kept pushing it away and patting it timidly all at the same time. The animal then ran around and around Lodi, keeping him a prisoner and almost knocking him off his feet. Ahead of us a child turned and whistled. The animal went bounding away."

e. ". . . I felt something rubbing against my hand. My heart almost stopped before I saw it was a small, mewing animal that meant no harm. I scratched its neck as I would have scratched the neck of a *pprrr* at home."

Discoveries

(1) The people in this place are tall compared to the Martians.
(2) The Martians met a cat.
(3) The children are trick or treating door-to-door.
(4) The children are wearing costumes.
(5) The Martians met a dog.

WORD ATTACK

Understanding Special Compound Words

One way of creating a new word is to join two words together with a hyphen. The new hyphenated word is a shortcut way of saying two complete ideas. When you try to understand the meaning of the hyphenated word, you have to keep the meanings of the two individual words in mind. For example, the woman who opens the door is described as "Goddess-tall." This hyphenated word is a shortcut way of saying the woman is as *tall* as a *goddess.*

▶ Write the meaning of each *italicized* word in the sentences below.

a. "I had never seen one any closer than ship's length away, staring *goggle-eyed* at us through the window of his aircraft."

b. "Lodi sounded the *clear-ahead* whistle."

c. "I have followed Lodi into many a *trouble-making, council-shaking* act, but I would not rob even a giant's child."

d. " '*Clang-heads!*' Lodi whispered heatedly."

e. "She kept murmuring at us, and we caught the *no-sack* concept. . . ."

f. "She went darting deeper into the house, while we stood there frantically communicating, all *mind-talking* at once. . . ."

g. "Lodi, who was too full of love to be afraid, kept his ears open, and says the woman *mind-named* the things as she placed them in the sacks."

h. " 'Oh, yes, your lungs are *ever-present*, your mouth is *ever-moving*, your belly *ever-calling* . . . . ' "

The Christmas Parade

Theodore Taylor

The Gonzagas had always watched the parade from the sidelines. But this year, they would be in it.

Maria stood in the doorway, holding her breath, and immediately George Gonzaga knew he had caught the thief. Poor Maria, who was twelve years old, had never been able to hide guilt.

"You did it! You did it!" he shouted, both angry and hurt.

Maria nodded, swallowing again. She felt awful, so ashamed, yet she was glad he had discovered the money was gone. He checked the health of his savings, down to the penny, once a week. Discovery was inevitable.

Dumbfounded, Gonzaga looked from Felicia, his wife, back to his daughter. Though she was sometimes flighty and foolish, the thin, black-haired girl had always seemed so faithful and pure. Now Maria was a thief, a common sneak thief. "Why?" Felicia asked, shaking her head in disbelief. The Gonzagas had never stolen from each other or anyone else. "Why?" Gonzaga echoed, but in rage. Fifteen dollars was a lot of money in this October many years ago.

"I entered us in the Christmas parade, Papa," Maria said in a tiny voice, almost a whisper.

Rafael, her older brother, laughed. "She's crazy."

Gonzaga's mouth dropped open. "You did *what?*" He was a stocky, gray-haired man and worked seven days a week, growing vegetables on almost every inch of their land, located in a long, fertile valley in California. Felicia worked beside him most of the time, as did Maria and Rafael when they weren't at school.

Maria swallowed once more and took a deep, deep breath. "I entered Rancho Gonzaga in the parade."

Rafael burst into laughter again. "Rancho Gonzaga?" he mocked, and walked out of the kitchen.

Felicia sighed and turned back to the stove. Gonzaga sat down heavily at the kitchen table. They all knew the Christmas parade of San Lazaro. Sponsored by the Chamber of Commerce, it

was held each year on the first Saturday night in December. There were a half-dozen bands from around the country; thirty to forty floats: beautiful horses in silver trappings, ridden by rich ranchers; old carriages with rich families; a Hollywood celebrity as parade master. The Gonzagas had always watched the parade from the sidelines, joining other Mexican-American families, all of them awed and wistful. The grand prize was a silver trophy and five hundred dollars.

"A float from Rancho Gonzaga, eh?" Gonzaga said, staring at his daughter. "Are you insane? They would laugh us off the street. We have a little truck farm here, not a rancho. Why did you do it, Maria?"

Maria took another deep breath. It was very hard to explain. "We were all in the school yard . . ."

"We?" Gonzaga exploded again.

Felicia, who had once been almost as pretty as Maria, returned to the table, spoon in hand, and was looking at her daughter with sadness. She was a serene woman and said "Ssssh" to her husband to calm him down.

". . . the other girls. They were all talking about the floats their families would enter. Louise Webster said they would have real flowers. Jane Thomas said theirs would be gold and silver. I felt left out, Papa, so I said we would have one, too. Then Louise Webster laughed at me. So I came home and took the money out of the jar . . ."

Anger beginning to ebb, Gonzaga sighed. "You should have asked me. I would have told you we cannot compete with these people, even if we wanted to. It takes much money, Maria. The big ranchos have it; the gas company has it; the automobile dealers have it. We do

not. Now, tomorrow, after school, you go to the Chamber of Commerce and tell them you made a mistake."

Tears came swiftly into Maria's eyes. "What will I say at school?"

"Tell them I decided not to enter the parade after all. Blame it all on me," Gonzaga said, tiredly.

Maria fled into her bedroom, and Gonzaga said, a bit defensively, to his wife. "She should not have done it, you know."

Felicia nodded. "I know." Then she went into the bedroom and sat down by her daughter to say the old litany soothingly. "I understand, Maria, and I know what it is like to be left out."

Maria wrenched up from the bed and ran through the kitchen and out into the backyard.

Gonzaga shook his head as Felicia reentered. "It is pride," she muttered, and went about fixing supper. Gonzaga knew the meaning of the word as much or more than any of them. Yet Maria had done a foolish thing.

Maria moved aimlessly about the yard for a moment, feeling destroyed, and then went into the small barn where Hernando and Francisco were feeding. In times past they had been of comfort. Sniffling, she slumped down near the wide doors and looked at them in the twilight shadows. She stared at Hernando, the hinny; then at Francisco, the ox. Why her father had to have a ridiculous crossbred donkey—an ugly hinny—and an ox she'd never know. If he couldn't afford a tractor, why couldn't he at least have a pair of ordinary mules? Sluggish old Francisco—she didn't believe there was another ox in the county, maybe not anywhere in California. Everyone laughed at the strange pair, she knew. Beyond that, they were laughing at the Gonzagas, she was certain. A few years ago she'd loved these animals very much, but now she was beginning to hate the sight of them.

Suddenly, she raged at Hernando, "You're not even a pure donkey, and you're stupid." The hinny rotated his head slightly to look at her with soft, loving eyes. "So are you stupid, Francisco." The ox raised his head with a look that might have been surprise.

Then Maria heard her mother calling her to supper. Dabbing at the moisture on her cheeks, she went into the house and sat down stiffly at the table. The family did not speak very much during the rest of the evening. Maria truthfully hoped morning would never come, and George Gonzaga's heart was heavy for a different reason, as was Felicia's. Morning did come, of course, and

Maria went off silently to school, avoiding Rafael when they walked down the road to the bus stop.

About noon Gonzaga started his battered, rusting, old sedan to drive into San Lazaro and market twelve hampers of red peppers he'd picked the previous day. The backseat had been removed long ago to haul vegetables, sacks of fertilizer, tools—not passengers. Gonzaga hoped to buy a truck in a year or so. After marketing the peppers, he was at a stoplight midway down Main Street, when a shiny white pickup slid beside him in the next lane. The timing couldn't have been worse. Webster, the cattle rancher next door, shouted, "Hey, Gonzaga, I hear you're putting in a float this year." He was grinning widely but probably had no ill will, Gonzaga thought. Yet in all the twelve years of the parade, no one of Mexican descent had ever

The Christmas Parade   **271**

entered a float. They did not even ride their horses in the parade, and several had fine mares. They did not feel welcome.

Gonzaga looked over at the ruddy-faced rancher. He had never liked this man, though they hadn't had any particular trouble as neighbors. Webster had made some half-hearted offers to buy the scant Gonzaga acres, but George had politely refused.

"What kind of float you gonna put in, Gonzaga?" Webster asked with amiable curiosity. "They cost a lot, I tell you. I should know."

Perhaps it was advice; perhaps it was something else. Gonzaga felt his pulse begin to quicken and his temper to simmer. "Yes, they do cost a lot, I've heard."

Webster said, seriously, "Tell you what. You need a designer. I'll give you mine. Florist over in Los Angeles. But he's expensive."

Controlling himself carefully, Gonzaga squinted at the rancher. The whole gossipy valley probably knew what Maria had done. Gonzaga nodded and meshed the gears of the rattling Dodge as Webster's new truck pulled on ahead.

It was then that Gonzaga angrily performed a U-turn and parked squarely in front of the Chamber of Commerce. He entered the building and went to the counter. A girl was sitting behind it. "Please, who is in charge of the parade?" Gonzaga asked.

"What do you want to know?"

"My name is Gonzaga. Three days ago my daughter entered us."

The girl smiled at the pudgy man in worn dungarees, muddy boots and straw hat. "And now you want your money back?"

"Oh, no," said Gonzaga quickly. "When she comes in this afternoon, tell her I came by to sign the papers."

The girl frowned. "There are no papers. We will mail you a parade number and the instructions next month."

"Okay, then. Rancho Gonzaga will be in the parade. That is definite."

The secretary shrugged. "Good luck."

Gonzaga departed hurriedly and on returning home told Felicia what he had done. She gasped but then began to laugh. They both laughed and embraced, feeling very close.

In midafternoon, George was plowing with Francisco in the upper sloping acreage when he glimpsed Maria running across the fields toward him, black hair flowing, feet leaping the rows. Even before she reached him, he saw the happy look on her face and heard her excited yelling. "You changed your mind, Papa! You changed your mind!"

She ran into his arms, and he grinned at her. "Yes, I did. I am as crazy as you are."

At supper they all asked about Gonzaga's plans for the float. He replied, uncertainly, "I have to think about it."

"It will be a beautiful float, won't it?" said Maria. "Even if we don't win, it will be a beautiful float."

Rafael had finally caught the spirit and said, "We'll be proud of it, won't we?"

"Yes," Gonzaga answered, with a helpless glance at Felicia.

They talked on a while longer; but as the evening wore on Gonzaga began to regret more and more his impulsive visit to the Chamber of Commerce. Now that he thought about it without emotion and anger, there were many problems. Most of the floats were towed by tractors. Some had engines built into them. He'd heard that the big ranches spent as much as three thousand dollars just for the one night. By bedtime Gonzaga was furious with himself, with everyone.

After an hour of tossing, he sat up in bed to say, "We have a budget of ten dollars."

Felicia sat up, too. "You can't do anything with ten dollars."

Gonzaga nodded grimly to himself in the darkness. That would discourage all of them. No float, no parade.

In the days that followed it seemed that every Mexican-American in the county found a way to get in touch with George Gonzaga and talk about the float. They met him in town or came to the farm. He began to feel trapped. Finally, he blew up again, telling Felicia, "You would think I have been appointed to represent them all. But do they offer money? No. Do they give me any ideas? No. They simply ask what I'm going to do. 'Hey, Gonzaga, what about that float?' "

He paused and roared, "We have no float."

Almost every night at the table the Gonzagas talked about the float, and every idea was discarded. In view of the meager budget, the suggestions of Maria and Rafael were far too expensive; Felicia thought they should get some friends together and do a fiesta scene. Sing and dance. But it would take a vehicle thirty feet long to do that. Gonzaga could make no contribution aside from suggesting a display of vegetables to represent the rancho—carrots, peppers, tomatoes, beans. Even Felicia voted against that.

By late November, Gonzaga was about to swallow his pride, along with Maria's, Rafael's, Felicia's and every other Mexican-American nearabout, and return to the Chamber of Commerce to announce that Rancho Gonzaga would not be entered after all. He knew Maria would be crushed, but better that than making fools of themselves before the entire valley.

His mind was almost made up when he entered the barn one chill evening to lock it up. There was a full moon, and some silver shafts of moonlight lay across the straw and animals. *Navidad*, he thought. That is it, *Navidad*. He stood looking for a moment and then rushed back into the house. "I know what to do," he yelled.

"About what?"

"The float! Where is your Bible?"

Felicia got out her old, thick, illustrated Spanish Bible, and Gonzaga leafed the pages excitedly. Toward the back there was a painting of the Nativity. Part of the stable appeared to be built in a cave. A donkey was visible, as was the head of a cow. Gonzaga said, happily, "That's what we'll do but without the cave. Why didn't we think of it before? It will cost us nothing."

Looking over his shoulder, Felicia said approvingly, "It is a good idea."

They got a flashlight and returned to the barn, comparing the painting with their own animals. "You see," said Gonzaga, "we have everything, even to Hernando." The hinny and the ox stared toward the oval of light. Gonzaga laughed triumphantly, and he and Felicia returned to the house, summoning Maria.

"Here it is," he said grinning. "Look, our float." His thick fingers pointed to the figures in the painting. "You'll be Mary. Rafael will be Joseph. I'll build part of the barn on the old flatbed wagon. Hernando will be here . . ." The finger tapped. "Francisco will tow it . . ."

Maria was stricken. The dumb hinny! The stupid ox! In dismay, she said, "Saint Catherine's always has that float."

"Why not two?" Felicia asked, sensibly. "The other one will not look like ours. They have no animals."

Maria groaned. "Everyone will laugh at Hernando and Francisco. Then they will laugh at us."

Very disappointed, Gonzaga eyed his daughter. "I don't think so. I am a farmer. These are our helpers. And you will be a beautiful Mary."

Voice rising, Maria said, "But the floats are supposed to be grand. We will have two dumb animals and part of a barn. And I don't want to be Mary."

When Rafael came home, he agreed with Maria. What's more, he did not want to be Joseph.

Gonzaga raged at them. "This is what we will do, and I want no more talk about it. Not a word."

On the last day of November, in his spare time, Gonzaga began to build the Nativity scene on the ancient flatbed that had been used for many things about the farm. He stripped boards from the barn so they would look old and removed part of the worn feed trough for the manger. He kept the painting nearby, and several times showed it to both Hernando and Francisco, telling them what was expected of them.

Meanwhile, Felicia was busy at her sewing machine. Spending less than the ten dollars Gonzaga had allotted, she made a white robe for Maria, an exact copy of the painting, and a striped robe of coarse cloth for Rafael. She made a headdress from a towel and a robe for her husband, who would guide Francisco. They went about their work defiantly and would not discuss the subject with the children.

On the first Saturday in December, about noon, Gonzaga hosed Francisco down and then washed Hernando. He curried them, talking to them all the while. "Hernando, do not bray while you are on the wagon. You just eat. That is all." To Francisco, he said, "Pull steadily, as you have always done." Looking at them, he could not understand why he had a feeling of approaching disaster, but he did.

The instructions had said that all floats must be in position at the east foot of Main Street by six P.M.; and shortly after three, Gonzaga hitched Francisco to the flatbed, tying Hernando behind, and began to walk to town. Felicia, Maria and Rafael were to follow later in the old sedan, bringing the robes and one of Maria's old dolls to represent the Christ Child.

As Gonzaga walked along the road, several cars and trucks slowed, the occupants staring at the odd sight of an ox pulling the flatbed with the flimsy barn section, a queer-looking donkey tied behind. Gonzaga himself realized it all looked a little idiotic.

Reaching San Lazaro at sunset, just about five, Gonzaga was immediately tempted to turn about and walk the dirt road back home. The other floats were things of beauty, particularly Webster's with its banks of fresh flowers. But he was glad to see that Webster's number was sixteen, well behind his own ninth position. Just then, Felicia arrived with Maria and Rafael. As they stepped out of the car, Gonzaga, forcing himself to be cheerful, walked over. "Everything is fine," he said. "You see, the night is beginning to help us. You'll be beautiful, Maria. So will you, Rafael." They barely answered.

Felicia, surveying the other floats, said, with slight grimness, "Ours is different. That is good."

Maria shivered in the twilight chill, and Gonzaga said, "Stay in the car until I call you," and then went about putting on his robe. He joked feebly with Felicia. "I look like an Arab."

In a few minutes, an official walked up to tell Gonzaga that the floats were beginning to line up and that he should move down the street into the proper spot. Mercifully, the official made no comment about the Rancho Gonzaga entry. Gonzaga then led Hernando up a ramp onto the flatbed and led Francisco a half block down to get into ninth position, between a fine float sponsored by a large ranch and one entered by the co-op. It was obvious that both floats had been built by designers and Gonzaga felt like tumbleweed between red roses.

Felicia stayed near him. She said, with some fierceness, "Whatever anyone thinks, our own people will know that we tried hard. They will applaud us, I am sure."

Gonzaga nodded tensely and lit the lantern that would cast an orange glow over Maria and the manger. "I plan to look straight ahead, close my ears to what they say and keep moving." But he appeared to be ready to fight any man who laughed.

Just before six Felicia returned to the car to get Maria and Rafael. A moment later they climbed up warily to take their places. Then Gonzaga and Felicia stood back to look at their float and were suddenly overwhelmed. The evening shadows made the scene almost a duplicate of the painting. Only the cow was missing. It was breathtakingly real, even Hernando munching on alfalfa near the Christ Child.

Felicia said to Maria, "I wish you could see yourself. You are beautiful. Just look down at Him. Stay still."

Maria, sensing what had happened, said, "I feel beautiful, I do."

Even Rafael had noticed what the night had done to the float. His sour look had vanished. He asked, "How am I?"

"You are both fine," said Gonzaga, moving proudly and confidently up to stand by Francisco.

Promptly at six the band began to play, and Gonzaga heard a long blast on a whistle. He waited until he saw the float ahead begin to move and then said to Francisco, "Now, we go."

The ox stayed absolutely motionless. Gonzaga, having had other such experiences, though they had been infrequent, said calmly, "Francisco, we go now," and grasped the handmade headstall. Francisco paid not the slightest attention. There was some laughter from the sidelines. The funny Mexican was having trouble with his ox, all predictable.

Gonzaga, keeping his voice down, said in Spanish, "Why are you doing this to me? We must go." Then Gonzaga jerked Francisco savagely. "Move," he shouted in English but Francisco did not budge. The laughter grew, along with appropriate remarks. Gonzaga glanced back at Maria and Rafael. They looked demolished. Again in Spanish he

snarled at Francisco, "You are disgracing us," and turned to drive a fist into the animal's heavy shoulder. The ox promptly sat down between the shafts, and the laughter of the crowd grew to a roar. Gonzaga wanted to vanish, to die.

The float ahead was now a half block down the street and a parade official wheeled up on his motorbike to shout "Get going, or we're going around you."

In an anguished voice, Gonzaga said, "I am trying," as he attempted to tug Francisco erect. But the ox had made up his mind not to move, and even divine powers would not have straightened his rear legs.

Felicia ran up to comfort Maria who was now weeping, and Rafael stood on the flatbed as if frozen, disgraced. The float behind slowly circled around them, and the parade began to move on. Yet the best and loudest show in town was still in number-nine position as Gonzaga pleaded with Francisco to cooperate, then cursed him, oaths flying out over the barn of Bethlehem.

At first there was only a trickle of brown faces toward the stranded flatbed; but then they began to increase in number as the Panaderos, the Echeverrias, the Castillos, the Gracias and many more gathered to advise and help their countryman. Until the day he died, George Gonzaga did not know who said, "Unhitch that silly ox and get him out of here." But having no better solution, Gonzaga quickly relieved Francisco of his duty. The ox came willingly.

It was Felicia who whispered to her husband, "Our friends are going to pull the wagon. Put Francisco up beside Hernando." Gonzaga was in such a state that he complied without thought, and in a moment Francisco was up where he wanted to be, where he always was this time of night—beside Hernando, munching feed. The painting in the Old Spanish Bible was now finished.

With twenty men on the shafts, the robed farmer walking at the head, the float of Rancho Gonzaga finally began to move along the main street of San Lazaro. Then a man named Guerrero, who had brought a guitar with him because he had to play at a café later that night, stepped in front of the float. In a clear, strong voice, he began to sing "Away in a Manger."

The words carried into the starry night above, and a certain magic proceeded along with the old wheels of the wagon.

No one in the county had ever seen a Nativity quite like it. Proud, solemn-faced men, instead of noisy tractors, were pulling the float. A hinny and an ox were on it. The section of barn truly looked as if it might have come from Bethlehem. The crowds along the street became quiet as the Gonzaga float approached, heralded by the carol. Within a few blocks it was evident that the humble had swept aside the grand.

To those who travel San Joaquin Valley in the month of December, it is worth an hour on the first Saturday night to see the San Lazaro parade and the traditional Chicano Nativity scene, pulled by twenty men. The farmer Gonzaga and his good wife, Felicia, are dead; but the oldest daughter of Maria is now Mary, and the oldest son of Rafael is Joseph, and the tall, dark-skinned man who proudly walks out in front of the silver-trophy float, singing "Away in a Manger," is Rafael himself.

Close Up

1. The Gonzagas are a proud but poor Mexican-American family. (a) What does Maria do with the money she takes from the family savings? (b) Why is her dream impractical?

2. George Gonzaga takes a more practical view of the situation. (a) What does he tell Maria she must do? (b) How does Webster stir up Gonzaga's pride and make him change his mind?

3. Gonzaga enters the barn and sees the ox and the hinny munching hay. (a) What does this scene remind him of? (b) What idea does it give him for the float?

4. All of the Mexican-Americans in the community are proud that the Gonzagas have a float in the parade. When the ox refuses to move, what do they do to show what the float means to all of them?

Setting

The setting of a story is the time and place where the events occur. One element that adds color to the setting is the detail of customs, or particular habits, of the characters in the particular story. For example, the custom of having a parade on the first Saturday night in December gives you a colorful picture of the setting, San Lazaro.

1. Reread paragraph 10 on pages 268–270. List three details that give a colorful picture of the parade.

2. Sometimes the customs of two groups of characters in a particular setting are in conflict. The rich ranchers of San Lazaro displayed grand, expensive floats in the parade. (a) Write a sentence describing the Gonzagas' float. (b) How was it different from the floats of the rich ranchers?

3. Did the Gonzagas' float become part of the custom of the San Lazaro Christmas parade? Find evidence in the story to support your answer.

Activities

1. Dramatize a press conference with the Gonzaga family. Have several students play reporters. These students should draw up questions to ask the Gonzagas. Have other students play each member of the family.

2. Think of a parade that has a special meaning for you. Make a model of the float you might enter in that parade.

INFERENCES

A motive is the reason why a character acts a certain way. Sometimes, the motives of characters are not clear. You have to use the information the author gives you to make inferences. For example, in "The Christmas Parade," you can use the information the author gives you to infer that Maria entered her family in the Christmas parade because she wanted to feel equal to her friends.

▶ Use evidence from the story to make inferences about the motives of the characters. Answer each question in a complete sentence.

   a. Why does Felicia tell George Gonzaga to calm down when he is upset with Maria?

   b. Why does Gonzaga tell Maria she can blame everything on him?

   c. Why does Maria hate the sight of the ox and the hinny?

   d. Why does the woman at the Chamber of Commerce assume Gonzaga wants his money back?

   e. Why is Gonzaga tempted to walk back home when he sees the other floats?

   f. Why do the other Mexican-Americans in the community help the Gonzagas?

WORD ATTACK

Finding Antonyms

An antonym is a word that means the opposite, or almost the opposite, of another word. For example, *miserable* is the opposite of *joyous* and *pride* is the opposite of *humility*. To understand the full meaning of some words, it is helpful to contrast them with words that mean the opposite. The meaning of the word *beautiful* is better understood when the word is placed alongside the word *ugly*. Thinking of antonyms can make the meaning of some words clearer and deeper.

▶ Match each word in the left-hand column with its antonym in the right-hand column. You may want to use a dictionary to help you.

a.	guilt	(1)	thin
b.	disbelief	(2)	hate
c.	stocky	(3)	far
d.	pride	(4)	grand
e.	love	(5)	gentleness
f.	expensive	(6)	belief
g.	close	(7)	humility
h.	humble	(8)	made proud
i.	darkness	(9)	innocence
j.	fierceness	(10)	cheap
k.	disgraced	(11)	light

Three Haiku

Richard Wright

The spring lingers on
In the scent of a damp log
Rotting in the sun

The crow flew so fast
That he left his lonely caw
Behind in the fields

In the falling snow
A laughing boy holds out his palms
Until they are white

Three Haiku

Gerald Vizenor

august heat
even the big green housefly
sits by the fan

upon the pine cones
first flakes of delicate snow
becoming drops of dew

fireflies blinking
one alights then disappears
in the dewy grass

Activity ▶ A haiku is a poem with only three lines. Usually, but not always in English, the first line contains five syllables; the second, seven syllables; and the last, five syllables. Try writing a haiku that describes one specific scene.

Haiku **283**

The Boomer Fireman's Fast Sooner Hound

Jack Conroy and Arna Bontemps

The Sooner hound would rather run than eat. But could he outrun the Cannonball?

In the days of the old railroad trains before diesel engines were ever thought of, the fireman was an important man. A Boomer fireman could get him a job most anytime on most any railroad and was never long for any one road. Last year he might have worked for the Frisco, and this year he's heaving black diamonds for the Katy or the Wabash. He traveled light, and traveled far, and didn't let any grass grow under his feet when they got to itching for greener pastures on the next road, or the next division, or maybe on the other side of the mountains. He didn't need furniture and he didn't need many clothes, and goodness knows he didn't need a family or a dog.

One day when one of these Boomer firemen pulled into the roadmaster's office looking for a job, there was that Sooner hound of his loping after him. That hound would sooner run than eat, and he'd sooner eat than fight or do something useful like catching a rabbit. Not that a rabbit would have any chance if the Sooner really wanted to nail him; but that crazy hound dog didn't like to

do anything but run, and he was the fastest thing on four legs.

"I might use you," said the roadmaster. "Can you get a boarding place for the dog?"

"Oh, he goes along with me," said the Boomer. "I raised him from a pup just like a mother or a father, and he ain't never spent a night or a day or even an hour far away from me. He'd cry like his poor heart would break, and raise such a ruckus nobody couldn't sleep, eat, or hear themselves think for miles about."

"Well, I don't see how that would work out," said the roadmaster. "It's against the rules of the road to allow a passenger in the cab, man or beast, or in the caboose, and I aim to put you on a freight run, so you can't ship him by express. Besides, he'd get the idea you wasn't nowhere about and pester folks out of their wits with his yipping and yowling. You look like a man that could keep a boiler popping off on an uphill grade, but I just don't see how we could work it if the hound won't listen to reason while you're on your runs."

"Why he ain't no trouble," said the Boomer. "He just runs alongside, and when I'm on a freight run, he chases around a little in the fields to pass the time away. It's a little bit tiresome on him having to travel at such a slow gait, but that Sooner would do anything to stay close by me—he loves me that much."

"Oh, is that so? Well, don't try to tell that yarn around here," said the road-master.

"I'll lay my first paycheck against a fin[1] that he'll be fresh as a daisy and his

---

1. a fin: A five dollar bill.

tongue behind his teeth when we pull into the junction. He'll run around the station a hundred times or so to limber up."

"It's a bet," said the roadmaster.

On the first run, the Sooner moved in what was a slow walk for him. He kept looking up into the cab where the Boomer was shoveling in the coal.

"He looks worried," said the Boomer. "He thinks the hog law is going to catch us—we're making such bad time."

The roadmaster was so sore at losing the bet, that he transferred the Boomer to a local passenger run and doubled the stakes. The Sooner speeded up to a slow trot; but he had to kill a lot of time, at that, not to get too far ahead of the engine.

Then the roadmaster got mad enough to bite off a drawbar. People got to watching the Sooner trotting alongside the train and began thinking it must be a mighty slow road. Passengers might just as well walk; they'd get there just as fast. And if you shipped a yearling calf to market, it'd be a bologna bull before it reached the stockyards. Of course, the trains were keeping up their schedule the same as usual, but that's the way it looked to people who saw a no-good, mangy Sooner hound beating all the trains without his tongue hanging out an inch or letting out the least little pant.

It was giving the road a black eye, all right. The roadmaster would have fired the Boomer and told him to hit the grit with his Sooner and never come back again; but he was stubborn from the word go, and hated worse than anything to own up he was licked.

"I'll fix that Sooner," said the road-master. "I'll slap the Boomer into the cab of the Cannonball, and if anything on four legs can keep up with the fastest thing on wheels, I'd admire to see it. That Sooner'll be left so far behind, it'll take nine dollars to send him a post card."

The word got around that the Sooner was going to try to keep up with the Cannonball. Farmers left off plowing, hitched up, and drove to the right of way to see the sight. It was like a circus day or the county fair. The schools all dismissed the pupils, and not a factory could keep enough men to make a wheel turn.

The roadmaster got right in the cab so that the Boomer couldn't soldier on the job to let the Sooner keep up. A clear track for a hundred miles was ordered for the Cannonball; and all the switches were spiked down till after that streak of lightning passed by. It took three men to see the Cannonball on that run; one to say "There she comes," one to say "There she is," and another to say "There she goes." You couldn't see a thing for steam, cinders, and smoke, and the rails sang like a violin for a half hour after she'd passed by into the next county.

Every valve was popping off and the wheels three feet in the air above the roadbed. The Boomer was so sure the Sooner would keep up, that he didn't stint the elbow grease; he wore the hinges off the fire door, and fifteen pounds of him melted and ran right down into his shoes. He had his shovel whetted to a nub.

The roadmaster stuck his head out of the cab window, and—whoosh!—off went his hat and almost his head. The suction like to have jerked his arms from their sockets as he nailed a-hold of the window seat.

It was all he could do to see, and gravel pinged against his goggles like hailstones; but he let out a whoop of joy.

"THE SOONER! THE SOONER!" he yelled. "He's gone! He's gone for true! Ain't *nowhere* in sight.

"I can't understand that," hollered the Boomer. "He ain't *never* laid down on me yet. It just ain't like him to lay down on me. Leave me take a peek."

He dropped his shovel and poked out his head. Sure enough, the Sooner was nowhere to be seen. The Boomer's wild and troubled gaze swept far and wide.

"Don't see him, do you?" the roadmaster demanded. "He's at least seventy-six miles behind."

The Boomer didn't answer. He just drew his head back into the cab and began to shovel coal. He shoveled without much spirit, shaking his head sadly. There was no need for hard work, anyhow, for the Cannonball was puffing into the station at the end of the run.

Before the wheels had stopped rolling, the roadmaster jumped nimbly to the ground. A mighty cheer was heard from a group of people near them.

"Here I am!" he shouted. "Where are the cameras? Do you want to take my picture in the cab?"

"Go way back and sit down!" a man shouted as he turned briefly toward the railroad official. "You might as well scrap that Cannonball. The Sooner has been here a good half hour, and time has been hanging heavy on his hands. Look at him!"

The Sooner was loping easily around a tree, barking at a cat which had taken refuge in the branches and was spitting angrily. The Sooner didn't look even a mite tired, and his tongue was behind his teeth.

"I'm through! Enough is enough, boys!" the roadmaster sputtered. "The rule about passengers in the cab is a dead duck from now on. Let the Sooner ride in the cab as often and as far as he wants to."

The Cannonball chugged out of the station with the Boomer waving his shovel in salute, and the Sooner yelping proudly beside him. The people cheered until the train disappeared around a bend.

Close Up

1. The Boomer fireman has never been separated from his Sooner hound. (a) Does the roadmaster believe the Sooner can keep up with the train, or does he think the Boomer is exaggerating? (b) What are the terms of the bet between the Boomer and the roadmaster?

2. Why does the roadmaster think the Sooner is "giving the road a black eye"?

3. (a) Why does the roadmaster assign the Boomer to work the Cannonball? (b) List three steps the roadmaster takes to win the bet.

4. When the Cannonball arrives at the station, what does the roadmaster do that shows he is certain he has won?

Setting

The setting in which people live can affect the type of stories they tell or write. The American frontier was a seemingly limitless expanse of land where almost anything seemed possible. It was a place of rapid change where settlements became small cities almost overnight. It was a place of opportunity, where fair competition determined who was best. It was a place of awesome dangers. The American response to these dangers was laughter.

The stories that grew out of this setting were *tall tales*. These were yarns filled with fantastic lies that could make you laugh. They also were filled with precise details that made you almost believe the lies. The characters in these yarns were common people who became heroes because of their great—but devilishly funny—deeds.

1. This yarn takes place on the American frontier. When does it take place?

2. The railroads played an important part in the development of the West. They were powerful and fast. What "no-good, mangy" creature takes on the railroad and wins?

3. The heroes in most tall tales are common people who prove their worth through some task. Why is it fitting that the dog in this story is a Sooner hound instead of a pedigreed?

Activity

▶ **Composition.** Find a collection of tall tales in the library. Write a paragraph summarizing one of these tales.

INFERENCES

Making Inferences About Exaggeration

Exaggeration makes something greater than it really is, or greater than it normally is. One type of exaggeration is the whopper—a big lie that no one is really expected to believe. Tall tales are filled with whoppers, or gross exaggerations. For example, the Sooner would "raise such a ruckus, nobody couldn't sleep, eat, or hear themselves think for miles about." When you read tall tales, you make inferences about which statements are accurate and which are exaggerations.

▶ Read the statements below. On a separate piece of paper, put an *E* by each statement that is an exaggeration.

   a. ". . . that crazy hound dog didn't like to do anything but run, and he was the fastest thing on four legs."

   b. "The roadmaster was so sore at losing the bet, that he transferred the Boomer to a local passenger run and doubled the stakes."

   c. "And if you shipped a yearling calf to market, it'd be a bologna bull before it reached the stockyards."

   d. "That Sooner'll be left so far behind, it'll take nine dollars to send him a post card."

   e. "The word got around that the Sooner was going to try to keep up with the Cannonball."

   f. "Passengers might just as well walk; they'd get there just as fast."

   g. ". . . he wore the hinges off the fire door, and fifteen pounds of him melted and ran right down into his shoes."

   h. "Then the roadmaster got mad enough to bite off a drawbar."

   i. "He dropped his shovel and poked out his head. Sure enough, the Sooner was nowhere to be seen."

   j. "(The Sooner) just runs alongside (the train); and when I'm on a freight run, he chases around a little in the fields to pass the time away."

WORD ATTACK

Understanding Figurative Expressions

Figurative expressions are groups of words that have a special meaning. These expressions cannot be interpreted word for word, that is, literally. In fact, the words in these expressions do not have their literal, or dictionary, meanings. For example, "He traveled light, and traveled far, and didn't *let any grass grow under his feet when they got to itching for greener pastures. . . .*" This expression has nothing to do with grass or itching feet. It is a figurative way of saying that the Boomer was always on the move.

▶ Read each sentence below. Then, in your own words, write the meaning of the *italicized* expression on a separate piece of paper.

   a. " 'You look like a man who could *keep a boiler popping off on an uphill grade.* . . .' "

   b. " 'I'll *lay my first paycheck against a fin* that he'll be *fresh as a daisy.* . . .' "

   c. "It was *giving the road a black eye,* all right."

   d. ". . . *time has been hanging heavy on his hands.*"

   e. " 'The rule about passengers in the cab *is a dead duck* from now on.' "

The Adventure of the Speckled Band

Lewis K. Parker

Based on a Short Story by Sir Arthur Conan Doyle

Characters

Narrator	Philip Armitage
Sherlock Holmes	Mr. Reynolds
Dr. Watson	Mrs. Sharp
Helen Stoner	Dr. Roylott
Julia Stoner	Mrs. Hudson

Narrator: It's a Tuesday morning, and the fog is just lifting from around 221 Baker Street where Sherlock Holmes and Dr. Watson reside. Usually they aren't early risers. But this morning a few surprises await them.

Mrs. Hudson (banging on Holmes's door): Mr. Holmes! Mr. Holmes! Wake up, sir. You have visitors.

Holmes (comes to his door, opens it a crack, looks out): Stop that blasted noise! Now what is it, Mrs. Hudson?

Mrs. Hudson (very politely): Two people to see you, sir.

Holmes (grumbling): All right, I suppose. I'll be right there. Mrs. Hudson, make sure a fire's in the parlor. And ask Dr. Watson to join me.

Mrs. Hudson: Yes, sir.

Narrator: She crosses the hallway and knocks on Dr. Watson's door.

Watson: (yawning): What's going on? What is it, Mrs. Hudson? A fire?

Mrs. Hudson (politely): No, sir. Visitors in the parlor, sir. Mr. Holmes requests you join him.

Watson (as he closes the door): At this hour? Why the sun's hardly up. I'll be there in . . . (His voice trails off as the door closes.)

Narrator: In a few minutes Holmes and Watson enter the parlor. A young man and woman are there. The man is comforting the woman.

Holmes (stepping forward): Hello. I'm Holmes and this is Watson. (He notices that the woman is shivering.)

Armitage (shakes hands with Holmes and Watson): My name's Philip Armitage, and this is my fiancée, Helen Stoner. She's the one who requests your help.

Holmes: Then let's proceed.

Watson: We're all attention, madam.

Helen (*calming down*): I'm living at my stepfather's house. He's Dr. Roylott, the last survivor of the oldest family in the area.

Watson: Yes, I've heard of the family.

Helen: Once the family was one of the richest in England; but over the years the fortune was gambled away. My stepfather, however, became a doctor. Then he went to India, where he was quite successful.

Armitage: Dr. Roylott killed a man in India, you know. Then he and his family came back to England.

Helen: That meant my mother, my twin sister, Julia, Dr. Roylott, and myself. After my mother's death a few years ago, Dr. Roylott gave up his medical practice. He shut himself up in the old house; and when he did go out, he got into fights with the villagers. Actually, his only friends are the gypsies who camp not far from our house. But he's received a few unusual gifts from old friends in India. These have all been strange animals. Sometimes Dr. Roylott's baboon and cheetah frighten me half to death.

Watson (*jokingly*): Dr. Roylott seems to have a very strange personality.

Holmes: What about your sister? Julia—was that her name?

Helen: Yes. Julia died two years ago, on the night before her wedding. (*Pauses and looks frightened.*) Tomorrow I'm going to be married and I'm afraid something will happen to me too.

Holmes: I see. Give me all the details concerning your sister's death.

Narrator: A terrified look comes into Helen's eyes as she relates the events of her sister's last night alive. As she speaks, Holmes and Watson can almost see the two girls sitting in Helen's room . . . .

Julia (*looking at a box of dishes*): Thank you so much for this lovely chinaware!

Helen: Everyone says it's good to start out with new dishes.

Julia (*gazing out the window at the storm*): Listen to that wind howl! But it doesn't really bother me. I can hardly wait for tomorrow when I'll come down the stairs and become Jason's bride!

Helen (*touching her sister's hands*): It's a dream come true, Julia. You'll soon be married—and away from this house.

Julia (*in a serious tone*): Helen, have you ever heard a whistle at night?

Helen: No. Why do you ask?

Julia: I've been awakened in the middle of the night a few times by a strange low whistle. (*Shivers*) But let's not think about that—it's probably my imagination.

Helen: Well, it's getting late, and you've a hundred things to do before tomorrow. You'd better be getting off to bed.

Narrator: Julia returns to her room, which is between Dr. Roylott's and Helen's rooms. The wind and rain continue to pound against the old house's shutters as Helen drops off to sleep. Before long she's awakened by the screaming of Mrs. Sharp, the family's half-deaf housekeeper.

Mrs. Sharp: Miss Helen! Miss Helen!

Helen (*opens her door*): What on earth is it, Mrs. Sharp?

Mrs. Sharp (*very upset*): It's Miss Julia. I heard terrible noises coming from her room.

Helen *(steps out into the hall and hears Julia screaming from inside her room; tries the door):* The door's locked. *(Hears a whistle and the clanging of some kind of metal.)* I can't hear Julia anymore! We'll have to break into the room.

Narrator: Mrs. Sharp and Helen break the lock. When the door flies open, they see Julia staggering around the room. Then she falls to the floor.

Helen *(rushing to Julia and holding her head):* Julia, what's wrong? Tell me.

Julia *(gasping):* It was . . . was . . . the speckled band!

Narrator: Julia points toward Dr. Roylott's room. Then she collapses . . . .

Helen: . . . and she was dead, Mr. Holmes. *(She sobs quietly.)*

Holmes *(lights up his pipe):* Are you sure about the whistle and the metallic sound?

Helen: Well, the house creaks a lot. I . . . I might not have heard anything.

Watson: I'm sure the coroner examined your sister's body. What killed her?

Helen: The coroner couldn't discover why she died. There were no marks on her body, and her door was locked from the inside. She was completely alone at the time.

Holmes *(puffing on his pipe):* Perhaps she died of fear. But the speckled band . . . what could that be? *(He pauses as he puffs again.)* Gypsies often wear spotted handkerchiefs around their heads. Could that be the speckled band? I wonder . . . hmmm. But, tell me, is there anything else?

Helen: Two weeks ago Dr. Roylott ordered some repair work done in my room, so I've moved into Julia's old room

for the time being. Last night I heard the same whistle Julia said she heard. I looked all around the room, but I saw nothing. That's why I came here today.

Armitage: We need your help, Mr. Holmes.

Holmes *(a frown on his face):* I'd like to investigate your room. If you don't mind, Watson and I will be at the estate this afternoon.

Narrator: Helen and Philip leave Holmes's house. As soon as they've left, another visitor barges through the door.

Roylott *(in a loud voice):* Which one of you is Holmes?

Holmes *(steps forward, offers his hand):* Why, I'm Holmes. But who are you?

Roylott *(brushes Holmes's hand away):* Dr. Grimesby Roylott.

Watson: Take a seat, sir.

Roylott *(growling):* I will do nothing of the kind. I just saw my stepdaughter and her worthless fiancé leaving here. What has she been saying to you?

Holmes *(ignoring the question):* A little cold for this time of year, don't you think?

Roylott *(glaring at Holmes):* What has she been saying to you?

Holmes *(calmly puffing on his pipe):* Do you think the flowers will bloom early this spring?

Roylott *(getting very angry):* You're Holmes, the meddler! Holmes, the busybody!

Holmes *(stepping forward and opening the door):* When you leave, please close the door. Drafts give us all colds.

Roylott *(stands in the doorway):* I'll go. But don't dare meddle in my affairs, I warn you! I'm a dangerous man to cross.

The Adventure of the Speckled Band **295**

Narrator: Roylott leaves and slams the door. On a hunch, Holmes pays a visit to the legal documents section of the village bank.

Holmes: I'd like some information about the will left by Mrs. Roylott.

Reynolds (looking up from a column of figures): I'm the chief legal documents expert here. You're Sherlock Holmes, aren't you?

Holmes: Yes, I am. Now I'd like that information.

Reynolds: You know, I can't allow you to read the will. That just isn't done—at least not without authority. But—I can read it to you. (Ruffles through file.)

Here it is. Mrs. Roylott's first husband was a Bengal Lancer, and he left quite a bit of money to her. She, in turn, included that money in her will. Hmmm, it's quite an ordinary will except for the marriage clause. It says that if either or both of Mrs. Roylott's daughters marries, the bulk of the estate would go to them. That would be a considerable amount of money.

Holmes: Do you have Dr. Roylott's bank account there?

Reynolds: You're asking for a lot of information. I can't give you the figures in his account. But I can tell you that Dr. Roylott has no income of his own. He's been using the estate money for several years.

Narrator: That afternoon Holmes, Watson, and Helen explore the old Roylott mansion while Dr. Roylott is still away in the village. Holmes notes that the repair work in Helen's room doesn't seem necessary. Then they enter Julia's room.

Holmes (looking around the room): Beautiful draperies. And an antique chest of drawers. Ah, what's this—a bell rope, eh? What does it ring?

Helen (pulling the rope): I don't know. Julia and I never used it. That's funny—it doesn't work.

Holmes (studying the rope): It should work. It looks new.

Helen: It is new. My stepfather had the bell rope and the ventilator shaft installed just before my sister died.

Holmes (looking at the bell rope more closely): It seems to be attached to a hook just above the opening for the ventilator. And the ventilator is strange—it doesn't open up to the outside. It seems to connect with the room next door.

Narrator: Holmes and Watson then enter Dr. Roylott's room.

Holmes (cautiously): What's this? A saucer of milk. Does your stepfather have a cat, Helen?

Helen (puzzled): Why, no.

Watson: Look at this, Holmes.

Holmes (examining the object): It's a small leash, curled around to make it even smaller. I'm beginning to understand. Helen, I think you're in great danger and we haven't much time left. But if you'll carry out my plan, you'll be safe and we'll catch your sister's murderer.

Narrator: Holmes explains his plan to Helen, and that evening she begins to carry out her part.

Helen (yawning): I feel sleepy this evening, Dr. Roylott. I've got many things to do before tomorrow.

Roylott: Perhaps you should retire to your room, my dear. Maybe I'll go to mine soon. I could use some rest myself. Sleep well.

Narrator: As soon as Dr. Roylott goes to his room, Helen places a lamp in

the window of Julia's room. This is a signal to Holmes and Watson, who aren't very far away.

Holmes *(whispering):* This could be dangerous, Watson.

Watson: I realize that.

Holmes: No doubt you saw all I did in the dead woman's room? Did you notice that the bed was fastened to the floor?

Watson: That's unusual.

Holmes: Yes, isn't it. Julia couldn't move her bed, and it would always be in a position just below the ventilator with the bell rope hanging down beside the bed.

Watson *(looking toward the house):* There's the light. Did you see that—it looked like a monster scampering across the lawn?

Holmes *(touching Watson on the shoulder):* That's only Dr. Roylott's ba-boon. Helen said he received animals from India. Let's go.

Narrator: Helen goes into her own room. Watson and Holmes enter the house and hide in the darkness of Julia's room. During the long night, the only sound is the occasional clanging of the village church clock. . . . Still Holmes and Watson wait. Finally they see a glimmer of light in the direction of the ventilator, and they smell burning oil.

Holmes *(whispering):* Someone's lit a lantern in the next room. Now if you hear a hiss or a whistle, turn on the lamp.

Narrator: In only a few minutes they hear a gentle soothing sound like that of a light jet stream escaping from a teakettle. Instantly Holmes springs at the sound, beating the air with his cane.

Holmes *(yelling):* Quick, turn on the lamp! There—did you see it?

Watson (puzzled): I'm sorry, Holmes, I didn't see a thing.

Narrator: Holmes darts out the door. Watson follows him into Dr. Roylott's room.

Roylott (gasping): Help me . . . please . . . I can't . . . can't . . . Aagggh!!

Narrator: Roylott's leaning against the wall. His eyes stare wildly at the ceiling. Holmes and Watson see some kind of spotted band around the top of Roylott's head. Slowly, Roylott slides down the wall and collapses.

Holmes (picking up the lantern and holding it toward Roylott): I'm afraid its too late. There, Watson—that's the speckled band.

Watson: What is it?

Holmes (pulls Watson back from touching the band): Not too close, Watson. Be careful!

Watson (amazed): Why, it moved. That's no band—it's a snake.

Holmes (lighting his pipe): Precisely, Watson. A swamp adder, to be exact. It's considered to be the deadliest snake in India.

Helen (coming into the room): I heard a noise . . . Oh, Dr. Roylott! Is he dead, Mr. Holmes?

Holmes (puffing on his pipe): I'm afraid so, Helen. It only takes about fifteen seconds to die after that snake bites.

Watson: How did you know it was Roylott who murdered Julia?

Holmes: There are many clues. We've already discussed the useless bell rope and ventilator shaft. As you can see, the rope was a bridge to the bed. And the whistle . . . (pauses)

Watson: Yes. What was that?

Holmes: Roylott received the snake from his friends in India. Then, using the leash, he trained it to come when he blew the whistle. You remember the saucer of milk I almost stepped on? Well, he probably used it to reward the snake. He would put the adder through the ventilator at the hour he thought best. The snake crawled down the rope and sooner or later it would bite the victim.

Helen: But what was the metallic sound I heard?

Holmes (leaving Roylott's room and slowly walking down the hall): Roylott put the snake in a metal box when it came back through the ventilator. He had just enough time to throw it in the box and slam the lid tight.

Helen: But what reason would he have had for killing Julia?

Holmes A very good reason, actually. He was using the estate funds for himself. If either of the daughters married, then most of his income would be cut off.

Watson (putting his arm around Helen): Well, Helen, now you can be married tomorrow in safety and in happiness.

Holmes (puffing on his pipe): I think we can consider this case closed. And just remember, he who sets a trap for others is often trapped himself.

1. (a) On what special night was Julia Stoner killed? (b) Why does Helen fear that she too will be killed?

2. When Holmes examines Helen's room, he notices that the repairs Dr. Roylott ordered are not necessary. Where do these repairs force Helen to sleep?

3. To save Helen, Holmes first must discover how Julia was killed. (a) What three unusual things does he notice about Julia's room? (b) What two clues does he find in Roylott's room?

4. Holmes examines the contents of Mrs. Roylott's will to find a motive. What does he find is Roylott's motive for killing Julia?

5. How does Roylott get caught in his own trap?

Setting

Certain details of the setting can affect the story. The details can help a character achieve certain goals or they can create problems a character must overcome. For example, the setting of this murder mystery is a locked room. This locked room presents special problems for both the murderer who commits the crime and the detective who tries to solve the crime.

1. "The Adventure of the Speckled Band" is called a locked-door mystery. (a) Where does the crime take place? (b) Why is it important that the crime take place at night when Julia cannot see what is happening?

2. What special problem does the locked door present?

3. (a) Besides the door, what other means of entry and exit to Julia's room is there? (b) How does discovering this help Holmes solve the murder?

Activities

1. Imagine you are presenting this play on the radio. Add a commercial message before, in the middle, and at the end of the play.

2. Draw a sketch of Dr. Roylott's room and Julia's room, showing the ventilator shaft and the rope above the bed.

INFERENCES

Making Inferences About Past and Future Actions

An inference about past actions is an intelligent guess you make about what a character did before the start of a story. An inference about future actions is an intelligent guess about what a character will do before a story is over. For example, when you infer that Holmes will solve the mystery, you make an inference about future actions.

▶ The following lines of dialogue allow you to make inferences about a character's past and future actions. Match the clues below with the inferences that result.

Dialogue

a. **Narrator:** . . . A young man and woman (Helen Stoner) are there. The man is comforting the woman.

b. **Helen:** . . . But he's (Dr. Roylott) received a few unusual gifts from old friends in India. These have all been strange animals.

c. **Helen:** Tomorrow I'm going to be married and I'm afraid something will happen to me too.

d. **Julia:** I've been awakened in the middle of the night a few times by a strange low whistle. (*Shivers*) But let's not think about that—it's probably my imagination.

e. **Holmes:** It's a small leash, curled around to make it even smaller. I'm beginning to understand.

Inferences

(1) Helen Stoner had an upsetting experience just before she came to Holmes for help.

(2) Holmes will be faced with a mystery involving an animal from India.

(3) Holmes has an idea and will soon solve the mystery.

(4) Something will probably happen to Julia during the night.

(5) Someone will try to murder Helen.

WORD ATTACK

Using Prefixes to Make Antonyms

A prefix is one or more letters attached to the front of a word to change its meaning. Attaching such prefixes as *il-*, *im-*, *in-*, *de-*, *dis-*, *un-*, and *anti-* to words makes them antonyms. **Antonyms are words that mean the opposite or almost the opposite of the original words.** For example, *unable* means the opposite of *able*. Attaching the prefix *im-* to the word *patient* makes the word *impatient*, the antonym of *patient*. You must be sure that the beginnings of words are really prefixes before you read them as antonyms. The letters *un-* in the word *understand* are not a prefix, nor are the letters *im-* in the word *important*.

---

1. Decide which of the following words contain prefixes. On a separate piece of paper, write the prefix in column 1. (If there is no prefix, write O.) Write the antonym in column 2. You may use a dictionary to help you.

    Word   (1)   (2)

    a. usually
    b. unusual
    c. into
    d. imagination
    e. illegal
    f. improper
    g. unheard
    h. immovable
    i. disconnect
    j. discuss

2. Add a prefix to each word below to form its antonym. You may want to use your dictionary to help you choose the correct prefix.

    a. social   f. toxin
    b. likely   g. legal
    c. mature   h. mortal
    d. logical   i. tidy
    e. freeze   j. willing

The Horse Looked at Him

MacKinlay Kantor

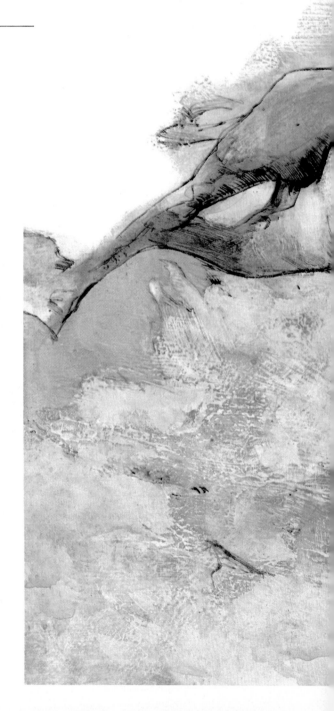

Jameson thought he saw something stirring on the burnt sullenness of the desert's face. He thought he saw a quiver among slopes of brown and red.

He opened his dry, cracked mouth. His mouth had been open for a long time, but he opened it wider. He tried to say, weakly, "Posse." Jameson never thought he'd see the day when he'd be glad to have a posse come smoking up to him. But he reckoned that if a man lived long enough, he saw different days from those he had expected to see.

But there was no posse. No quiver in the blue, no twisting and dividing in the brown . . . .

Jameson turned his head and felt the vast, round flame of sky searing his eyeballs. He managed to lift his hand, and in the scant shade granted by swollen fingers, he tried to find some buzzards. He couldn't find any buzzards. Nothing lived on this dry pan of desertion—nothing lived here but Jameson and Poco.

The man twisted the upper part of his body, and sighed. Poco's head lay against the burning shale a few feet away. When Jameson stirred, the little horse moved his neck with the agony of a movement five hundred times repeated. There were flies eating slowly away at Poco's ears. His ears twitched them off now and again, but the flies came back.

"How you doing?" Jameson wanted to ask his horse.

Poco wasn't doing so well. He had done well for the five years Jameson had ridden him. He had taken Jameson bustling out of towns, slapping along narrow mountain roads when the bullets squealed around them. And there was the night in Dundee when the wise little horse waited silently beside a dark doorway, aloof from the stampede of pursuing hoofs, and finally carried Jameson away with two bullets in his arm.

There were marks on Poco too. There was a dark streak along his sorrel shoulder, where lead had branded him with the only brand he wore. There was a knobby place on one hock, and the contour of one inquisitive ear had been misshapen long before the flies ever sat there.

Jameson said to the horse, "Reckon you'd like to drink. So would I."

He stole Poco from the Maxwell ranch, clear over south of the Estella Plata range, when Poco was only a colt. Jameson had raised Poco on a bottle, so to speak—taught him to blow his nose and keep his clothes buttoned. He was the only kid Jameson had ever had.

Now the heat-warped fingers of the man's hand stole down to find his revolver butt, as they had stolen a dozen times before. He thought, nothing in this country. Nothing for fifty miles. I ought to have known better than to ride across. But we made it, other times. No water.

His hand trembled as he exposed the cylinder and saw the solitary undented cartridge cap which reposed on the surface of powder-grimed steel. One chamber was vacant—Jameson never kept a shell under his hammer. There were five shiny little wafers looking at him. The rims of four were marred by hammer strokes.

He put the gun back in its holster again, and felt around his cartridge belt. His raw fingers rubbed across empty sockets. Jameson had known men who wore two cartridge belts, but he had never worn more than one. He had never expected that posse to cling to his trail across the desert with such wolfish tenacity.

The blue sky came down and struck him across the face. It was a red sky—now it was yellow—now white. "Sky," he wanted to ask, "do you see any posses? I sure would like to see one."

Poco's ears fluttered again, and he tried to whinny. Still there was moisture in his muzzle, and one bubble formed there, and then it went away. It was mighty strange that there could be any moisture in either of them, after the hot day and the cold night, and the day before that.

Jameson said, "One of us went wrong. That was a bad slide. I reckon you might have seen that crack in the rocks, but I ain't blaming you. You seen plenty I've never seen."

His mind went away from him for a while, and came speeding back amid the hearty hoofs of phantom horses. There were men in this fantasy—enemies who

came to gather him in, and all the time they laughed at him.

The mystic enemies said, "Why did you do it, Jimmy Jameson? You ain't never killed anyone. Time was when you were mighty charitable with what you took off the road. You're a bad man, but a lot of people like you."

They said, in this parched dream that formed within his mind, "It wouldn't have been hanging. We're the Law. We know. We've burned powder and shoved lead at each other, but you ain't really got a bad name. Maybe you'd have spent a couple of years behind bars, but that's all. You shouldn't have tried the Llano Diablo. No water in the Llano Diablo. Nobody goes there."

In his thoughts the posse circled him, and then dismounted to pat Poco's red-hot flank and to moisten Jameson's own lips with cool, wet salve from a canteen. "You're an awful idiot," said the posse. "Here you are—your horse has got a broken back, and it looks as if both your legs is busted too. Can't either of you move. Can't even crawl. Not even coyotes go out on the Llano Diablo."

Now he awoke from his dream, and he had the gun in his hand. Twice he put the muzzle against his own temple, and twice he fought successfully to keep his finger from tightening. His horse watched him with glazing eyes: Again it tried to lift its head.

"No," Jameson thought, "I can't! It's bad for me, but I reckon it's double bad for you."

Once more the desert became a pasture, and in it he saw a lush green place where Poco trotted toward him, stiff-legged, knobby-kneed, his eyes young and coltish. "Sugar?" said Jameson to his darling. "You don't get none. I ain't going to ruin your teeth. I got a piece of apple here . . . ." and his hands played with the thick, wiry mane. "Reckon someday you'll be a fine horse."

The sky changed from white back into yellow and orange. The shadow of a steep stone ridge grew longer; it went past the two suffering shapes—the swollen mass of living horseflesh—the dry-skinned, crippled man who lay beside it.

"Not another night," said Jameson. "I can't stand it. Pity there ain't two shells. I never realized I didn't have another loading for this gun."

Again the muzzle found his temple, but the horse still looked at him.

Jameson breathed softly. "OK," he croaked. He remembered something about the *Bible* and a merciful man being merciful to his beast. But Jameson would never in his life call Poco a beast.

He inched forward suffering horrors until he felt the metal barrel sinking against Poco's ear cavity, soft and warm and silky despite all endurances.

"Be seeing you," he said, and pulled the trigger.

The gun jumped loose from his hand. His first thought was that the flies wouldn't be bothering Poco any longer.

He did not know how many dreams possessed him, but not many. The night came closer every second. And then his ears picked out a faint scrambling, a sound of sliding gravel. Hoof rims scraped the burnished gray rocks not far away.

They rode up; they were angels in leather and flannel; they wore guns.

They would carry Jimmy Jameson behind the bars, but still they were angels.

The sheriff was on his knees beside him.

"Can't understand it," Jameson whispered. "So late. Nobody comes to Llano Diablo."

The sheriff looked at the dead horse. He shook his head, even while his hands moved to his water bottle.

"One shell," said Jameson. "It was him or me. Poco needed a break."

The brown, lined face of the sheriff bent closer, and there were other faces behind. Water touched Jameson's dry lips.

"Guess you got a break yourself," the sheriff said. "We hadn't come across your trail, and we agreed to ride back. We were just turning our horses, behind that hill, when we heard you shoot."

Close Up

1. Jameson and Poco are trapped in the desert, their bodies broken from a fall among the rocks. How long have they been without water?

2. Jameson says, " . . . if a man lived long enough, he saw different days from those he had expected to see." (a) What does this statement mean? (b) Why does he now want to see a posse?

3. Jameson remembers something about "a merciful man being merciful to his beast." (a) What does Jameson do that shows he is a merciful man? (b) How does this merciful action save Jameson's life?

Setting

The setting of a story may reveal the best or the worst in a character. For example, a battlefield setting may show some apparently meek characters to be heroic, while it may reveal seemingly heroic types to be cowardly.

1. Reread the first four paragraphs of the story. Write down three groups of words that give you a good picture of the setting.

2. No one freely rides into the Llano Diablo. (a) How many miles is it across? (b) What does it lack that is necessary to life?

3. The barren and desolate setting forces Jameson to make a decision. (a) What is his decision? (b) How does his decision show that Jameson has good qualities?

Activities

1. **Composition.** Imagine you are Poco. Write a paragraph telling about your first meeting with Jameson. Tell how Jameson appeared to you, and what kind of person he seemed to be.

2. A monologue is a speech by one character. Imagine you are Jameson. Prepare a monologue that reveals the best in your nature.

INFERENCES

Making Inferences About Characters

When you make an inference about a character, you make an intelligent guess about what this character is like. Sometimes you are told what a character is like. Other times, you can infer what a character is like by looking at how the character acts. An important clue that helps you make inferences is the way the character treats others. For example, you are told that Jameson is a bad man. By reading between the lines and examining the way he treats Poco, you can make the inference that he is also a kind man.

▶ Which of the following details help you infer that there is good in Jameson?

  a. Jameson has been in trouble with the law for at least five years.

  b. Jameson stole Poco from the Maxwell ranch.

  c. Jameson treated Poco with tenderness—as though Poco were his child.

  d. Jameson never kept a shell under his hammer.

  e. Jameson never killed anyone.

  f. Jameson was charitable with what he took off the road.

  g. Jameson was suffering; but he didn't use his one bullet on himself.

  h. Jameson was used to being pursued by posses.

  i. Jameson was glad that "the flies wouldn't be bothering Poco any longer."

  j. Jameson had escaped from posses by riding across Llano Diablo other times.

WORD ATTACK

Understanding Verbs That Appeal to the Five Senses

Verbs are the words that show action in sentences. The horse *streaked* across the desert. Jameson *crashed* to the ground. The verbs may be vivid and sharp. They may create a vivid impact by appealing to one or more of the five senses (sight, hearing, taste, touch, and smell). For example, in the sentence, "The sun flamed above the desert sand," the word *flamed* appeals to the senses of touch (burning) and sight.

1. Read the sentences below. Look up the meaning of each *italicized* verb. Then decide which senses each verb appeals to.
   a. "He had taken Jameson *bustling* out of towns, *slapping* along narrow mountain roads when the bullets *squealed* around them."
   b. "There was a dark streak along his sorrel shoulder, where lead had *branded* him with the only brand he wore."
   c. "Jameson turned his head and felt the vast, round flame of sky *searing* his eyeballs."
   d. "He had never expected that posse to *cling* to his trail across the desert with such wolfish tenacity."
   e. "Jameson breathed softly. 'OK,' he *croaked*."

2. Why is the verb *smoking* a particularly good image in the following sentence: "Jameson never thought he'd see the day when he'd be glad to have a posse come *smoking* up to him"?

Apartment House

Gerald Raftery

A filing-cabinet of human lives
Where people swarm like bees in tunneled hives,
Each to his own cell in the towered comb,
Identical and cramped—we call it home.

The City

Langston Hughes

In the morning the city
Spreads its wings
Making a song
In stone that sings.

5 In the evening the city
Goes to bed
Hanging lights
Above its head.

Close Up

1. Both these poems are about city living. (a) To what does Gerald Raftery compare an apartment building? (b) How do you feel about city living after reading his poem?

2. (a) To what creature does Hughes compare the city? (b) How do you feel about the city after reading his poem?

Spectral Beast in the Night

Arthur Tofte

Andy looked down at his dog. There was no question about it—his big seventy-pound golden retriever had been in a battle. Patches of his golden hair had been torn away leaving raw, bloody flesh below. There were several cuts across his face. One leg seemed to be lame. Even his expression was pitiful.

How had it happened?

It couldn't have been a dog fight. Champ knew every dog within miles and was friendly with all of them. The wounds weren't the kind a cat might have inflicted. Andy knew that the great forest beyond his father's farm had the usual assortment of wild animals—deer, rabbits, squirrels, muskrats, even a few foxes and raccoons, and a family or two of beavers. None of them was the type that would have tangled with Champ.

A wolf might have. Even a bear, or a wolverine. But nothing like them had been seen in the great forest for over fifty years.

"What was it, Champ-boy?" Andy asked, as he carefully washed the wounds and applied bandages. The dog's eyes looked up at him beseechingly, as though trying to tell him what had caused the rips and tears.

That night, instead of having Champ sleep in his shelter next to the house, Andy brought him up to his room. Andy's father was away for the night, arranging for a loan to buy seeds and supplies for the coming year.

"Pa won't like it," his mother had said, when Andy asked permission to keep the dog in his room overnight.

"Aw, Ma," Andy's sister, Ellen, put in a plea for him. "Can't you see Champ is hurt bad? He might need help during the night."

"Thanks, sis," Andy smiled at his eleven-year-old sister, four years younger than he was.

"Pa needn't know," she added. "I won't tell."

"All right, Andy," his mother said with a smile. "I see you did a pretty good job of bandaging him. In the morning, I'll see what I can do for him."

That night Andy had trouble going to sleep. Champ lay on the rug next to his bed. Every once in a while, the dog would give a yelp of pain, then sigh wearily. Andy knew there wasn't much more he could do . . . except wonder what kind of creature had fought with Champ.

Suddenly he sat up in bed. Champ was moaning. The boy turned on the light and stared at the dog. Apparently he was having a nightmare, probably fighting the battle again.

But there was something strange about it. Champ, who was normally the bravest of all creatures, awoke now and was cowering in fear. He was obviously afraid of something . . . something that had fought with him, something outside the house.

Andy strode to the window and looked out. It was still dark and he couldn't see anything. But something was making Champ act as he had never acted before.

The boy looked over at his warm bed. Probably he should slip back under the covers and wait for morning to do any investigating.

Whatever was frightening Champ was frightening Andy. There had to be an answer. Was there really something strange and weird out there? Better wait until daylight. But could he wait?

He felt it now—a pulling at him to go out into the night. Almost as though he were still half-asleep, he slipped into pants and a heavy wool shirt. Then he went to the corner closet and picked up his .22 rifle.

He gave Champ a pat on the head and told him to stay! Then, as quietly as he could, he made his way down the stairs to the back door. He listened for two or three minutes before opening it. Once he thought he heard heavy breathing; then he realized it was only his own.

Slowly he opened the door and peered out. There was only a three-quarter moon to give a scary thin light to the scene. He could see the big red hay barn, so red in the daytime, so dark now. He could make out the outline of the cattle barn and tractor shed next to it. All were in their proper places. But somehow they looked different. It wasn't just the dark of the night that gave them an eerie look. It was something else—something unreal, uncanny, and alien.

He slowly slipped out, closing the door behind him. Now, if ever, he wished he had Champ at his side. He shivered with fear. He took a deep breath. Even the air seemed heavy and depressing. A light fog helped to add to the thickness of the dark.

Like fingers plucking at his brain, a feeling came to him to go to the stream that crossed the farm. Holding his gun tightly in his hand, he headed that way even though he saw the fog was heavier there.

His feet struck a patch of mud. In his desire to be as quiet as he could, he had neglected to put on boots. The mud was oozing up between his toes. He usually liked to go barefoot, but tonight the mud felt like quicksand.

Then he reached the stream. On the bank was a big old elm that had died and had been chopped down. It had never been cleared away.

With a spurt of terror, he climbed up on the log and tried to peer around. It was almost light enough to see. For several minutes he looked, but mostly he listened.

The stream always had been a laughing friend to Andy. The water came down from the hills clear and pure. Now, as he looked and listened, the stream became something else. Strange glugging sounds seemed to come from it. It was like the sound of cattle caught in wet sand, struggling to pull themselves free.

It was a kind of a suction sound, frightening and unreal.

Standing on the fallen elm log, looking and listening, Andy was now sure something was out there and coming down the stream toward him.

He had spent all of his fifteen years living on the farm. He had always said that nothing on the farm could ever frighten him, but he was frightened now.

What he saw slowly emerging from the fog was the faintest of outlines. It was not coming fast. Instead it seemed to be plodding along, step-by-step, pushing its way through the water. The splash, as it lifted its long legs, came more clearly to him. For long seconds he stood paralyzed by the fearsome sight.

In the dim light, he still could not see what it was. It had to be big to be able to walk in the middle of the stream. *Very big.*

Without quite realizing what he was doing, he raised his rifle and aimed it in the direction of the approaching creature. But he did not fire. He still could not see well enough to risk a shot.

He tried not to panic. One of the bigger branches of the dead elm offered a higher perch. Quickly he climbed. It was about eight or ten feet above the ground.

He peered off toward the east. A light glow was beginning to show. Day was not too far off. But would daylight help? While it would reveal what sort of beast he faced, it would also show the beast where *he* was.

He looked back at the stream. Whatever was approaching was now only forty or fifty feet away—close enough for him to see that it had form. But what was it?

A new shiver of fear ran through him as he tried to make it out. It had a pale, spectral, ghostlike appearance. There came back to him stories he had heard old-timers tell of a strange, mysterious creature that had once roamed through the great forest. But no one had seen it since pioneer days. Could this be it, a survival of those early days when men lived close to nature?

The sound of its slow movement through the water could now be heard more plainly. Andy also could hear the beast's angry snorting.

He had always believed that ghostly creatures didn't make noise. This one most certainly did. He shuddered as he watched with horror as the fog, the darkness, and the misty shape combined to blind him to what it really looked like. If only Champ were here to protect him. Champ would know what to do.

Would there be time to get down from the elm and dash back to the house? Flight was the only thing he could think of. He knew his little .22 would be useless against a thing that was only half-real, or maybe not real at all.

The creature had stopped. Evidently it had sighted him.

Andy groaned in despair. Again he raised his gun. With trembling hands, he tried to aim. He knew it was no use. The light was still too poor, and he was shaking too badly.

With a bellowing roar, the beast plunged forward through the water, splashing furiously as it came. In desperation, Andy aimed his gun and fired, emptying it in his hurry. Still the creature came on.

Andy cried out, horror-stricken at the huge, misty shape charging toward him. Was this something he was dreaming? Surely there was no creature like this anywhere on Earth—so real and yet so unreal.

He closed his eyes, unable to watch any longer. Then he heard it!

From the direction of the house, he heard the rising sound of Champ's familiar booming voice. The dog's long-haired, golden body did not appear out of the still-hovering fog until he was less than fifty feet away. He was coming at top speed, his long tail straight out behind him. His growl was strong and full.

With terror-stricken eyes, Andy watched as Champ plunged straight at the huge creature. The beast lowered its head and prepared to crush the dog in its rage. At the last second Champ moved sideways and snapped at one of the beast's rear legs. For only a second or two he held the leg firmly in his teeth. Then, before the huge animal could twist around, Champ had leaped back out of danger.

What surprised and shocked Andy was to see Champ, apparently completely recovered from his injuries. There were no torn patches of fur, not even any bandages. And from the way he dodged in and out, he was the Champ of old—ferociously leading the creature back away from the tree where Andy was clinging precariously.

As the light improved, Andy could see that the beast had only four legs and one head. But the pale, spectral look remained.

In a few minutes, Champ had worked the creature back into the stream. As he watched from his perch, Andy saw the two animals gradually fade from his sight. Even the sound of their fighting—the creature's bellowing and Champ's booming voice—diminished, until he could hear nothing. At that moment the sun slipped up over the eastern horizon.

Andy climbed down from the tree and hurried back to the house. It had been a miracle. When he left Champ, the dog was hardly able to move. What he had seen was Champ at his very best. And somehow he had driven the strange beast away.

The boy quietly opened the door. He left it open for Champ to get back in. Then he moved carefully and silently up the stairs to his room.

Going in, he went to the window to look out. Daylight had come. Then he turned back; he couldn't believe what he saw!

There, on his rug, lay Champ, moaning and whimpering, just as Andy had left him. Obviously he hadn't moved. The bandages were still around his wounds. Even now, as the dog looked up at his master, he tried to struggle to his feet, only to fall back in weakness.

Andy sank to his knees next to his dog and hugged him. His eyes filled with tears.

What really had happened? Was it all a bad dream? No, it couldn't be. There was mud on his feet. His .22 was empty.

The beast? What was it? Something from another time, another place, come back by accident?

And Champ? Had Champ's love for him been so strong that he could send his spirit out to battle with the spirit-beast?

Something strange had happened. Looking into the dog's love-filled eyes, he knew Champ would tell him if he could only speak. *If* he could only speak. . . .

Close Up

1. Champ comes home badly beaten and frightened. Why does Andy have trouble determining what animal hurt Champ?

2. Andy is awakened by Champ's moaning. Why does Andy go out into the night?

3. Andy sees an awesome creature emerging from the dense fog. (a) Why is he sure it must be very big? (b) What does he think the creature might be?

4. Champ arrives to battle the creature and protect Andy. How does Champ's appearance tell you that something supernatural is happening?

5. As the sun rises, Champ and the beast fade away. (a) What does Andy find when he returns to his room? (b) How does he know he didn't have a nightmare?

Setting and Mood

The setting of a story may create a special mood or feeling. Some settings create a mood of fear. For example, if the setting of a story is a barren forest, thick with fog or mist, you might feel afraid and expect frightening events to occur. Mood also may be heightened by image-producing words.

1. The setting of this story is a great forest. What stories do the old-timers tell about this place?

2. Andy thought he would never be afraid of the forest. How does the fog make the forest unfamiliar and unreal?

3. Image-producing words also help create a mood of fear. Words and phrases help you see the scene the author wants to create. Below is a list of phrases from the story. Which ones help create a mood of fear?
   a. bravest of all creatures
   b. scary, thin light
   c. thickness of dark
   d. mud felt like quicksand
   e. glugging sounds
   f. bellowing roar
   g. pale, spectral and ghost-like
   h. angry snorting
   i. misty shape
   j. familiar, booming voice
   k. long-haired, with a golden body
   l. strong and full growl

Activity

▶ **Composition.** Write a paragraph describing a scary setting. Be sure to include many image-rich words.

INFERENCES

Some stories contain both realistic (like life) and supernatural, or unreal, details. It is important not to confuse the two.

▶ Label each one of the following happenings as either *fantastic* (highly unusual and difficult to explain) or *realistic* (could happen without any supernatural power at work—easy to explain).

a. Champ had lost a fight, but not to another dog or to any typical forest animal.

b. Patches of Champ's golden hair had been torn away.

c. Andy's mother permitted Champ to sleep in Andy's room that night.

d. All of the farm buildings looked different that night. They looked unreal and alien.

e. Strange glugging sounds seemed to come from the stream.

f. Something was walking down the middle of the stream, which was too deep for farm or forest animals.

g. Andy raised his rifle and aimed at the slowly approaching creature.

h. Champ appeared out of the fog and saved Andy from the beast, although Champ was badly injured when Andy had left him.

i. When Andy got home, his boots were muddy and his .22 was empty.

j. Champ was still lying in Andy's room, badly injured, although Andy had just seen him healthy and able to drive off the huge beast.

WORD ATTACK

Understanding Adverbs

An adverb is a word that often modifies a verb or an adjective. That is, an adverb gives you more information about the action by answering one of the following questions: Where? When? How? To what extent? Take this sentence: He *vaguely* could see a creature emerging from the fog. The adverb *vaguely* tells you *how* he could see. Often you can spot an adverb by its *-ly* ending.

▶ Use a dictionary to find the meaning of each of the following *italicized* adverbs.

a. "The dog's eyes looked up at him *beseechingly*, as though trying to tell him what had caused the rips and tears."

b. "Every once in a while, the dog would give a yelp of pain, then sigh *wearily*."

c. "He was *obviously* afraid of something. . . something that had fought with him, something outside the house."

d. "The splash, as it lifted its long legs, came more *clearly* to him."

e. "*Evidently* it had sighted him."

f. "With a bellowing roar, the beast plunged forward through the water, splashing *furiously* as it came."

g. "And from the way he dodged in and out, he was the Champ of old—*ferociously* leading the creature back away from the tree. . . ."

h. ". . . where Andy was clinging *precariously*."

i. "As he watched from his perch, Andy saw the two animals *gradually* fade from his sight."

j. "What surprised and shocked Andy was to see Champ, *apparently* . . . recovered from his injuries."

The Tinker and the Ghost

Ralph Steele Boggs and
Mary Gould Davis

A Spanish Ghost Story

On the wide plain not far from the city of Toledo, there once stood a great gray Castle. For many years before this story begins, no one had dwelt there, because the Castle was haunted. There was no living soul within its walls; and yet, on almost every night in the year, a thin, sad voice moaned and wept and wailed through the huge, empty rooms. And on All Hallows' Eve, a ghostly light appeared in the chimney, a light that flared and died and flared again against the dark sky.

Learned doctors and brave adventurers had tried to banish the ghost. And the next morning, they had been found in the great hall of the Castle, sitting lifeless before the empty fireplace.

Now, one day in late October, there came to the little village that nestled around the Castle walls a brave and jolly tinker whose name was Esteban. And while he sat in the market place mending the pots and pans, the good wives told him about the haunted Castle. It was All

Hallows' Eve, they said; and if he would wait until nightfall, he could see the strange, ghostly light flare up from the chimney. He might, if he dared go near enough, hear the thin, sad voice echo through the silent rooms.

"If I dare!" Esteban repeated scornfully. "You must know, good wives, that I—Esteban—fear nothing, neither ghost nor human. I will gladly sleep in the Castle tonight, and keep this dismal spirit company."

The good wives looked at him in amazement. Did Esteban know that if he succeeded in banishing the ghost, the owner of the Castle would give him a thousand gold *reales*?[1]

Esteban chuckled. If that was how matters stood, he would go to the Castle at nightfall and do his best to get rid of the thing that haunted it. But he was a man who liked plenty to eat and drink, and a fire to keep him company. They must bring to him a load of firewood, a side of bacon, a flask of wine, a dozen fresh eggs, and a frying pan. This the good wives gladly did. And as the dusk fell, Esteban loaded these things on the donkey's back and set out for the Castle. And you may be very sure that not one of the village people went very far along the way with him!

It was a dark night with a chill wind blowing and a hint of rain in the air. Esteban unsaddled his donkey and set him to graze on the short grass of the deserted courtyard. Then he carried his food and his firewood into the great hall. It was dark as pitch there. Bats beat their soft wings in his face, and the air felt cold and musty. He lost no time in piling some of his sticks in one corner of the huge stone fireplace and in lighting them. As the red and golden flames leaped up the chimney, Esteban rubbed his hands. Then he settled himself comfortably on the hearth.

"*That* is the thing to keep off both cold and fear," he said.

Carefully slicing some bacon, he laid it in the pan and set it over the flames. How good it smelled! And how cheerful the sound of its crisp sizzling!

He had just lifted his flask to take a deep drink of the good wine when down the chimney there came a voice—a thin, sad voice—and "*Oh, me!*" it wailed, "*Oh, me! Oh, me!*"

Esteban swallowed the wine and set the flask carefully down beside him.

"Not a very cheerful greeting, my friend," he said, as he moved the bacon on the pan so that it should be equally brown in all its parts. "But bearable to a man who is used to the braying of his donkey."

And, "*Oh, me!*" sobbed the voice. "*Oh, me! Oh, me!*"

Esteban lifted the bacon carefully from the hot fat and laid it on a bit of brown paper to drain. Then he broke an egg into the frying pan. As he gently shook the pan so that the edges of his egg should be crisp and brown and the yolk soft, the voice came again. Only this time it was shrill and frightened.

"*Look out below,*" it called. "*I'm falling!*"

"All right," answered Esteban. "Only don't fall into the frying pan."

With that, there was a thump, and there on the hearth lay a man's leg! It was a good enough leg and it was clothed in half of a pair of brown corduroy trousers.

---

1. reales (rā-ä′lāz) n.: Coins of Spain.

Esteban ate his egg, a piece of bacon, and drank again from the flask of wine. The wind howled around the Castle and the rain beat against the windows.

Then, *"Look out below,"* called the voice sharply. *"I'm falling!"*

There was a thump, and on the hearth there lay a second leg, just like the first!

Esteban moved it away from the fire and piled on more sticks. Then he warmed the fat in the frying pan and broke into it a second egg.

And, *"Look out below!"* roared the voice. And now it was no longer thin, but strong and lusty. *"Look out below! I'm falling!"*

"Fall away," Esteban answered cheerfully. "Only don't spill my egg."

There was a thump, heavier than the first two, and on the hearth there lay a trunk. It was clothed in a blue shirt and a brown corduroy coat.

Esteban was eating his third egg and the last of the cooked bacon, when the voice called again; and down fell first one arm and then the other.

"Now," thought Esteban, as he put the frying pan on the fire and began to cook more bacon. "Now there is only the head. I confess that I am rather curious to see the head."

And, "LOOK OUT BELOW!" thundered the voice. "I'M FALLING—FALLING!"

And down the chimney there came tumbling a head!

It was a good enough head, with thick black hair, a long black beard, and dark eyes that looked a little strained and anxious. Esteban's bacon was only half-cooked. Nevertheless, he removed the pan from the fire and laid it on the hearth. And it is a good thing that he did, because, before his eyes, the parts of the body joined together, and a living man—or his ghost—stood before him! And *that* was a sight that might have startled Esteban into burning his fingers with the bacon fat.

"Good evening," said Esteban. "Will you have an egg and a bit of bacon?"

"No, I want no food," the ghost answered. "But I will tell you this, right here and now. You are the only man, out of all those who have come to the Castle, to stay here until I could get my body together again. The others died of sheer fright before I was half finished."

"That is because they did not have sense enough to bring food and fire with them," Esteban replied coolly. And he turned back to his frying pan.

"Wait a minute!" pleaded the ghost. "If you will help me a bit more, you will save my soul and get me into the Kingdom of Heaven. Out in the courtyard, under a cypress tree, there are buried three bags—one of copper coins, one of silver coins, and one of gold coins. I stole them from some thieves and brought them here to the Castle to hide. But no sooner did I have them buried, than the thieves overtook me, murdered me, and cut my body into pieces. But they did not find the coins. Now, you come with me and dig them up. Give the copper coins to the Church, the silver coins to the poor, and keep the gold coins for yourself. Then I will have paid for my sins and can go to the Kingdom of Heaven."

This suited Esteban. So he went out into the courtyard with the ghost. And you should have heard how the donkey brayed when he saw them!

When they reached the cypress tree in a corner of the courtyard, "Dig," said the ghost.

"Dig yourself," answered Esteban.

So the ghost dug, and after a time the three bags of money appeared.

"Now, will you promise to do just what I asked you to do?" asked the ghost.

"Yes, I promise," Esteban answered.

"Then," said the ghost, "Strip my garments from me."

This Esteban did, and instantly the ghost disappeared, leaving his clothes lying there on the short grass of the courtyard. It went straight up to Heaven and knocked on the Gate. St. Peter opened it and, when the spirit explained that he had paid for his sins, gave him a cordial welcome.

Esteban carried the coins into the great hall of the Castle, fried and ate another egg, and then went peacefully to sleep before the fire.

The next morning, when the village people came to carry away Esteban's body, they found him making an omelette out of the last of the fresh eggs.

"Are you alive?" they gasped.

"I am," Esteban answered. "And the food and the firewood lasted through very nicely. Now I will go to the owner of the Castle and collect my thousand gold *reales*. The ghost has gone for good and all. You will find his clothes lying out in the courtyard."

And before their astonished eyes, he loaded the bags of coins on the donkey's back and departed.

First he collected the thousand gold *reales* from the grateful lord of the Castle. Then he returned to Toledo, gave the copper coins to the *cura*[2] of his church, and faithfully distributed the silver ones among the poor. And on the thousand *reales* and the golden coins he lived in idleness and great contentment for many years.

---

2. cura (cyŏo-rá) n.: A clergyman who assists the pastor.

1. Esteban is "a man who likes plenty to eat and drink and a fire to keep him company." What supplies does he request?

2. While Esteban prepares his meal, the ghost begins to wail. Does Esteban's reaction show that he is more concerned with the ghost or with having a good meal? Why?

3. (a) What does the ghost want Esteban to do? (b) What sin must the ghost pay for?

4. (a) How does Esteban use the reward money? (b) Did you expect him to use it this way? Why or why not?

Setting and Mood

When events in the story are the opposite of what you expected, humor sometimes results. Some settings make you anticipate certain events. For example, when the setting of a story is a haunted castle, you expect the characters to react with terror. Humor results when you find the characters to be more concerned about food than about their lives.

1. This story is humorous because you expect Esteban to act one way, and he acts just the opposite. (a) How would you expect Esteban to act when he hears the ghostly voice say, "*Oh, me!*"? (b) How does he react?

2. (a) What does Esteban do while the body of the ghost falls piece by piece? (b) Why is this behavior unusual?

3. What does Esteban say to the ghost that is unusual, once the parts of the ghost's body are all joined together?

4. The ghost explains where the coins are buried and tells Esteban to dig. (a) Do you expect a person to talk back to a ghost? (b) What does Esteban say to the ghost?

Activities

1. **Composition.** Be the castle owner and write a newspaper advertisement for someone to remove a ghost from your castle.

2. **Composition.** Write a paragraph about one of the following topics, or make up your own topic:
   a. a vampire who prefers milk to blood
   b. a cowardly lion tamer
   c. an astronaut who is afraid of heights
   d. a frog turned into a prince

INFERENCES

Making Inferences About Tone

Tone is the attitude or feeling of the author toward what he or she has written or said. For example, the tone may be joking or serious, or it may be angry or admiring. When you read, you can infer the author's tone by looking carefully at the author's choice of words and details, and by determining the author's purpose.

1. How would you describe the tone of this story?
   a. serious and inspirational
   b. convincing or persuasive
   c. light-hearted and comical
   d. angry and resentful

2. Which of the following details support your inference about the writer's tone?
   a. Esteban liked nothing better than having plenty to eat and drink and a fire to keep him company.
   b. Esteban promised to do what the ghost asked.
   c. Esteban greeted the ghost by offering him an egg and a bit of bacon.
   d. When the people came to carry Esteban's body away, they found him eating an omelette.
   e. The villagers found the ghost's clothing lying out in the courtyard.

3. What do you think was the author's purpose for writing this story?
   a. to convince you that tinkers are not frightened by ghosts
   b. to entertain and amuse you
   c. to frighten you
   d. to inform you about eating customs in Spain

WORD ATTACK

Using Context to Find the Meaning of Unfamiliar Words

Sometimes you need to look up unfamiliar words in a dictionary. However, in many cases, you can find the meaning of those words by looking at the context—the other words surrounding the word you do not know. You may find clues to the meaning in the rest of the sentence, or in surrounding sentences.

▶ Use context to answer the questions following the excerpts below.

a. "And on All Hallows' Eve, a *ghostly* light appeared in the chimney, a light that flared and died and flared again against the dark sky."

What did the light look like?

b. ". . . a brave and jolly *tinker* whose name was Esteban. And while he sat in the market place mending the pots and pans . . ."

What is a tinker?

c. "As the red and golden flames leaped up the chimney, Esteban rubbed his hands. Then he settled himself comfortably on the *hearth*."

What must a hearth be?

d. "But he was a man who liked plenty to eat and drink, and a fire to keep him company. They must bring to him a load of firewood, a *side* of bacon, a *flask* of wine, . . ."

Would a side of bacon be a large or small piece for one man?

What must a flask be?

e. "It was a good enough leg and it was clothed in half a pair of brown *corduroy* trousers."

What must corduroy be?

The Tinker and the Ghost   **327**

In the Fog

Milton Geiger

Characters

The Doctor

Zeke

Eben

Filling Station Attendant

Sets: *A signpost on Pennsylvania Route 30. A rock or stump in the fog. A gas station pump.*

Night. At first we can only see fog drifting across a dark scene devoid[1] of detail. Then, out of the fog, there emerges toward us a white roadside signpost with a number of white painted signboards pointing to right and to left. The marker is a Pennsylvania State Route—marked characteristically "PENNA-30." *Now, a light as from a far headlight sweeps the signs.*

An automobile approaches. The car pulls up close. We hear the car door open and slam, and a man's footsteps

---

1. devoid: Lacking; empty.

approaching on the concrete. Now the signs are lit up again by a more localized, smaller source of light. The light grows stronger as the man, offstage, approaches. The Doctor enters, holding a flashlight before him. He scrutinizes[2] the road marker. He flashes his light up at the arrows. We see the legends on the markers. Pointing off right there are markers that read: York, Columbia, Lancaster; pointing left the signs read: Fayetteville, McConnellsburg, Pennsylvania Turnpike.

The Doctor's face is perplexed and annoyed as he turns his flashlight on a folded road map. He is a bit lost in the fog. Then his flashlight fails him. It goes out!

Doctor: Darn! *[He fumbles with the flashlight in the gloom. Then a voice is raised to him from offstage.]*

Eben *[offstage, strangely]:* Turn around, mister. . . . *[The Doctor turns sharply to stare offstage.]*

Zeke *[offstage]:* You don't have to be afraid, mister. . . .

[The Doctor sees two men slowly approaching out of the fog. One carries a lantern below his knees. The other holds a heavy rifle. Their features are utterly indistinct as they approach, and the rifleman holds up his gun with quiet threat.]

Eben: You don't have to be afraid.

Doctor *[more indignant than afraid]:* So you say! Who are you, man?

Eben: We don't aim to hurt you none.

Doctor: That's reassuring. I'd like to know just what you mean by this? This gun business! Who are you?

---

2. **scrutinizes** (skro͞ot′n-īz′əz) *v.:* Examines closely.

Zeke *[mildly]:* What's your trade, mister?

Doctor: I . . . I'm a doctor. Why?

Zeke *[to Eben]:* Doctor.

Eben *[nods; then to Doctor]:* Yer the man we want.

Zeke: Ye'll do proper, we're thinkin'.

Eben: So ye'd better come along, mister.

Zeke: Aye.

Doctor: Why? Has—anyone been hurt?

Eben: It's for you to say if he's been hurt nigh to the finish.

Zeke: So we're askin' ye to come along, doctor.

[The Doctor looks from one to another in indecision and puzzlement.]

Eben: In the name o' mercy.

Zeke: Aye.

Doctor: I want you to understand— I'm not afraid of your gun! I'll go to your man all right. Naturally, I'm a doctor. But I demand to know who you are.

Zeke *[patiently]:* Why not? Raise yer lantern, Eben. . . .

Eben *[tiredly]:* Aye.

[Eben lifts his lantern. Its light falls on their faces now, and we see that they are terrifying. Matted beards, clotted with blood; crude head bandages, crusty with dirt and dry blood. Their hair, stringy and disheveled. Their faces are lean and hollow-cheeked; their eyes sunken and tragic. The Doctor is shocked for a moment—then bursts out——]

Doctor: Good Lord!—

Zeke: That's Eben; I'm Zeke.

Doctor: What's happened? Has there been an accident or . . . what?

Zeke: Mischief's happened, stranger.

Eben: Mischief enough.

Doctor [*looks at rifle at his chest*]: There's been gunplay—hasn't there?

Zeke [*mildly ironic[3]*]: Yer tellin' us there's been gunplay!

Doctor: And I'm telling you that I'm not at all frightened! It's my duty to report this, and report it I will!

Zeke: Aye, mister. You *do* that.

Doctor: You're arrogant about it now! You don't think you'll be caught and dealt with. But people are losing patience with you men. . . You . . . you moonshiners![4] Running wild . . . a law unto yourselves . . . shooting up the countryside!

Zeke: Hear that, Eben? Moonshiners.

Eben: Mischief's happened, mister, we'll warrant that. . . .

Doctor: And I don't like it!

Zeke: Can't say we like it better'n you do, mister. . . .

Eben [*strangely sad and remote*]: What must be, must.

Zeke: There's no changin' or goin' back, and all 'at's left is the wishin' things were different.

Eben: Aye.

Doctor: And while we talk, your wounded man lies bleeding, suppose—worthless though he may be. Well? I'll have to get my instrument bag, you know. It's in the car.

[*Eben and Zeke part to let Doctor pass between them. The Doctor reenters, carrying his medical bag.*]

Doctor: I'm ready. Lead the way.

[*Eben lifts his lantern a bit and goes first. Zeke prods the Doctor ever so*

gently and apologetically, but firmly with the rifle muzzle. The Doctor leaves. Zeke strides off slowly after them.*]

[*A wounded man is lying against a section of stone fence. He, too, is bearded, though very young, and his shirt is dark with blood. He breathes but never stirs otherwise. Eben enters, followed by the Doctor and Zeke.*]

Zeke: Ain't stirred a mite since we left 'im.

Doctor: Let's have that lantern here! [*The Doctor tears the man's shirt for better access to the wound.*]

Doctor [*softly*]: Dreadful! Dreadful. . .!

Zeke's voice [*off-scene*]: Reckon it's bad in the chest like that, hey?

Doctor [*taking pulse*]: His pulse is positively racing . . . !

Doctor: How long has he been this way?

Zeke: A long time, mister. A long time. . . .

Doctor [*to Eben*]: You! Hand me my bag.

[*Eben puts down lantern and hands bag to Doctor. The Doctor opens bag and takes out a couple of retractors.[5] Zeke holds lantern close now.*]

Doctor: Lend me a hand with these retractors. [*He works on the man.*] All right . . . when I tell you to draw back on the retractors—draw back.

Eben: Aye.

Zeke: How is 'e, mister?

Doctor [*preoccupied*]: More retraction. Pull them a bit more. Hold it. . . .

Eben: Bad, ain't he?

---

3. ironic (ī-rŏn′ĭk) *adj.*: Meaning the opposite of what is said.

4. moonshiners: Persons who make illegal whiskey during the night.

---

5. retractors: Instruments to hold apart the edges of a wound during an operation.

Doctor: Bad enough. The bullet didn't touch any lung tissue far as I can see right now. There's some pneumothorax[6] though. All I can do now is plug the wound. There's some cotton and gauze wadding in my bag. Find it. . . .

[Zeke probes about silently in the bag and comes up with a small dark box of gauze.]

Doctor: That's it. [Works a moment in silence.] I've never seen anything quite like it.

Eben: Yer young, doctor. Lots o' things you've never seen.

Doctor: Adhesive tape!

[Zeke finds a roll of three-inch tape and hands it to the Doctor, who tears off longs strips and slaps them on the dressing and pats and smooths them to man's chest. Eben replaces equipment in Doctor's bag and closes it with a hint of the finality to come. A preview of dismissal, so to speak.]

Doctor [at length]: There. So much for that. Now then—[Takes man's shoulders.] Give me a hand here.

Zeke [quiet suspicion]: What fer?

Doctor: We've got to move this man.

Zeke: What fer?

Doctor [stands; indignantly]: We've got to get him to a hospital for treatment; a thorough cleansing of the wound; irrigation.[7] I've done all I can for him here.

Zeke: I reckon he'll be all right 'thout no hospital.

Doctor: Do you realize how badly this man's hurt!

---

6. pneumothorax (no͞o′mō-thôr′ăks′) n.: Condition caused by injury to the lining of the lungs.
7. irrigation: Application of a continuous stream of liquid to an affected part for cleansing.

Eben: He won't bleed to death, will he?

Doctor: I don't think so—not with that plug and pressure dressing. But bleeding isn't the only danger we've got to——

Zeke [interrupts]: All right, then. Much obliged to you.

Doctor: This man's *dangerously* hurt!

Zeke: Reckon he'll pull through now, thanks to you.

Doctor: I'm glad you feel that way about it! But I'm going to report this to the Pennsylvania State Police at the first telephone I reach!

Zeke: We ain't stoppin' ye, mister.

Eben: Fog is liftin', Zeke. Better be done with this, I say.

Zeke [nods, sadly]: Aye. Ye can go now, mister . . . and thanks.

Zeke [continues]: We never meant a mite o' harm, I can tell ye. If we killed, it was no wish of ours.

Eben: What's done is done. Aye.

Zeke: Ye can go now, stranger. . . .

[Eben hands Zeke the Doctor's bag. Zeke hands it gently to the Doctor.]

Doctor: Very well. You haven't heard the last of this, though!

Zeke: That's the truth, mister. We've killed, aye; and we've been hurt for it. . . .

Eben: Hurt bad.

[The Doctor's face is puckered with doubt and strange apprehension.]

Zeke: We're not alone, mister. We ain't the only ones. (Sighs.) Ye can go now, doctor . . . and our thanks to ye. . . .

[The Doctor leaves the other two, still gazing at them in strange enchantment and wonder and a touch of indignation.]

Eben's voice: Thanks, mister. . . .

Zeke's voice: In the name o' mercy. . . . We thank you. . . .

Eben: In the name o' mercy.

Zeke: Thanks, mister. . . .

Eben: In the name o' kindness. . . .

[The two men stand with their wounded comrade at their feet—like a group statue in the park. The fog thickens across the scene. Far off the long, sad wail of a locomotive whimpers in the dark.]

[The scene now shifts to a young Attendant standing in front of a gasoline pump taking a reading and recording it in a book as he prepares to close up. He turns as he hears the car approach on the gravel drive.]

[The Doctor enters.]

Attendant *[pleasantly]*: Good evening, sir. *[Nods off at car.]* Care to pull 'er up to this pump, sir? Closing up.

Doctor *[impatiently]*: No. Where's your telephone, please? I've just been held up!

Attendant: Pay station inside, sir. . . .

Doctor: Thank you! *[The Doctor starts to go past the Attendant.]*

Attendant: Excuse me, sir. . . .

Doctor *[stops]*: Eh, what is it, what is it?

Attendant: Uh . . . what sort of looking fellows were they?

Doctor: Oh—two big fellows with a rifle; faces and heads bandaged and smeared with dirt and blood. Friend of theirs with a gaping hole in his chest. I'm a doctor, so they forced me to attend him. Why?

Attendant: *Those* fellers, huh?

Doctor: Then you know about them!

Attendant: I guess so.

Doctor: They're armed and they're desperate!

Attendant: That was about two or three miles back, would you say?

Doctor *[fumbling in pocket]*: Just about—I don't seem to have the change. I wonder if you'd spare me change for a quarter . . . ?

Attendant *[makes change from metal coin canister at his belt]*: Certainly, sir. . . .

Doctor: What town was that back there, now?

Attendant *[dumps coins in other's hand]*: There you are, sir.

Doctor *[impatient]*: Yes, thank you. I say—what town was that back there, so I can tell the police?

Attendant: That was . . . Gettysburg, mister. . . .

Doctor: Gettysburg . . . ?

Attendant: Gettysburg and Gettysburg battlefield. . . . *[Looks off.]* When it's light and the fog's gone, you can see the gravestones. Meade's men . . . Pickett's men, Robert E. Lee's. . . .

[The Doctor is looking off with the Attendant; now he turns his head slowly to stare at the other man.]

Attendant *[continues]*: On nights like this—well—you're not the first those men've stopped . . . or the last. *[Nods off.]* Fill'er up, mister?

Doctor: Yes, fill 'er up. . . .

Close Up

1. When the doctor stops to check his location and the road signs, he is approached by two strangers who come out of the fog. Although the doctor is annoyed and somewhat frightened, he goes with the strangers. Why?

2. The doctor assumes the strangers are moonshiners, people who make and sell whiskey illegally. (a) What do the strangers say when the doctor threatens to report them? (b) Why does the doctor think they say this?

3. Many of the strangers' statements have double meanings. They say one thing but imply much more. What does Eben really mean when he tells the doctor, "Yer young, doctor. Lots o' things you've never seen"?

4. The doctor later stops his car to call the police. (a) Where does he learn that he was? (b) Who does he learn that the men were?

Setting and Mood

Darkness or weather conditions such as rain or fog often create a mood of mystery because details of the surroundings are hidden.

1. The doctor is lost somewhere on the Pennsylvania Turnpike. What weather conditions prevent him from knowing exactly where he is?

2. The only lights on the road are from passing cars and the doctor's flashlight. (a) What happens to the flashlight? (b) Do you think this makes the setting more mysterious? Why or why not?

3. The fog also seems to muffle the noise. The only sound heard is the "long sad wail of a locomotive that whimpers in the dark." (a) Do you think this sound adds to the mood of mystery? Why or why not? (b) Why is it appropriate that you do not hear car traffic noise from the Turnpike?

Activities

1. If you were to record this play as a radio drama, what sound effects would you need?

2. Imagine you are the costume designer for a production of this play. Sketch costume designs for two characters. (You might want to do some research on Civil War uniforms.)

INFERENCES

Making Inferences About Time

You can infer the time period of a story by using certain clues. Among these clues are clothing styles, equipment (tools and supplies), and the way characters speak.

1. When the play begins, the setting is present-day Pennsylvania. List three clues that help you infer this time period.

2. By reading between the lines, you find that the time period changes from the present to the past, as the strangers emerge from the fog. Which of the following clues help you to make this inference?
   a. The strangers have unusual names—Zeke and Eben.
   b. One stranger carries an old lantern and another carries a heavy rifle.
   c. The strangers are crusty with dirt and dry blood.
   d. Zeke and Eben speak in an old-fashioned style. They say "Ain't stirred a mite since we left 'im" and "Mischief's happened mister, we'll warrant that. . . ."
   e. The strangers' faces are lean.

3. The light bulb was not invented until 1879. Why do you think the doctor's flashlight goes out as soon as the time changes to the past?

4. Knowing the exact place of the story helps you to infer the time period. (a) Where does the doctor meet the strangers? (b) How does knowing the history of this place help you infer the time period?

WORD ATTACK

Understanding Dialect

Language changes. At one time the word *aye* was commonly used. Now *aye* has been replaced by *yes*. Language also differs from culture to culture, and from place to place. Differences in word use and word pronunciation within a language are called dialect differences. In Boston, for example, the r in the word *park* is not pronounced. Bostonians go for a walk in the "pock" or "pock" their cars. In some parts of the South, it is not unusual to hear the words *you all* blended together. Some people drop the -ing sound off words. They might say, "I've been walkin' all day." To make their characters more realistic, authors sometimes write in the dialect their characters would use. Authors also use an *apostrophe* (walkin') on some words to show that some letters are missing from the way the word is usually spelled.

▶ The *italicized* words and phrases are written in the dialect of the characters in the play, "In the Fog." Rewrite each sentence in standard English.

   a. "We don't *aim* to hurt you *none*."
   b. "*Ye'll* do *proper*, we're *thinkin'*."
   c. "So we're *askin'* *ye* to come along, doctor."
   d. "Raise *yer* lantern, Eben. . . ."
   e. "*Mischief's* happened, stranger."
   f. "Can't say we like it *better'n* you do, mister. . . ."
   g. "There's no *changin'* or *goin'* back, and all *'at's* left is the *wishin'* things were different."
   h. "*Ain't* stirred a *mite* since we left *'im*."
   i. "What *fer*?"
   j. "What's done is done. *Aye*."

REVIEW QUIZ

On the Selections

1. In "The Great Cross-Tunisia Raccoon Chase," Anwar gives Peter a fennec. What is a fennec?

2. In "The Word," Cleel says, "I had never seen one any closer than ship's length away, staring goggle-eyed at us through the window of his aircraft." To whom does the pronoun *one* refer?

3. List two ways in which the Gonzagas' float in "The Christmas Parade" differs from the other floats.

4. In "The Boomer Fireman's Fast Sooner Hound," the people judge that the train must be very slow. What evidence do they use to back up their judgment?

5. In "The Adventure of the Speckled Band," Dr. Roylott pays Holmes a visit. Do you infer from his visit that he is concerned about Helen's safety? Why or why not?

6. In "The Horse Looked At Him," what is the only brand that Poco wears?

7. In "Apartment House," to what does the poet compare the house?

8. In "Spectral Beast in the Night," Andy shows he loves Champ by risking the dangers of the night-time forest. What does Champ do that shows he loves Andy?

9. In "The Tinker and the Ghost," what do the good wives say that causes Esteban to spend a night in the castle?

10. In "In the Fog," Zeke tells the doctor that mischief has happened. (a) What does the doctor think Zeke means by mischief? (b) What does Zeke really mean?

On Inference

1. Read the following list of details. Then infer whether Peter opened Rex's cage door because he liked Anwar or because he wanted to show up Anwar:
   a. Peter thought Anwar was showing off when Anwar spoke in French.
   b. Peter smugly told Anwar that Tunis is small compared to New York.
   c. Peter's eyes almost popped when Anwar told him Tunis is 3000 years old.

2. List three details from "The Word" that help you infer the time—Halloween.

3. Read the following passage. Then infer Jameson's past action—that is, decide what he had just done.

   > "And there was the night in Dundee when the wise little horse waited silently beside a dark doorway, aloof from the stampede of pursuing hoofs, and finally carried Jameson away with two bullets in his arm."

4. Which three of the following details best support Holmes' inference that Roylott is the type of man who could commit murder?
   a. Roylott had lived in India.
   b. Roylott had once killed a man.
   c. Roylott needed money badly.
   d. Roylott had been married to Helen's mother.
   e. Roylott often got into fights.

5. Which one of the following details do you infer is fantastic rather than realistic?
   a. The doctor lost his way in the fog.
   b. The doctor's intrument bag was in the car.
   c. Two men, who spoke as though they were from another time, stepped out of the fog.

COMPOSITION

Description A good descriptive paragraph helps you form a clear picture of something. It makes you feel as though you are actually there, seeing the events, or the characters, or the setting for yourself.

You can write a good descriptive paragraph by using vivid details that appeal to the five senses. By using figurative language and precise verbs, adverbs, and adjectives, you can create a strong impression.

▶ Write a descriptive paragraph using one of the ideas below.
   a. You are Peter Pappas. You want to tell Anwar about a town in the United States in order to impress him. Write a good descriptive paragraph that will help him visualize the town.
   b. You have discovered the spaceship in which the Martians have landed. Write a paragraph describing the ship. Try to include details that create a mood of mystery.
   c. In "The Horse Looked at Him," the author creates a vivid picture of a man trapped on a hot, sun-baked desert. Write a paragraph describing a person trapped on a snow-covered mountain.
   d. Write a paragraph describing the tinker in "The Tinker and the Ghost." Choose words and details that create the impression that the tinker is a jolly fellow.
   e. Take a good look at the street on which you live. Imagine how it looked one hundred years ago or how it will look one hundred years from now. Write a paragraph describing it.

BEFORE GOING ON

Skimming   Skimming is a reading skill that helps you get a quick overview of the content in a reading selection. Skimming is useful for finding out whether or not you want to spend the time reading a selection slowly and carefully. Skimming helps you get some general ideas about the subject of the selection.

A good technique for skimming is to know, first of all, why you are skimming. (Are you thinking the content of the selection might be interesting reading, or do you have some general questions about Kachinas?) When you know your purpose:

1. Study the title to see what information you get from it.

2. Read the first and last paragraphs of the selection.

3. Run your finger down the middle of each page, letting your eyes search the lines of print quickly and letting your mind register key words and impressions.

4. After you finish the last page, collect your thoughts and decide whether or not you have satisfied your purpose. If you have not, repeat the process.

▶ Skim "Kachinas: Sacred Drama of the Hopis" and then answer the questions below.
  a. What does the title lead you to suspect the selection is about?
  b. Would you be interested in reading this selection more slowly and more carefully?
  c. Would this selection help you write a paper for your history class on Hopi customs?
  d. List three things you learned from this selection.

Further Reading

Kachinas: Sacred Drama of the Hopis

Lonnie Dyer

Each December along the high, wind-swept mesas of northern Arizona, a sharp, insistent call shatters the winter calm of a Hopi Indian village. It's a familiar cry from the spirit world of the tribe's ancestors, and it's answered by the echoing voices of every villager: "Kachina! Kachina! Kachina!"

From every corner of the pueblo, Hopi men, women, and children cease work or play and stream into the plaza or onto the rooftops to watch the season's first appearance of the masked, costumed spirit chief.

Like an old man, Soyal Kachina totters on the road to the plaza. He wears

a brown woven shirt, a white kilt and white blanket, and a sash of black yarn across his chest. His simple leather mask has no elaborate painting, merely a tuft of dyed red horsehair on top, with an eagle feather tied to it. An old fox-skin collar keeps out the winter chill. With his right hand, he rattles a dried gourd in rhythm to his stumbling walk. In his left hand, he carries a pouch of cornmeal and four prayer sticks. He moves with great effort. Each tribesman reaches out to him in symbolic help, bending his or her body as if sharing the hard journey, and calling out proud words of encouragement.

When at last Soyal Kachina reaches the plaza, he stops at the entrance to the *kiva* (clubhouse) where the winter ceremonies will soon begin. Standing the four prayer sticks at the door, he draws cornmeal from his pouch and tosses it into the *kiva* from four directions. Turning, he approaches a shrine, sprinkles cornmeal upon it and dances in four places. Then he leaves the village as he came, with a faltering, uncertain gait.

On the narrow road, he is met by a Hopi man who presents him with a blue prayer stick, which he accepts humbly. Then Soyal Kachina disappears down the side of the mesa.

The sacred drama of the Kachinas has begun again, as it has for nearly 2,000 years, to insure rain, good crops, and prosperity for the Hopi tribe.

After the winter solstice, many Kachinas will come to live in the village for six months. They'll offer prayers, sprinkle cornmeal in chosen places, offer medicine to the sick, sing ancient songs, and dance ancient dances. And they will give dolls to young Hopis made especially in a Kachina image. No time is

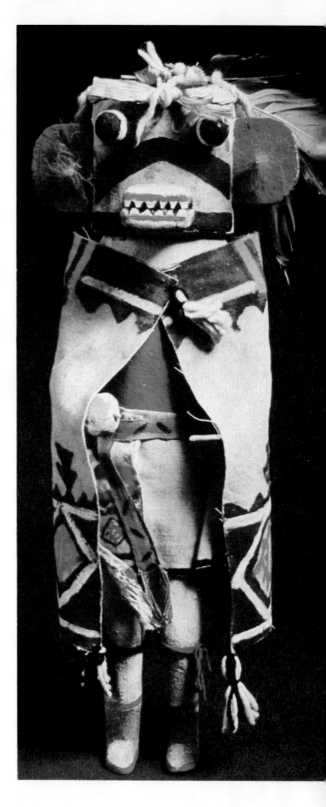

more important in Hopi life than this. It's a time of memory, celebration, and worship; of teaching, discipline, and prayer. Without Kachinas, Hopis believe the tribe would not survive, for like their counterpart in the Christian religion, saints, Kachinas protect, guide, and comfort the Hopi people.

Kachina means many things to a Hopi: a divine ancestral spirit representing nature in plants, animals, and clouds; the masked, painted impersonator of these spirits; and the handcarved dolls given to the young. Each Kachina is distinguished by his costume, coloring, songs, dance steps, call, and bearing. All these things symbolize his personality and powers.

Kachinas are actually spirits; therefore they usually remain unseen. They are made visible, though, by men who have been properly trained and initiated as Kachina impersonators. Female Kachinas are called *Kachin-manas*, but they are always impersonated by men. Every Hopi youngster between the ages of seven and twelve years old who is thought to be wise enough, is instructed in Kachina ritual. Every boy and man takes an active part, as do many girls, but only men can impersonate Kachinas. Although a human dresses as a Kachina, it is believed that he who wears the Kachina mask loses his own identity and becomes the spirit he impersonates.

Because Hopis have no written language, Kachina dolls are used to pass tribal lore and religion down through generations. Given to the young during special dances, Kachina dolls are then hung in the home as constant reminders of Hopi ancestry and heritage. Though too young to understand their meaning, infants are given Kachina paddle dolls as toys, so that from birth they are familiar with Hopi custom.

In winter, Kachina ceremonies are held in the village *kivas*, but when the weather becomes warm in the spring, dancing and singing move outdoors. Most ceremonies have 25 or more Kachinas. Sometimes as many as 125 perform at one time. A chanting chorus usually keeps time to a beating tom-tom, and prayer sticks are planted at holy places.

Kachina ceremonies include not only entertainment and pageantry but also humor. Some of the most popular Kachinas are the clowns. Painted with black-and-white stripes, they cavort and play tricks on spectators to keep them from becoming too sad. Clowns can safely break the most rigid taboos, too. They love to dance around, jump on, and ridicule the mudhead Kachina, who is covered with mud because he once broke tribal law. Mudhead and other special Kachinas teach and remind the Hopi that punishment comes with lawbreaking.

Over many years, Kachina dolls have evolved from plain blocks of wood with simple painted faces to finely carved works of art, often sporting a riot of colors and symbols. Dolls used in ceremonies and given as gifts are sacred and cannot be sold, but many Hopi craftsmen now make dolls especially for sale. Many natural history museums have Kachina dolls in their gift shops.

Because the Hopi are a people whose life on the dry mesas is difficult and uncertain, they find strength, honor, dignity, and peace in their Kachina beliefs. Wherever he or she may wander— at home among the pueblos, alone on the plains, or in alien white man's cities— every Hopi carries close to his heart the traditions and strength of Kachinas.

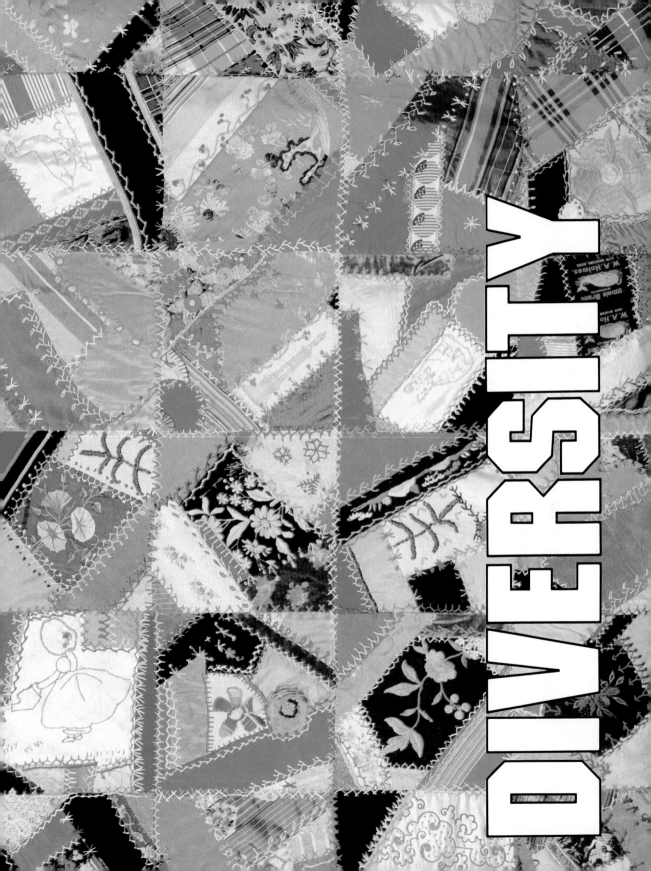

DIVERSITY

Anansi, the African Spider

Adapted by Barbara Winther

Three folk tales from West Africa

I. How Anansi Brought the Stories Down

Characters

Three Storytellers

Nyame, the Sky-god

Anansi, the Spiderman

Crocodile

Monkey

Before rise: Three Storytellers enter before curtain. Each carries African rattle. They stand at one side of stage.

1st Storyteller: We are storytellers from an Ashanti village in Africa.

2nd Storyteller: We are going to tell you three stories about Anansi, the Spiderman.

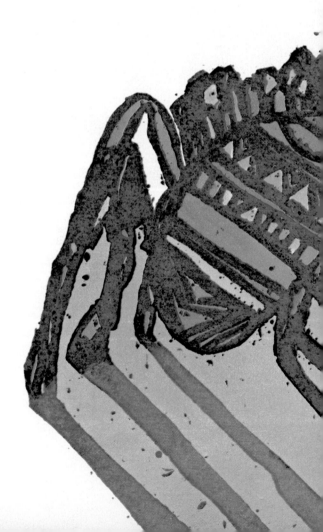

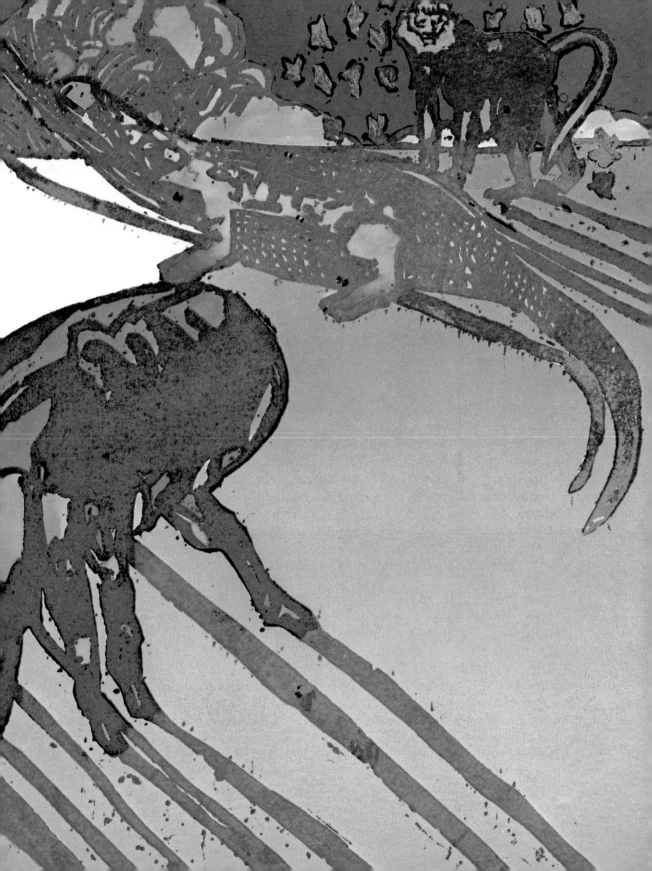

3rd Storyteller: Anansi is a sly, clever spider. For this is his way of living among larger, stronger animals. (*2nd and 3rd Storytellers sit.*)

1st Storyteller: The story I will tell is called, "How Anansi Brought the Stories Down." (*Shakes rattle and curtain opens. Storytellers remain onstage.*)

———————————————

(*Setting: Forest of equatorial Africa. Kola nut tree and berry bush are near center. Hornets' nest hangs from bush, and calabash gourd is on ground. Tall stool is up center.*)

(*At rise: Nyame is sitting on stool, which represents his home in the sky. Anansi enters as if climbing.*)

1st Storyteller: It all happened near the beginning of time, not long after animals were on the earth. Anansi thought it might be fun to tell stories in the evening. But Nyame, the Sky-god, was the owner of all the stories. (*Sits.*)

Nyame: Here comes Anansi, climbing into my sky.

Anansi: Good day to you, Sky-god.

Nyame: *All* my days are good, Anansi.

Anansi: But of course. It is only we poor earth creatures who have bad days.

Nyame: I'm not going to change that. If that's why you've come, go home.

Anansi: No, I'm here for another reason. I want to buy your stories.

Nyame (*thundering*): What? Buy my stories? (*Anansi cringes.*) You dare climb into my sky and ask me to sell you my stories? Great kings have tried to buy them. My stories are not for sale.

Anansi: Don't be angry with me, Sky-god. I'm just a little spider trying to make my way in life. (*Pleading gently*) Isn't there any way I might talk you into giving up your stories?

Nyame (*growling*): What a bother you are.

Anansi: Why? Because I don't give up easily?

Nyame: Oh, all right, Spiderman. If you can show me a crocodile with no teeth, an empty hornets' nest, and a quiet monkey, I'll give you my stories.

Anansi: Sky-god, those things don't exist.

Nyame: But if you're as clever as some say, then you can *make* them exist. Now, go away. I must plan the weather for next week.

Anansi (*pantomiming climbing down*): A crocodile with no teeth, an empty hornets' nest, and a quiet monkey. That will take some doing. (*Sits as Crocodile enters crawling.*)

Crocodile: Hungry! Hungry! (*Opens mouth wide*) I'm so hungry I could eat anything. I'm only happy when I'm eating more and more. (*Crosses stage, peering around for food. Anansi watches thoughtfully, looks offstage, then claps some of his legs together.*)

Anansi: I've got an idea! (*Calling*) Say, Crocodile, I know where you can get a meal.

Crocodile (*hurrying to Anansi*): Where, where, where?

Anansi (*pointing offstage*): Over there.

Crocodile: I don't see anything but a big, green rock.

Anansi: *I* see a plump juicy frog that looks like a rock.

Crocodile: Yum, yum! A plump juicy frog. I see it now. That frog is trying to trick me into thinking it's a rock.

Anansi: Why don't you sneak up quietly on that rock—I mean frog, open your mouth wide, and clamp your jaws shut as hard as you can.

Crocodile: That's just what I'll do. Yum, yum! *(Sneaks offstage. Anansi watches Crocodile's actions offstage. Sound of loud crunch is heard, followed by scattered pings. Crocodile shouts from offstage.)* Ouch! That's the toughest frog I've ever eaten!

Anansi: Aha! *(Calling to Nyame)* Did you see that, Sky-god?

Nyame *(with rumbling laugh)*: Yes, Anansi. Greed broke the crocodile's teeth. Now, find an empty hornets' nest. *(Anansi looks around.)*

Anansi *(spying nest in bush)*: Ah, there's a hornets' nest. *(He crosses to nest. Sound of buzzing hornets is heard.)* But it's full of hornets. *(Picks up calabash gourd, takes off top, and looks inside.)* This calabash gourd looks almost like a hornets' nest. That gives me an idea. *(Yelling)* Hornets, hornets, your home is too small. *(Sound of buzzing is repeated.)* See this? I've brought you a bigger, more beautiful home. Just take a peek and see how much better off you'll be in here. *(Holds up gourd. Buzzing continues. Anansi pantomimes watching hornets enter gourd, one by one. He suddenly bangs down lid and buzzing sound stops.)* Aha! *(Calling to Nyame)* Did you see that, Sky-god?

Nyame *(laughing as before)*: Yes, Anansi. Dissatisfaction emptied the hornets' nest. Find a quiet monkey and my stories are yours.

Anansi: This is going to be the hardest job of all. *(Monkey enters as if swinging from tree to tree.)*

Monkey: Chitter, chitter, chatter. Look how pretty I am. Chitter, chitter, chatter. *(Stops to preen and pose.)* What a perfectly gorgeous monkey I am!

Anansi: I have an idea. *(Sighs loudly, in mock sorrow.)*

Monkey: Hello, Anansi. Is something wrong with you?

Anansi *(sighing again)*: It's not possible. It simply can't be done.

Monkey: What can't be done?

Anansi: There's a great reward for the animal who can stuff its mouth with twenty kola nuts and still talk.

Monkey: Twenty kola nuts? *(Indicates tree)* Like the ones on this tree?

Anansi: Yes, and no one can do it.

Monkey: What's the reward?

Anansi: The animal who succeeds becomes king of the jungle for a week.

Monkey *(excitedly)*: Oh, oh, oh! I must have that reward!

Anansi: But you can't do it.

Monkey: Yes, I can. Just watch me. *(Rushes over to tree and pantomimes stuffing nuts into mouth as Anansi counts quickly from one to twenty.)*

Anansi: Excellent! Excellent! Now talk to me. *(Monkey waves hands as if trying to speak, then points to cheeks, jumps up and down with distress, and finally exits. Anansi calls to Nyame.)* Did you see that, Sky-god?

Nyame *(laughing as before)*: Yes, Anansi. Vanity too made the monkey speechless. I see you understand the ways of the world, Spiderman. From this day on, the Sky-god stories will be known as yours. *(Curtain closes behind Storytellers.)*

Anansi, the African Spider   **351**

II. The First Talking Drum

Characters

Three Storytellers

Forest King

Anansi, the Spiderman

Antelope

Leopard

Crocodile

Monkey

Before Rise: Three Storytellers are sitting onstage. 2nd Storyteller rises.

2nd Storyteller: I will tell you a story called, "The First Talking Drum." *(Shakes rattle. Curtain opens.)*

(Setting: Same as Scene 1. Hornets' nest, stool, and calabash gourd are not onstage.)

(At rise: King and Anansi are talking in pantomime.)

2nd Storyteller: In the early days, there was one Forest King. When he wanted to tell his subjects anything, it took weeks for messengers to reach the farthest villages. This made the King very unhappy.

King: There must be a quicker way. What would I do if an enemy attacked? I would be defeated before help could come.

Anansi: What you need, mighty Forest King, is something to make such a loud noise that everyone in the forest will hear it.

King: But, Spiderman, I know of nothing that can make such a loud noise.

Anansi: I can't think of anything either. But I'll have a meeting with some of the animals. We might come up with an idea. *(King nods and exits one way; Anansi bows and exits the other.)*

2nd Storyteller: That evening the animals met in a secret place in the forest. *(Anansi enters, followed by Crocodile, Antelope, Leopard, and Monkey. Monkey immediately sits down and falls asleep.)*

Anansi: And so, my friends, that's the situation. We must think of the loudest noisemaker there is.

Crocodile: Nyame, the Sky-god, can make thunder. That's the biggest noise I know.

Anansi: True, Crocodile. But Nyame wouldn't let anyone borrow his thunder.

Antelope, Leopard and Crocodile *(ad-lib):* That's right. Of course. Yes. *(Etc. Voices wake Monkey, who nods, then falls asleep again.)*

Leopard: I have some loud cousins. You know—those lions.

Antelope *(leaping up in terror):* Oh, those lions make such frightful roars! We antelope can hear them miles away.

Anansi: I'll admit your cousins are loud, Leopard. But I've never met a lion who was willing to carry a message for anyone. *(Animals ad-lib agreement.)*

Crocodile: Sh-h-h! Listen! *(Animals freeze. Sound of drum beating in distance is heard. Monkey snores.)* Don't listen to Monkey snoring. Listen to the drum beating.

Antelope: It's coming from the village. They must be having a dance.

Anansi: Hm-m-m. A drum makes a loud sound.

Anansi, the African Spider　**353**

Leopard: It can be heard for miles.

Crocodile: But a drum only beats out a rhythm for dancing.

Anansi: Well, why couldn't a drum talk? Different beats could mean different things. And if a drummer were really skilled, he could beat out the sound of a voice.

Crocodile and Leopard *(to each other)*: A talking drum?

Anansi *(waving legs excitedly)*: Yes! Yes! That's it! A giant drum to carry messages far away.

Animals *(ad-lib, excitedly)*: He's got it! A talking drum! Great idea! *(Etc. Noise wakes Monkey again.)*

Monkey: I wish you animals would stop waking me up.

Anansi: It's time you woke up, Monkey. We are all going to make a talking drum for the Forest King.

Crocodile: We crocodiles will find the biggest log by the river.

Leopard: We leopards will use our sharp teeth to hollow out the log.

Antelope: We antelope will give a fine skin to stretch over the drum and thongs to tie down the sides.

Anansi: And I will decorate the drum. What will you do, Monkey?

Monkey *(yawning and scratching)*: I'll pick some berries from this shrub. Then, I'll sit under this tree, and eat them, and watch the rest of you work. *(Others sigh in disgust and exit. Monkey pantomimes picking berries, eating, and chattering.)*

2nd Storyteller: The animals worked very hard making the giant talking drum. All except Monkey. *(Sounds of chomping, chewing, pounding, creaking, and groaning are heard.)* At last the giant talking drum was finished. *(Anan-si, Crocodile, Leopard, and Antelope shove and pull drum onstage. Monkey watches.)*

Anansi: Now that the drum is made, it must be taken to the village and given to the Forest King.

Antelope: That's a long way to travel.

Crocodile: This is a heavy drum.

Leopard: Who shall carry the drum?

Crocodile: Antelope is the fastest. He should carry it.

Antelope: No! Leopard is the strongest. He should carry it.

Leopard: No! Crocodile has the best jaws. He should carry it.

Crocodile: No! I can't go so far from the river.

Anansi: Wait! I know who should carry the drum to the King. It should be the job of the laziest animal. *(Animals ad-lib agreement.)*

Monkey *(leaping up and rushing over)*: Now, see here! I don't feel like doing anything. I'm just going to sit here and eat and talk and *(Voice trails off as he sees other animals staring at him)*— and rest.

Anansi: Well, well, Monkey. We didn't say you were the laziest. You're the one who just admitted it.

Monkey *(sighing)*: You win, Spider-man. All right. I'm the one who has to carry the giant talking drum all the way to the King. *(Starts pushing drum off while others laugh and pat Anansi on back.)*

2nd Storyteller: To this day the talking drum can be heard in the African forest. And when Monkey hears it, he stops his chattering. He sits still and remembers how lazy he was! *(Curtain.)*

III. Tall-Tale Man

Characters

Three Storytellers

Tall-Tale Man

Leopard

Antelope

Anansi, the Spiderman

(Before rise: Three Storytellers are sitting onstage. 3rd Storyteller rises.)

3rd Storyteller: Our last story is called, "Tall-Tale Man." *(Shakes rattle. Curtain opens.)*

(Setting: Same as Scene 2.)

(At rise: Tall-Tale Man is sitting under tree, staring up.)

3rd Storyteller: There once was a man who told tales that were so tall they could not possibly be true. Yet he insisted they were the honest truth. *(Sits; Leopard enters.)*

Leopard *(to Tall-Tale Man):* Good day, sir. Why are you staring up into the tree?

Tall-Tale Man: I'm waiting for the magic kola nuts to fall.

Leopard: Magic kola nuts?

Tall-Tale Man: Oh, yes. Last week I caught two nuts from this tree. They turned into two cows. I took the two cows to the Frog King and he gave me two canoes. But two old bull elephants stole the canoes while I was asleep. And so I'm trying to catch some more magic nuts.

Leopard *(in disbelief):* That's an unbelievable story!

Tall-Tale Man: You must believe me, Leopard. I swear it's true.

Leopard: You should be ashamed of yourself. I won't stay here and listen to any more of your false stories. (*Exits in a huff.*)

Tall-Tale Man (*laughing*): Ho, ho, ho! I really fooled the leopard. (*Looks off*) Aha! Here comes Antelope. I'll fool him too. (*Stares up into tree; Antelope comes bounding in.*)

Antelope (*to Tall-Tale Man*): Good day, sir. Is there something important in that tree?

Tall-Tale Man: I'm waiting for the magic kola nuts to fall.

Antelope: Magic kola nuts?

Tall-Tale Man: Oh, yes. Last week I caught two nuts from this tree. They turned into two cows. I took the two cows to the Frog King and he gave me two canoes. But two old bull elephants stole the canoes while I was asleep. And so I'm trying to catch some more magic nuts.

Antelope: What a ridiculous story!

Tall-Tale Man: You must believe me, Antelope. I swear it's true.

Antelope: Sir, it is bad of you to tell such tall tales and call them true. Someone should teach you a lesson. (*Exits in a huff.*)

Tall-Tale Man (*laughing*): Ho, ho, ho! I really fooled the antelope. (*Looks off*) Ah, ha! Here comes Anansi, the Spiderman. I'll fool him, too. (*Stares up into tree.*)

Anansi (*entering*): Good day, sir. What's so important in the tree?

Tall-Tale Man: I'm waiting for the magic kola nuts to fall.

Anansi: Magic kola nuts?

Tall-Tale Man: Oh, yes. Last week I caught two nuts from this tree. They turned into two cows. I took the two cows to the Frog King and he gave me two canoes. But two old bull elephants stole the canoes while I was asleep. And so I'm trying to catch some more magic nuts.

Anansi: My, my! Next time hide your canoes so the two bull elephants won't find them.

Tall-Tale Man (*startled*): You mean you believe me?

Anansi: Why, of course. And I'll tell you why. Last week I planted a field of okra. It grew so tall it touched the sky. I made seven hundred pots of soup and fed five villages. But two bull elephants came along and squashed the field with two enormous canoes. Then the Frog King stole the canoes and left two magic kola nuts in their place. I planted the magic kola nuts. And that's how *that* tree got here.

Tall-Tale Man (*stunned*): That's an impossible story!

Anansi: You must believe me, sir. I swear it's true.

Tall-Tale Man: I won't stay here and listen to any more of your silly tall tales. (*Exits in disgust.*)

Anansi (*to audience*): I have a moral to this tale. He who dishes it out should be able to eat it! Goodbye. (*Starts to exit as curtain closes. Storytellers rise and start to exit, shaking their rattles, keeping step to beat.*)

Storytellers (*chanting*):
Anansi, the Spiderman,
Clever and sly.
Though nobody fools him,
Many still try.
(*Last two lines of chant are repeated until Three Storytellers are all offstage.*)

Close Up

1. In the first tale, Anansi wants to buy the Sky-god's stories. (a) What three things does Nyame ask Anansi to show him? (b) Does he believe Anansi can accomplish this task? Why or why not?

2. (a) What trick does Anansi use to show Nyame an empty hornets' nest? (b) What trick does Anansi use to show a quiet monkey?

3. Greed makes the crocodile lose all its teeth. (a) What makes hornets leave their nest? (b) What makes the monkey quiet?

4. (a) In the second tale, who comes up with the idea for the talking drum? (b) How does Anansi trick the monkey into carrying the drum?

5. In the third tale, Tall-Tale Man tries to fool all the animals. How does Anansi trick Tall-Tale Man?

Moral

The moral of a story is its message or lesson about some part of life. It usually gives good, practical advice about human behavior. Many folk tales end with a moral that can be stated in one sentence. For example, "Slow and steady wins the race," and "Don't bite the hand that feeds you."

1. Anansi states the moral for the third tale. What is it?

2. Which statement below sums up the lesson of the third tale?
   a. Don't serve more food than you can eat.
   b. Don't tease other people unless you can take some teasing yourself.
   c. Don't eat with your eyes.

3. Make up a moral for the second tale. Express your moral in a sentence that sums up the lesson that the second tale teaches.

Activities

1. Anansi, the Spiderman, is a heroic character from Ashanti culture. His superpower is his tremendous cunning. Make a list of superheroes from American culture. Next to each superhero, list his or her superpower. For example, Wonderwoman—super strength. Perhaps you can bring a comic strip about a superhero into class.

2. **Composition.** Imagine you are a superhero. Write a paragraph about your adventures.

MAIN IDEA

Finding Topic Sentences

A paragraph is a group of sentences about one idea. A paragraph is indented and is usually more than one sentence long.

A paragraph may have a topic sentence. **The topic sentence tells the main idea of the paragraph.** The topic sentence may appear at the beginning of a paragraph, or in the middle or end of the paragraph. All of the other sentences in the paragraph add information to the idea expressed in the topic sentence. For example, the topic sentence is printed in *italics* in the following paragraph. Notice how the other sentences add information to this idea.

> *The Ashanti people of West Africa tell many stories about Anansi, the Spider.* These stories are known as *Anansesem*, or spider tales. In these stories, Anansi uses cunning to outwit the other creatures. Often, he gains prizes that benefit all the creatures.

▶ Copy each paragraph below on a separate piece of paper. Then underline the topic sentence in each paragraph.

a. Anansi thought it would be fun to tell stories in the evening. This would help the animals pass the time. But Anansi knew no stories. Only Nyame knew stories.

b. Have you ever seen an empty hornets' nest? Have you met a crocodile without teeth? Do you think a monkey can stop chattering? Nyame would give Anansi his stories only if Anansi found these three impossible things.

c. The forest was large. The Forest King needed a quick way to get messages to the farthest villagers. This would help him protect the forest against enemies.

d. Anansi wanted to give Tall-Tale Man some of his own medicine. He pretended to believe Tall-Tale Man's story. Then Anansi told an even taller story. This story shocked Tall-Tale Man, who walked away in disgust.

WORD ATTACK

Using a Pronunciation Key

A dictionary or glossary shows you how to pronounce words you do not know. First the dictionary lists the regular spelling of the word. Then, in parentheses, it shows the word as it is spelled with pronunciation symbols. For example, cringe (krĭnj).

Each symbol is listed in a pronunciation key, and is illustrated with words whose pronunciation most people know. For example, the pronunciation key on page 478 tells you how to read the symbols (krĭnj). The k is pronounced as in kick, the r as in roar, the i as in pit, the n as in no, and the j as in judge.

There is no short cut for finding the pronunciation of a word. First, you must look up the word in a dictionary or glossary. Second, you must see how it is spelled with pronunciation symbols. Then, you must look up the symbols you are unsure of in the pronunciation key.

---

1. Look up each of the following words in the glossary. Then, on a separate piece of paper, write the pronunciation symbols you find in parentheses next to each word.
a.	antelope	f.	gorgeous
b.	calabash	g.	pantomime
c.	dissatisfaction	h.	preen
d.	equatorial	i.	situation
e.	gourd	j.	vanity

2. Study the pronunciation key on page 478. Use it to interpret the symbols you wrote in Exercise **1.** Then read each word from Exercise **1** aloud.

3. Write a sentence for each of the ten words in Exercise **1.** Read each sentence aloud.

Snow Igloo

Ruth Boellstorff

(1) The sled was loaded at last.

(2) Steve lashed a rope across the covering canvas and knotted it tightly, then checked the ivory slabs on the runners to be sure they weren't loose. It was a good sled, he admitted grudgingly to himself, strong and graceful as a seal.

(3) Now, his father came with the dogs, leaping and straining at their leashes. In the confusion, Black Fox jostled against One-Ear, the old lead dog. One-Ear turned on the younger dog, snarling and baring his teeth. Steve grabbed his leash and held him until the other dogs were hitched in their places. Then his father hooked One-Ear in position at the head of the line.

(4) "Are you ready, Makpuk?" asked his father.

(5) "Ready," the boy answered, taking his place on the sled. Why couldn't his father call him Steve, he thought, instead of always using his Eskimo name? Everyone else called him Steve, in the new way.

(6) Striding now to the rear of the sled,

his father gripped the handles firmly. "Mush!" he called. "Mush-mush!"

(7) The dogs leaped ahead, yelping with excitement. Clinging to the handles, the driver ran along behind; then as the dogs quieted and settled into a steady trot, he stepped onto the sled runners to ride. *Areegah*, it was fine! The snow was smooth and hard; the dogs were running easily behind One-Ear, their tails waving over their backs. The village was not many miles away. They should be safely home by nightfall.

(8) Steve, riding on the load, listened to the slurr of the runners, the breathing of the dogs, and the padding of their flying feet. Growing chilly, he hunched his shoulders and drew his head further into his fur hood.

(9) "Are you cold, Makpuk?" called his father, slowing the team. "Maybe you should jump off and run awhile."

(10) Trotting along beside the sled, Steve soon was warm. "Let me drive now, Father. Please. I know I can handle the dogs."

(11) His father hesitated, then brought the team to a halt. "Very well. The dogs know the way home. I am tired and will be glad to ride for a time."

(12) Steve grasped the handles of the sled. "Mush!" he shouted.

(13) One-Ear looked around at the sound of the different voice, and then resumed his gait. The other dogs followed in line behind him.

(14) "This is great!" Steve thought happily. Running behind the sled part of the time, then riding the runners, he felt very grown-up. Maybe dog teams weren't so bad after all.

(15) Many times he had urged his father to buy a snowmobile, one like many people in the village had. But his father

always replied, "No, Makpuk. It is not good to give up all the old Eskimo ways."

(16) "But Father," Steve protested, "we are different now. Airplanes come to our village. We can earn much money working for the *tannik*. We have stoves and lights in our houses. And radios. We have outboard motors on our *umiaks*."

(17) "Yes, son you are right. Many changes have come to the Eskimo people, and some are very good. But there are things that do not change. Our land does not change. Its cold, its darkness, its dangers are the same as before. That is why it saddens me to see the old ways forgotten, the old skills lost."

(18) So it was a dog team, not a snowmobile, that Steve was guiding westward toward the village. Absorbed in his thoughts, he did not notice the darkening sky until his father motioned for him to look back. Behind them rose a dark wall. Was a storm coming?

(19) Even as he watched, a sharp flake stung his cheek. Another! His father leaped from the sled and, running beside him, reached for the sled handles. "Let me have the team now. You ride," he said.

(20) Steve scrambled onto the load and crouched low, holding tightly to the rope that anchored the canvas. The menacing wall rose higher in the sky. Then with a shriek, the storm was upon them.

(21) Faster and faster ran the dogs. The wind was stinging and bitter. The snow fell in heavy, choking curtains.

(22) "Whoa!" Steve heard his father shout. He saw him go quickly to each dog in turn, passing his hands over the dogs' eyes to clear them of frozen snow, then lifting each paw to check for ice balls between their toes.

(23) The sled moved on again, more slowly. Suddenly the wind roared to a new fury, flinging sharp ice pellets like keen-edged knives. One-Ear stopped abruptly, throwing the rest of the team into confusion. One or two of the dogs started ahead again, but One-Ear had curled into a tight ball in the snow. In moments, each dog had wound himself up tightly, with his furry tail covering his nose and eyes.

(24) "Father!" cried Steve. "What shall we do?"

(25) "We must take shelter ourselves. And quickly." Reaching under the sled canvas, his father pulled out his old snow knife. "We must make a snow igloo," he said. "My father taught me."

(26) As Steve hurried to secure the dogs to the sides of the sled, he could see his father through the blur of the storm. With deft strokes, he was cutting slabs of frozen snow, slashing the ends at a slant. These he set on edge like beveled white dominoes standing in a circle. Another ring of blocks rose on the first. *Alepah,* the wind was cold!

(27) "Can I help, Father?" Steve shouted through the storm as he secured the last leash.

(28) "Bring the sleeping bags from the sled, and the stove. And the tea!" his father called.

(29) As Steve struggled up with the load, his father was fitting the last block of snow in place at the top of the igloo. They crawled at once through the opening left and pulled the waiting block of snow into place behind them.

(30) They could not stand erect inside, but crouched on the sleeping bags, slapping their arms against their chests to warm themselves and laughing with relief to be out of the storm. Soon they had snow melting on the alcohol burner for hot tea. The warmth from the flame and the moisture from their breathing caused a glaze of ice to form on the snow walls.

(31) "The ice seals the snow. We must make an opening for fresh air." Steve watched his father cut carefully through the dome above their heads. "We must not let this hole get choked with snow or we will die!"

(32) They crawled into their caribou sleeping bags, warm and safe, and lay listening to the wind. Was it slackening just a little?

(33) "Father?"

(34) "Yes, Makpuk, my son."

(35) "How is it, Father, that you speak always of the old ways of the Eskimo. Yet you want me to go to school each day. You want me to learn the ways of the outside world."

(36) "Yes, son, that is right. You must learn to take your place in the world of which Alaska is now a part. But the old Eskimo world is still with us. We must learn to live in both worlds."

(37) The sounds of the storm were quieting. "Let us sleep now, my son. Tomorrow we will go home."

(38) Drowsily, Steve watched as his father thrust the knife upward once more, clearing the opening for air. Old wisdom, old skills had saved their lives.

(39) "I guess Father is right," he thought. "An Eskimo needs to know the ways of the new world. But never should he scorn the old."

Close Up

1. Steve's father calls him Makpuk. Why doesn't Steve want his father to call him by his Eskimo name?

2. Steve wants his father to use the new ways instead of the old ways. What does Steve wish his father would use instead of a dog sled?

3. Why does Steve's father feel the old ways should not be forgotten, and the old skills should not be lost?

4. A storm approaches. (a) Who is the first to recognize the warning signals? (b) What skill does he use to save lives?

5. What has Steve learned by the end of the story?

Theme

The theme of a story is its central idea or insight into life. In some stories, you can discover the theme by asking yourself what the characters learn about life. In fact, one character may make a *key statement* that points to the theme of the story.

1. At the beginning of "Snow Igloo," Steve believes that modern ways and skills should replace the old ways. What happens that makes him change his mind?

2. At the end of the story, Steve makes a key statement about what he has learned. What does he say?

3. Steve's key statement helps you understand the theme. Steve talks about Eskimos in particular. The theme deals with people in general. Which statement below best expresses the theme?
   a. People need to adapt to the changing world, but they also need to treasure their heritage.
   b. People should stay apart from the changes taking place in the modern world.
   c. Ancient Eskimo skills are superior to modern science and technology.

Activities

1. Have a craft show. Bring in objects made completely by hand. Tell how each was made. You might ask your grandparents or other older people in your neighborhood for help.

2. Find out how to make an igloo. Share your findings with your class.

MAIN IDEA

Noting Changes Signaled by Paragraphs

A new paragraph signals a change. Sometimes, the new paragraph moves you from the narrative of the story to the words spoken by one character. Other times, the new paragraph changes the focus to a different time, to a different place, or to a different character.

1. There are thirty-nine paragraphs in this story. How many paragraphs introduce the actual words spoken by Steve or his father?

2. The fifth paragraph focuses on Steve. Does the sixth paragraph change to a different time, a different place, or a different character?

3. (a) The tenth paragraph focuses on what character? (b) The eleventh paragraph changes the focus to what character?

4. The event in the fourteenth paragraph happens in the present. Does the event in the fifteenth paragraph happen in the past or in the future?

5. Most of this story happens outside. Which paragraph moves the story inside the igloo?

WORD ATTACK

Noting Comparisons

Comparisons show how two objects are alike. Authors often use comparisons to create vivid pictures. For example, an author might compare a dog sled team to "a train with the engine and all the cars puffing smoke billows."

1. In the following sentences what is being compared to what?
   a. "It was a good sled, he admitted grudgingly to himself, strong and graceful as a seal."
   b. "The menacing wall rose higher in the sky. Then with a shriek, the storm was upon them."
   c. "Suddenly the wind roared to a new fury, flinging sharp ice pellets like keen-edged knives."
   d. ". . . One-Ear had curled into a tight ball in the snow."
   e. "These (slabs of frozen snow) he set on edge like beveled white dominoes standing in a circle."

2. Comparisons are based on the likeness between two things.
   a. How is a good sled like a seal?
   b. How is a storm like a wall?
   c. How are ice pellets like knives?
   d. How is One-Ear like a ball?
   e. How are the slabs of frozen snow like dominoes?

Honor Society

Senator Daniel K. Inouye
with Lawrence Elliott

Daniel thought they would question him about his interests and his schoolwork. Instead, he found they were only interested in the clothes he wore.

Mrs. King's class was the top tenth-grade class at McKinley High. I don't know how I got into it, but from the very first day I wanted out. In place of all my old buddies, I found myself rubbing shoulders with kids who kept trying to pretend that their skin was white and that their eyes were blue.

In those days, McKinley High School was jokingly called "Tokyo High." All public schools in Hawaii were supposed to be open to everyone regardless of race, color, or creed. But thanks to a clever system of segregation, nearly all of us at McKinley were of Japanese ancestry and poor.

No one could transfer out of McKinley into an English Standard School—which always had better facilities and better teachers—without passing an examination. The written part of the test was fair and gave everyone an equal chance. But not the oral part. Students whose parents came from Japan or China always had great trouble pronouncing the "th," "r," and the "l" sounds. So only a handful of Japanese or Chinese kids ever got into the English Standard Schools, and these few got in only because their parents were rich enough to give them private tutoring so they could pass the oral test.

McKinley's honor society. My mother and father glowed with pride. I tried to pretend that it didn't matter to me one way or the other; but the truth is that I was excited, too.

I had to be interviewed by the Student Council before I was accepted. When it was time for the interview, I marched up and stood before the Council. Four seniors trying to look as serious as bankers sat behind a long table. They didn't ask me to sit down.

"Why do you think you should belong to an honor society?" one senior asked.

I shrugged. "It was Mrs. King's idea."

"Why don't you wear shoes?" asked a Japanese kid I had known for five years.

"Because I only have one pair," I told him. "They have to last." It was a silly question; he knew I only had one pair. He also knew that the shoes had been bought two years ago, and had been two sizes too big so I wouldn't grow out of them, and that I'd had to stuff the toes with paper to keep them on.

But that silly question was only the beginning.

"Why don't you wear a tie?" they asked. "Why don't you wear a white shirt?"

I didn't know what to say. I looked from one senior to the other. What was this all about? I thought they were going to interview me about my interests and ideas, about my schoolwork. Why did they care what clothes I wore?

"Are you going to answer the question?"

"My shirt is for church," I said.

"Don't you care how you look in school?"

I was too young and unknowing to be troubled by the idea of Tokyo High. Only the kids in my class bothered me. Sometimes it seemed that the only person who ever talked to me was the teacher, Mrs. King. When she did, I was suddenly able to see beyond the narrow life I had known and to feel that being a clerk, or even a beach boy, was not the greatest and only hope for a kid like me. She took me seriously, which is something no one—not even I—had ever done.

In the middle of the year, Mrs. King recommended me for membership in

I looked down at my sport shirt and my denim pants and bare feet. "My clothes are clean," I mumbled. "I don't know what's wrong."

"What about your friends?" one of them asked, and he rattled off a list of kids from my neighborhood. "Are *they* your friends?"

"Yes," I said. "What's the matter with them?"

"Delinquents!" the seniors answered.

"Because they don't wear shoes?" I said. "Because they're poor? They're no more delinquents than I am. Or you are."

All the disappointment, all the fear suddenly boiled up in anger, and I began to shout. "Hey, listen, I thought this interview was for an honor society. But if all you're looking for is a guy who wears white shirts and shoes, you don't want me and I sure don't want you. I wouldn't trade one of my friends for your honor society or all four of you!"

For a long, long time afterward I felt angry every time I remembered that humiliating interview, and I remembered it often. And that wasn't the end of it. I had to tell my parents that I hadn't been accepted into the honor society. But I couldn't tell them the real reason because they would have blamed themselves. So I stammered out a weak explanation that didn't fool them at all, and their eyes grew sad and there was no more for any of us to say.

Mrs. King found out about my unhappy meeting with the Student Council. She was so deeply hurt by what had happened that not once in my next year at McKinley High did she recommend another candidate for the honor society.

I should explain that I was not rejected because of racial prejudice. It was not my Japanese ancestry that the Council was against. They were angry because I did not *hide* that ancestry by dressing and acting like white people in Hawaii. My worst critics on the Council were the Japanese members. They agreed with others in the Japanese community in Hawaii who tried to please their white neighbors by acting as if they, too, were white. These Japanese people resented those of us who would not conform to their twisted ideas of what made an American, and they never missed a chance to crack down on us.

But the most important effect of the episode was that it left me with a resolve to "show those guys." Never before had I felt so determined to make something of myself. As a matter of fact, I think I can say that those four snobbish seniors are partly responsible for whatever success I've had. For many years afterward, I attacked and overcame every obstacle in my path just so I could prove that shoes and neckties are no measure of a man.

1. One of Daniel Inouye's high school teachers greatly influences his life. How does she treat Daniel Inouye that is unlike the way he has ever been treated before?

2. (a) Is Daniel pleased about the recommendation to the honor society? (b) What is the only thing that stands in the way of his being accepted?

3. (a) At the Student Council interview, how does Daniel react to the questions? (b) What does he do?

4. Daniel is not accepted into the honor society. (a) Why does he make up a feeble excuse to his parents? (b) Can his parents guess the real reason anyway? Why or why not?

5. Daniel is determined to make a success of his life. What have the Student Council members made him determined to prove?

Theme

The theme of a story is often suggested rather than stated. Sometimes you can discover the theme by looking at how the main character has changed and what he or she has learned about life.

1. What does Daniel first learn about himself from his teacher, Mrs. King?

2. Daniel learns his second lesson at the Student Council interview. How does he feel about character judgments based on clothes people wear?

3. Daniel learns his third lesson from the Student Council members. Why do they want him to conform to their notions of what Americans should be like?

4. These three lessons point to the theme of this story. Which statement below best represents the theme?
   a. People are what they appear to be.
   b. A person can overcome obstacles and prove that deeds, not clothes, are the measure of a man or woman.
   c. Anyone who works hard will succeed.

Activity

▶ **Composition.** Many people have overcome obstacles and gained success. Write a paragraph about a person whose achievements you admire.

MAIN IDEA

Distinguishing Between Topic and Main Idea

The subject of a paragraph is called the topic. Usually, the topic is stated in one word, or a very few. For example, the topic of a paragraph may be "school" or "high-school life."

The main idea of a paragraph is the most important information a paragraph gives about the topic. The main idea usually is stated as a complete sentence. For example, the main idea of a paragraph about school may be, "School is one place where you learn to get along with other people."

---

1. Read each paragraph below. Then write the topic of each paragraph. Remember, the topic is what the paragraph is about.
   a. "Mrs. King's class was the top tenth-grade class at McKinley High. I don't know how I got into it, but from the very first day I wanted out. In place of all my old buddies, I found myself rubbing shoulders with kids who kept trying to pretend that their skin was white and that their eyes were blue."
   b. "In those days, McKinley High School was jokingly called 'Tokyo High.' All public schools in Hawaii were supposed to be open to everyone regardless of race, color, or creed. But thanks to a clever system of segregation, nearly all of us at McKinley were of Japanese ancestry and poor."
   c. "But the most important effect of the episode was that it left me with a resolve to 'show those guys.' Never before had I felt so determined to make something of myself. As a matter of fact, I think I can say that those four snobbish seniors are partly responsible for whatever success I've had. For many years afterward, I attacked and overcame every obstacle in my path just so I could prove that shoes and neckties are no measure of a man."

2. Which statement below best expresses the main idea of paragraph **1 a?**
   a. Daniel's buddies were not in Mrs. King's class.
   b. Daniel did not want to be in Mrs. King's class.

3. Which statement expresses the main idea of paragraph **1 b?**
   a. Public schools were mixed in name only; but in fact, McKinley High was segregated.
   b. Daniel went to a school nicknamed "Tokyo High."

4. Which statement below best expresses the main idea of paragraph **1 c?**

    a. The episode made Daniel resolve to make something of himself.

    b. The seniors on the Council were snobbish.

WORD ATTACK

Understanding Figurative Expressions

Figurative expressions are made up of words that do not have their usual or dictionary meaning. In fact, if you gave the words in these expressions their usual meanings, the expressions would be humorous or full of nonsense. For example, can you imagine yourself *with your heart in your mouth* or *looking like the last rose of summer?*

▶ Read each sentence below. Think about the meaning of the *italicized* words. On a separate piece of paper, put L next to the sentence if the italicized words are used literally—that is, if they mean exactly what they say. Put F next to the sentence if the italicized words are used figuratively; that is, without their usual meaning.

    a. The coach was *rubbing* his *shoulders* because they ached.

    b. We were *rubbing shoulders* with people from many cultures.

    c. Her parents *glowed with pride* when she won the prize.

    d. The candle *glowed in the dark.*

    e. Only a *handful* of Japanese students belonged to the honor society.

    f. The child had a *handful* of white pebbles.

    g. The water *boiled* on the stove top.

    h. Daniel *boiled* with anger.

    i. The rubber band was *twisted* into knots.

    j. Their ideas were *twisted* and confused.

The New Girl

Nan Gilbert

Ann Cameron first saw Bianca on the November day when the little Mexican girl enrolled at Carthage Junior High School. Foreigners were not often seen in this small Iowa town, so all the students stared when the new girl was brought into the study hall. Bianca stared right back, a wide, friendly smile flashing white in her brown face.

Miss Peterson, who was in charge of the study hall, picked up her pencil and asked, "Your name, please?"

"Bianca Guadaloupe Marita Francesca Rosalita Malenche Quiroso," she announced proudly. She laughed without embarrassment at the teacher's surprised look. "It's a mouthful, no? I am named for three saints, two grandmothers, and one rich granduncle."

"Will you repeat your name?" asked Miss Peterson quietly. A snicker welled up from the front row of students. Bianca's smile widened in friendly response as she again rattled off the list of her names. The snickers swelled into a loud roar. Miss Peterson straightened her shoulders and stood up.

"Quiet, please!" she ordered. "Bianca, please take that vacant seat in the last row for this period."

Bianca came beaming down the aisle. As she sat down across from Ann, she whispered excitedly, "My name is Bianca Guadaloupe Marita—and yours?"

"Ann Cameron," Ann whispered hurriedly, her cheeks red with embarrassment. Ann, who blushed when anyone even looked in her direction, felt very uncomfortable. She knew that the laughing eyes of everyone in the study hall were directed at her and Bianca, waiting for something to happen.

"Ann? No more to it than that?" puzzled Bianca. "It is a pretty name. But had you no grandmothers nor granduncles? Well, no matter. Up in Minnesota we have worked all summer at the canneries, my mamma, my papa, and my brothers. Because of the new baby,

Benito, we are not going on to our home in Texas until my mamma is more strong.''

"We must be quiet now," Ann whispered desperately. "Here, why don't you look over these books of mine until you get your own? And I'll give you some paper and a pencil."

"Oh, *gracias!* thank you!" Bianca glowed. "Already you are my good friend, for friendship is giving! So now I, too, give!" And she took a tiny carved figure out of a pocket in her skirt.

"See, it is a little Madonna with her small babe! Is it not sweet? Take it; it is yours. My papa makes them in the evenings. He is always busy carving. My mamma says if he had no bit of wood to fashion, he would surely carve the roof over our heads."

With wild relief Ann welcomed the bell that meant she could escape to class. Such an experience! Would every study-hall hour from now on be as bad as this one?

Every study-hall hour! Before the week was out, Ann would have felt lucky if the study hall had been the only place she had to put up with Bianca. For Bianca, with her wide, trusting smile and her never-ending chatter, thought happily that Ann was her friend. And she attached herself tighter than adhesive tape.

But what could Ann do? She was too kind-hearted to be rude. She could not turn her back on a strange girl so far from home, or tell her to go bother somebody else. Yet she winced whenever she saw Bianca running to meet her in the morning.

"Oh, Ann, here you are," Bianca would cry. "See what I brought you!" Once it was some sort of pancake rolled around a peppery mixture. It stung Ann's throat and made her whoop and strangle when she tried to gulp it hurriedly before anybody saw her.

"An enchilada. Is it not good?" Bianca beamed, patting Ann's back. "Tomorrow I will bring you a tamale!"

Bianca's cheerful comments, which were meant to be encouraging, were as embarrassing as her gifts. Like the day in assembly when she asked, "Why do you not sing louder, Ann? You have such a sweet voice but no bigger than a bird cheep! Lift it, Ann, see? Like me."

Everywhere Ann went, there was Bianca. And everywhere Bianca went, a trail of giggles followed.

"Laughter is so fine, is it not?" Bianca would say, pleased, while Ann's ears burned. "Why do you not laugh more, Ann? Laughter makes the warm happiness that one feels in the center of the stomach."

"Of the heart," Ann corrected automatically.

Bianca shook her head strongly. "Too much is made of the heart, I think. It is the stomach that has the feelings. Does it not push up the laughter? And shake with the sobs? No, the glow, it is in the stomach! What do we do after school tonight, Ann?"

"I have to go to a class meeting, Bianca," Ann said hurriedly, though until that moment she had not planned to attend. Nobody had ever asked Ann's opinion in class meeting, and certainly she had never dared offer one. There really was not much reason for being present.

"Class meeting!" Bianca thrilled happily. "So I must go, too! Is it all right if I go with you, Ann? So you can explain all my questions?"

Ann gave a big, though silent, sigh. There was nothing she could do about the situation.

She decided to make the best of it.

"All right, Bianca," she agreed. "Four o'clock."

The meeting was held in the gym. Dick Wheeler, freshman-class president and object of Ann's secret hero worship, presided casually.

"Guess you all know what this meeting is about. It is our turn to decorate the gym for the Christmas party next week, so we have to decide what to do."

"Christmas party? Ah, ah, I love Christmas!" exclaimed Bianca.

"*Shh!*" begged Ann.

Dick went on. "I suppose we want the usual Christmas tree in the middle of the floor, and crepe paper things hanging from the balcony, and evergreen boughs—"

"If you've got it all figured out," a boy called out dryly, "what are we here for?"

Dick bristled. "Got any better ideas? Isn't Christmas always a tree and a guy in a Santa Claus suit?"

Bianca had been jiggling about in growing excitement that suddenly brought her to her feet. "In my town there is no Santa," she burst out. "But oh, the fiesta we make! For nine days before Christmas!"

Ann tugged at her skirt in dismay. "Bianca, *shhh!*"

"Each night in our homes we make the *posada*," Bianca rushed on, not paying any attention to Ann. "We act out the procession to the inn where Mary and Joseph begged shelter. We do it with candles and singing, all lovely and solemn! And afterwards, there is no more of the solemn, for then comes the piñata!

The piñata? This is a big, big jar dressed like a clown, or a rooster, or a fat lady— what you like. Stuffed with gifts it is, and hung from the ceiling. And someone is blindfolded and spun till he doesn't know right from left nor up from down. Then he takes three whacks at the air with his broomstick. And if he strikes the piñata—*crrrrack!*—down spill gifts, like

a giant cloudburst, for all to scramble after!"

It was the longest of all Bianca's long speeches. Her eyes glowed like black diamonds. Her brown skin was flooded with color. Ann, looking up at her, had a sudden understanding of how homesick a person might be, so far away from all of the dear, familiar holiday customs.

And then Dick Wheeler, with a patient look on his face, sighed. "Very interesting. Now if that's over, let's get on with our meeting. The girls can make the crepe paper streamers—"

The warm color drained from Bianca's cheeks, and the wide smiling mouth drooped a little at the corners. Ann's kind heart gave a painful thump, and suddenly she could not bear that Bianca should be so silent. For weeks Ann had wanted nothing else, but now that it had happened, she found it was awful!

For the first time in her life, she scrambled to her feet in a class meeting. She did not know what she was going to say, but she had to say something— anything to fill the silence left by Bianca.

"My goodness, Dick, you're running on about your old crepe paper when Bianca has just given us the sharpest idea any class ever had! Why, it would be wonderful to fix up a real Mexican Christmas for the party, with a—a piñata like she said and a procession and the gym decorated like a fiesta! I guess you aren't used to new ideas, Dick Wheeler, not to see it right off. Why, if you don't grab it, you must be stupid!"

The words were out—sharp words she couldn't take back! Ann, listening to them echo through the gym, felt that she would never dare set foot in Carthage Junior High again.

And then—was it possible? Another voice was filling the silence. It was Dick Wheeler's.

"Say, Ann, maybe you're right. Come to think about it, it does have possibilities. Big possibilities. And with Bianca here to tell us how to do it—— How about it, class, want to take a vote?"

Under cover of the roar of "Ayes!" Bianca piped up happily, "You see, Ann? It's as I told you. All you need is to lift your voice!"

Suddenly Ann, glancing quickly at Bianca, realized something. All these days she had thought she had been looking out for Bianca. But perhaps it was Bianca who had really been looking out for Ann.

But then it did not matter at all, for there was so much joy surrounding Ann that it made a rich, warm, Christmasy glow inside her. And yes—Bianca was right—the glow was definitely in the stomach!

Close Up

1. Bianca is a warm, friendly person. (a) What do the students do when they hear Bianca's long name? (b) How does Bianca react?

2. Why doesn't Ann tell Bianca she doesn't want her for a friend?

3. (a) Why do Bianca's cheerful and encouraging suggestions embarrass Ann? (b) What does Bianca suggest that Ann do with her voice?

4. Why does Bianca decide to go to the class meeting?

5. (a) What does Ann do to defend Bianca when Dick Wheeler ignores her suggestion? (b) How does Ann feel after she speaks up?

Theme

Sometimes you can discover the theme by using the special qualities or personality traits of the characters in the story as clues. For example, when a cheerful character appears in the midst of a group of gloomy characters, you may find that the theme of the story is about the importance of cheerfulness.

1. This story is about two characters, Ann and Bianca. Bianca is confident and outspoken. How is Ann different from Bianca?

2. At first, Ann is embarrassed because Bianca is not afraid to speak out. What happens at the class meeting that makes Ann value Bianca's outspokenness?

3. In this story, it is important that Bianca speaks out. Use that clue to choose the statement that best expresses the theme of the story.
   a. You must never trust a friend.
   b. Timid people do not speak out at class meetings, even when they should.
   c. People shouldn't be afraid to lift their voices and speak out.
   d. Nobody is perfect.

Activities

1. Dramatize the scene at the class meeting.

2. Find out how to make a piñata. Build one for a class party.

MAIN IDEA

Ordering the Importance of Ideas

The main idea of a paragraph is the most important thing said about the topic of the paragraph. The less important ideas in the paragraph back up or support the main idea. For example, in the following paragraph the main idea is in *italics*. The two supporting ideas are enclosed by parentheses.

> *Mexican fiestas are great parties for young and old.* (During the party, someone is almost certain to get the older folks singing a favorite song. The youngsters are almost certain to gets lots of treats.)

▶ Read each paragraph below. Then choose the main idea from the statements following each paragraph.

> "Ann Cameron first saw Bianca on the November day when the little Mexican girl enrolled at Carthage Junior High School. Foreigners were not often seen in this small Iowa town, so all the students stared when the new girl was brought into the study hall. Bianca stared right back, a wide, friendly smile flashing white in her brown face."

a. Ann first saw Bianca in November.
b. Bianca stared back at the students and smiled.
c. The students stared at Bianca.

> " 'Will you repeat your name?' asked Miss Peterson quietly. A snicker welled up from the front row of students. Bianca's smile widened in friendly response as she again rattled off the list of her names. The snickers swelled into a loud roar. Miss Peterson straightened her shoulders and stood up."

d. Miss Peterson asked Bianca to repeat her name.
e. Bianca did not seem to pay attention when the students laughed.
f. Miss Peterson stood up.

> "Suddenly Ann, glancing quickly at Bianca, realized something. All these days she had thought she had been looking out for Bianca. But perhaps it was Bianca who had really been looking out for Ann."

g. Ann realized that Bianca may have been looking out for her.
h. Ann glanced quickly at Bianca.

WORD ATTACK

Understanding Spanish Words

Languages borrow words from each other. The English language has borrowed a number of words from Spanish. Most native English speakers, for example, know that *amigo* means "friend"; that a *patio* is an outside addition to a house; that a *sombrero* is a hat, and so on.

1. After reading "The New Girl," you should be able to match the following Spanish words with their definitions. Look back at the story if necessary.

Spanish Words		Definitions	
a.	gracias	(1)	a party
b.	posada	(2)	a jar stuffed with gifts
c.	piñata	(3)	a pancake rolled around meat or cheese
d.	fiesta	(4)	thanks
e.	enchilada	(5)	a procession or parade

2. Write a sentence for each Spanish word above.

Unfolding Bud

Naoshi Koriyama

One is amazed
By a water-lily bud
Unfolding
With each passing day,
5 Taking on a richer color
And new dimensions.

One is not amazed,
At a first glance,
By a poem,
10 Which is as tight-closed
As a tiny bud.

Yet one is surprised
To see the poem
Gradually unfolding,
15 Revealing its rich inner self,
As one reads it
Again
And over again.

Close Up

1. Why can someone be amazed by a water-lily bud?
2. How is a poem like a tiny bud?
3. What does the poem reveal as it unfolds?

The Medicine Bag

Virginia Driving Hawk Sneve

My kid sister Cheryl and I always bragged about our Sioux grandpa, Joe Iron Shell. Our friends, who had always lived in the city and only knew about Indians from movies and TV, were impressed by our stories. Maybe we exaggerated and made Grandpa and the reservation sound glamorous; but when we'd return home to Iowa after our yearly summer visit to Grandpa, we always had some exciting tale to tell.

We always had some authentic Sioux article to show our listeners. One year Cheryl had new moccasins that Grandpa had made. On another visit he gave me a small, round, flat, rawhide drum which was decorated with a painting of a warrior riding a horse. He taught me a real Sioux chant to sing while I beat the drum with a leather-covered stick that had a feather on the end. Man, that really made an impression.

We never showed our friends Grandpa's picture. Not that we were ashamed of him, but because we knew that the glamorous tales we told didn't go with the real thing. Our friends would have laughed at the picture, because Grandpa wasn't tall and stately like TV Indians. His hair wasn't in braids, but

hung in stringy, gray strands on his neck; and he was old. He was our great-grandfather, and he didn't live in a tipi, but all by himself in a part log, part tar-paper shack on the Rosebud Reservation in South Dakota. So when Grandpa came to visit us, I was so ashamed and embarrassed, I could've died.

There are a lot of yippy poodles and other fancy little dogs in our neighborhood; but they usually barked singly at the mailman from the safety of their own yards. Now it sounded as if a whole pack of mutts were barking together in one place.

I got up and walked to the curb to see what the commotion was. About a block away I saw a crowd of little kids yelling, with the dogs yipping and growling around someone who was walking down the middle of the street.

I watched the group as it slowly came closer, and saw that in the center of the strange procession was a man wearing a tall black hat. He'd pause now and then to peer at something in his hand and then at the houses on either side of the street. I felt cold and hot at the same time as I recognized the man. "Oh, no!" I whispered. "It's Grandpa!"

I stood on the curb, unable to move even though I wanted to run and hide. Then I got mad when I saw how the yippy dogs were growling and nipping at the old man's baggy pant legs, and how wearily he poked them away with his cane. "Stupid mutts," I said as I ran to rescue Grandpa.

When I kicked and hollered at the dogs to get away, they put their tails between their legs and scattered. The kids ran to the curb where they watched me and the old man.

"Grandpa," I said and felt pretty dumb when my voice cracked. I reached for his beat-up old tin suitcase, which was tied shut with a rope. But he set it down right in the street and shook my hand.

"*Hau, Takoza,* Grandchild," he greeted me formally in Sioux.

All I could do was stand there with the whole neighborhood watching and shake the hand of the leather-brown old man. I saw how his gray hair straggled from under his big black hat, which had a drooping feather in its crown. His rumpled black suit hung like a sack over his stooped frame. As he shook my hand, his coat fell open to expose a bright-red, satin shirt with a beaded bolo tie[1] under the collar. His getup wasn't out of place on the reservation; but it sure was here, and I wanted to sink right through the pavement.

"Hi," I muttered with my head down. I tried to pull my hand away when I felt his bony hand trembling, and looked up to see fatigue in his face. I felt like crying. I couldn't think of anything to say, so I picked up Grandpa's suitcase,

took his arm, and guided him up the driveway to our house.

Mom was standing on the steps. I don't know how long she'd been watching, but her hand was over her mouth and she looked as if she couldn't believe what she saw. Then she ran to us.

"Grandpa," she gasped. "How in the world did you get here?"

She checked her move to embrace Grandpa and I remembered that such a display of affection is unseemly to the Sioux and would embarrass him.

"*Hau,* Marie," he said as he shook Mom's hand. She smiled and took his other arm.

As we supported him up the steps, the door banged open and Cheryl came bursting out of the house. She was all smiles, and was so obviously glad to see Grandpa that I was ashamed of how I felt.

"Grandpa!" she yelled happily. "You came to see us!"

Grandpa smiled and Mom and I let go of him as he stretched out his arms to my ten-year-old sister, who was still young enough to be hugged.

"*Wicincala,* little girl," he greeted her and then collapsed.

He had fainted. Mom and I carried him into her sewing room, where we had a spare bed.

After we had Grandpa on the bed, Mom stood there helplessly patting his shoulder.

"Shouldn't we call the doctor, Mom?" I suggested, since she didn't seem to know what to do.

"Yes," she agreed with a sigh. "You make Grandpa comfortable, Martin."

I reluctantly moved to the bed. I knew Grandpa wouldn't want to have Mom undress him, but I didn't want to,

---

1. bolo tie: A string tie fastened with a sliding device.

either. He was so skinny and frail that his coat slipped off easily. When I loosened his tie and opened his shirt collar, I felt a small leather pouch that hung from a thong around his neck. I left it alone and moved to remove his boots. The scuffed old cowboy boots were tight, and he moaned as I put pressure on his legs to jerk them off.

I put the boots on the floor and saw why they fit so tight. Each one was stuffed with money. I looked at the bills that lined the boots and started to ask about them; but Grandpa's eyes were closed again.

Mom came back with a basin of water. "The doctor thinks Grandpa is suffering from heat exhaustion," she explained as she bathed Grandpa's face. Mom gave a big sigh, "*Oh hinh*, Martin. How do you suppose he got here?"

We found out after the doctor's visit. Grandpa was angrily sitting up in bed while Mom tried to feed him some soup.

"Tonight you let Marie feed you, Grandpa," spoke my dad, who had gotten home from work just as the doctor was leaving. "You're not really sick," he said as he gently pushed Grandpa back against the pillows. "The doctor said you just got too tired and hot after your long trip."

Grandpa relaxed, and between sips of soup he told of his journey. Soon after our visit to him, Grandpa decided that he would like to see where his only living descendants lived and what our home was like. Besides, he admitted sheepishly, he was lonesome after we left.

I knew everybody felt as guilty as I did—especially Mom. Mom was all Grandpa had left. So even after she married my dad, who's a white man and

teaches in the college in our city, and after Cheryl and I were born, Mom made sure that every summer we spent a week with Grandpa.

I never thought that Grandpa would be lonely after our visits, and none of us noticed how old and weak he had become. But Grandpa knew, and so he came to us. He had ridden on buses for two and a half days. When he arrived in the city, tired and stiff from sitting for so long, he set out, walking, to find us.

He had stopped to rest on the steps of some building downtown, and a policeman found him. The cop, according to Grandpa, was a good man who took him to the bus stop and waited until the bus came, and told the driver to let Grandpa out at Bell View Drive. After Grandpa got off the bus, he started walking again. But he couldn't see the house numbers on the other side when he walked on the sidewalk, so he walked in the middle of the street. That's when all the little kids and dogs followed him.

I knew everybody felt as bad as I did. Yet I was proud of this eighty-six-year-old man, who had never been away from the reservation, having the courage to travel so far alone.

"You found the money in my boots?" he asked Mom.

"Martin did," she answered, and roused herself to scold. "Grandpa, you shouldn't have carried so much money. What if someone had stolen it from you?"

Grandpa laughed. "I would've known if anyone tried to take the boots off my feet. The money is what I've saved for a long time—a hundred dollars—for my funeral. But you take it now to buy groceries so that I won't be a burden to you while I am here."

"That won't be necessary, Grandpa," Dad said. "We are honored to have you with us, and you will never be a burden. I am only sorry that we never thought to bring you home with us this summer and spare you the discomfort of a long trip."

Grandpa was pleased. "Thank you," he answered. "But do not feel bad that you didn't bring me with you, for I would not have come then. It was not time." He said this in such a way that no one could argue with him. To Grandpa and the Sioux, he once told me, a thing would be done when it was the right time to do it, and that's the way it was.

"Also," Grandpa went on, looking at me, "I have come because it is soon time for Martin to have the medicine bag."

We all knew what that meant. Grandpa thought he was going to die, and he had to follow the tradition of his family to pass the medicine bag, along with its history, to the oldest male child.

"Even though the boy," he said still looking at me, "bears a white man's name, the medicine bag will be his."

I didn't know what to say. I had the same hot and cold feeling that I had when I first saw Grandpa in the street. The medicine bag was the dirty leather pouch I had found around his neck. "I could never wear such a thing," I almost said aloud. I thought of having my friends see it in gym class, at the swimming pool, and could imagine the smart things they would say. But I just swallowed hard and took a step toward the bed. I knew I would have to take it.

But Grandpa was tired. "Not now, Martin," he said, waving his hand in dismissal, "it is not time. Now I will sleep."

So that's how Grandpa came to be with us for two months. My friends kept asking to come see the old man, but I put them off. I told myself that I didn't want them laughing at Grandpa. But even as I made excuses, I knew it wasn't Grandpa that I was afraid they'd laugh at.

Nothing bothered Cheryl about bringing her friends to see Grandpa. Every day after school started, there'd be a crew of giggling little girls or round-

eyed little boys crowded around the old man on the patio, where he'd gotten in the habit of sitting every afternoon.

Grandpa would smile in his gentle way and patiently answer their questions, or he'd tell them stories of brave warriors, ghosts, animals; and the kids listened in awed silence. Those little guys thought Grandpa was great.

Finally, one day after school, my friends came home with me because

nothing I said stopped them. "We're going to see the great Indian of Bell View Drive," said Hank, who was supposed to be my best friend. "My brother has seen him three times, so he oughta be well enough to see us."

When we got to my house, Grandpa was sitting on the patio. He had on his red shirt; but today he also wore a fringed leather vest that was decorated with beads. Instead of his usual cowboy

boots, he had solidly beaded moccasins on his feet that stuck out of his black trousers. Of course, he had his old black hat on—he was seldom without it. But it had been brushed and the feather in the beaded headband was proudly erect, its tip a brighter white. His hair lay in silver strands over the red shirt collar.

I stared just as my friends did, and I heard one of them murmur, "Wow!"

Grandpa looked up, and when his eyes met mine, they twinkled as if he was laughing inside. He nodded to me and my face got all hot. I could tell that he had known all along I was afraid he'd embarrass me in front of my friends.

"*Hau, hoksilas,* boys," he greeted and held out his hand.

My buddies passed in a single file and shook his hand as I introduced them. They were so polite, I almost laughed. "How, there, Grandpa," and even a "How-do-you-do, sir."

"You look fine, Grandpa," I said as the boys sat on the lawn chairs or on the patio floor.

"*Hanh,* yes," he agreed. "When I woke up this morning it seemed the right time to dress in the good clothes. I knew that my grandson would be bringing his friends."

"You guys want some lemonade or something?" I offered. No one answered. They were listening to Grandpa as he started telling how he'd killed the deer from which his vest was made.

Grandpa did most of the talking while my friends were there. I was so proud of him, and amazed at how respectfully quiet my buddies were. Mom had to chase them home at supper time. As they left they shook Grandpa's hand again and said to me:

"Martin, he's really great!"

"Yeah, man! Don't blame you for keeping him to yourself."

"Can we come back?"

But after they left, Mom said, "No more visitors for a while, Martin. Grandpa won't admit it, but his strength hasn't returned. He likes having company, but it tires him."

That evening, Grandpa called me to his room before he went to sleep. "Tomorrow," he said, "when you come home, it will be time to give you the medicine bag."

I felt a hard squeeze from where my heart is supposed to be and was scared, but I answered, "OK, Grandpa."

All night I had weird dreams about thunder and lightning on a high hill. From a distance I heard the slow beat of a drum. When I woke up in the morning, I felt as if I hadn't slept at all. At school it seemed as if the day would never end and, when it finally did, I ran home.

Grandpa was in his room, sitting on the bed. The shades were down and the place was dim and cool. I sat on the floor in front of Grandpa; but he didn't even look at me. After what seemed a long time he spoke.

"I sent your mother and sister away. What you will hear today is only for a man's ears. What you will receive is only for a man's hands." He fell silent and I felt shivers down my back.

"My father in his early manhood," Grandpa began, "made a vision quest to find a spirit guide for his life. You cannot understand how it was in that time, when the great Teton Sioux were first made to stay on the reservation. There was a strong need for guidance from *Wakantanka,* the Great Spirit. But too many of the young men were filled with despair and hatred. They thought it was

hopeless to search for a vision when the glorious life was gone, and only the hated confines of a reservation lay ahead. But my father held to the old ways.

"He carefully prepared for his quest with a purifying sweat bath and then he went alone to a high butte top to fast and pray. After three days, he received his sacred dream—in which he found, after long searching, the white man's iron. He did not understand his vision of finding something belonging to the white people; for in that time, they were the enemy. When he came down from the butte to cleanse himself at the stream below, he found the remains of a campfire and the broken shell of an iron kettle. This was a sign which reinforced his dream. He took a piece of the iron for his medicine bag, which he had made of elk skin years before, to prepare for his quest.

"He returned to his village, where he told his dream to the wise old men of the tribe. They gave him the name *Iron Shell*; but neither did they understand the meaning of the dream. This first Iron Shell kept the piece of iron with him at all times and believed it gave him protection from the evils of those unhappy days.

"Then a terrible thing happened to Iron Shell. He and several other young men were taken from their homes by the soldiers, and sent far away to a white man's boarding school. He was angry and lonesome for his parents and the young girl he had wed before he was taken away. At first Iron Shell resisted the teachers' attempts to change him, and he did not try to learn. One day it was his turn to work in the school's blacksmith shop. As he walked into the place, he knew that his medicine had brought him there to learn and work with the white man's iron.

"Iron Shell became a blacksmith and worked at the trade when he returned to the reservation. All of his life he treasured the medicine bag. When he was old, and I was a man, he gave it to me; for no one made the vision quest any more."

Grandpa quit talking and I stared in disbelief as he covered his face with his hands. His shoulders were shaking with quiet sobs, and I looked away until he began to speak again.

"I kept the bag until my son, your mother's father, was a man and had to leave us to fight in the war across the ocean. I gave him the bag, for I believed it would protect him in battle; but he did not take it with him. He was afraid that he would lose it. He died in a faraway place."

Again Grandpa was still and I felt his grief around me.

"My son," he went on after clearing his throat, "had only a daughter and it is not proper for her to know of these things."

He unbuttoned his shirt, pulled out the leather pouch, and lifted it over his head. He held it in his hand, turning it over and over as if memorizing how it looked.

"In the bag," he said as he opened it and removed two objects, "is the broken shell of the iron kettle, a pebble from the butte, and a piece of the sacred sage.[2]" He held the pouch upside down and dust drifted down.

"After the bag is yours, you must put a piece of prairie sage within and never open it again until you pass it on to your son." He replaced the pebble and the piece of iron, and tied the bag.

I stood up, somehow knowing I should. Grandpa slowly rose from the bed and stood upright in front of me holding the bag before my face. I closed my eyes and waited for him to slip it over my head. But he spoke.

"No, you need not wear it." He placed the soft leather bag in my right hand and closed my other hand over it. "It would not be right to wear it in this time and place where no one will understand. Put it safely away until you are again on the reservation. Wear it then, when you replace the sacred sage."

Grandpa turned and sat again on the bed. Wearily he leaned his head against the pillow. "Go," he said, "I will sleep now."

"Thank you, Grandpa," I said softly, and left with the bag in my hands.

That night Mom and Dad took Grandpa to the hospital. Two weeks later, I stood alone on the lonely prairie of the reservation and put the sacred sage in my medicine bag.

---

2. sage: A plant some think to have healing powers.

Close Up

1. (a) What Sioux objects does Martin show his friends to impress them? (b) Why does he think his friends would not be impressed by Grandpa?

2. Although Martin is embarrassed by Grandpa, he is also impressed by Grandpa's courage. (a) Do you think it took courage for Grandpa to visit his family? Why or why not? (b) What is the main purpose of his visit?

3. Grandpa's father obtained the medicine bag during a vision quest. (a) Why did he need guidance from the Great Spirit? (b) What did he find in his dream?

4. The quest taught Grandpa's father how to live in the modern world. But the medicine bag helped all his descendants hold on to the traditions of the Sioux world. What does Martin do at the end of the story that shows he plans to honor his Sioux heritage?

Theme

The theme is not always stated in the story. At times, it is implied. Sometimes you can find the implied theme by studying the problem the main character faces. The solution he or she finds to the problem often points to the theme.

1. The medicine bag creates a problem for Martin. At first, why doesn't he want to wear the medicine bag?

2. Martin accepts the medicine bag after he understands how much it means to his grandfather. When Grandpa talks about the bag, what does he do to show how important that bag is to him?

3. (a) Do you think Martin accepts the medicine bag because he doesn't want to hurt his grandfather, or because he has come to treasure the bag and what it stands for? (b) What evidence can you give to support your answer?

4. Martin solves his problem when he learns to treasure his heritage. His solution points to the theme of this story. Which statement best expresses the theme?
   a. People shouldn't laugh at the way other people dress.
   b. A gift isn't valuable unless it costs a lot of money.
   c. Many people lead fuller lives when they treasure their heritage.

MAIN IDEA

Ordering the Importance of Ideas

A paragraph usually contains several ideas about one topic. The most important idea about the topic is the main idea. The other ideas in the paragraph are related to the main idea. They support, or back up, the main idea. For example, read the following paragraph:

"We always had some authentic Sioux article to show our listeners. One year Cheryl had new moccasins that Grandpa had made. On another visit he gave me a small, round, flat, rawhide drum which was decorated with a painting of a warrior riding a horse. He taught me a real Sioux chant to sing while I beat the drum with a leather-covered stick that had a feather on the end. Man, that really made an impression."

The main idea is, Martin and Cheryl had authentic Sioux articles. Four ideas support this statement. (1) Cheryl had moccasins that Grandpa had made. (2) Martin had a rawhide drum. (3) They knew a real Sioux chant. (4) They had a leather-covered stick with a feather on it.

▶ Read each paragraph below. Then read each group of three statements that follows the paragraph. On a separate piece of paper, write M by the statement that expresses the main idea. Write S by each statement that supports the main idea.

"We never showed our friends Grandpa's picture. Not that we were ashamed of him, but because we knew that the glamorous tales we told didn't go with the real thing. Our friends would have laughed at the picture, because Grandpa wasn't tall and stately like TV Indians. His hair wasn't in braids, but hung in stringy, gray strands on his neck; and he was old. He was our great-grandfather, and he didn't live in a tipi, but all by himself in a part log, part tar-paper shack on the Rosebud Reservation in South Dakota. So when Grandpa came to visit us, I was so ashamed and embarrassed, I could've died."

a. Grandpa wasn't stately and tall like TV Indians.
b. Martin and Cheryl told marvelous tales about Grandpa that did not fit the real person.
c. Grandpa didn't live in a tipi but in a part-log, part-tar-paper shack.

"He carefully prepared for his quest with a purifying sweat bath and then he went alone to a high butte top to fast and pray. After three days, he received his sacred dream—in which he found, after long searching, the white man's iron. He did not understand his vision of finding something belonging to the white people; for in that time, they were the enemy. When he came down from the butte to cleanse himself at the stream below, he found the remains of a campfire and the broken shell of an iron kettle. This was a sign which reinforced his dream. He took a piece of the iron for his medicine bag, which he had made of elk skin years before, to prepare for his quest."

    d.   He did not understand what his dream meant.
    e.   He found an iron kettle that reinforced his dream.
    f.   In his vision he found the white man's iron.

WORD ATTACK

Using Word Stems for Word Building

Many new words are built by adding prefixes or suffixes to smaller words or word stems. For example, *reservation* was built by adding a suffix to *reserve*. To reserve something is to set it aside for a particular purpose. A reservation is a place that has been set aside for a particular purpose.

1.   Use each word in parentheses to build a word that fits in the blank. You will have to change the spelling of some of the smaller words slightly. Check a dictionary to be sure you have the correct spelling for each word you build.

    a.   Their grandfather taught the children how important the _____ (preserve) of their culture was.

    b.   Grandpa's arrival in town caused quite a _____ (motion).

    c.   Mother wanted to _____ (brace) Grandpa when she saw him.

    d.   Grandpa and the people around him walked down the street in a strange _____ (process).

    e.   The children were surprised to find that their friends were very _____ (press) by their grandfather's knowledge.

    f.   Mother felt much _____ (affect) for her grandfather.

    g.   The vision made a big _____ (press) on Iron Shell.

    h.   Martin had to _____ (place) the sacred sage.

    i.   Grandpa thought it _____ (seem) to show his feelings.

    j.   Martin did not want to _____ (play) the medicine bag.

2.   Write new sentences using each word you formed above.

The Fallen Star

Grace Nies Fletcher

"You couldn't expect a gift horse to be perfect, and Tod would have to take his chances."

Ever since Tod Brown was six, he had hungered and thirsted after a horse of his own; when he couldn't get a real one, he rode anyway. Every Sunday night when it came time for the Gene Autry program, he'd put on his dime-store cowboy suit with the black cardboard sombrero, mount a dining-room chair turned upside down in front of the radio, and canter madly all through the program. He'd already hung around the neighbor's stable across the street enough to know what to do. He'd throw his leg over the saddle, make a little chirruping sound in his throat, and his cheeks would grow red and his gray eyes would shine as off they'd go, out of the living room and up the night-dark village street, the little blonde boy on the big horse cantering happily with the wind singing past their ears. Watching him, you could almost hear the thunder of hooves as he did.

"He gets so excited he doesn't sleep.

I don't know what we're going to do," his mother worried when she came back to the living room from tucking him in for the night. She asked his father, "You think we'll ever be able to buy him a horse, Fred?"

"It isn't just affording an old nag," Fred Brown explained heavily. "What would we do with a horse on a fifty-foot lot? No barn, no pasture .... Tod might just as well find out early that he wasn't born with a silver spoon in his mouth. He'll get over it."

Tod didn't get over it. Most of his friends as he grew older belonged to the 4-H Riding Club, who let him help take care of their horses. He even liked doing the dirty jobs, forking out the stalls, cleaning the horses' hooves. He polished lovingly the saddles he couldn't afford to buy. In return, often the other kids would offer him a ride. So he came to know the feel of a strong, real horse's body between his legs, the whip of sun and wind across his face, and the sweet harmony of motion that comes only when a horse and rider move as one along a greening country road, at peace with the world and with each other.

But by the time he was thirteen Tod realized if he was ever going to own a horse, he'd have to earn it for himself. He was a tall weed of a lad with feet too big for his body and a voice that broke from high C to low G. But unlike most uncertain adolescents, he knew what he wanted . . . a Morgan mare. "Morgans have guts and sense and if you get 'em young enough, you can train 'em to do almost anything," he told his mother earnestly. All during the long hot summer he worked stubbornly, saving his money. He picked beans at the Italian truck farm, fought off mosquitoes in the raspberry patch as he packed the fragile fruit carefully for market, cut lawns, and browbeat the neighbors into buying magazines till by fall he actually had $87.96 "horse money" in the bank.

"If I had a barn to keep her in, I could maybe get a mare from one of those summer camps to keep for the winter," he told his mother. "They let you have 'em from now till June. With hay at $35 a ton and a bag of grain $4.78, I could feed a horse for quite a while . . . if I had one."

He glanced sharply at her to see if she was laughing at him for feeding a horse he didn't have, on oats and grain he hadn't bought, in a barn that wasn't built yet. But instead, queerly, she looked more as if she wanted to cry. He heard the clatter of hooves outside in the street and ran to the open kitchen window. It was the 4-H Club riding by and one of them yelled to him.

"Hey, Tod! We're going up to the stone bridge on an all-day picnic. Wanna come?"

"Gee, sure." Frantically Tod tore out the door, grabbed his battered bike from the garage and pedaled madly to keep up with the horses. Soon they were all moving together down Main Street under the arching elms in the most perfect democracy there is, youngsters in a small New England town, with the riders clattering ahead and Tod trailing behind on his bike, his face radiant because he'd been asked on a horse picnic.

"Is that the most pathetic sight you ever saw? It's a crime Tod hasn't a horse," one of the neighbors said to another as they watched the little cavalcade go by. Her own three sons were in that group, each riding his own horse, and she knew how Tod felt, loving horse flesh the way he did; it was a disease for which the only cure was possession. She'd heard yesterday of a man who wanted a good home for an old Morgan mare, but Tod had no place to keep her, unless . . . . She turned excitedly to the neighbor who lived right across the street from the Browns, demanding, "If Tod got a horse, could he keep it in your barn?"

"Of course, he could. But where . . . ."

The other woman explained about the old Morgan that was to be given away because its best days were over, adding, "I have an old McClallan saddle we don't use; it's hard as a tax collector but Tod wouldn't mind. Let's phone around, see what we can find for him."

The whole town knew about Tod's horse fund and were glad to help, so by nightfall he had been offered not only an ancient Morgan mare but a box stall, a saddle and bridle, and even enough hay to keep her for four months. The local vet offered to go get the mare from a nearby town at half price, his contribution. Tod and the Browns simply couldn't believe it. It didn't seem real that he was actually going to have a horse of his own, even when he stood in the door of the barn across the street from his home and watched the horse truck coming up the driveway. Tod was shaking all over with excitement as he saw the vet backing out the bay mare, nervous and skittish from her ride.

"Well, Tod, here she is. Her name's Star," the vet said, handing the boy her halter rope. "She ain't no filly; she's twenty five if she's a day; but Morgans are tough. Look out she doesn't stumble. That left foreleg looks to me like she might've bowed a tendon one time . . . ."

He stopped because Tod wasn't hearing a word. He was just standing there, his shining gray eyes lost in the old mare's liquid brown ones, like some-one seeing a dream walking. Easy to see where she got her name, from that white star on her forehead. "Star!" he said softly, and she pricked up her ears. She was a Morgan, all right. Look at her long shoulders, her deep wide chest. But you'd never think a horse could have so much gray· hair! There was a line of it running under her ears, and her neck was peppered with it. She must be awful old. Tod gulped, uncertainly. Suddenly the mare caught sight of the carrot he'd stuffed into his back dungaree pocket, and when he didn't give it to her at once, she arched her neck, pawed with her forefoot, begging.

"Look!" Tod gasped to the vet. "She knows tricks!" He held out the carrot to her and the touch of her soft wet lips made her seem real at last, his own Morgan mare. "A clever old horse is the smartest thing there is," Tod said loudly, as if the vet had contradicted him. "Come on, Star!" As he led her into the stall that was to be her home, the old mare lifted her feet jauntily to match the fierce pride in Tod's voice.

From that instant Tod and Star were separated only when it was absolutely necessary for him to eat, sleep, or go to school. The whole Brown house smelt of hay, horse liniment, . . . and happiness. He had no fear of her at all. The very first day after he got her, Tod rode Star on an all-day picnic up Nobscot Mountain with the rest of the 4-H'ers. But when he didn't get home by dusk, his mother was frantic with worry. After all, most of Tod's riding to date had been in his own mind, and he hadn't the faintest idea what Star might shy at . . . cars? . . . a piece of paper blowing? She was so relieved when she saw them coming up the street with Tod still in his saddle that she ran up the hill to the barn to meet them.

"Star kept right up with the rest," Tod told her happily as he slid from the saddle, so stiff he could hardly stand. "She can jump, too. We came down by the back way. I tried to hold her in, but she went right over a fence after the others, light as a leaf."

"It's a mercy her whole front end didn't give way!" his mother gasped. "She's too old to jump."

"She knows what she can do," Tod boasted. "Don't you, Girl?"

But she stumbled over the threshold of her stall and his mother remembered nervously a steeplechase she'd seen in the movies where a horse stumbled, fell, and the rider didn't get up because his thigh was broken. She shook herself mentally, remembering all life was

pretty dangerous these days. You couldn't expect a gift horse to be perfect, and Tod would have to take his chances. It was silly to worry when he was so happy.

She had to admit that Star was a great help. It used to be a major operation to get Tod up mornings, but now he shot out of bed at six when the alarm went off so he'd have time to feed, groom, and visit with Star before he went to school. He brushed her coat till it gleamed like brown satin, cleaned and oiled her hooves as carefully as if she had been a racehorse instead of a tired old nag, soaped her saddle till he could roll up the skirts like cloth. He even braided her foretop. He spent his carefully hoarded cash to buy her a dark-blue blanket with white bands, and kept a daily record on a sheet tacked to her stall door of how much he fed her. When Star, who was by years the oldest horse there, won two red ribbons and a yellow one at the 4-H Gymkana, Tod tacked the colors to her door as proudly as if she'd won the Kentucky Derby. He even brushed his own hair . . . a minor miracle . . . in order to look nice when he rode her every day after school.

"It's the first time in his life he's accepted full responsibility for anything and carried it through," his mother told his father with great satisfaction. "Star's the best thing that ever happened to him."

And then the blow fell. Star had arrived in September, and the weeks had flown by until now it was late December and very cold, below zero for days as it so often is in New England at Christmas time. One morning when Tod's mother made his bed, she noticed there was no top sheet.

"Oh, that ole thing," Tod muttered uneasily when she asked him about it. "I tore it up to make bandages for Star's legs. They're kind of stiff these cold mornings. But she's perfectly all right," he added hastily. "I think she remembers where her leg was hurt before and puts on a limp just to hear me say, 'Poor Star.' " But his mother could see he was worried. He borrowed his father's liniment from the medicine chest and stayed up at the barn so long that night rubbing Star's legs they had to go call him for supper. And that night after his mother put out his light, he kept her talking about Star to reassure himself.

"I bet she's the smartest horse in the world," he told his mother. "Did you know you can talk to her without words? It was a kind of private language between the two of them," he explained. "Star understood the tone of your voice, the nudge of your heel, the tightening of your muscles when you rode, so that often she knew which way you wanted to turn before you did yourself." Then his voice broke as he asked anxiously, "How long does a horse live, Mom?"

"I don't know," she told him. Coldness touched her for she knew that if anything happened to Star, it'd make Tod sick too, literally. Maybe she could save enough out of her housekeeping money to have the vet look at Star's legs, go over her thoroughly when Tod was at school and find out what the score really was.

But tragedy struck too fast. The very next afternoon when Tod was out riding in the snow with the rest of the 4-H Club, Star's bad leg gave way and she fell. Tod rolled out of the saddle in time so he wasn't hurt and they managed to get the old mare up, but she limped painfully back to the barn, almost walking on her pastern. The vet looked grave when he saw her.

"Must be the same leg she hurt before," the vet said. Tod nodded and waited anxiously for the verdict; he winced when the mare reared as the vet touched her leg. He asked, "Is it . . . bad?"

"Could be. Yeah." Then seeing the boy's face grow white, stark terror rise in his gray eyes, the vet added hastily, to keep him busy, "That leg's swelling. I'll give you some medicine to rub in later and lend you some proper bandages."

For hours in the icy barn, Tod put on cold compresses till his hands were so numb he couldn't feel them anymore; and then his mother took over, helped him bind on the gray bandages. But by next morning two more of Star's legs were so swollen that she lay there in her stall, unable to get up. Tod refused to go to school. He worked over her all day and would have stayed all night if his parents had let him, but his mother insisted upon his coming down for a hot meal. "But Star can't eat. It'd choke me," Tod protested. When he ate finally, his dinner came up faster than it went down.

"What are you going to do?" his mother asked his father. "Let him go back up to that icy barn?"

"Better let him do it," his father advised. "This has hit him pretty hard, but he's almost fourteen. He'll have to work it out himself."

Tod fought against going back to school the next day, but his parents won. "If he can't study, at least he'll be warm," his mother figured. She was washing the breakfast dishes when she looked out the kitchen window and saw the vet coming up the back steps slowly, as if he didn't want to. He came into the kitchen, sat down and twisted his shapeless hat unhappily in his hands as he told her, "That mare ought to be shot. Even if she gets well enough to walk again, she isn't safe for Tod to ride. She's apt to fall on him and break his neck."

Tod's mother drew a deep, shaking breath. "You can't cure her?"

"Can you cure old age?" he asked her. "She's nearer thirty than twenty five, and she's got arthritis and that bowed tendon . . . she's in agony. Probably has been for weeks. I hate like heck to say so, but it isn't fair not to put her out of her misery." He got to his feet, started for the door, muttering, "But thank God I don't have to be the one to tell Tod!"

Tod's mother couldn't finish her housework. Though she knew they couldn't afford it, she sent for a second vet to look at Star, just to make sure; and he was even more emphatic that the mare should be put to sleep. Mrs. Brown was so distracted that she called her husband at his office. He came home to talk it over, but there was only one decision possible; if it was a matter of the boy's life or the horse's, there wasn't any question what had to be done.

"It doesn't seem possible you could get so attached to any animal in so short a time," Tod's mother mourned. She shivered. "It's . . . it's just like shooting one of the family!" Only, of course, it wasn't just any horse; it was Star, Tod's first horse, for which he'd waited since he was six, the smartest horse in the world, with whom he spoke a language deeper than words . . . . She gasped, "I can't tell him. I can't!"

But she had to. Tod took it so quietly that at first she thought he hadn't heard.

He just stood there looking at her as still as if he'd been turned to stone. His voice was stony too as he asked, "You mean Star's hurt so she can't get well?"

His mother nodded, speechless at the agony in his eyes. *If only you could ease this pain for him like you used to his baby cuts and bruises.* She asked, "Where you going, Son?" But he rushed from the room without answering. As he shot by the window, she saw that his face was working. *He didn't want you to see him being "chicken."* She watched him run up the hill as if a posse were after him, to his fallen Star. *Probably you'd better not tell him Star was being shot till it was all over; then he wouldn't have to bear it twice, in fact and in his imagination.*

Nobody slept very well that night, and the next morning before Tod appeared at breakfast, his mother asked his father, "When are you going to . . . do it?"

"It's better to get it over with fast," his father said. "I'll call the Society for Prevention of Cruelty to Animals today. It'll be all over by the time Tod gets home from school." He put down the coffee cup he'd been pretending to drink from, grabbed his hat, and for the first time in years went off without kissing his wife.

Tod went up to the barn to feed Star before he left for school. When he came down again, his mother was frightened. His face was so expressionless; it was unnatural for a child his age to hold himself in so. He said, "I gave her all the feed there was left in the box—six quarts. All old horses love to eat. She's up today, so I left her window open so she can see out to the street. She loves to watch people passing by."

He spoke as if this were just any other day. *Of course, how could he know it wasn't?* "That's fine," his mother said. But as he went off to school swinging his green flannel bookbag, she couldn't help wondering what had come over him to make him take Star's illness so quietly all at once? There was something queer here. She herself was so nervous she dropped a cup and broke it when the telephone rang. It was her husband saying everything was all set; the society with the long name had promised to send someone to take care of Star this morning.

"Be sure the boy is gone," the society had warned, "because we have to shoot the horse right there, and then cart it away. But our man is an expert. She'll never know what hit her."

Tod's mother couldn't keep away from the window, wanting to see the truck when it came and not wanting to. It came about half past eleven, a big green truck without any markings. She watched it go up the hill to the barn, and then in a very short time, the truck came down again and it was all over. So short a breath between life and death; between the ecstatic whinnying when Star heard Tod's step in the barn, between her following him around the paddock like a pet dog . . . and nothing. *Would there be any blood stains? What would the man do with the mare's halter?* She decided she'd better go to the barn and make sure everything was all right before Tod came home.

Her feet made no sound on the soft snow as she went up the hill and there was no one about; it was all as quiet as a funeral. The barn door was open and she stood for a moment looking in. The blue and white blanket Tod had bought for Star so proudly lay in a crumpled heap on the floor, and the halter was lying on top of it. But there was no other sign the man had been there with his gun; no sound even, nothing moving, alive; only the morning sunlight pouring yellow through the dusty window Tod had left open because Star liked to look out . . . . And then her heart leaped into her throat as she heard something stir beyond, in Star's stall. Maybe the man hadn't done what he came for after all!

She tiptoed over, peered inside fearfully. Tod was lying there face-down, spread-eagled on the extra-soft bed of straw he'd spread for Star this morning; and his whole body was shaken with great silent sobs. *He hadn't gone to school at all,* she realized numbly; *he just knew, and must have heard his father and me talking this morning. Had seen it all? Or had he come . . . after? What could you say to him?* Suddenly, looking at him sprawled out defenseless, she knew she had no right to be here at all; this was holy ground. There were some sorrows too deep to be spoken of; they had to be borne alone. She tiptoed away quietly and left him there.

The next half hour was the longest of her life. She busied herself making the cookies he liked best, chocolate chip, but she burned the first batch because she couldn't see. *It just didn't seem fair; Tod had worked so hard and waited so long, and now he couldn't ride again with the gang. Much better if Star had never come.* It was exactly lunch time when she heard his step at the door, the thud as he hurled his bookbag on the kitchen floor. She turned, half-afraid, to look at him. But his head was high, and it seemed to her that some of the sunlight that had flooded Star's empty stall lingered in his blonde rumpled hair.

He said slowly, "Star's gone. You know something, Mom? She lived a good life. She always ran for me on willing feet . . . and she was loved. She won't be cold any more and her feet won't hurt."

It was Star he was thinking of, not his own loss; that had carried him through. As he went quietly to his room and shut the door, his mother's heart gave a great leap of pride, for her son had gone up the hill to his fallen Star a little boy . . . but he had come down a man grown.

1. (a) At the beginning of the story, what three reasons prevent Tod from having a horse? (b) What does Tod do to get a horse?

2. (a) How is Star different from the horse Tod has dreamed of? (b) What does Tod say that shows he is pleased with the horse anyway?

3. (a) When does Tod first become concerned about Star's leg? (b) What does he do to make her more comfortable?

4. (a) What happens when Tod rides Star in the snow with the 4-H Club? (b) Why doesn't the vet think Star can be cured?

5. (a) On the day Star is to be put out of her misery, what does Tod do that shows he knows what will happen to Star? (b) When does his mother learn that Tod has known all along what would happen to Star?

6. Tod overcomes his grief when he thinks that Star "won't be cold any more, and her feet won't hurt." Do you think this shows he really cares for Star? Why or why not?

Theme

Sometimes the theme is not directly stated. It is suggested, or implied, through characters and events. At times, the title of the story provides a clue to the theme. For example, you probably know the book or the movie *Gone with the Wind*. The title provides you with a clue to the book's theme. It tells you that the theme says something about things that have passed, or have gone with the wind.

1. All of Tod's hopes and dreams center around Star. When Star falls, Tod's hopes and dreams fall with her. (a) Do you think the word *Star* in the title could have a double meaning? (b) What else could it mean besides the horse's name? (Clue: Have you ever wished on a star or thanked your lucky stars?)

2. The title gives you a clue to the theme. It tells you that the theme says something about a person's fallen hopes and dreams. Which statement best expresses the theme?
    a. People who place their hopes on horses will be disappointed.
    b. As people grow and mature, they learn to consider only their own dreams and hopes.
    c. As people grow and mature, they learn to put others before themselves.

MAIN IDEA

Finding Implied Main Ideas

The main idea is the most important idea about the topic of the paragraph. Sometimes the main idea is not stated in the paragraph. You have to read closely, add up all the details, and state the main idea in your own words.

For example, in the following paragraph, the main idea is not stated. By reading carefully and adding up the details, you can state the main idea: The neighbor is trying to think of a way to get the Morgan mare for Tod.

> " 'Is that the most pathetic sight you ever saw? It's a crime Tod hasn't a horse,' one of the neighbors said to another as they watched the little cavalcade go by. Her own three sons were in that group, each riding his own horse, and she knew how Tod felt, loving horse flesh the way he did; it was a disease for which the only cure was possession. She'd heard yesterday of a man who wanted a good home for an old Morgan mare, but Tod had no place to keep her, unless . . . . She turned excitedly to the neighbor who lived right across the street from the Browns, demanding, 'If Tod got a horse, could he keep it in your barn?' "

▶ In each of the following paragraphs, the main idea is not stated. Read each paragraph carefully. Then state the main idea in your own words.

   a.   "He stopped because Tod wasn't hearing a word. He was just standing there, his shining gray eyes lost in the old mare's liquid brown ones, like someone seeing a dream walking. Easy to see where she got her name, from that white star on her forehead. 'Star!' he said softly, and she pricked up her ears. She was a Morgan, all right. Look at her long shoulders, her deep wide chest. But you'd never think a horse could have so much gray hair! There was a line of it running under her ears, and her neck was peppered with it. She must be awful old. Tod gulped, uncertainly. Suddenly the mare caught sight of the carrot he'd stuffed into his back dungaree pocket, and when he didn't give it to her at once, she arched her neck, pawed with her forefoot, begging."

   b.   "For hours in the icy barn, Tod put on cold compresses till his hands were so numb he couldn't feel them anymore; and then his mother took over, helped him bind on the gray bandages. But by the next morning two more of Star's legs were so swollen that she lay there in her stall, unable to get up. Tod refused to go to school. He worked over her all day and would have stayed all night if his parents had let him, but his mother insisted upon his coming down for a hot meal. 'But Star can't eat. It'd choke me.' Tod protested. When he ate finally, his dinner came up faster than it went down.''

c.   "He spoke as if this were just any other day. *Of course, how could he know it wasn't?* 'That's fine,' his mother said. But as he went off to school swinging his green flannel bookbag, she couldn't help wondering what had come over him to make him take Star's illness so quietly all at once? There was something queer here. She herself was so nervous she dropped a cup and broke it when the telephone rang. It was her husband saying everything was all set; the society with the long name had promised to send someone to take care of Star this morning."

WORD ATTACK

Understanding Words Used as Nouns and Verbs

A noun is a word that names a person, a place, a thing, or an idea. A verb is a word that expresses action. Sometimes a word may be used as either a noun or a verb. For example, "There were *mushrooms* growing in the backyard," and "The problem *mushroomed* out of proportion." The meaning of a word in a sentence depends on whether it is used as a noun or a verb.

▶ Read the sentences below. Decide whether the *italicized* word is used as a noun or a verb. On a separate piece of paper, write *n.* or *v.* next to each sentence. Then look up each italicized word in the dictionary, and write its definition.

a. Each of the boys had his own *mount.*
b. Tod would *mount* his horse and go for a ride.
c. They hired someone to *fork* hay.
d. He let the food slip off his *fork.*
e. Star would *prick* up her ears when she heard Tod.
f. Tod felt a *prick* of sadness when he thought of Star.
g. They took sandwiches spiced with salt and *pepper* on the picnic.
h. The horse's coat was *peppered* with silver.
i. Tod's mother wanted to *stall* Star's fate.
j. Star and Tod were in the *stall.*

The Whale

Theodore Roethke

There was a most Monstrous Whale:
He had no Skin, he had no Tail.
When he tried to Spout, that Great Big Lubber,
The best he could do was Jiggle his Blubber.

The Hippo

Theodore Roethke

A Head or Tail—which does he lack?
I think his Forward's coming back!
He lives on Carrots, Leeks, and Hay;
He starts to yawn—it takes all Day—

5 Some time I think I'll live that way.

Squirrel

Felice Holman

Scolding
Holding
Boldly raiding
Plotting
5 Waiting
Ambuscading[1]
Highly climbing
And descending
Digging
10 Hiding
And forgetting.

---

1. ambuscading (ăm′bə-skād′ĭng) *v.*: Ambushing.

Activity ▶ Write a short poem describing an animal. You might want to try ending each line with an *-ing* verb form.

An Appropriate Time for Tears

Cynthia Irace

When Grandpa died, I remember everyone cried. Everyone but me, that is. I suppose I should have, but I just couldn't, and I really didn't know why. You probably wouldn't think of Grandpa's dying of a heart attack as such an important public event. But he headlined the newspapers, which were filled with his pictures and articles on his life from early boyhood to his death. And most of all, on his fame. I wish now I'd cried when Grandpa died.

It was to me, of all Gramps' twelve grandchildren, that he left his track shoes, which were really an old pair of sneakers: Gramps had been a famous track star in his youth, and his yellow track shoes with the black stripes were the sneakers he had worn when he won his first meet in high school. I'd been told how he had treasured the track shoes more than anything else he'd ever owned. They were a kind of good-luck

charm for him as his endurance and speed increased unbelievably throughout his high school years and beyond. Of course, his feet had grown out of those sneakers before he'd gotten much wear out of them; so he packed them safely away in their practically brand-new condition.

I was in awe when his track shoes were presented to me in the old brown shoe box, and along with them Grandpa's journal. I had admired my grandfather's talent, and my eternal dream was to be a track star too. Everyone said I was a better-than-average runner, and Grandpa used to clock me as I ran around my high school track. I was going to miss Gramps, not having him out there watching me run. But now I had his track shoes.

It was amazing that they fitted, and I only hoped I'd get off to a good start with them before I outgrew them. I was sure they would bring me the fame that they had brought Gramps. Gramps was superstitious, as most athletes seem to be, and his track shoes were his lucky piece. When I was given those shoes, I guess the superstition came with them—or at least something did. I felt it was a miracle that they fitted me so perfectly. I knew they'd bring me luck.

Although I had faith in myself and the sneakers, I was prepared for a disaster the day of my first race. The guys on the team did not like me. They just wouldn't accept me, and they usually made practice fairly uncomfortable. But running was my life; and I knew I had it in me to be the best runner there ever was, maybe even better than Grandpa. I knew he'd have liked that. Gramps acted as my father too. I don't remember when Dad died; I was only a baby at the time. However, Gramps did everything he possibly could for me, just as my real dad would have done.

I had never worn the sneakers to practice. I had others I wore then because I didn't want to wear these out. They had to last for as long as they possibly could. And I vowed never to dispose of them, even when they became completely worn out. This treasure would always remain. I wished it were possible to press them between the pages of my journal. However, I would have to be content instead to place the sneakers safely away on the top shelf of my closet, and keep their luck in my memory.

The guys smirked at my sneakers when they first saw them. Sure, they were old-fashioned; but they had been Gramps' once, and to me they were unique. I think the guys were jealous that I was related to the famous Henry Campion, but I didn't care. I just had to win this first race—for Grandpa, for myself and for the team—even though they sarcastically chuckled at me and my track shoes. And we did it! Our school won the meet; and I came in first in my race, making phenomenal time.

Every meet my high school competed in that year we won! And my teammates became much friendlier with each new victory. Finally I felt as if I was really a part of the team. I realized it was probably just because we were winning, but I let it pass. After all, how could one not be friends with one's own teammates?

I was feeling so great about everything when the blow fell. Well, it didn't really suddenly fall—I had known all along that it was bound to happen. Then it did. I couldn't imagine anything bad happening at that point in my life. I was friends with the guys on the team, my grades in school were good, my speed and endurance were increasing and we had won all our meets of the season. Then my feet grew. Of course, they didn't grow overnight. I was aware that my track shoes were feeling tighter; but I tried not to pay attention. I wanted to believe it was just the summer heat that had made my feet expand or swell or something. But it was true—the sneakers just didn't fit anymore. I wanted to cry, but I didn't.

Instead, I opened Grandpa's journal to the place where he had written about his growing out of the track shoes. I had saved this part of his journal to read when it happened to me. I guess I'd hoped he had written some words of encouragement or reassurance, maybe something he would have said to me if he were alive, about the situation with which I found myself confronted.

Though I didn't know quite what it was I was hoping to find when I began reading, I guess Gramps knew when he wrote it, because I found it. It was dated June 2, 1915, when Gramps was fifteen years old; and what he wrote I'll always remember:

"Panic set in today. Whoa, God, I first thought. Our last and most important meet is in two days; and God, do you know what finally happened? I had to pack my good-luck charm away. I just can't squeeze into those track shoes anymore; and even if I could, they'd do me more harm than good because they are just too tight. I'm going out to buy a new pair tomorrow, and they'll take over where my old racers left off. My first reaction was panic, but now I realize those yellow and black track shoes got me started all right; but my engine is still running strong and will continue. They just gave me the initial—though much needed—push. Once an athlete, always an athlete. We're going to win that last meet, and I'm going to run my best ever."

I immediately went out to buy a new pair of track shoes. Looking in the window of the sporting goods store, I saw a pair of yellow and black Puma track shoes. They were sharp; but somehow they weren't Gramps' old sneakers. I knew no shoes would be the same, so I figured I might as well buy a completely different pair. I tried on many kinds and finally settled for a bright red pair. "How much are these?" I asked the store clerk.

"Twenty-seven fifty," he replied.

I knew Gramps had never had to pay that for a pair of sneakers. It would have seemed an absurdity to pay that even for a fine pair of racers when he was a kid.

However, I paid it, carried the track shoes home in their brand-new shoe box, and put them on the floor of my closet.

I knew I was going to pass Gramps' sneakers on to one of my children; and I only wondered how many more times they'd be handed down. I supposed they'd be passed down until they were worn out completely. I debated within my own mind what would wear out first, the yellow and black track shoes or the line of descendants who would be runners. The shoes seemed eternal. I wondered if the line of runners in our family would be eternal too. I certainly hoped so.

I became increasingly more successful with my running. Gramps had been right. The winning was in my feet, not in the shoes; and my red track shoes carried me just as swiftly around the track in all the races I wore them in. And now my dream had expanded. I wanted to run and represent the United States in the Olympics in three years. Well, actually, my dream hadn't expanded; it had just become more real. I'd always wanted to be an Olympic runner, only now I felt I really could do it; and I knew I had to be willing to work very hard.

I underwent rigorous training. The coach helped to keep me going, especially toward the trials' end, when I felt I hadn't enough energy to pull through. If I lost, as so many did, I would be losing everything I'd worked toward in a matter of minutes. My body felt hollow; my head seemed suspended in my chest through it all. We each knew any one of us could be eliminated at any time, and it was an icy thought. Hopes were so easily shattered. The competition was intense; and it was so often disheartening to see athletes lose out in the trials after having trained their entire lives to make it to the

Olympic Games. However, each competitor who was eliminated was a good sport about it.

Mom cried whenever she watched me practice. She couldn't take my pained expression, a mixture of anguish and anticipation, as I ran pantingly past her. I'd be reaching for a finish line that always seemed miles away, never getting closer. But it always did, and that's what made it all worthwhile. What a feeling of conquest and victory when my feet stepped over the last yard each time. The tears would dribble down Mom's cheeks while she watched my face turn red and then go white as I covered another yard. She would cry harder tears of laughter and joy as I crossed the finish line and run to hug me and hold me up at the same time. We would both be thrilled.

I knew that she thought of her father whenever she saw me run. Those yellow and black track shoes must have really brought him back for her when I used to wear them to run. They had been a wonder machine.

I made it through the trials, and then it was on to the Olympic Games. I may not have been continually smiling on the outside during the training; but I was constantly beaming on the inside. I couldn't believe that I'd finally made it to the United States Olympic Team.

Three years had passed. I was no longer wearing the bright red sneakers, and hadn't been for a long time. The track shoes I wore now were just like all the others, but my feet were different. My feet, like Gramps', were winning feet. I had worked hard and improved fantastically as I had trained for the Olympics.

Mom had been going with me everywhere to watch me run. She was almost as excited about it all as I was. I knew what she was thinking as the day neared for us to leave for the games. She was wishing Gramps could be there to see me run. I knew he was there. He had been with me at every race, and I knew he would be at this one too. It wasn't something I could have explained; it was just a feeling which I was sure about. I would be running for Gramps, and he knew it. He would be there beside me at the starting line and beside me all the way to the finish line, whispering words of insight and incentive in my ear.

And suddenly there I was, representing my own country, thousands of miles away in a foreign land. It seemed that half of America came to watch their athletes and the kid whose running career had begun with a pair of almost antique track shoes. The crowd was cheering, and I knew it was behind me all the way.

I wish now I'd cried when Gramps died. I loved Gramps; but I just couldn't cry then. I guess it was because I really could not believe he was dead—and he wasn't really. He was still alive in me and he would go on living. No, I didn't cry when Gramps died; but as I stood in the Olympic Stadium, the tears trickled down my cheeks as I waited for my name and country to be announced. This was a more appropriate time for tears—tears of joy not sorrow, because I knew Gramps was proud.

The announcement swelled out across the stadium: "First place, from the United States of America—Mary Alice Laracy!" Gramps and I received our gold medal, just as I had planned.

Close Up

1. (a) How does Mary Alice hope to follow in her grandfather's footsteps? (b) What does her grandfather leave her to help her fulfill her ambition?

2. (a) What happens to Mary Alice's confidence when she outgrows Grandfather's sneakers? (b) How does Grandfather help her from the pages of his journal?

3. Mary Alice could not cry tears of sorrow when her grandfather died because she could not believe he was really dead. (a) How does she feel that she has kept him alive? (b) Why does she cry when she wins the Olympics?

Theme

A symbol is something that means more than its dictionary definition. It is something real in itself. But it also suggests many other ideas. For example, a fireplace or hearth is an actual object. But it also suggests the ideas of family love, togetherness, and security. When a symbol appears in a story, it often provides a clue to the theme.

1. One object appears repeatedly in "An Appropriate Time for Tears." What is this object?

2. When Mary Alice inherits her grandfather's sneakers, she also inherits her grandfather's strength and determination. What will Mary Alice pass on when she gives the sneakers to one of her children?

3. Do you think the sneakers are a good symbol? Why or why not?

4. The sneakers provide a clue to the theme. Write a sentence that you think states the theme.

Activities

1. Find out who Wilma Rudolph was and who Jesse Owens was. Look for their names in an encyclopedia or in the library card catalog. Share your information with the class.

2. Make a list of or bring in pictures of symbols you meet in everyday life.

MAIN IDEA

Finding the Main Idea

The main idea is the most important idea about the topic of a paragraph. For example, the topic of the following paragraph is Grandfather's track shoes. The main idea is that Grandfather left Mary Alice his most treasured possession, his track shoes.

> "It was to me, of all Gramps' twelve grandchildren, that he left his track shoes, which were really an old pair of sneakers: Gramps had been a famous track star in his youth, and his yellow track shoes with the black stripes were the sneakers he had worn when he won his first meet in high school. I'd been told how he had treasured the track shoes more than anything else he'd ever owned. They were a kind of good-luck charm for him as his endurance and speed increased unbelievably throughout his high school years and beyond. Of course, his feet had grown out of those sneakers before he'd gotten much wear out of them; so he packed them safely away in their practically brand-new condition."

► State the main idea of each paragraph below.

a. "I became increasingly more successful with my running. Gramps had been right. The winning was in my feet, not in the shoes; and my red track shoes carried me just as swiftly around the track in all the races I wore them in. And now my dream had expanded. I wanted to run and represent the United States in the Olympics in three years. Well, actually, my dream hadn't expanded; it had just become more real. I'd always wanted to be an Olympic runner, only now I felt I really could do it; and I knew I had to be willing to work very hard."

b. "Mom cried whenever she watched me practice. She couldn't take my pained expression, a mixture of anguish and anticipation, as I ran pantingly past her. I'd be reaching for a finish line that always seemed miles away, never getting closer. But it always did, and that's what made it all worthwhile. What a feeling of conquest and victory when my feet stepped over the last yard each time. The tears would dribble down Mom's cheeks while she watched my face turn red and then go white as I covered another yard. She would cry harder tears of laughter and joy as I crossed the finish line and run to hug me and hold me up at the same time. We would both be thrilled."

WORD ATTACK

Using a Dictionary to Find Word Origins

Dictionaries tell you how to spell a word and what a word means. They also tell you about the origins of a word—which language the word originally came from.

English is made up of many words that come from Latin and Greek. After the definition of a word, a dictionary usually includes information in brackets. This information tells you which language the word came from, and what it originally meant. For example, after the definition for the word *panic*, you might find the following information: [fr. Gk. *panikos*, of Pan, a Greek god who terrorizes people]. The abbreviation, Gk., means Greek; and L. means Latin.

---

1. Look up each of the following words in the dictionary. Write Gk. after each word that originally came from Greek. Write L. after each word that originally came from Latin. Then write what each word originally meant.

   a. athlete
   b. miracle
   c. unique
   d. sarcasm
   e. phenomena

   f. victory
   g. eternal
   h. fantastic
   i. antique
   j. stadium

2. Write a sentence using each word above.

The Power of Light

Isaac Bashevis Singer

The plan for escape was risky. But remaining in Warsaw meant certain death.

In World War II, when the Nazis had bombed and burned the Warsaw[1] ghetto,[2] in one of the ruins a boy and a girl were hiding—David, fourteen years old, and Rebecca, thirteen.

It was winter and bitter cold outside. For weeks Rebecca had not left the dark, partially-collapsed cellar that was their hiding place; but every few days, David would go out to search for food. In the bombing all the stores had been destroyed, and David sometimes found stale bread, cans of preserved food, or whatever else had been buried. Making his way through the ruins was dangerous. Sometimes bricks and mortar would fall down, and he could easily lose his way. But if he and Rebecca did not want to die from hunger, he had to take the risks.

That day was one of the coldest. Rebecca sat on the ground wrapped in all

the garments she possessed; still she could not get warm. David had left many hours before, and Rebecca listened in the darkness for the sound of his return, knowing that if he did not come back, nothing remained to her but death.

Suddenly she heard heavy breathing and the sound of a bundle being dropped. David had made his way home. Rebecca could not help but cry, "David!"

"Rebecca!"

In the darkness they embraced and kissed. Then David said, "Rebecca, I found a treasure."

"What kind of treasure?"

"Cheese, potatoes, dried mushrooms, and a package of candy—and I have another surprise for you."

"What surprise?"

"Later."

Both were too hungry for long talk. Ravenously they ate the frozen potatoes, the mushrooms, and part of the cheese. They each had one piece of candy. Then Rebecca asked, "What is it now, day or night?"

---

1. Warsaw (wôr'sô) n.: The capital of Poland.
2. ghetto (gĕt'ō) n.: A section of a city to which Jews were restricted.

"I think night has fallen," David replied. He had a wristwatch and kept track of day and night and also of the days of the week and the month. After awhile Rebecca asked again, "What is the surprise?"

"Rebecca, today is the first day of Chanukah, and I found a candle and some matches."

"Chanukah tonight?"

"Yes."

"Oh, my God!"

"I am going to bless the Chanukah candle," David said.

He lit a match and there was light. For the first time Rebecca saw their hiding place—bricks, pipes, and the uneven ground. He lighted the candle. Rebecca blinked her eyes. For the first time in weeks she saw David. His hair was matted and his face streaked with dirt, but his eyes shone with joy. In spite of the starvation and persecution, David had grown taller, and he seemed older than his age and manly. Young as both of them were, they had decided to marry if they could manage to escape from war-ridden Warsaw. As a token of their engagement, David had given Rebecca a shining penny he found in his pocket on the day when the building where both of them lived was bombed.

Now David pronounced the benediction over the Chanukah candle, and Rebecca said, "Amen." They had both lost their families, and they had good reason to be angry with God for sending them so many afflictions; but the light of the Chanukah candle brought peace into their souls. That glimmer of light, surrounded by so many shadows, seemed to say without words: Evil has not yet taken complete dominion. A spark of hope is still left.

For weeks, David and Rebecca had pondered about escaping from Warsaw. But how? The ghetto was watched by the Nazis day and night. Each step was dangerous. Rebecca kept delaying their departure. It would be easier in the summer, she often said; but David knew that in their predicament they had little chance of lasting until then. Somewhere in the forest, there were young men and women called partisans who fought the Nazi invaders. David wanted to reach them. Now, by the light of the Chanukah candle, Rebecca suddenly felt renewed courage. She said, "David, let's leave."

"When?"

"When you think it's the right time," she answered.

"The right time is now," David said. "On Chanukah the moon never shines. I have a plan."

For a long while David explained to Rebecca the details of his plan. It was more than risky. The Nazis had enclosed the ghetto with barbed wire and posted guards armed with machine guns on the surrounding roofs. At night searchlights lit up all possible exits from the destroyed ghetto. But in his wanderings through the ruins, David had found an opening to a sewer which he thought might lead to the other side. David told Rebecca that their chances to remain alive were slim. They could drown in the dirty water or freeze to death. Also the sewers were full of hungry rats. But Rebecca consented to take the risks; to remain in the cellar for the winter would mean certain death.

When the Chanukah light began to sputter and flicker before going out, David and Rebecca gathered their few belongings. She packed the remaining food in a kerchief, and David took a piece

of lead pipe for a weapon, his matches, and a compass.

In moments of great danger people become unusually courageous. David and Rebecca were soon on their way through the ruins. They came to passages so narrow, they had to crawl on hands and knees. But the food they had eaten, and the joy the Chanukah candle had awakened in them, gave them the courage to continue. After some time David found the entrance to the sewer. Luckily the sewage had frozen, and it seemed that the rats had left because of the extreme cold. From time to time David and Rebecca stopped to rest and to listen. Then David lit a match and looked at the compass. After a while they crawled on, slowly and carefully. Suddenly they stopped in their tracks. From above they could hear the ringing of a trolley car. They had reached the other side of the ghetto. All they needed now was to find a way to get out of the sewer and to leave the city as quickly as possible.

Many miracles seemed to happen that Chanukah night. Because the Nazis were afraid of enemy planes, they had ordered a complete blackout. Because of the bitter cold, there were fewer Gestapo guards. Despite the curfew, David and Rebecca managed to leave the sewer and to steal out of the city without being caught. At dawn they reached a forest where they were able to rest and have a bite to eat.

Even though the partisans were not very far from Warsaw, it took David and Rebecca a week to reach them. They walked at night and hid during the days—sometimes in ditches and sometimes in barns. The peasants stealthily helped the partisans and those who were running away from the Nazis. From time to time David and Rebecca got a piece of bread, a few potatoes, a radish, or whatever the peasants could spare. In one village they encountered a Jewish partisan who had come to get food for his group. He belonged to the *Haganah*, an organization that sent men from Israel to rescue Jewish refugees from the Nazis in occupied Poland. This young man brought David and Rebecca to the other partisans who roamed the forest. It was the last day of Chanukah, and that evening the partisans lit eight candles. Some of them played dreidel on the stump of an oak tree, while others kept watch.

From the day David and Rebecca met the partisans, their life became like a tale in a story book. They joined more and more refugees who all had but one desire—to settle in the land of Israel. They did not travel by train or bus. They walked. They slept in stables, in burnt-out houses, and wherever they could hide from the enemy. To reach their destination, they had to cross Czechoslovakia, Hungary, and Yugoslavia. Somewhere at the seashore in Yugoslavia, in the middle of the night, a small boat manned by a crew of the *Haganah* waited for them, and all the refugees with their meager belongings were packed into it. This all happened silently and in great secrecy because the Nazis occupied Yugoslavia.

But their dangers were far from over. Even though it was spring, the sea was stormy, and the boat was too small for such a long trip. Nazi planes spied the boat and tried to sink it with bombs, and Nazi submarines were lurking in the depths. There was nothing the refugees could do besides pray to God, and this time God seemed to have heard their prayers because they managed to land safely.

The Jews of Israel greeted them with a love that made them forget their suffering. They were the first refugees who had reached the Holy Land, and they were offered all the help and comfort that could be given. Rebecca and David found relatives in Israel who accepted them with open arms; and although they had become quite emaciated, they were basically healthy and recovered quickly. After some rest they were sent to a special school where foreigners were taught modern Hebrew. Then David was able to enter the academy of engineering in Haifa, and Rebecca, who excelled in languages and literature, studied in Tel Aviv—but they always met on weekends. When Rebecca was eighteen, she and David were married. They found a small house with a garden in Ramat Gan, a suburb of Tel Aviv.

I know all this because David and Rebecca told me their story on a Chanukah evening in their house in Ramat Gan about eight years later. The Chanukah candles were burning, and Rebecca was frying potato pancakes for all of us. David and I were playing dreidel with their little son Menahem Eliezer; and David told me that his large wooden dreidel was the same one the partisans had played with on that Chanukah evening in the forest in Poland. Rebecca said to me, "If it had not been for the Chanukah candle David brought to our hiding place, we wouldn't be sitting here today. That small light awakened in us a hope and strength we didn't know we possessed. We'll give the dreidel to Menahem Eliezer when he is old enough to understand what we went through and how miraculously we were saved."

1. Why are David and Rebecca hiding in the dark, cold ruins of a Warsaw ghetto?

2. David leaves the hiding place only to search for food. (a) What does he find in addition to food? (b) How does this find help them escape to freedom?

3. Before reaching the Holy Land, their final destination, David and Rebecca endure great hardship and danger. How does the Chanukah candle help them to overcome every obstacle along the way?

Theme

Sometimes a simple object appears repeatedly in a story. When this happens, ask yourself, "Is there more to the object than meets the eye? Does the object suggest meanings other than its dictionary meaning?" If the answer to both these questions is yes, the object may be a symbol. Often a symbol is a key to the story's theme.

1. What object does this story mention often?

2. When David and Rebecca first light the candle, they find that it brings peace to their souls. What does it seem to say to them?

3. David and Rebecca escape through passages so narrow they have to crawl on their hands and knees. What gives them the courage to continue?

4. At the end of the story, what does Rebecca say would have happened if it hadn't been for the candle?

5. The Chanukah candle represents hope and courage. This symbol also points to the theme. Which statement below best expresses the theme of the story?
   a. Hope and courage exist in all of us; but sometimes we need something to remind us they are there.
   b. If you need courage and hope, all you need to do is light up a Chanukah candle.

Activities

1. **Composition.** Write three questions you would like to ask David and Rebecca.

2. Another name for Chanukah is "Feast of Lights." Find out more about this celebration and share your information with the class.

MAIN IDEA

Finding Supporting Details

The main idea in some paragraphs is a simple statement. Much of the remainder of the paragraph may be devoted to supporting that statement with details. These are called *supporting details*.

▶ The main idea in each paragraph below is *italicized*. Find one or more supporting details. The first paragraph is done for you. The supporting details are printed in **boldface**.

a. "For a long while David explained to Rebecca the details of his plan. *It was more than risky.* **The Nazis had enclosed the ghetto with barbed wire and posted guards armed with machine guns on the surrounding roofs. At night searchlights lit up all possible exits from the destroyed ghetto.** But in his wanderings through the ruins, David had found an opening to a sewer which he thought might lead to the other side. **David told Rebecca that their chances to remain alive were slim. They could drown in the dirty water or freeze to death. Also the sewers were full of hungry rats.** But Rebecca consented to take the risks; to remain in the cellar for the winter would mean certain death."

b. "*That day was one of the coldest.* Rebecca sat on the ground wrapped in all the garments she possessed; still she could not get warm. David had left many hours before, and Rebecca listened in the darkness for the sound of his return, knowing that if he did not come back, nothing remained to her but death."

c. "It was winter and bitter cold outside. For weeks Rebecca had not left the dark, partially-collapsed cellar that was their hiding place; but every few days, *David would go out to search for food.* In the bombing all the stores had been destroyed, and David sometimes found stale bread, cans of preserved food, or whatever else had been buried. Making his way through the ruins was dangerous. Sometimes bricks and mortar would fall down, and he could easily lose his way. But if he and Rebecca did not want to die from hunger, he had to take the risks."

d. "When the Chanukah light began to sputter and flicker before going out, *David and Rebecca gathered their few belongings.* She packed the remaining food in a kerchief, and David took a piece of lead pipe for a weapon, his matches, and a compass."

WORD ATTACK

Using Context Clues

The words surrounding an unknown word often provide clues to its meaning. These clues are called *context clues*. For example, look at the following sentence: Since she hadn't eaten for days, she was *famished*. The context clue, she hadn't eaten for days, should help you to see that *famished* means "extremely hungry."

▶ In each of the following sentences there is an *italicized* word which is defined by context clues. Select the word or words from the list below that are reasonable definitions for each italicized word.

(1) symbol
(2) organization to rescue Jewish refugees
(3) people fighting to drive out occupying forces
(4) extremely thin
(5) a prayer; blessing
(6) control over the earth
(7) greedily
(8) hardships

a. "Now David pronounced the *benediction* over the Chanukah candle, and Rebecca said, 'Amen.'"

b. "That glimmer of light, surrounded by so many shadows, seemed to say without words: Evil has not yet taken complete *dominion*."

c. "Somewhere in the forest, there were young men and women called *partisans* who fought the Nazi invaders."

d. "Both were too hungry for long talk. *Ravenously* they ate the frozen potatoes, the mushrooms, and part of the cheese."

e. "He belonged to the *Haganah*, an organization that sent men from Israel to rescue Jewish refugees from the Nazis in occupied Poland."

f. "As a *token* of their engagement, David had given Rebecca a shining penny he found in his pocket on the day when the building where both of them lived was bombed."

g. "Rebecca and David found relatives in Israel who accepted them with open arms, and although they had become quite *emaciated*, they were basically healthy and recovered quickly."

Gentleman
of Río en Medio

Juan A. A. Sedillo

It took months of negotiation to come to an understanding with the old man. He was in no hurry. What he had the most of was time. He lived up in Río en Medio, where his people had been for hundreds of years. He tilled the same land they had tilled. His house was small and wretched, but quaint. The little creek ran through his land. His orchard was gnarled and beautiful.

The day of the sale he came into the office. His coat was old, green and faded. I thought of Senator Catron, who had been such a power with these people up there in the mountains. Perhaps it was one of his old Prince Alberts.[1] He also wore gloves. They were old and torn and his fingertips showed through them. He carried a cane, but it was only the skeleton of a worn-out umbrella. Behind him walked one of his innumerable kin—a dark young man with eyes like a gazelle.

The old man bowed to all of us in the room. Then he removed his hat and gloves, slowly and carefully. Chaplin[2] once did that in a picture, in a bank—he was the janitor. Then he handed his things to the boy, who stood obediently behind the old man's chair.

There was a great deal of conversation, about rain and about his family. He was very proud of his large family. Finally we got down to business. Yes, he would sell, as he had agreed, for twelve hundred dollars, in cash. We would buy, and the money was ready. "Don Anselmo," I said to him in Spanish, "we have made a discovery. You remember that we sent that surveyor, that engineer, up there to survey your land so as to make the deed. Well, he finds that you own more than eight acres. He tells us that your land extends across the river and that you own almost twice as much as you thought." He didn't know that. "And now, Don Anselmo," I added, "these Americans are *buena gente*,[3] they are good people, and they are willing to pay you for the additional land as well, at the same rate per acre, so that instead of twelve hundred dollars you will get almost twice as much, and the money is here for you."

The old man hung his head for a moment in thought. Then he stood up and stared at me. "Friend," he said, "I do not like to have you speak to me in that manner." I kept still and let him have his say. "I know these Americans are good people, and that is why I have agreed to sell to them. But I do not care to be insulted. I have agreed to sell my house and land for twelve hundred dollars and that is the price."

I argued with him but it was useless. Finally he signed the deed and took the money, but refused to take more than the amount agreed upon. Then he shook hands all around, put on his ragged gloves, took his stick and walked out with the boy behind him.

A month later my friends had moved into Río en Medio. They had replastered the old adobe house, pruned the trees, patched the fence, and moved in for the summer. One day they came back to the office to complain. The children of the village were overrunning their property. They came every day and played under the trees, built little play

---

1. Prince Albert: A long, double-breasted coat, sometimes called a cutaway.
2. Chaplin: "Charlie" Chaplin was an actor and comedian who appeared in many early movies.

3. buena gente (bwā′nä hən′tä).

fences around them, and took blossoms. When they were spoken to they only laughed and talked back good-naturedly in Spanish.

I sent a messenger up to the mountains for Don Anselmo. It took a week to arrange another meeting. When he arrived he repeated his previous preliminary performance. He wore the same faded cutaway, carried the same stick and was accompanied by the boy again. He shook hands all around, sat down with the boy behind his chair, and talked about the weather. Finally I broached the subject. "Don Anselmo, about the ranch you sold to these people. They are good people and want to be your friends and neighbors always. When you sold to them you signed a document, a deed, and in that deed you agreed to several things. One thing was that they were to have the complete possession of the property. Now, Don Anselmo, it seems that every day the children of the village overrun the orchard and spend most of their time there. We would like to know if you, as the most respected man in the village, could not stop them from doing so in order that these people may enjoy their new home more in peace."

Don Anselmo stood up. "We have all learned to love these Americans," he said, "because they are good people and good neighbors. I sold them my property because I knew they were good people, but I did not sell them the trees in the orchard."

This was bad. "Don Anselmo," I pleaded, "when one signs a deed and sells real property, one sells also everything that grows on the land; and those trees, every one of them, are on the land and inside the boundaries of what you sold."

"Yes, I admit that," he said. "You know," he added, "I am the oldest man in the village. Almost everyone there is my relative; and all the children of Río en Medio are my *sobrinos*[4] and *nietos*,[5] my descendants. Every time a child has been born in Río en Medio, since I took possession of that house from my mother, I have planted a tree for that child. The trees in that orchard are not mine, Señor, they belong to the children of the village. Every person in Río en Medio born since the railroad came to Santa Fe owns a tree in that orchard. I did not sell the trees because I could not. They are not mine."

There was nothing we could do. Legally we owned the trees; but the old man had been so generous, refusing what amounted to a fortune for him. It took most of the following winter to buy the trees, individually, from the descendants of Don Anselmo in the valley of Río en Medio.

---

4. sobrinos (soo-bre′nōz).
5. nietos (ne-ā′tōz).

Close Up

1. Reread the first two paragraphs of this story. List three details that show that Don Anselmo is poor.

2. Don Anselmo makes a deal to sell his property to the Americans. What do the Americans find out about the size of the property?

3. Don Anselmo refuses the extra money from the Americans. (a) Which do you think he values more, his honor or the money? (b) What evidence can you give to support your answer?

4. (a) After they buy the property, what problem do the Americans have with the children of the village? (b) Why doesn't Don Anselmo try to keep the children away from the trees?

5. How do the Americans solve their problem?

Theme

Sometimes a character performs a significant act that gives you a key to the theme of the story.

1. Don Anselmo performs two acts that appear very important in this story. First, he refuses to take more money for his property. Why is he insulted by the Americans' offer?

2. Second, he refuses to sell the trees in the orchard. Do you think it would have been honorable for Don Anselmo to take back the trees and sell them to the Americans? Why or why not?

3. These two acts tell you that Don Anselmo is a man who cherishes his sense of honor. They are also a key to the theme. Which statement below is the best summary of the theme of this story?
   a. People with money can buy everything, including happiness.
   b. Money is at the base of all our problems.
   c. A person's sense of worth or honor does not depend on the amount of money he or she has.

Activity

▶ Find a picture of Charlie Chaplin. Then draw a picture of Don Anselmo to show how he looked like Charlie Chaplin.

MAIN IDEA

Supporting details back up the main idea of the paragraph. For example, suppose the main idea is that a man is quite wealthy. The supporting details might be: (1) He wears expensive clothes; (2) he lives in a mansion; and (3) he has a butler and a maid.

▶ Read each paragraph below. Then read the main idea stated after each paragraph. Find the supporting details.

a.   "The day of the sale he came into the office. His coat was old, green and faded. I thought of Senator Catron, who had been such a power with these people up there in the mountains. Perhaps it was one of his old Prince Alberts. He also wore gloves. They were old and torn and his fingertips showed through them. He carried a cane, but it was only the skeleton of a worn-out umbrella. Behind him walked one of his innumerable kin—a dark young man with eyes like a gazelle."

Main Idea: Don Anselmo was a poor man.

b.   " 'Yes, I admit that,' he said. 'You know,' he added, 'I am the oldest man in the village. Almost everyone there is my relative; and all the children of Río en Medio are my *sobrinos* and *nietos,* my descendants. Every time a child has been born in Río en Medio, since I took possession of that house from my mother, I have planted a tree for that child. The trees in that orchard are not mine, Señor, they belong to the children of the village. Every person in Río en Medio born since the railroad came to Santa Fe owns a tree in that orchard. I did not sell the trees because I could not. They are not mine.' "

Main Idea: The people in the village owned the trees in the orchard.

WORD ATTACK

Understanding Homophones

Homophones are words that are pronounced alike; but they are spelled differently, and they have different meanings. You hear homophones every day. For example, the words *son* and *sun* are homophones. They are pronounced the same but they have different meanings. The word *son* means "a male child." The word *sun* means "the star around which the earth revolves."

▶ Choose the correct homophone that fits in each sentence below. You may use a dictionary to help you.
   a. Don Anselmo came to the meeting on (thyme, time).
   b. The young man was (one, won) of his kin.
   c. Don Anselmo (wore, war) a hat and gloves and carried a cane.
   d. He made a slight (bough, bow) when he met the Americans.
   e. At the meeting, Don Anselmo agreed to (sell, cell) his property.
   f. He would not take a (cent, scent, sent) more than the Americans had originally offered.
   g. The Americans wanted to live in (piece, peace) on the land.
   h. During the (weak, week), children came to play under the trees.
   i. The Americans did not (no, know) that the trees belonged to the children.
   j. They offered to (buy, by, bye) each tree.

Everybody Does It

Lou Derman and Bill Davenport

**From an Episode
of *All in the Family***

Characters

Archie Bunker

Edith, his wife

Gloria, their daughter

Mike, Gloria's husband

Irene, a family friend

*Int. dining room. About 6 P.M. Archie
has just arrived home carrying a piece of
plywood.*

    Edith: What's that for?

    Archie: I'm gonna build you an
overhang for the back porch. That way,
when you're luggin' the garbage in the
rain you won't get wet.

    Edith: Oh, Archie, that's so thought-
ful. I bet I got the best husband in the
world.

    Archie: Hey . . . hey . . . hey . . . do I
see a fifth place at the table?

    Edith: Yeah, it's for Irene. I ain't
hardly seen her since she got that fork-
lifting job at your plant.

Archie: But I see her at work every day.

Edith: Please, Archie, I feel sorry for Irene. She's all by herself. Frank's on the road all the time.

Archie: I don't blame him.

(First Mike, then Gloria, arrives home.)

Gloria: What's that wood doin' here?

Archie: I'm buildin' an overhang for your mother over the kitchen door. And I'm gonna need your help tomorrow, Meathead, nailin' that up.

Mike: Okay, but we're gonna have to buy some nails. I used the last one fixing the cellar step.

Archie: We don't have to buy nothin'. *(He crosses to his lunchbox, takes two boxes of nails out.)* 'Cause I picked up a few nails at work today.

Gloria: What do you mean, you picked up a few nails?

Archie: I mean, they was there, so I picked them up, and now they are here.

Mike: But they don't belong to you.

Archie: They do now.

Mike: But, just taking something like that—that's stealing.

Archie: What're you talkin' about? When you take somethin' from work, that ain't stealin'. That's what you call your fringe benefits. . . . Everybody does it.

Mike: No, they don't. And if they do, it's wrong.

Archie: Listen, your big companies are smart enough to buy more than they need, so the workers will have somethin' to take home. That's how they prevent stealin'.

Gloria: Michael's right, Daddy. It's not honest.

Archie: Why are you always turnin' against your father?

Gloria: You're the one that taught me. Never take anything that didn't belong to me. And I never have.

Mike: Wait a minute, Gloria. What about those little lipsticks you bring home from the cosmetics counter?

Gloria: They don't count! They're just samples.

Mike: You're rationalizing, Gloria.

Gloria: Michael—we give those things away free to the customers, and I just took a few for myself.

Mike: Are you a customer?

Gloria: No, but—g— *(She stares at Mike for a beat. He just looks back at her.)* I'm a crook! You're right, Michael. I'm a crook!

Archie: Don't be callin' yourself no crook. This meathead, he'd be takin' things home from work—if he had any work!

(Irene arrives, and she and Archie at once strike sparks over a matter of religion.)

Mike: Irene, let me ask you something. Do you ever take things from the plant?

Irene: What?

Archie: He's buggin' me because I'm buildin' somethin' out back, and I borrowed a few nails from the plant.

Mike: You mean you took a couple of *boxes.* Irene, do you think it's okay to take things from the plant?

Irene: No. I'm afraid I was raised by strictly honest parents.

Archie: Who do you think I was raised by, Bonnie and Clyde? All I took was a few lousy nails!

Edith (*enters from kitchen, holding electric drill*): Archie, what was this doing in your lunchbox?

Archie (*gets up, takes drill from her*): Edith, gimme that drill! Don't be snoopin' around in my lunchbox.

Irene: Archie! That's a company drill. Did you take that home from work?

Archie: I didn't take nothin'! I borrowed it from the plant! I'm bringin' it back Monday morning, and don't you say nothin' about it.

Irene: Archie, you're taking an awful risk. Don't you know what those signs mean all over the plant: "Pilferers Will Be Prosecuted"? It means no stealing.

Archie: I didn't steal nothin'. Look Irene, no preachin', huh? If I want a sermon with my dinner, I'll go down to the Salvation Army! Now shaddup!

(*The abuse from Archie escalates, and Irene leaves before dinner. Angry with Archie, Edith at first rebels, and refuses to serve dinner. But she finally relents.*)

SOUND: PHONE RINGS

Mike (*into phone*): No, operator, Michael Stivic isn't here. He won't be home until Sunday. You're welcome. Thank you. Goodbye. (*Hangs up, returns to table.*)

Archie: What the heck was that all about?

Mike: It's a code I worked out with a friend of mine in Chicago. I'm trying to find an apartment for him, and that's my way of telling him to call me back Sunday.

Gloria: Oh, I get it. That way, the phone call doesn't cost anything.

Mike: Right!

Archie: Hey, you stole a phone call!

Mike (*defensively*): I didn't even make a phone call.

Archie: What was that, a smoke signal?

Mike: Arch, I didn't talk to my friend, just the operator.

Archie: But you got your message through. And you didn't pay for it.

Mike: Oh, the poor phone company. Do you know how much profit they made last year?

Gloria: Now *you're* rationalizing, Michael.

Archie: No he ain't. He's stealin'!

Mike (*looks at them both for a beat*): You're right. I've gotta admit it, you're right. (*Sighs.*) I guess I'm a victim of the system, too.

Archie: Listen to this! When he takes somethin', he's a victim. When I take somethin', I'm a crook!

Fade Out.

Close Up

1. Archie and Mike disagree about almost everything. When Archie takes nails home from work, Mike accuses him of stealing. (a) What does Archie mean when he says that taking things home are "fringe benefits"? (b) Do you think the company would agree with Archie? Why or why not?

2. Gloria agrees with Mike. But Mike accuses her of stealing lipsticks from the store where she works. (a) What excuse does Gloria give for taking lipsticks? (b) Why is this a poor excuse?

3. Throughout this episode, Mike has been very self-satisfied. (a) How does Archie show that Mike is guilty of stealing too? (b) What is Mike's defense?

Theme

Some stories contain both a major and a minor theme. This means that two messages, or ideas, are present in the story at the same time. The major theme is the most important idea that the author is trying to get across. The minor theme is a less important idea that grows out of the major theme.

1. The major theme is about stealing. Do you think it says that stealing is all right because "everybody does it" or that stealing is wrong even though "everybody does it"? Give evidence to support your answer.

2. The minor theme says something about hypocrisy, which means pretending to be virtuous when you are as guilty as anyone else. Who is a hypocrite in this episode?

3. Which statement best summarizes the minor theme?
   a. People should examine their own faults before they accuse others of faults.
   b. Hypocrisy is all right because everybody is hypocritical sometimes.

Activities

1. Put this episode on as a class play.

2. Imagine you are a writer for a weekly guide to television. Write three sentences telling your readers what this show is about.

MAIN IDEA

Understanding Conflicting Main Ideas

The main idea of a paragraph is the most important thing it says about a topic. Two paragraphs may be about the same topic. But the main idea of each paragraph may be completely different. For example, two paragraphs may be about snakes. The main idea of one paragraph may be that snakes make good house pets. The main idea of the other paragraph may be that snakes sometimes are terrifying creatures.

▶ Imagine Archie and Mike each wrote a paragraph about stealing. Find the main idea in each paragraph. Then list two details that support each main idea.

a. Archie's paragraph.

> Taking things home from work isn't really stealing. It's just getting your fringe benefits. Everyone takes things home from work, and companies build this loss into their budgets. If the company paid me more money, I could buy what I wanted. But since they pay me so little, the only way I can get what I need is to "borrow" it from the job. You would do the same thing if you were in my position.

b. Mike's paragraph.

> When you take something home from the job, the company loses money. If the company loses money, they raise their prices. Who pays the raised prices? We do. If the company continues to lose money, they lay off people. Who gets hurt? We do. When you take something home from the job, you are stealing not only from the company, but from all of us.

WORD ATTACK

Understanding Dialect

Most people pronounce some words a little differently from the way the dictionary shows pronunciation. They leave out letters, they run sounds together, and they change the sound of certain letters. Sometimes writers try to record the way people really speak. They use an apostrophe when they show a word with a letter left out. For example, *'cause* for *because*. Sometimes, they run words together. They show two words as one word. For example, they write "gotta" for "got to," because some people do speak that way.

▶ Read the sentences below. Write the word or words each *italicized* word represents in standard speech.

a. "I'm *gonna* build you an overhang for the back porch."

b. "When you take *somethin'* from work, that *ain't* *stealin'*."

c. "Edith, *gimme* that drill."

d. "I've *gotta* admit it, you're right."

e. "Don't be *snoopin'* around in my lunchbox."

f. "Now *shaddup!*"

REVIEW QUIZ

On the Selections

1. Anansi uses a calabash gourd to trick the hornets. What is a calabash gourd? What other object does it look like?

2. In "Snow Igloo," Steve's father builds an igloo. What can happen if the hole in the dome of the igloo gets plugged with ice?

3. In "Honor Society," Daniel Inouye is not accepted as a member of the society. Does the committee base its judgment on the facts they find in Daniel's school record, or on the opinion they form after looking at the clothes he wears?

4. Do you think Ann Cameron showed courage when she stood up and defended Bianca at the class meeting? Why or why not?

5. In "The Medicine Bag," how does Grandpa show he knows that Martin is embarrassed to bring his friends to meet him?

6. In "The Fallen Star," Tod wants a Morgan mare. He says that "if you get them young enough, you can teach them almost anything." How is Star different from the Morgan Tod wanted?

7. In "An Appropriate Time for Tears," Mary Alice says that Gramps isn't really dead. How is he alive?

8. In "The Power of Light," three objects are important: a penny, a candle, and a dreidel. Choose one object and write a sentence telling why it is important.

9. Read the following sentences: "His (Don Anselmo's) coat was old, green and faded. I thought of Senator Catron, who had been such a power with these people up there in the mountains. Perhaps it was one of his old Prince Alberts. *He* also wore gloves." Does the italicized pronoun *He* refer to Senator Catron, Don Anselmo, or Prince Albert?

10. In "Everybody Does It," Mike accuses Archie and Gloria of stealing. Who doesn't Mike accuse of stealing?

On Main Idea

1. What is the topic of the following paragraph?

"He returned to his village, where he told his dream to the wise old men of the tribe. They gave him the name *Iron Shell*, but neither did they understand the meaning of the dream. This first Iron Shell kept the piece of iron with him at all times and believed it gave him protection from the evils of those unhappy days."

2. Find the topic sentence in the following paragraph.

"Yes, son, you are right. Many changes have come to the Eskimo people, and some are very good. But there are things that do not change. Our land does not change. Its cold, its darkness, its dangers are the same as before. That is why it saddens me to see the old ways forgotten, the old skills lost."

3. Find the topic sentence in the following paragraph.

"For a long, long time afterward, I felt angry every time I remembered that humiliating interview, and I remembered it often. And that wasn't the end of it. I had to tell my parents that I hadn't been accepted into the honor society. But I couldn't tell them the real reason because they would have blamed themselves. So I stammered out a weak explanation that didn't fool them at all; and their eyes grew sad and there was no more for any of us to say."

4. In your own words, state the main idea of the following paragraph.

"She had to admit that Star was a great help. It used to be a major operation to get Tod up mornings, but now he shot out of bed at six when the alarm went off so he'd have time to feed, groom, and visit with Star before he went to school. He brushed her coat till it gleamed like brown satin, cleaned and oiled her hooves as carefully as if she had been a race horse instead of a tired old nag, soaped her saddle till he could roll up the skirts like cloth; he even braided her foretop. He spent his carefully hoarded cash to buy her a dark-blue blanket with white bands, and kept a daily record on a sheet tacked to her stall door of how much he fed her. When Star, who was by years the oldest horse there, won two red ribbons and a yellow one at the 4-H Gymkana, Tod tacked the colors to her door as proudly as if she'd won the Kentucky Derby. He even brushed his own hair . . . a minor miracle . . . in order to look nice when he rode her every day after school."

COMPOSITION

Exposition   An expository paragraph gives information or explains something. In fact, the word *exposition* comes from the Latin word meaning "to expound or explain." Often, an expository paragraph begins with a topic sentence. The rest of the paragraph contains details that are arranged in a logical order. These details support the main idea expressed in the topic sentence.

1. Write an expository paragraph about one of the following topics.
   a. Building an igloo
   b. A new pair of sneakers
   c. A family heirloom
   d. Taking care of a horse (dog, cat, etc.)

2. Use one of the following topic sentences to begin your expository paragraph.
   a. Anansi is a folkhero of the Ashanti people.
   b. Qualifying for the Olympics requires rigorous training.
   c. _____ is a holiday that holds special meaning for me.
   d. Knowing that someone believes in you can help you achieve seemingly impossible goals.

BEFORE GOING ON

Skimming for Main Ideas

When you skim for main ideas, read the title of the selection first. Then read the first and last two paragraphs. Then read the selection by letting your eyes sweep across the lines of print and down the pages. Stop and read carefully only when you come to main ideas.

▶ See how well you skimmed for main ideas. Put *T* by each statement that is true. Put *F* by each statement that is false.

a. Scientists think we will find our future in the sea.
b. Exploring the sea is mostly for fun.
c. We hope to learn more and more about the sea.
d. Untrained fishermen and divers tell us most about the sea's resources.
e. There are many kinds of oceanographers.
f. Fishermen will learn to farm the sea as farmers farm the land.
g. Sea plants are beautiful but they have no value other than their beauty.
h. Pure drinking water may be the most valuable thing of all to come from sea water.
i. Robots may be used to mine the sea.
j. Most of the equipment for mining the sea has already been invented.
k. Scientists hope to be able to control the weather by studying the sea.

Further Reading

The Sea— The Key to Our Future

D. X. Fenten

Scientists think we will find our future in the sea. The land we live on is getting too crowded. There is not enough for everyone to eat. There is not enough water for everyone to drink. Metals and minerals are becoming harder to find. The sea has a lot of everything. It has enough of all these things for everyone and enough to spare.

We really know very little about the sea. Our scientists and engineers have only just started to learn about the sea. Up to now only about one-tenth of the ocean bottom has been mapped. Only a little more than that has ever been seen. In the next few years we hope to learn more and more about the sea and everything that is in it.

What we learn about the sea and its rich harvest will come from the hard work of a special group of scientists called oceanographers. They study the oceans and everything about them.

There are many kinds of oceanographers. An oceanographic biologist studies animals and plants that live in the

sea. An oceanographic geophysicist studies the movement of the oceans—the tides, the waves, and the things that make up the water. The oceanographic meteorologist studies how the sea affects the weather. As you can see, oceanography is a team science. Each scientist does something to help all the others.

Every new thing we learn about the sea helps us harvest more from the sea. Fishing will be even more important than it is today. We will catch and eat ten times the amount of fish we do today. Oceanographers will explore the deeper parts of the sea and find many new kinds of fish for us to eat. They will learn more and more about the sea. With this information, computers and sonar equipment will lead fishing boats right to large schools of fish.

In the next few years fishermen will learn to farm the sea just as farmers do the land. Fish will be hatched in special pools and put into the sea. There they will grow and have more fish. Other fish will be carefully bred so they are bigger, and there will be more to eat on each fish. Parts of the ocean that have few fish will have fish put there to live and grow. This is called stocking. Fishermen will put large numbers of baby fish into the sea and will leave them there to grow big enough to catch.

Sea plants will also become more and more important as we learn more and more about them. A lot of seaweed will be planted and harvested. Seaweed is very rich in iodine, which we all need to live. Other chemicals and drugs also come from seaweed and other sea plants. Some day there will be sea plant farms in the oceans just as there are corn and wheat farms on the land. More and more sea plants will be harvested for food and we will learn new ways to use these plants.

Both sea plants and sea animals will give us drugs to cure and prevent deadly diseases. As we learn more about the sea and the things that live in the sea, we hope to find the chemicals and drugs that will cure terrible diseases like cancer, cerebral palsy and others.

The larger sea animals, including the sea mammals, will also be bred and raised for food, just as cows and sheep are today. Large herds of sea animals will be fed, cared for, and brought to market as food. All the sea animals will be protected, so only a certain amount can be killed for food, furs and oil each year.

Scientists and engineers will find ways for us to get more minerals, metals, chemicals and other valuable things from the sea. Special filtering stations will be set up so we can get many more chemicals from the water more quickly and more easily. Sea water will be pumped through a special, very fine filter. As the water goes through, one of its chemicals will not be able to get through the filter. That chemical, bromine for example, will be left behind. At the next filter, the salt will be left behind. And at the next filter, the gold will be left behind. After it passes through all the filters, the water will be pure. This may be the most valuable thing of all to come from the sea water—pure drinking water. With special stations like these, we will be able to get cheap drinking water and minerals from each gallon of sea water.

It will also be easier to get other minerals from the sea. Scientists are working on tools and equipment so people can dive and work deeper under the water. Where it is too deep, and people cannot work, robots will work. People will control the robots who will work deep under the water.

Oil wells will go down deeper and bring back more and more oil. Today platforms can operate in water more than 100 feet deep and drill to a depth of 20,000 feet. Ways will be found to bring up many more manganese nodules from the floor of the sea. All kinds of minerals and metals will be mined from the sea. Much of it will be mined with equipment that has not even been invented yet.

One of the most important harvests from the sea will not be something you can see or hold in your hand. It will be something we learn about. Scientists know that most of our weather comes from the sea. By learning more about the seas, their temperature, waves, and tides, we will learn what causes our weather. We will learn what to look for so we can tell what kind of weather is coming. The next thing we hope to learn is how to change the weather. Then we can always have what we want and need. We will be able to have enough rain, enough sun, and enough wind to grow enough food for everyone. We will be able to soften the severe weather hurricanes, tornadoes, and cyclones. As we learn more and more about the sea, we will learn more and more about making the weather work for us and not against us.

The next few years will be exciting in our world. Many new things will happen on land, in space, and in the sea. We will learn more and more about the world in which we live. And as we learn, we will see many new and wonderful things.

The sea may hold our future.

Gilead

Zenna Henderson

"Be as different as you can. But don't let anyone see—don't let anyone know!"

Part One

I don't know when it was that I found out that our family was different from other families. There was nothing to point it out. We lived in a house very like the other houses in Socorro. Our pasture lot sloped down just like the rest through arrowweed and mesquite trees to the sometime Rio Gordo that looped around town. And on occasion our cow bawled just as loudly across the river at the Jacobses' bull as all the other cows in all the other pasture lots. And I spent as many lazy days as any other boy in Socorro lying on my back in the thin shade of the mesquites, chewing on the beans when work was waiting somewhere. It never occurred to me to wonder if we were different.

I suppose my first realization came soon after I started to school and fell in love—with the girl with the longest pig-tails and the widest gap in her front teeth of all the girls in my room. I think she was seven to my six.

My girl and I had wandered down behind the school woodshed, under the cottonwoods, to eat our lunch together, ignoring the chanted "Peter's got a gir-ul! Peter's got a gir-ul!" and the whittling fingers that shamed me for showing my love. We ate our sandwiches and pickles and then lay back, arms doubled under our heads, and blinked at the bright sky while we tried to keep the crumbs from our cupcakes from falling into our ears. I was so full of lunch, contentment, and love that I suddenly felt I just had to do something spectacular for my ladylove. I sat up, electrified by a great idea and by the knowledge that I could carry it out.

"Hey! Did you know that I can fly?" I scrambled to my feet, leaving my love sitting gape-mouthed in the grass.

"You can't neither fly! Don't be crazy!"

"I can too fly!"

"You can not neither!"

"I can so! You just watch!" And lifting my arms I swooped up to the roof of the shed. I leaned over the edge and said, "See there? I can, too!"

"I'll tell teacher on you!" she gasped, wide-eyed, staring up at me. "You ain't supposed to climb up on the shed."

"Oh, poof," I said, "I didn't climb. Come on, you fly up, too. Here, I'll help you."

And I slid down the air to the ground. I put my arms around my love and lifted. She screamed and wrenched away from me and fled shrieking back to the schoolhouse. Somewhat taken aback by her desertion, I gathered up the re-mains of my cake and hers and was perched comfortably on the ridgepole of the shed, enjoying the last crumbs, when teacher arrived with half the school trailing behind her.

"Peter Merrill! How many times have you been told not to climb things at school?"

I peered down at her, noting with interest that the spit curls on her cheeks had been jarred loose by her hurry and agitation, and one of them was straightening out, contrasting oddly with the rest of her shingled bob.

"Hang on tight until Stanley gets the ladder!"

"I can get down," I said, scrambling off the ridgepole. "It's easy."

"Peter!" teacher shrieked. "Stay where you are!"

So I did, wondering at all the fuss.

By the time they got me down and teacher yanked me by one arm back up to the schoolhouse I was bawling at the top of my voice, outraged and indignant because no one would believe me, even my girl denying obstinately the evidence of her own eyes. Teacher, annoyed at my persistence, said over and over, "Don't be silly, Peter. You can't fly. Nobody can fly. Where are your wings?"

"I don't need wings," I bellowed. "People don't need wings. I ain't a bird!"

"Then you can't fly. Only things with wings can fly."

So I alternately cried and kicked the schoolhouse steps for the rest of the noon hour, and then I began to worry for fear teacher would tattle to Dad. After all, I had been on forbidden territory, no matter how I got there.

As it turned out, she didn't tell Dad, but that night after I was put to bed I suddenly felt an all-gone feeling inside me. Maybe I couldn't fly. Maybe teacher was right. I sneaked out of bed and cautiously flew up to the top of the dresser and back. Then I pulled the covers up tight under my chin and whispered to myself, "I can so fly," and sighed heavily. Just another fun stuff that grownups didn't allow, like having cake for breakfast or driving the tractor.

And that was all of that incident, except that when teacher met Mother and me at the store that Saturday she ruffled my hair and said, "How's my little bird?" Then she laughed and said to Mother, "He thinks he can fly!"

I saw Mother's fingers tighten whitely on her purse, and she looked down at me with all the laughter gone from her eyes. I was overflooded with incredulous surprise mixed with fear and dread that made me want to cry, even though I knew it was Mother's emotions and not my own that I was feeling.

Mostly Mother had laughing eyes. She was the laughingest mother in Socorro. She carried happiness inside her as if it were a bouquet of flowers, and she gave part of it to everyone she met. Most of the other mothers seemed to have hardly enough to go around to their own families. And yet, there were other times, like at the store, when laughter fled and fear showed through—and an odd wariness. Other times she made me think of a caged bird, pressing against the bars. Like one night I remember vividly.

Mother stood at the window in her ankle-length flannel nightgown, her long dark hair lifting softly in the draft from the rattling window frames. A high wind was blowing in from a spectacular thunderstorm in the Huachucas. I had been awakened by the rising crescendo and was huddled on the sofa wondering if I was scared or excited as the house shook with the constant thunder. Dad was sitting with the newspaper in his lap.

Mother spoke softly, but her voice came clearly through the tumult.

"Have you ever wondered what it would be like to be up there in the middle of the storm with clouds under your feet and over your head and lightning lacing around you like hot golden rivers?"

Dad rattled his paper. "Sounds uncomfortable," he said.

But I sat there and hugged the words to me in wonder. I knew! I remembered! " 'And the rain like icy silver hair lashing across your lifted face,' " I recited as though it were a loved lesson.

Mother whirled from the window and stared at me. Dad's eyes were on me, dark and troubled.

"How do you know?" he asked.

I ducked my head in confusion. "I don't know," I muttered.

Mother pressed her hands together, hard, her bowed head swinging the curtains of her hair forward over her shadowy face. "He knows because I know. I know because my mother knew. She knew because our People used to——" Her voice broke. "Those were her words——"

She stopped and turned back to the window, leaning her arm against the frame, her face pressed to it, like a child in tears.

"Oh, Bruce, I'm sorry!"

I stared, round-eyed in amazement, trying to keep tears from coming to my eyes as I fought against Mother's desolation and sorrow.

Dad went to Mother and turned her gently into his arms. He looked over her head at me. "Better run on back to bed, Peter. The worst is over."

I trailed off reluctantly, my mind filled with wonder. Just before I shut my door, I stopped and listened.

"I've never said a word to him, honest." Mother's voice quivered. "Oh, Bruce, I try so hard, but sometimes—oh sometimes!"

"I know, Eve. And you've done a wonderful job of it. I know it's hard on you, but we've talked it out so many times. It's the only way, honey."

"Yes," Mother said. "It's the only way, but—oh, be my strength, Bruce! Bless the Power for giving me you!"

I shut my door softly and huddled in the dark in the middle of my bed until I felt Mother's anguish smooth out to loving warmness again. Then for no good reason I flew solemnly to the top of the dresser and back, crawled into bed and relaxed. And remembered. Remembered the hot golden rivers, the clouds over and under, and the wild winds that buffeted like foam-frosted waves. But with all the sweet remembering was the reminder, *You can't because you're only eight. You're only eight. You'll have to wait.*

And then Bethie was born, almost in time for my ninth birthday. I remember peeking over the edge of the bassinet at the miracle of tiny fingers and spun-sugar hair. Bethie, my little sister. Bethie, who was whispered about and stared at when Mother let her go to school, though mostly she kept her home even after she was old enough. Because Bethie was different—too.

When Bethie was a month old, I smashed my finger in the bedroom door.

I cried for a quarter of an hour, but Bethie sobbed on and on until the last pain left my finger.

When Bethie was six months old, our little terrier, Glib, got caught in a gopher trap. He dragged himself, yelping, back to the house dangling the trap. Bethie screamed until Glib fell asleep over his bandaged paw.

Dad had acute appendicitis when Bethie was two, but it was Bethie who had to be given a sedative until we could get Dad to the hospital.

One night Dad and Mother stood over Bethie as she slept restlessly under sedatives. Mr. Tyree-next-door had been cutting wood and his ax slipped. He lost a big toe and a pint or so of blood, but as Doctor Dueff skidded to a stop on our street, it was into our house that he rushed first and then to Mr. Tyree-next-door who lay with his foot swathed and propped up on a chair, his hands pressed to his ears to shut out Bethie's screams.

"What can we do, Eve?" Dad asked. "What does the doctor say?"

"Nothing. They can do nothing for her. He hopes she will outgrow it. He doesn't understand it. He doesn't know that she——"

"What's the matter? What makes her like this?" Dad asked despairingly.

Mother winced. "She's a Sensitive. Among my People there were such—but not so young. Their perception made it possible for them to help sufferers. Bethie has only half the Gift. She has no control."

"Because of me?" Dad's voice was ragged.

Mother looked at him with steady loving eyes. "Because of us, Bruce. It was the chance we took. We pushed our luck after Peter."

So there we were, the two of us—different—but different in our differences. For me it was mostly fun, but not for Bethie.

We had to be careful for Bethie. She tried school at first, but skinned knees and rough rassling and aching teeth and bumped heads sent her home exhausted and shaking the first day, with hysteria hanging on the flick of an eyelash. So Bethie read for Mother and learned her numbers and leaned wistfully over the gate as the other children went by.

It wasn't long after Bethie's first day in school that I found a practical use for my difference. Dad sent me out to the woodshed to stack a cord of mesquite that Delfino dumped into our back yard from his old wagon. I had a date to explore an old fluorspar mine with some other guys and bitterly resented being sidetracked. I slouched out to the woodpile and stood, hands in pockets, kicking the heavy rough stove lengths. Finally I carried in one armload, grunting under the weight, and afterward sucking the round of my thumb where the sliding wood had peeled me. I hunkered down on my heels and stared as I sucked. Suddenly something prickled inside my brain. If I could fly, why couldn't I make the wood fly? And I knew I could! I leaned forward and flipped a finger under half a dozen sticks, concentrating as I did so. They lifted into the air and hovered. I pushed them into the shed, guided them to where I wanted them, and distributed them like dealing a pack of cards. It didn't take me long to figure out the maximum load, and I had all the wood stacked in a wonderfully short time.

I whistled into the house for my flashlight. The mine was spooky and dark, and I was the only one of the gang with a flashlight.

"I told you to stack the wood." Dad looked up from his milk records.

"I did," I said, grinning.

"Cut the kidding," Dad grunted. "You couldn't be done already."

"I am, though," I said triumphantly. "I found a new way to do it. You see——" I stopped, frozen by Dad's look.

"We don't need any new ways around here," he said evenly. "Go back out there until you've had time to stack the wood right!"

"It is stacked," I protested. "And the kids are waiting for me!"

"I'm not arguing, son," said Dad, white-faced. "Go back out to the shed."

I went back out to the shed—past Mother, who had come in from the kitchen and whose hand half went out to me. I sat in the shed fuming for a long time, stubbornly set that I wouldn't leave till Dad told me to.

Then I got to thinking. Dad wasn't usually unreasonable like this. Maybe I'd done something wrong. Maybe it was bad to stack wood like that. Maybe—my thoughts wavered as I remembered whispers I'd overheard about Bethie. Maybe it—it was a crazy thing to do—an insane thing.

I huddled close upon myself as I considered it. Crazy means not doing like other people. Crazy means doing things ordinary people don't do. Maybe that's why Dad made such a fuss. Maybe I'd done an insane thing! I stared at the ground, lost in bewilderment. What was different about our family? And for the first time I was able to isolate and recognize the feeling I must have had for a long time—the feeling of being on the

outside looking in—the feeling of apartness. With this recognition came a wariness, a need for concealment. If something was wrong, no one else must know—I must not betray. . .

Then Mother was standing beside me. "Dad says you may go now," she said, sitting down on my log.

"Peter——" She looked at me unhappily. "Dad's doing what is best. All I can say is: remember that whatever you do, wherever you live, different is dead. You have to conform or—or die. But Peter, don't be ashamed!" Then swiftly her hands were on my shoulders and her lips brushed my ear. "Be different!" she whispered. "Be as different as you can. But don't let anyone see—don't let anyone know!" And she was gone up the back steps, into the kitchen.

As I grew further into adolescence, I seemed to grow further and further away from kids my age. I couldn't seem to get much of a kick out of what they considered fun. So it was that with increasing frequency in the years that followed I took Mother's whispered advice, never asking for explanations I knew she wouldn't give. The wood incident had opened up a whole vista of possibilities—no telling what I might be able to do—so I got in the habit of going down to the foot of our pasture lot. There, screened by the brush and greasewood, I tried all sorts of experiments, never knowing whether they would work or not. I sweated plenty over some that didn't work—and some that did.

I found that I could snap my fingers and bring things to me, or send them short distances from me without bothering to touch them as I had the wood. I roosted regularly in the tops of the tall cottonwoods, swan-diving ecstatically

down to the ground, warily, after I got too ecstatic once and crash landed on my nose and chin. By headaching concentration that left me dizzy, I even set a small campfire ablaze. Then blistered and charred both hands unmercifully by confidently scooping up the crackling fire.

Then I guess I got careless about checking for onlookers, because some nasty talk got started. Bub Jacobs spread rumors about me. I learned bitterly then what Mother had told me. Different is dead—and one death is never enough. You die and die and die.

Then one day I caught Bub cutting across the foot of our wood lot. He saw me coming and hit for tall timber, already smarting under what he knew he'd get if I caught him. I started full speed after him, then plowed to a stop. Why waste effort? If I could do it to the wood, I could do it to a blockhead like Bub.

He let out a scream of pure terror as the ground dropped out from under him. His scream flatted and strangled into silence as he struggled in midair, convulsed with fear of falling and the terrible thing that was happening to him. And I stood and laughed at him, feeling myself a giant towering above stupid dopes like Bub.

Sharply, before he passed out, I felt his terror, and an echo of his scream rose in my throat. I slumped down in the dirt, sick with sudden realization, knowing with a knowledge that went beyond ordinary experience that I had done something terribly wrong. I had used whatever powers I possessed to terrorize unjustly.

I knelt and looked up at Bub, crumpled in the air, higher than my head, higher than my reach, and swallowed painfully as I realized that I had no idea how to get him down. He wasn't a stick of wood to be snapped to the ground. He wasn't me, to dive through the air. I hadn't the remotest idea how to get a human down.

Half dazed, I crawled over to a shaft of sunlight that slit the cottonwood branches overhead and felt it rush through my fingers like something to be lifted—and twisted—and fashioned and used! Used on Bub! But how? How? I clenched my fist in the flood of light, my mind beating against another door that needed only a word or look or gesture to open, but I couldn't say it, or look it, or make it.

I stood up and took a deep breath. I jumped, batting at Bub's heels that dangled a little lower than the rest of him. I missed. Again I jumped and the tip of one finger flicked his heel and he moved sluggishly in the air. Then I swiped the back of my hand across my sweaty forehead and laughed—laughed at my stupid self.

Cautiously, because I hadn't done much hovering, mostly just up and down, I lifted myself up level with Bub. I put my hands on him and pushed down hard. He didn't move.

I tugged him up and he rose with me. I drifted slowly and deliberately away from him and pondered. Then I got on the other side of him and pushed him toward the branches of the cottonwood. His head was beginning to toss and his lips moved with returning consciousness. He drifted through the air like a waterlogged stump, but he moved and I draped him carefully over a big limb near the top of the tree, anchoring his arms and legs as securely as I could. By the time his eyes opened and he clutched frenziedly for support, I was standing down at the foot of the tree, yelling up at him.

"Hang on, Bub! I'll go get someone to help you down!"

So for the next week or so people forgot me, and Bub squirmed under "Who treed you, feller?" and "How's the weather up there?" and "Get a ladder, Bub, get a ladder!"

Even with worries like that it was mostly fun for me. Why couldn't it be like that for Bethie? Why couldn't I give her part of my fun and take part of her pain?

Close Up

1. (a) When does Peter first learn that he can fly? (b) Why does he get an "all-gone" feeling later that night?

2. (a) When Peter's mother learns that he has flown, she feels frightened. How does Peter know how she feels? (b) When Peter's mother describes flying in the middle of a storm, Peter remembers what it is like. How is Peter able to remember?

3. (a) Peter and his sister Bethie are different from other people. How are they also different from one another? (b) What does Mother mean when she says that Bethie has only "half the gift"?

4. (a) Peter uses his special powers to finish his chores early. Why does his father make him restack the wood? (b) How does Peter feel when he uses his powers to get even with Bub?

Part Two

Then Dad died, swept out of life by our Rio Gordo as he tried to rescue a fool Easterner who had camped on the bone-dry white sands of the river bottom in cloudburst weather. Somehow it seemed impossible to think of Mother by herself. It had always been Mother and Dad. Not just two parents but Mother-and-Dad, a single entity. And now our thoughts must limp to Mother-and, Mother-and. And Mother—well, half of her was gone.

After the funeral Mother and Bethie and I sat in our front room, looking at the floor. Bethie was clenching her teeth against the stabbing pain of Mother's fingernails gouging Mother's palms.

I unfolded the clenched hands gently and Bethie relaxed.

"Mother," I said softly, "I can take care of us. I have my part-time job at the plant. Don't worry. I'll take care of us."

I knew what a trivial thing I was offering to her anguish, but I had to do something to break through to her.

"Thank you, Peter," Mother said, rousing a little. "I know you will——" She bowed her head and pressed both hands to her dry eyes with restrained desperation. "Oh, Peter, Peter! I'm enough of this world now to find death a despair and desolation instead of the solemnly sweet calling it is. Help me, help me!" Her breath labored in her throat and she groped blindly for my hand.

"If I can, Mother," I said, taking one hand as Bethie took the other. "Then help me remember. Remember with me."

And behind my closed eyes I remembered. Unhampered flight through a starry night, a flight of a thousand happy people like birds in the sky, rushing to meet the dawn—the dawn of the Festival. I could smell the flowers that garlanded the women and feel the quiet exultation that went with the Festival dawn. Then the leader sounded the magnificent opening notes of the Festival song as he caught the first glimpse of the rising sun over the heavily wooded hills. A thousand voices took up the song. A thousand hands lifted in the Sign. . . .

I opened my eyes to find my own

fingers lifted to trace a sign I did not know. My own throat throbbed to a note I had never sung. I took a deep breath and glanced over at Bethie. She met my eyes and shook her head sadly. She hadn't seen. Mother sat quietly, eyes closed, her face cleared and calmed.

"What was it, Mother?" I whispered.

"The Festival," she said softly. "For all those who had been called during the year. For your father, Peter and Bethie. We remembered it for your father."

"Where was it?" I asked. "Where in the world——?"

"Not in this——" Mother's eyes flicked open. "It doesn't matter, Peter. You are of this world. There is no other for you."

"Mother," Bethie's voice was a hesitant murmur, "what do you mean, 'remember'?"

Mother looked at her and tears swelled into her dry burned-out eyes.

"Oh, Bethie, Bethie, all the burdens and none of the blessings! I'm sorry, Bethie, I'm sorry." And she fled down the hall to her room.

Bethie stood close against my side as we looked after Mother. "Peter," she murmured, "what did Mother mean, 'none of the blessings'?"

"I don't know," I said.

"I'll bet it's because I can't fly like you."

"Fly!" My startled eyes went to hers. "How do you know?"

"I know lots of things," she whispered. "But mostly I know we're different. Other people aren't like us. Peter, what made us different?"

"Mother?" I whispered. "Mother?"

"I guess so," Bethie murmured. "But how come?"

We fell silent and then Bethie went to the window where the late sun haloed her silvery blond hair in fire.

"I can do things, too," she whispered. "Look."

She reached out and took a handful of sun, the same sort of golden sunslant that had flowed so heavily through my fingers under the cottonwoods while Bub dangled above me. With flashing fingers she fashioned the sun into an intricate glowing pattern. "But what's it for," she murmured, "except for pretty?"

"I know," I said, looking at my answer for lowering Bub. "I know, Bethie." And I took the pattern from her. It strained between my fingers and flowed into darkness.

The years that followed were casual, uneventful years. I finished high school, but college was out of the question. I went to work in the plant that provided work for most of the employables in Socorro.

Mother built up quite a reputation as a midwife—a very necessary calling in a community which took literally the injunction to multiply and replenish the earth and which lay exactly seventy-five miles from a hospital, no matter which way you turned when you got to the highway.

Bethie was in her teens and, with Mother's help, was learning to control her visible reactions to the pain of others, but I knew she still suffered as much as, if not more than, she had when she was smaller. But she was able to go to school most of the time now and was becoming fairly popular in spite of her quietness.

So all in all we were getting along quite comfortably and quite ordinarily except—well, I always felt as though I were waiting for something to happen or for someone to come. And Bethie must have, too, because she actually watched and listened—especially after a particularly bad spell. And even Mother. Sometimes as we sat on the porch in the long evenings she would cock her head and listen intently, her rocking chair still. But when we asked what she heard she'd sigh and say, "Nothing. Just the night " And her chair would rock again.

Of course, I still indulged my differences. Not with the white fire of possible discovery that they had kindled when I first began, but more like the feeding of a small flame just "for pretty." I went farther afield now for my "holidays," but Bethie went with me. She got a big kick out of our excursions, especially after we found, by means of a heart-stopping accident, that though she couldn't go up, she could control her going down. After that it was her pleasure to have me carry her up as far as I could and she would come down, sometimes taking an hour to make the descent, often weaving about her the intricate splendor of her sunshine patterns.

It was a rustling russet day in October when our world ended—again. We talked and laughed over the breakfast table, teasing Bethie about her date the night before. Color was high in her usually pale cheeks, and with all the laughter and brightness, the tingle of fall, everything just felt good.

But between one joke and another, the laughter drained out of Bethie's face and the pinched set look came to her lips.

"Mother!" she whispered, and then she relaxed.

"Already?" asked Mother, rising and finishing her coffee as I went to get her coat. "I had a hunch today would be the day. Reena would ride that jeep up Peppersauce Canyon this close to her time."

I helped her on with her coat and hugged her tight.

"Bless-a-mama," I said, "when are you going to retire and let someone else snatch the fall and spring crops of kids?"

"When I snatch a grandchild or so for myself," she said, joking, but I felt her sadness. "Besides, she's going to name this one Peter—or Bethie, as the case may be." She reached for her little black bag and looked at Bethie. "No more yet?"

Bethie smiled. "No," she murmured.

"Then I've got plenty of time. Peter, you'd better take Bethie for a holiday. Reena takes her own sweet time and being just across the road makes it bad on Bethie."

"Okay, Mother," I said. "We planned one anyway, but we hoped this time you'd go with us."

Mother looked at me, hesitated and turned aside. "I—I might sometime."

"Mother! Really?" This was the first hesitation from Mother in all the times we'd asked her.

"Well, you've asked me so many times and I've been wondering. Wondering if it's fair to deny our birthright. After all, there's nothing wrong in being of the People."

"What people, Mother?" I pressed. "Where are you from? Why can——?"

"Some other time, son," Mother said. "Maybe soon. These last few months I've begun to sense—yes, it wouldn't hurt you to know even if nothing could ever come of it; and perhaps soon something can come, and you will have to know. But no," she chided as we clung to her. "There's no time now. Reena might fool us after all and produce before I get there. You kids scoot, now!"

We looked back as the pickup roared across the highway and headed for Mendigo's Peak. Mother answered our wave and went in the gate of Reena's yard, where Dalt, in spite of this being their sixth, was running like an anxious puppy dog from Mother to the porch and back again.

It was a day of perfection for us. The relaxation of flight for me, the delight of hovering for Bethie, the frosted glory of the burning-blue sky, the russet and gold of grasslands stretching for endless miles down from the snow-flecked blue and gold Mendigo.

At lunchtime we lolled in the pleasant warmth of our favorite baby box canyon that held the sun and shut out the wind. After we ate we played our favorite game, Remembering. It began with my clearing my mind so that it lay as quiet as a hidden pool of water, as receptive as the pool to every pattern the slightest breeze might start quivering across its surface.

Then the memories would come— strange un-Earthlike memories that were like those Mother and I had had when Dad died. Bethie could not remember with me, but she seemed to catch the memories from me almost before the words could form in my mouth.

So this last lovely "holiday" we remembered again our favorite. We walked the darkly gleaming waters of a mountain lake, curling our toes in the liquid coolness, loving the tilt and sway of the waves beneath our feet, feeling around us from shore and sky a dear familiarity that was stronger than any Earth ties we had yet formed.

Before we knew it, the long lazy afternoon had fled and we shivered in the sudden chill as the sun dropped westward, nearing the peaks of the Huachucas. We packed the remains of our picnic in the basket, and I turned to Bethie, to lift her and carry her back to the pickup.

She was smiling her soft little secret smile.

"Look, Peter," she murmured. And flicking her fingers over her head she shook out a cloud of snowflakes, gigantic whirling tumbling snowflakes that clung feather-soft to her pale hair and melted, glistening, across her warm cheeks and mischievous smile.

"Early winter, Peter!" she said.

"Early winter, punkin!" I cried and snatching her up, boosted her out of the little canyon and jumped over her, clearing the boulders she had to scramble over. "For that you walk, young lady!"

But she almost beat me to the car anyway. For one who couldn't fly, she was learning to run awfully light.

Twilight had fallen before we got back to the highway. We could see the headlights of the scurrying cars that seldom even slowed down for Socorro. "So this is Socorro, wasn't it?" was the way most traffic went through.

We had topped the last rise before the highway when Bethie screamed. I almost lost control of the car on the rutty road. She screamed again, a wild tortured cry as she folded in on herself.

"Bethie!" I called, trying to get through to her. "What is it? Where is it? Where can I take you?"

But her third scream broke off short

and she slid limply to the floor. I was terrified. She hadn't reacted like this in years. She had never fainted like this before. Could it be that Reena hadn't had her child yet? That she was in such agony—but even when Mrs. Allbeg had died in childbirth Bethie hadn't—I lifted Bethie to the seat and drove wildly homeward, praying that Mother would be. . . .

And then I saw it. In front of our house. The big car skewed across the road. The kneeling cluster of people on the pavement.

The next thing I knew I was kneeling, too, beside Dr. Dueff, clutching the edge of the blanket that mercifully covered Mother from chin to toes. I lifted a trembling hand to the dark trickle of blood that threaded crookedly down from her forehead.

"Mother," I whispered. "Mother!"

Her eyelids fluttered and she looked up blindly. "Peter." I could hardly hear her. "Peter, where's Bethie?"

"She fainted. She's in the car," I faltered. "Oh, Mother!"

"Tell the doctor to go to Bethie."

"But, Mother!" I cried. "You——"

"I am not called yet. Go to Bethie."

We knelt by her bedside, Bethie and I. The doctor was gone. There was no use trying to get Mother to a hospital. Just moving her indoors had started a dark oozing from the corner of her mouth. The neighbors were all gone except Gramma Reuther, who always came to troubled homes and had folded the hands of the dead in Socorro from the founding of the town. She sat now in the front room holding her worn Bible in quiet hands, after all these years no longer needing to look up the passages of comfort and assurance.

The doctor had quieted the pain for Mother and had urged sleep upon Bethie, not knowing how long the easing would last, but Bethie wouldn't take it.

Suddenly Mother's eyes were open.

"I married your father," she said clearly, as though continuing a conversation. "We loved each other so, and they were all dead—all my People. Of course, I told him first, and oh, Peter! He believed me! After all the time of having to guard every word and every move I had someone to talk to——someone to believe me. I told him all about the People and lifted myself and then I lifted the car and turned it in mid-air above the highway—just for fun. It pleased him a lot but it made him thoughtful, and later he said, 'You know, honey, your world and ours took different turns way back there. We turned to gadgets. You turned to the Power.'"

Her eyes smiled. "He got so he knew when I was lonesome for the Home. Once he said, 'Homesick, honey? So am I. For what this world could have been. Or maybe—God willing—what it may become.'

"Your father was the other half of me." Her eyes closed, and in the silence her breath became audible. a harsh straining sound. Bethie crouched with both hands pressed to her chest, her face dead white in the shadows.

"We discussed it and discussed it," Mother cried. "But we had to decide as we did. We thought I was the last of the People. I had to forget the Home and be of Earth. You children had to be of Earth, too, even if——That's why he was so stern with you, Peter. Why he didn't want you to—experiment. He was afraid you'd do too much around other people if you found out——" She stopped and lay panting. "Different is dead," she whispered, and lay scarcely breathing for a moment.

"I knew the Home." Her voice was heavy with sorrow. "I remember the Home. Not just because my People remembered it, but because I saw it. I was born there. It's gone now. Gone forever. There is no Home. Only a band of dust between the stars!" Her face twisted with grief and Bethie echoed her cry of pain.

Then Mother's face cleared and her eyes opened. She half propped herself up in her bed.

"You have the Home, too. You and Bethie. You will have it always. And your children after you. Remember, Peter? Remember?"

Then her head tilted attentively and she gave a laughing sob. "Oh, Peter! Oh, Bethie! Did you hear it? I've been called! I've been called!" Her hand lifted in the Sign and her lips moved tenderly.

"Mother!" I cried fearfully. "What do you mean? Lie down. Please lie down!" I pressed her back against the pillows.

"I've been called back to the Presence. My years are finished. My days are totaled."

"But Mother," I blubbered like a child, "what will we do without you?"

"Listen!" Mother whispered rapidly, one hand pressed to my hair. "You must find the rest. You must go right away. They can help Bethie. They can help you, Peter. As long as you are separated from them, you are not complete. I have felt them calling the last year or so, and now that I am on the way to the Presence I can hear them clearer, and clearer." She paused and held her breath. "There is a canyon—north. The

ship crashed there, after our life slips—here, Peter, give me your hand." She reached urgently toward me and I cradled her hand in mine.

And I saw half the state spread out below me like a giant map. I saw the wrinkled folds of the mountains, the deceptively smooth roll of the desert up to the jagged slopes. I saw the blur of timber blunting the hills and I saw the angular writhing of the narrow road through the passes. Then I felt a sharp pleasurable twinge, like the one you feel when seeing home after being away a long time.

"There!" Mother whispered as the panorama faded. "I wish I could have known before. It's been lonely——

"But you, Peter," she said strongly. "You and Bethie must go to them."

"Why should we, Mother?" I cried in desperation. "What are they to us or we to them that we should leave Socorro and go among strangers?"

Mother pulled herself up in bed, her eyes intent on my face. She wavered a moment and then Bethie was crouched behind her, steadying her back.

"They are not strangers," she said clearly and slowly. "They are the People. We shared the ship with them during the Crossing. They were with us when we were out in the middle of emptiness with only the fading of stars behind and the brightening before to tell us we were moving. They, with us, looked at all the bright frosting of stars across the blackness, wondering if on one of them we would find a welcome.

"You are woven of their fabric. Even though your father was not of the People——"

Her voice died, her face changed. Bethie moved from in back of her and lowered her gently. Mother clasped her hands and sighed.

"It's a lonely business," she whispered "No one can go with you. Even with them waiting it's lonely."

In the silence that followed, we heard Gramma Reuther rocking quietly in the front room. Bethie sat on the floor beside me, her cheeks flushed, her eyes wide with a strange dark awe.

"Peter, it didn't hurt. It didn't hurt at all. It—healed!"

But we didn't go. How could we leave my job and our home and go off—where? Looking for—whom? Because—why? It was mostly me, I guess, but I couldn't quite believe what Mother had told us. After all, she hadn't said anything definite. We were probably reading meaning where it didn't exist. Bethie returned again and again to the puzzle of Mother and what she had meant, but we didn't go.

And Bethie got paler and thinner, and it was nearly a year later that I came home to find her curled into an impossibly tight ball on her bed, her eyes tight shut, snatching at breath that came out again in sharp moans.

I nearly went crazy before I at last got through to her and uncurled her enough to get hold of one of her hands. Finally, though, she opened dull dazed eyes and looked past me.

"Like a dam, Peter," she gasped. "It all comes in. It should—it should! I was born to——" I wiped the cold sweat from her forehead. "But it just piles up and piles up. It's supposed to go somewhere. I'm supposed to do something! Peter Peter Peter!" She twisted on the bed, her distorted face pushing into the pillow.

"What does, Bethie?" I asked, turning her face to mine. "What does?"

"Glib's foot and Dad's side and Mr. Tyree-next-door's toe——" and her voice faded down through the litany of years of agony.

"I'll go get Dr. Dueff," I said hopelessly.

"No." She turned her face away. "Why build the dam higher? Let it break. Oh, soon soon!"

"Bethie, don't talk like that," I said, feeling inside me my terrible aloneness that only Bethie could fend off now that Mother was gone. "We'll find something—some way——"

"Mother could help," she gasped. "A little. But she's gone. And now I'm picking up mental pain, too! Reena's afraid she's got cancer. Oh, Peter Peter!" Her voice strained to a whisper. "Let me die! Help me die!"

Both of us were shocked to silence by her words. Help her die? I leaned against her hand. Go back into the Presence with the weight of unfinished years dragging at our feet? For if she went, I went, too.

Then my eyes flew open and I stared at Bethie's hand. What Presence? Whose ethics and mores were talking in my mind?

And so I had to decide. I talked Bethie into a sleeping pill and sat by her even after she was asleep. And as I sat there all the past years wound through my head. The way it must have been for Bethie all this time and I hadn't let myself know.

Just before dawn I woke Bethie. We packed and went. I left a note on the kitchen table for Dr. Dueff saying only that we were going to look for help for Bethie and would he ask Reena to see to the house. And thanks.

Close Up

1. When Dad dies, how does Peter help Mother ease her sorrow?

2. (a) What does Peter find out about the Festival? (b) What does he find out about Bethie?

3. Finally, Mother tells Peter about the People. (a) Why did she keep this knowledge from him originally? (b) Why does she now tell him to find the People?

4. An allusion is a reference in one work of literature to something that is well known in another work of literature, history, the arts, etc. For example, the title of this story is an allusion to the Bible: "Is there no balm in Gilead; is there no physician there? Why then is *not* the health of the daughter of my people recovered?" (Jeremiah 9:22). (a) Why does Bethie seek balm, which is something that heals? (b) Why does Peter seek balm?

5. Why do you think this story is called "Gilead"?

Part Three

I slowed the pickup over to the side of the junction and slammed the brakes on.

"Okay," I said hopelessly. "You choose which way this time. Or shall we toss for it? Heads straight up, tails straight down! I can't tell where to go, Bethie. I had only that one little glimpse that Mother gave me of this country. There's a million canyons and a million side roads. We were fools to leave Socorro. After all, we have nothing to go on but what Mother said. It might have been delirium."

"No," Bethie murmured. "It can't be. It's got to be real."

"But, Bethie," I said, leaning my weary head on the steering wheel, "you know how much I want it to be true, not only for you but for myself, too. But look. What do we have to assume if Mother was right? First, that space travel is possible—was possible nearly fifty years ago. Second, that Mother and her People came here from another planet. Third, that we are, bluntly speaking, half-breeds, a cross between Earth and heaven knows what world. Fourth, that there's a chance—in ten million—of our finding the other People who came at the same time Mother did, presupposing that any of them survived the Crossing.

"Why, any one of these premises would brand us as crazy crackpots to any normal person. No, we're building too much on a dream and a hope. Let's go back, Bethie. We've got just enough gas money along to make it. Let's give it up."

"And go back to what?" Bethie asked, her face pinched. "No, Peter. Here."

I looked up as she handed me one of her sunlight patterns, a handful of brilliance that twisted briefly in my fingers before it flickered out.

"Is that Earth?" she asked quietly. "How many of our friends can fly? How many—" she hesitated, "how many can Remember?"

"Remember!" I said slowly, and then I whacked the steering wheel with my fist. "Oh, Bethie, of all the stupid——! Why, it's Bub all over again!"

I kicked the pickup into life and turned on the first faint desert trail beyond the junction. I pulled off even that suggestion of a trail and headed across the nearly naked desert toward a clump of ironwood, mesquite, and catclaw that marked a sand wash against the foothills. With the westering sun making shadow lace through the thin foliage, we made camp.

I lay on my back in the wash and looked deep into the arch of the desert sky. The trees made a typical desert pattern of warmth and coolness on me, warm in the sun, cool in the shadow, as I let my mind clear smoother, smoother, until the soft intake of Bethie's breath as she sat beside me sent a bright ripple across it.

And I remembered. But only Mother-and-Dad and the little campfire I had gathered up, and Glib with the trap on his foot and Bethie curled, face to knees on the bed, and the thin crying sound of her labored breath.

I blinked at the sky. I had to Remember. I just had to. I shut my eyes and concentrated and concentrated, until I was exhausted. Nothing came now, not even a hint of memory. In despair I relaxed, limp against the chilling sand. And all at once unaccustomed gears shifted and slipped into place in my mind and there I was, just as I had been, hovering over the life-sized map.

Slowly and painfully I located Socorro and the thin thread that marked the Rio Gordo. I followed it and lost it and followed it again, the finger of my attention pressing close. Then I located Vulcan Springs Valley and traced its broad rolling to the upsweep of the desert, to the Sierra Cobreña Mountains. It was an eerie sensation to look down on the infinitesimal groove that must be where I was lying now. Then I hand-spanned my thinking around our camp spot. Nothing. I probed farther north, and east, and north again. I drew a deep breath and exhaled it shakily. There it was. The Home twinge. The call of familiarity.

I read it off to Bethie. The high thrust of a mountain that pushed up baldly past its timber, the huge tailings dump across the range from the mountain. The casual wreathing of smoke from what must be a logging town, all forming sides of a slender triangle. Somewhere in this area was the place.

I opened my eyes to find Bethie in tears.

"Why, Bethie!" I said. "What's wrong? Aren't you glad——?"

Bethie tried to smile but her lips quivered. She hid her face in the crook of her elbow and whispered. "I saw, too! Oh, Peter, this time I saw, too!"

We got out the road map and by the fading afternoon light we tried to translate our rememberings. As nearly as we could figure out, we should head for a place way off the highway called Kerry Canyon. It was apparently the only inhabited spot anywhere near the big bald mountain. I looked at the little black dot in the kink in the third-rate road and wondered if it would turn out to be a period to all our hopes or the point for the beginning of new lives for the two of us. Life and sanity for Bethie, and for me. . . . In a sudden spasm of emotion I crumpled the map in my hand. I felt blindly that in all my life I had never known anyone but Mother and Dad and Bethie. That I was a ghost walking the world. If only I could see even one other person that felt like our kind! Just to know that Bethie and I weren't all alone with our unearthly heritage!

I smoothed out the map and folded it again. Night was on us and the wind was cold. We shivered as we scurried around looking for wood for our campfire.

Kerry Canyon was one business street, two service stations, two saloons, two stores, two churches, and a handful of houses flung at random over the hillsides that sloped down to an area that looked too small to accommodate the road. A creek which was now thinned to an intermittent trickle that loitered along, waited for the fall rains to begin. A sudden speckling across our windshield suggested it hadn't long to wait.

We rattled over the old bridge and half through the town. The road swung up sharply over a rusty single-line railroad and turned left, shying away from the bluff that was hollowed just enough to accommodate one of the service stations.

We pulled into the station. The uniformed attendant came alongside.

"We just want some information," I said, conscious of the thinness of my billfold. We had picked up our last tankful of gas before plunging into the maze of canyons between the main highway and here. Our stopping place would have to be soon, whether we found the People or not.

"Sure! Sure! Glad to oblige." The attendant pushed his cap back from his forehead. "How can I help you?"

I hesitated, trying to gather my thoughts and words—and some of the hope that had jolted out of me since we had left the junction. "We're trying to locate some—friends—of ours. We were told they lived out the other side of here, out by Baldy. Is there anyone——?"

"Friends of them people?" he asked in astonishment. "Well, say now, that's interesting! You're the first I ever had come asking after them."

I felt Bethie's arm trembling against mine. Then there was something beyond Kerry Canyon!

"How come? What's wrong with them?"

"Why, nothing, Mac, nothing. Matter of fact, they're dern nice people. Trade here a lot. Come in to church and the dances."

"Dances?" I glanced around the steep sloping hills.

"Sure. We ain't as dead as we look," the attendant grinned. "Come Saturday night we're quite a town. Lots of ranches around these hills. Course, not much out Cougar Canyon way. That's where your friends live, didn't you say?"

"Yeah. Out by Baldy."

"Well, nobody else lives out that way." He hesitated. "Hey, there's something I'd like to ask."

"Sure. Like what?"

"Well, them people pretty much keep themselves to themselves. I don't mean they're stuck-up or anything, but— well, I've always wondered. Where they come from? One of them overrun countries in Europe? They're foreigners, ain't they? And seems like most of what Europe exports any more is DP's.[1] Are them people some?"

"Well, yes, you might call them that. Why?"

"Well, they talk just as good as anybody and it must have been a war a long time ago because they've been around since my Dad's time, but they just—feel different." He caught his upper lip between his teeth reflectively. "Good different. Real nice different." He grinned again. "Wouldn't mind shining up to some of them gals myself. Don't get no encouragement, though."

"Anyway, keep on this road. It's easy. No other road going that way. Jackass Flat will beat the tar outa your tires, but you'll probably make it, less'n comes up a heavy rain. Then you'll skate over half the country and most likely end up in a ditch. Slickest mud in the world. Real cold out there on the flat when the wind starts blowing. Better bundle up."

"Thanks, fella," I said. "Thanks a lot. Think we'll make it before dark?"

"Oh, sure. 'Tain't so awful far but the road's lousy. Oughta make it in two–three hours, less'n like I said, comes up a heavy rain."

We knew when we hit Jackass Flat. It was like dropping off the edge. If we had thought the road to Kerry Canyon was bad we revised our opinions, but fast. In the first place, it was choose your own ruts. Then the tracks were deep sunk in heavy clay generously mixed with sharp splintery shale and rocks as big as your two fists that were like a gigantic gravel as far as we could see across the lifeless expanse of the flat.

But to make it worse, the ruts I chose kept ending abruptly as though the cars that had made them had either backed away from the job or jumped over. Jumped over! I drove in and out of ruts, so wrapped up in surmises that I hardly noticed the rough going until a cry from Bethie aroused me.

"Stop the car!" she cried. "Oh, Peter! Stop the car!"

I braked so fast that the pickup swerved wildly, mounted the side of a rut, lurched, and settled sickeningly down on the back tire which sighed itself flatly into the rising wind.

"What on earth!" I yelped, as near to being mad at Bethie as I'd ever been in my life. "What was that for?"

Bethie, white-faced, was emerging from the army blanket she had huddled in against the cold. "It just came to me. Peter, supposing they don't want us?"

"Don't want us? What do you mean?" I growled, wondering if that lace doily I called my spare tire would be worth the trouble of putting it on.

"We never thought. It didn't even occur to us. Peter, we—we don't belong. We won't be like them. We're partly of Earth—as much as we are of whatever else. Supposing they reject us? Supposing they think we're undesirable——?" Bethie turned her face away. "Maybe we don't belong anywhere, Peter, not anywhere at all."

I felt a chill sweep over me that was not of the weather. We had assumed so blithely that we would be welcome. But how did we know? Maybe they wouldn't want us. We weren't of the People. We

---

1. DP's.: Displaced persons. During World War Two, many people were forced to flee their homelands in order to save their lives. Some of these people immigrated to the United States.

weren't of Earth. Maybe we didn't belong—not anywhere.

"Sure they'll want us," I forced out heartily. Then my eyes wavered away from Bethie's and I said defensively, "Mother said they would help us. She said we were woven of the same fabric——"

"But maybe the warp[2] will only accept genuine woof.[3] Mother couldn't know. There weren't any—half-breeds—when she was separated from them. Maybe our Earth blood will mark us——"

"There's nothing wrong with Earth blood," I said defiantly. "Besides, like you said, what would there be for you if we went back?"

She pressed her clenched fists against her cheeks, her eyes wide and vacant. "Maybe," she muttered, "maybe if I'd just go on and go completely insane it wouldn't hurt so terribly much. It might even feel good."

"Bethie!" my voice jerked her physically. "Cut out that talk right now! We're going on. The only way we can judge the People is by Mother. She would never reject us or any others like us. And that fellow back there said they were good people."

I opened the door. "You better try to get some kinks out of your legs while I change the tire. By the looks of the sky we'll be doing some skating before we get to Cougar Canyon."

But for all my brave words it wasn't just for the tire that I knelt beside the car,

and it wasn't only the sound of the lug wrench that the wind carried up into the darkening sky.

I squinted through the streaming windshield, trying to make out the road through the downpour that fought our windshield wiper to a standstill. What few glimpses I caught of the road showed a deceptively smooth-looking chocolate river, but we alternately shook like a giant maraca,[4] pushed out sheets of water like a speedboat, or slithered aimlessly and terrifyingly across sudden mud flats that often left us yards off the road. Then we'd creep cautiously back until the soggy squelch of our tires told us we were in the flooded ruts again.

Then all at once it wasn't there. The road, I mean. It stretched a few yards ahead of us and then just flowed over the edge, into the rain, into nothingness.

"It couldn't go there," Bethie murmured incredulously. "It can't just drop off like that."

"Well, I'm certainly not dropping off with it, sight unseen," I said, huddling deeper into my army blanket. My jacket was packed in back and I hadn't bothered to dig it out. I hunched my shoulders to bring the blanket up over my head. "I'm going to take a look first."

I slid out into the solid wall of rain that hissed and splashed around me on the flooded flat. I was soaked to the knees and mud-coated to the shins before I slithered to the drop-off. The trail—call that a road?—tipped over the edge of the canyon and turned abruptly to the right, then lost itself along a shrub-grown ledge that sloped downward even

---

2. warp (wôrp) n.: In weaving, the threads that run lengthwise.
3. woof (wo͞of) n.: In weaving, the threads that run crosswise. These threads form right angles with the warp.

---

4. maraca (mə-rä′kə) n.: A rattle-like instrument made from a hollow gourd.

as it paralleled the rim of the canyon. If I could get the pickup over the rim and onto the trail it wouldn't be so bad. But—I peered over the drop-off at the turn. The bottom was lost in shadows and rain. I shuddered.

Then quickly, before I could lose my nerve, I squelched back to the car.

"Pray, Bethie. Here we go."

There was the suck and slosh of our turning tires, the awful moment when we hung on the brink. Then the turn. And there we were, poised over nothing, with our rear end slewing outward.

The sudden tongue-biting jolt as we finally landed, right side up, pointing the right way on the narrow trail, jarred the cold sweat on my face so it rolled down with the rain.

I pulled over at the first wide spot in the road and stopped the car. We sat in the silence, listening to the rain. I felt as though something infinitely precious were lying just before me. Bethie's hand crept into mine and I knew she was feeling it, too. But suddenly Bethie's hand was snatched from mine and she was pounding with both fists against my shoulder in most un-Bethie-like violence.

"I can't stand it, Peter!" she cried hoarsely, emotion choking her voice. "Let's go back before we find out any more. If they should send us away! Oh, Peter! Let's go before they find us! Then we'll still have our dream. We can pretend that someday we'll come back. We can never dream again, never hope again!" She hid her face in her hands. "I'll manage somehow. I'd rather go away, hoping, than run the risk of being rejected by them."

"Not me," I said, starting the motor. "We have as much chance of a welcome as we do of being kicked out. And if they can help you—say, what's the matter with you today? I'm supposed to be the doubting one, remember? You're the mustard seed of this outfit!" I grinned at her, but my heart sank at the drawn white misery of her face. She almost managed a smile.

The trail led steadily downward, lapping back on itself as it worked back and forth along the canyon wall, sometimes steep, sometimes almost level. The farther we went the more rested I felt, as though I were shutting doors behind or opening them before me.

Then came one of the casual miracles of mountain country. The clouds suddenly opened and the late sun broke through. There, almost frighteningly, a huge mountain pushed out of the featureless gray distance. In the flooding light the towering slopes seemed to move, stepping closer to us as we watched. The rain still fell, but now in glittering silver-beaded curtains; and one vivid end of a rainbow splashed color recklessly over trees and rocks and a corner of the sky.

I didn't watch the road. I watched the splendor and glory spread out around us. So when, at Bethie's scream, I snatched back to my driving, all I took down into the roaring splintering darkness was the thought of Bethie and the sight of the other car, slanting down from the bobbing top branches of a tree, seconds before it plowed into us broadside, a yard above the road.

Close Up

1. (a) Why does Peter begin to doubt that the People really exist? (b) How does Bethie convince him that Mother's story is true?

2. (a) How does Peter use his special powers to find a path to the People? (b) What does he mean when he wonders if the dot in the kink of the road will "turn out to be a period to all our hopes or the point for the beginning"?

3. Peter says that the ruts in the road end so abruptly, it looks as if the cars that made them jumped from rut to rut. Why does this make him think that he is near the People?

4. As they near their goal, Bethie wants to turn back. (a) What does she fear? (b) What does she mean when she says, "But maybe the warp will only accept genuine woof"?

5. Peter says that Bethie has been "the mustard seed of this outfit." This is an allusion to the Bible: " . . . If ye have faith as a grain of mustard seed, ye shall say unto this mountain, 'Remove hence to yonder place'; and it shall remove; and nothing shall be impossible unto you" (Matthew 17:20). How has Bethie been like a mustard seed?

Part Four

I thought I was dead. I was afraid to open my eyes because I could feel the rain making little puddles over my closed lids. And then I breathed. I was alive, all right. A knife jabbed itself up and down the left side of my chest and twisted itself viciously with each reluctant breath I drew.

Then I heard a voice.

"Thank the Power they aren't hurt too badly. But, oh, Valancy! What will Father say?" The voice was young and scared.

"You've known him longer than I have," another girl-voice answered. "You should have some idea."

"I never had a wreck before, not even when I was driving instead of lifting."

"I have a hunch that you'll be grounded for quite a spell," the second voice replied. "But that isn't what's worrying me, Karen. Why didn't we know they were coming? We always can sense Outsiders. We should have known——"

"Q.E.D.[5] then," said the Karen-voice.

"'Q.E.D.'?"

"Yes. If we didn't sense them, then they're not Outsiders——" There was the sound of a caught breath and then, "Oh, what I said, Valancy! You don't suppose!" I felt a movement close to me and heard the soft sound of breathing. "Can it really be two more of us? Oh, Valancy, they must be second genera-

tion—they're about our age. How did they find us? Which of our Lost Ones were their parents?"

Valancy sounded amused. "Those are questions they're certainly in no condition to answer right now, Karen. We'd better figure out what to do. Look, the girl is coming to."

I was snapped out of my detached eavesdropping by a moan beside me. I started to sit up. "Bethie——" I began, and all the knives twisted through my lungs. Bethie's scream followed my gasp.

My eyes were open now, but good, and my leg was an agonized burning ache down at the far end of my consciousness. I gritted my teeth but Bethie moaned again.

"Help her, help her!" I pleaded to the two fuzzy figures leaning over as I tried to hold my breath to stop the jabbing.

"But she's hardly hurt," Karen cried. "A bump on her head. Some cuts."

With an effort I focused on a luminous clear face—Valancy's—whose

---

5. Q.E.D.: In this context, the abbreviation means they can only reach one conclusion.

deep eyes bent close above me. I licked the rain from my lips and blurted foolishly, "You're not even wet in all this rain!" A look of consternation swept over her face. There was a pause as she looked at me intently and then said, "Their shields aren't activated, Karen. We'd better extend ours."

"Okay, Valancy." And the annoying sibilant wetness of the rain stopped.

"How's the girl?"

"It must be shock or maybe internal——"

I started to turn to see, but Bethie's sobbing cry pushed me flat again.

"Help her," I gasped, grabbing wildly in my memory for Mother's words.

"She's a—a Sensitive!"

"A Sensitive?" The two exchanged looks. "Then why doesn't she——?"

Valancy started to say something, then turned swiftly. I crooked my arm over my eyes as I listened.

"Honey—Bethie—hear me!" The voice was warm but authoritative. "I'm going to help you. I'll show you how, Bethie."

There was a silence. A warm hand clasped mine and Karen squatted close beside me.

"She's sorting her," she whispered. "Going into her mind. To teach her control. It's so simple. How could it happen that she doesn't know——?"

I heard a soft wondering "Oh!" from Bethie, followed by a breathless "Oh, thank you, Valancy, thank you!"

I heaved myself up onto my elbow, fire streaking me from head to foot, and peered over at Bethie. She was looking at me, and her quiet face was happier than smiles could ever make it. We stared for the space of two relieved tears, then she said softly, "Tell them now, Peter. We can't go any farther until you tell them."

I lay back again, blinking at the sky where the scattered raindrops were still falling, though none of them reached us. Karen's hand was warm on mine and I felt a shiver of reluctance. If they sent us away . . . ! But then they couldn't take back what they had given to Bethie, even if—I shut my eyes and blurted it out as bluntly as possible.

"We aren't of the People—not entirely. Father was not of the People. We're half-breeds."

There was a startled silence.

"You mean your mother married an Outsider?" Valancy's voice was filled with astonishment. "That you and Bethie are ——?"

"Yes, she did and yes we are!" I retorted. "And Dad was the best——" My belligerence ran thinly out across the sharp edge of my pain. "They're both dead now. Mother sent us to you."

"But Bethie is a Sensitive——" Valancy's voice was thoughtful.

"Yes, and I can fly and make things travel in the air and I've even made fire. But Dad——" I hid my face and let it twist with the increasing agony.

"Then we can!" I couldn't read the emotion in Valancy's voice. "Then the People and Outsiders—but it's unbelievable that you——" Her voice died.

In the silence that followed, Bethie's voice came fearful and tremulous, "Are you going to send us away?" My heart twisted to the ache in her voice.

"Send you away! Oh, my people, my people! Of course not! As if there were any question!" Valancy's arm went tightly around Bethie, and Karen's hand closed warmly on mine. The tension that had been a hard twisted knot inside me dissolved, and Bethie and I were home.

Then Valancy became very brisk.

"Bethie, what's wrong with Peter?"

Bethie was astonished. "How did you know his name?" Then she smiled. "Of course. When you were sorting me!" She touched me lightly along my sides, along my legs. "Four of his ribs are hurt. His left leg is broken. That's about all. Shall I control him?"

"Yes," Valancy said. "I'll help."

And the pain was gone, put to sleep under the persuasive warmth that came to me as Bethie and Valancy came softly into my mind.

"Good," Valancy said. "We're pleased to welcome a Sensitive. Karen and I know a little of their function because we are Sorters. But we have no full-fledged Sensitive in our Group now."

She turned to me. "You said you know the inanimate lift?"

"I don't know," I said. "I don't know the words for lots of things."

"You'll have to relax completely. We don't usually use it on people. But if you let go all over we can manage."

They wrapped me warmly in our blankets and lightly, a hand under my shoulders and under my heels, lifted me carrying-high and sped me through the trees, Bethie trailing from Valancy's free hand.

Before we reached the yard, the door flew open and warm yellow light spilled out into the dusk. The girls paused on the porch and shifted me to the waiting touch of two men. In the wordless pause before the babble of question and explanation I felt Bethie beside me draw a deep wondering breath and merge like a raindrop in a river into the People around us.

But even as the lights went out for me again, and I felt myself slide down into comfort and hunger-fed belongingness, somewhere deep inside of me was a core of something that couldn't quite— no, wouldn't quite dissolve—wouldn't yet yield itself completely to the People.

Close Up

1. (a) How do Karen and Valancy help Bethie after the accident? (b) What are Sorters?

2. (a) How do Karen and Valancy react when they learn that Peter and Bethie's father was human? (b) Why do you think they react this way?

3. At the end of the story, Bethie feels at one with the People, while Peter still feels somewhat separate. (a) What happened to Bethie that explains why she feels this way? (b) How do you think Peter will feel when this happens to him?

GLOSSARY

ă	pat		ŏ	pot
ā	pay		ō	toe
âr	care		ô	paw, for
ä	father		oi	noise
b	**bib**		oͦo	took
ch	**church**		o͞o	boot
d	**deed**		ou	**out**
ě	pet		p	**pop**
ē	**bee**		r	roar
f	**fife**		s	sauce
g	**gag**		sh	**ship, dish**
h	**hat**		t	**tight**
hw	**which**		th	**thin, path**
ĭ	pit		th	**this, bathe**
ī	pie		ŭ	cut
îr	pier		ûr	urge
j	**judge**		v	**valve**
k	**kick**		w	**with**
l	lid, needle		y	**yes**
m	**mum**		z	**zebra, dismal, exile**
n	**no, sudden**		zh	vision
ng	thing		ə	about, item, edible, gallop, circus

adj.	adjective	*n.*	noun	*prep.*	preposition
adv.	adverb			*v.*	verb

From *The American Heritage Dictionary of the English Language.* © 1979 by Houghton Mifflin Company. Reprinted by permission of Houghton Mifflin Company.

A

a ban don (ə-băn′dən) v.: To give up; to desert.

ab nor mal (ăb-nôr′məl) adj.: Not normal; unnatural.

ab surd i ty (ăb-sûrd′ĭ-tē, ăb-zûrd′ĭ-tē) n.: Total nonsense or foolishness.

ad just (ə-jŭst′) v.: To adapt or conform.

ad-lib (ăd-lĭb′) v.: To speak off the top of one's head, or in an improvised fashion.

a do be (ə-dō′bē) n.: Building material, made from sun-dried clay and straw. —adj.: Made from adobe.

aer ie (âr′ē, ăr′ē, ĭr′ē) n.: The nest of a bird that preys on other animals, such as an eagle, built in a high place.

af fec tion (ə-fĕk′shən) n.: Fondness; warm, tender feeling for another.

af flic tion (ə-flĭk′shən) n.: Misfortune; cause of suffering or pain.

ag i tate (ăj′ə-tāt′) v.: To upset, excite, or disturb. —**ag i ta tion,** n.

a li en (ā′lē-ən, āl′yən) adj.: Unfamiliar; strange; from a different place or culture.

al lot (ə-lŏt′) v.: To assign or give out.

a loft (ə-lôft′, ə-lŏft′) adv.: In the air or in flight.

a mi a ble (ā′mē-ə-bəl) adj.: Good-natured; friendly, agreeable.

an a con da (ăn′ə-kŏn′də) n.: Large, nonpoisonous snake of tropical South America that coils around and crushes its victims.

an ces try (ăn′sĕs′trē) n.: **1.** Line of descent. **2.** One's ancestors—the people from whom one is descended.

an guish (ăng′gwĭsh) n.: Agony, heartache, or turmoil; great mental or physical pain. —**an guished,** adj.

an gu lar (ăng′gyə-lər) adj.: **1.** Stiff or awkward. **2.** Sharp, rough-edged.

an tag o nize (ăn-tăg′ə-nīz′) v.: To make angry.

an te lope (ăn′tə-lōp′) n.: Swift, small, long-horned animal of Africa and Asia; similar to a deer.

an tic (ăn′tĭk) n.: Prank; silly action.

a pol o get i cal ly (ə-pŏl′ə-jĕt′ĭ-kəl-ē) adv.: Repentfully; in a way that admits one was wrong or at fault.

ap pa ra tus (ăp′ə-rā′təs, ăp′ə-răt′əs) n.: Equipment or materials used for a specific task or function.

ap pli ance (ə-plī′əns) n.: Electrical device, usually designed for household use.

ap pre hen sive (ăp′rĭ-hĕn′sĭv) adj.: Fearful or uneasy about what will happen.

a quat ic (ə-kwŏt′ĭk, ə-kwăt′ĭk) adj.: Living or growing in water.

ar chives (är′kīvz) n.: Place where public or historic records are kept.

ar dent (är′dənt) adj.: Passionate, devoted, enthusiastic.

ar rest ing (ə-rĕs′tĭng) adj.: **1.** Commanding, authoritative. **2.** Able to capture one's attention.

ar ro gant (ăr′ə-gənt) adj.: **1.** Proud and scornful. **2.** Overbearing.

as sess (ə-sĕs′) v.: To examine and judge.

as sort ment (ə-sôrt′mənt) n.: A collection or variety.

at ta ché (ăt′ə-shā′, ă-tā′shā′) n.: Person having a specific assignment on a diplomatic staff.

at test (ə-tĕst′) v.: To confirm; to declare something to be true or accurate.

at ti tude (ăt′ə-tōōd′, ăt′ə-tyōōd′) n.: Way of looking at things; frame of mind.

au ra (ôr′ə) n.: A distinctive quality or characteristic.

au then tic (ô-thĕn′tĭk) adj.: Genuine; of proven origin.

B

ban ish (băn′ĭsh) v.: To drive away or exile.

bank (băngk) v.: To tilt, usually an airplane.

bar ren (băr′ən) adj.: Empty; unadorned.

bar ri er (băr′ē-ər) n.: Obstacle; anything that prevents passage.

belch (bĕlch) *v.*: To spew forth or eject through the mouth.

bel low (bĕl′ō) *v.*: To roar; to shout in a deep voice. —**bel lowing,** *adj.*

ben e dic tion (bĕn′ə-dĭk′shən) *n.*: Prayer asking for a divine blessing, usually at the end of a religious service.

be seech ing ly (bĭ-sēch′ĭng-lē) *adv.*: In a pleading or begging manner.

bev el (bĕv′əl) *v.*: To cut or shape at an angle. —**bev eled,** *adj.*

bi ol o gist (bī-ŏl′ə-jĭst) *n.*: An expert in biology, which is the study of living organisms.

birth right (bûrth′rīt′) *n.*: A right or possession belonging to a person at birth, such as the right to an inheritance.

black out (blăk′out′) *n.*: In wartime, the extinguishing of all lights that might be seen by enemy aircraft during a night attack.

bleak (blēk) *adj.*: Unsheltered from wind and weather; bare and cheerless; dreary.

brace (brās) *v.*: To push firmly against for support.

brawn (brôn) *n.*: Muscular strength.

bris tle (brĭs′əl) *v.*: To stiffen or tense with anger or resentment.

broach (brōch) *v.*: To introduce or bring up for discussion.

bur den (bûrd′n) *n.*: A difficult thing to bear; a heavy responsibility.

bur ly (bûr′lē) *adj.*: Husky in build; strong, muscular.

bur nish (bûr′nĭsh) *v.*: To polish to a high gloss or finish. —**bur nished,** *adj.*

by stand er (bī′stăn′dər) *n.*: Person observing but not participating in an event.

C

ca jole (kə-jōl′) *v.*: To coax or persuade with flattery or false promises.

cal a bash (kăl′ə-băsh′) *n.*: A tropical tree or vine that produces a hard, round fruit. —*adj.*: Of or pertaining to a calabash.

cal cu late (kăl′kyə-lāt′) *v.*: To compute; to arrive at by using mathematical processes.

can ter (kăn′tər) *n.*: Horse's gait that is faster than a trot and slower than a gallop. —*v.*: To move at a canter.

ca per (kā′pər) *v.*: To leap about joyfully or playfully; to frolic.

cas u al ly (kăzh′ōō-əl-ē) *adv.*: In a relaxed fashion; informally.

ca ter er (kā′tər-ər) *n.*: Person or company hired to provide food for a party or banquet.

ca vort (kə-vôrt′) *v.*: To romp about and make merry.

cen sus (sĕn′səs) *n.*: Official number or count of a population. —*adj.*: Of or pertaining to a census.

char ac ter is ti cal ly (kăr′ĭk-tə-rĭs′tĭk-lē) *adv.*: In a distinctive or distinguishing way; typically.

char ter (chär′tər) *n.*: The hiring of a commercial vehicle, especially an airplane, for private use. —*adj.*: Relating to a charter.

chide (chīd) *v.*: To scold or voice disapproval.

chor tle (chôrt′l) *v.*: To chuckle with glee (made up of the words *chuckle* and *snort*).

clan (klăn) *n.*: Group of people descended from the same ancestor.

cloak (klōk) *n.*: Loose outer garment thrown over the shoulders.

comb (kōm) *n.*: Short for *honeycomb.*

com mer cial (kə-mûr′shəl) *adj.*: Having mass appeal; able to be sold to a lot of people.

com mo tion (kə-mō′shən) *n.*: Excitement, to-do, fuss; noisy disturbance.

com pli cate (kŏm′plĭ-kāt′) *v.*: To make more complex or difficult.

com ply (kəm-plī′) *v.*: To conform to a rule or request (used with *with*).

com pound (kŏm′pound) *n.*: Fenced-in area containing several buildings.

com put er (kəm-pyōō′tər) *n.*: An electronic device that can record, store, and feed back information and quickly perform mathematical or logical calculations.

con fed er ate (kən-fĕd′ər-ĭt) *n.*: Ally; accomplice.

con fine (kŏn′fīn′) *n.*: Border; boundary.

con form (kən-fôrm′) *v.*: To act in accordance or agreement with; to alter, adapt, or change one's views or actions to fit in with another's views or actions.

con found (kən-found′, kŏn-found′) *v.*: **1.** To confuse. **2.** To defeat.

con jure (kŏn′jər, kən-jŏŏr′) *v.*: To create or call up by magic.

con sent (kən-sĕnt′) v.: To agree.

con tent ment (kən-tĕnt′mənt) n.: Satisfaction; happiness with what one has.

con tour (kŏn′tŏor) n.: Outline or shape.

con tract (kən-trăkt′) v.: To pull together or reduce in size.

con tro ver sy (kŏn′trə-vûr′sē) n.: Dispute or debate in which differing opinions are expressed.

co or di nate (kō-ôr′də-nāt′) v.: To make two or more things work in harmony.

co or di na tion (kō-ôr′də-nā′shən) n.: Ability of muscles to work smoothly together to perform a specific task.

cor dial (kôr′jəl) adj.: Sincerely warm, gracious.

cor o ner (kôr′ə-nər, kŏr′ə-nər) n.: Public official who investigates deaths not clearly due to natural causes.

corpse (kôrps) n.: Dead body.

cos tum er (kŏs-tōo′mər, kŏs-tyōo′mər) n.: Person who makes, rents, or sells costumes.

coun ter part (koun′tər-pärt′) n.: Thing or person that closely resembles another or has a like role.

cow er (kou′ər) v.: To shrink away or crouch; to recoil.

cre ma tion (krĭ-mā′shən) n.: The act of burning a corpse.

cre ma to ri um (krē′mə-tôr′ē-əm, krē′mə-tōr′ē-əm) n.: Furnace for cremating corpses.

cres cen do (krə-shĕn′dō, krə-sĕn′dō) n.: Gradual increase in volume, as in a swelling of sound.

crit i cize (krĭt′ə-sīz′) v.: To find fault with.

cryp tic (krĭp′tĭk) adj.: Having a hidden meaning; puzzling, mystifying.

crys tal lize (krĭs′tə-līz′) v.: To become clear or definite; to jell.

cun ning (kŭn′ĭng) adj.: Clever, artful.

cur few (kûr′fyōo) n.: Order requiring people to remain indoors after a certain time of day.

cy clone (sī′klōn) n.: Windstorm marked by rotating columns of air and heavy rains.

D

deft (dĕft) adj.: Skillful, adept; well-coordinated, especially in using one's hands.

de lin quent (dĭ-lĭng′kwənt) n.: Person who behaves in a criminal way.

de mol ish (dĭ-mŏl′ĭsh) v.: To tear down or destroy.

de nom i na tor (dĭ-nŏm′ə-nā′tər) n.: Common trait or characteristic.

de plore (dĭ-plôr′, dĭ-plōr′) v.: **1.** To regret or feel sorry for. **2.** To strongly disapprove of.

de pressed (dĭ-prĕst′) adj.: Flattened down, sunken.

dep u tize (dĕp′yə-tīz′) v.: To appoint as deputy or substitute.

der e lict (dĕr′ə-lĭkt) n.: Something that has been abandoned, usually a ship that has been abandoned at sea.

des o late (dĕs′ə-lĭt) adj.: Deserted; no longer inhabited.

des o la tion (dĕs′ə-lā′shən) n.: Wretchedness; total misery.

des per a tion (dĕs′pə-rā′shən) n.: Quality of having been driven to the edge; feeling of hopelessness, or extreme despair. —**des per ate,** adj.

de ter mi na tion (dĭ-tûr′mə-nā′shən) n.: **1.** Quality of having made up one's mind. **2.** A fixed purpose or strong resolve. —**de ter mined,** adj.

di a lect (dī′ə-lĕkt′) n.: Regional version of a language, with differences in vocabulary, pronunciations, etc.

di am e ter (dī-ăm′ə-tər) n.: Straight line passing through the center of a circle; the length of such a line.

die sel (dē′zəl, dē′səl) n. [short for diesel engine]: An engine in which the ignition fluid is sparked by heat produced by compressed air.

din (dĭn) n.: Loud noise; clamor.

di shev eled (dĭ-shĕv′əld) adj.: Untidy, messy.

dis mal (dĭz′məl) adj.: Gloomy, dreary, depressing, bleak.

dis pel (dĭs-pĕl′) v.: To drive away, scatter.

dis play (dĭs-plā′) n.: Demonstration, showing, or exhibition.

dis pose (dĭs-pōz′) v.: To get rid of (used with of).

dis qual i fy (dĭs-kwŏl′ə-fī′) v.: To make ineligible; to eliminate.

dis sat is fac tion (dĭs-săt′ĭs-făk′shən) n.: Discontent, disappointment, or displeasure; a sense of unfulfillment.

dis traught (dĭs-trôt′) adj.: Deeply worried, anxious, or upset.

di vert (dĭ-vûrt′, dī-vûrt′) v.: To distract some-one's attention; to steer a person or thing away from a set course or direction.

doc u ment (dŏk′yə-mənt) v.: To support or prove by means of written, factual evidence.

do min ion (də-mĭn′yən) n.: Control, power, rule.

don (dŏn) v.: To put on, dress in.

do nate (dō′nāt′, dō-nāt′) v.: To contribute, or give something free of charge, usually to a fund or cause.

droll (drōl) adj.: Odd; comical or laughable.

dum found (dŭm′found) v.: To astonish, stun, or surprise.

E

ebb (ĕb) v.: To lessen or weaken; to diminish.

ec stat ic (ĕk-stăt′ĭk) adj.: Rapturous, overjoyed.

ee rie (îr′ē) adj: Weird, mysterious, spooky.

el o quence (ĕl′ə-kwəns) n.: Persuasive and effec-tive use of language.

e lude (ĭ-lōōd′) v.: To manage to avoid or escape by means of cunning or physical skill.

e ma ci ate (ĭ-mā′shē-āt′) v.: To become thin, usu-ally from starvation.

em brace (ĕm-brās′, ĭm-brās′) v.: To wrap one's arms around; to hug.

em phat ic (ĕm-făt′ĭk) adj.: 1. Forceful. 2. Defi-nite.

en chi la da (ĕn′chə-lä′də) n.: A rolled tortilla, a type of crepe or pancake that is stuffed with meat or cheese and served with chile sauce.

en com pass ing ly (ĕn-kŭm′pəs-ĭng′lē) adv.: In an all-embracing way.

en dur ance (ĕn-dŏŏr′əns, ĕn-dyŏŏr′əns) n.: Abil-ity to outlast, withstand, or put up with hard-ships.

en sue (ĕn-sōō′, ĭn-sōō′) v.: To take place or occur immediately afterward; to follow from.

en thu si ast (ĕn-thōō′zē-ăst′, ĭn-thōō′zē-ăst′) n.: Person who is greatly interested in, or preoccu-pied with, a certain subject or practice; a de-voted follower.

e qua to ri al (ē′kwə-tôr′ē-əl, ē′kwə-tōr′ē-əl, ĕk′wə-tôr′ē-əl) adj.: Of or pertaining to the earth's equator, or to conditions, such as cli-mate, that exist there.

e rupt (ĭ-rŭpt′) v.: To break out suddenly.

es ca late (ĕs′kə-lāt′) v.: To increase, or to become more intense.

es tate (ĕ-stāt′, ĭ-stāt′) n.: All of one's property or holdings; usually refers to a country mansion and its surrounding land.

e ter nal (ĭ-tûr′nəl) adj.: Lasting forever; unend-ing.

et i quette (ĕt′ə-kĕt′, ĕt′ə-kĭt) n.: Established social rules and customs.

e vac u ate (ĭ-văk′yōō-āt′) v.: To leave or depart, usually for safety reasons.

e val u ate (ĭ-văl′yōō-āt′) v.: To judge the worth of; to appraise.

ex ceed ing ly (ĕk-sē′dĭng-lē, ĭk-sē′dĭng-lē) adv.: Extremely.

ex clam a to ry (ĕks-klăm′ə-tôr′ē, ĕks-klăm′ə-tōr′ē, ĭks-klăm′ə-tōr′ē) adj.: Characterized by an abrupt or excited comment or outcry.

ex cur sion (ĕk-skûr′zhən, ĭk-skûr′zhən) n.: Brief outing.

ex ile (ĕg′zīl′, ĕk′sīl′) n.: Forced removal or dis-missal from one's country or home.

ex ot ic (ĕg-zŏt′ĭk, ĭg-zŏt′ĭk) adj.: Strangely or excitingly different from the usual; charmingly unfamiliar or intriguing.

ex pe di tion (ĕk′spə-dĭsh′ən) n.: Journey arranged for a specific purpose, usually by an organized group.

ex tinct (ĕk-stĭngkt′, ĭk-stĭngkt′) adj.: No longer existing.

ex trav a gance (ĕk-străv′ə-gəns, ĭk-străv′ə-gəns) n.: Wasteful spending.

ex u ber ant (ĕg-zōō′bər-ənt, ĭg-zōō′bər-ənt) adj.: Full of joy and high spirits.

F

fa cil i ty (fə-sĭl′ə-tē) n.: Building, area, or equip-ment that serves a special purpose.

fad (făd) n.: Something that is very popular, but only for a brief time, such as hoola-hoops or miniskirts; a current craze.

fal ter (fôl′tər) v.: To move unsteadily, or halting-ly; to stumble. —**fal tering**, adj.

fan tas tic (făn-tăs′tĭk) adj.: Remarkable or extraordinary in concept or appearance; incred-ible, unbelievable.

fash ion (făsh′ən) v.: To give a certain form to; to mold or shape into something else.

fas tid i ous (fă-stĭd′ē-əs, fə-stĭd′ē-əs) *adj.*: Hard to please or satisfy.

fe ro cious (fə-rō′shəs) *adj.*: Fierce or savage. —**fe ro cious ly**, *adv.*

fi an cé (fē′än-sā′, fē-än′sā′) *n.*: A man engaged to be married.

fi an cée (fē′än-sā′, fē-än′sā′) *n.*: A woman engaged to be married.

flank (flăngk) *n.*: Part of the body between the ribs and hip, especially of a horse.

flask (flăsk, fläsk) *n.*: Broad, flat, curved container of liquor, usually carried in a pocket.

flaw (flô) *n.*: Weakness; fault, defect.

flight y (flī′tē) *adj.*: Impulsive, moved by sudden whims; frivolous.

flinch (flĭnch) *v.*: To recoil in fear, pain, or surprise; to wince.

for feit (fôr′fĭt) *v.*: To lose; to have to surrender or give up something, usually as a penalty.

for ma tion (fôr-mā′shən) *n.*: Way in which a group of aircraft are positioned in flight.

for mi da ble (fôr′mə-də-bəl) *adj.*: Awesome, frightening, impressive; appearing impossible to conquer or defeat.

fran ti cal ly (frăn′tĭk-lē) *adv.*: Desperately.

fraud (frôd) *n.*: Act of trickery or deceit.

fu gi tive (fyoo′jə-tĭv) *n.*: Runaway; usually someone in hiding from the law.

fu se lage (fyoo′sə-läzh′, fyoo′zə-läzh′) *n.*: Central part of an airplane, holding the crew, passengers, and cargo.

G

gait (gāt) *n.*: Manner of moving, especially the way and rate of speed at which an animal moves.

gan gling (găng′glĭng) *adj.*: Tall, thin, lanky in build; awkward or ungraceful.

gauz y (gôz′ē) *adj.*: Having the properties of gauze, a thin, transparent fabric.

gawk (gôk) *v.*: To stare at stupidly or gape at.

gear (gîr) *v.*: To adjust something to suit or match something else.

ghast ly (găst′lē, gäst′lē) *adj.*: Frightening; dreadful.

gloat (glōt) *v.*: To regard with great or excessive delight, often in a smug or offensive manner.

gor geous (gôr′jəs) *adj.*: Very beautiful or handsome.

gourd (gôrd, gōrd, goord) *n.*: Hard, hollow, dried-out shell of a vine-growing fruit; usually used as a bowl or cup.

gris ly (grĭz′lē) *adj.*: Gruesome, ghastly.

gulch (gŭlch) *n.*: Narrow canyon or ravine cut out by a stream.

gul li ble (gŭl′ə-bəl) *adj.*: Easily fooled or deceived; liable to believe anything.

gut tur al (gŭt′ər-əl) *adj.*: Having a harsh or rasping vocal quality.

H

hal lu ci na tion (hə-loo′sə-nā′shən) *n.*: An illusion; the act of perceiving as real something that is imaginary.

hal ter (hôl′tər) *n.*: Rope or leather headpiece used on cows or horses.

heark en (här′kən) *v.*: To listen.

heath er (hĕth′ər) *n.*: A small, hardy shrub with evergreen leaves and clusters of purplish-pink flowers.

hi jack (hī′jăk′) *v.*: To seize a vehicle (such as a plane) by force.

hoax (hōks) *n.* Any act intended to deceive; for example, a practical joke or fraud.

hog wash (hôg′wŏsh′, hôg′wôsh′, hŏg′wôsh′) *n.*: Any worthless, nonsensical comments.

hov er (hŭv′ər, hŏv′ər) *v.*: To stay in or over one place while in flight (as if suspended in air); to linger or wait.

hu mil i ate (hyoo-mĭl′ē-āt′) *v.*: To humble; to disgrace or shame. —**hu mil i ating**, *adj.*

hu mil i a tion (hyoo-mĭl′ē-ā′shən) *n.*: Disgrace, shame.

hur ri cane (hûr′ə-kān′) *n.*: Tropical windstorm marked by heavy rains and rotating winds over seventy-five miles per hour.

hys ter i a (hĭ-stĕr′ē-ə) *n.*: Uncontrollable emotion, such as fear or excitement; panic. —**hys ter i cal**, *adj.*

I

ich thy ol o gy (ĭk′thē-ŏl′ə-jē) *n.*: Branch of biology dealing with the study of fishes. —**ich thy ol o gist**, *n.* —**ich thy ic**, *adj.*

ich thy or nis (ĭk′thē-ôr′nĭs) *n.*: Any of an order of extinct, fish-eating, toothed birds.

ich thy o saur (ĭk′thē-ə-sôr′) *n.*: One of an order of extinct, salt-water reptiles that had fish-like bodies and long snouts.

ig nite (ĭg-nīt′) *v.*: To set fire to; to spark.

ig ni tion (ĭg-nĭsh′ən) *n.*: Switch that sparks the fuel that starts the engine in a car. —*adj.*: Of or pertaining to an ignition.

im per a tive (ĭm-pĕr′ə-tĭv) *adj.*: Urgent; absolutely necessary.

im per son ate (ĭm-pûr′sə-nāt′) *v.*: To pretend to be someone else. —**im per son a tor,** *n.*

im plic it ly (ĭm-plĭs′ĭt-lē) *adv.*: Unquestioningly; without any doubts.

im press (ĭm-prĕs′) *v.*: To affect strongly or influence deeply. —**im pres sion,** *n.*

im pu dent (ĭm′pyə-dənt) *adj.*: Rude, brash, disrespectful.

im pul sive (ĭm-pŭl′sĭv) *adj.*: Not calculated or planned; spur of the moment.

in ac tiv ity (ĭn′ăk-tĭv′ə-tē) *n.*: Lack of motion; idleness.

in com pre hen si ble (ĭn′kŏm-prĭ-hĕn′sə-bəl) *adj.*: Incapable of being understood.

in cred i ble (ĭn-krĕd′ə-bəl) *adj.*: Unbelievable; fantastic.

in cred u lous (ĭn-krĕj′ə-ləs) *adj.*: Disbelieving; skeptical.

in de ci sion (ĭn′dĭ-sĭzh′ən) *n.*: State of being uncertain, or unable to make up one's mind.

in dig nant (ĭn-dĭg′nənt) *adj.*: Rightly offended by something unjust or mean. —**in dig nant ly,** *adv.*

in dis tinct (ĭn′dĭs-tĭngkt′) *adj.*: Unclear; not sharply defined or outlined.

in dom i ta ble (ĭn-dŏm′ə-tə-bəl) *adj.*: Incapable of being conquered or defeated.

in ert (ĭn-ûrt′) *adj.*: Lacking the ability to move; inactive.

in ev i ta ble (ĭn-ĕv′ə-tə-bəl) *adj.*: Unpreventable, unavoidable.

in hab i tant (ĭn-hăb′ə-tənt) *n.*: One who lives in a place; a resident.

in i ti ate (ĭ-nĭsh′ē-āt′) *v.*: **1.** To introduce to something for the first time, usually to a new field or new skill. **2.** To accept as a member in a club or group, by means of a special ceremony.

in nu mer a ble (ĭ-nōō′mər-ə-bəl, ĭ-nyōō′mər-ə-bəl) *adj.*: Numberless; having too many to count.

in quis i tive (ĭn-kwĭz′ə-tĭv) *adj.*: Curious, inquiring; eager to know or learn.

in sis tent (ĭn-sĭs′tənt) *adj.*: Demanding attention; urgent.

in stinct (ĭn′stĭngkt′) *n.*: An inborn or unlearned response.

in suf fi cient (ĭn′sə-fĭsh′ənt) *adj.*: Inadequate; not enough.

in ten si fy (ĭn-tĕn′sə-fī′) *v.*: To become stronger; to heighten or increase.

in ten tion (ĭn-tĕn′shən) *n.*: Plan or purpose; determination to do a specific thing.

in ter mit tent (ĭn′tər-mĭt′ənt) *adj.*: Periodic, or at intervals; not continuous.

in ter sperse (ĭn′tər-spûrs′) *v.*: To scatter or sprinkle something at regular intervals.

in ter val (ĭn′tər-vəl) *n.*: Period of time between two events.

in tra mu rals (ĭn′trə-myōōr′əlz) *n.*: Competitive games played with students from your own school.

in tri cate (ĭn′trĭ-kĭt) *adj.*: Complex or involved; full of elaborate or puzzling details.

in var i a ble (ĭn-vâr′ē-ə-bəl) *adj.*: Lacking variation or change; constant. —**in var i a bly,** *adv.*

is let (ī′lĭt) *n.*: Small island.

J

jab ber (jăb′ər) *v.*: To speak rapidly or unintelligibly.

jaun ti ly (jôn′tĭ-lē, jän′tĭ-lē) *adv.*: In a brisk, carefree way.

jest (jĕst) *v.*: To joke; to clown around.

jest er (jĕs′tər) *n.*: In medieval times, the person who was hired to jest and amuse, or play the fool, at court.

jos tle (jŏs′əl) *v.*: To push or shove in a particularly rough way.

K

ken nel (kĕn′əl) *n.*: Place where dogs are bred or boarded. —*adj.*: Of or pertaining to a kennel.

kiln (kĭl, kĭln) *n.*: Oven for hardening or drying substances, such as clay, bricks, or grain.

kilt (kĭlt) *n.*: Pleated, knee-length skirt worn by Scotsmen; any similar garment.

L

lash (lăsh) v.: To bind or fasten with a rope or cord.

latch (lăch) v.: To get hold of; to attach oneself to something.

leg end (lĕj′ənd) n.: Words, usually on a map or chart, that identify or point out things; captions.

li a ble (lī′ə-bəl) adj.: Likely.

lim ber (lĭm′bər) v.: To make one's muscles supple or agile; to loosen up.

lin guis tics (lĭng-gwĭs′tĭks) n.: Science of language. —adj.: Of or pertaining to linguistics.

lit a ny (lĭt′n-ē) n.: Something that is recited over and over again, usually a prayer.

lit er al ly (lĭt′ər-ə-lē) adv.: Really or actually.

lit ter (lĭt′ər) n.: Term for all the offspring (more than one) born to an animal at a single birth. (The term usually is applied to cats.)

loathe (lōth, lōth) v.: To hate or greatly dislike.

lo cal ize (lō′kə-līz′) v.: To confine within a given area or part. —**lo cal ized**, adj.

loch (lŏk) n.: Scottish for lake.

loft i ly (lôft′ĭ-lē) adv.: In a superior or high-handed way.

log (lôg, lŏg) n.: Written record of events, usually of a ship's daily speed and progress.

lurk (lûrk) v.: To sneak or slink about.

lust y (lŭs′tē) adj.: Full of health and strength; hearty; vigorous.

M

ma caw (mə-kô′) n.: A type of tropical-American parrot that has showy plumage and a long tail.

mag ne to (măg-nē′tō) n. [short for magnetoelectric machine]: Machine using magnets to produce the electric current that starts an engine.

mal ice (măl′ĭs) n.: Spite; ill will; a desire to see others suffer.

mane (mān) n.: Long, heavy hair growing along the necks of certain animals, particularly horses and lions.

ma neu ver (mə-nōō′vər, mə-nyōō′vər) v.: To make a calculated, or deliberate, change in one's position. —**ma neu vers**, n.

man gy (mān′jē) adj.: **1.** Resembling mange, a skin disease characterized by loss of hair and itching. **2.** Shabby.

man i fest (măn′ə-fĕst′) n.: List of passengers or cargo on an airplane or ship.

marge (märj) n.: Margin, edge, rim.

mar row (măr′ō) n.: **1.** Soft, fatty substance found inside bones. **2.** The essence, or innermost being of something.

mart en (märt′n) n.: Weasel-like, flesh-eating mammal found in northern wooded areas.

mas cot (măs′kŏt, măs′kət) n.: Person, animal, or object kept for good luck.

med dle (mĕd′l) v.: To intrude or interfere in someone else's affairs.

me di e val (mē′dē-ē′vəl, mĕd′ē′vəl) adj.: Characteristic of or belonging to the Middle Ages, the period of history dating from A.D. 476 to 1453.

men ace (mĕn′ĭs) v.: To threaten; to act in a threatening manner. —**men acing**, adj.

me sa (mā′sə) n.: Flat, high stretch of land with steep, sloping sides.

mesh (mĕsh) v.: To fit in with, or come together.

me thod i cal (mə-thŏd′ĭ-kəl) adj.: Orderly; characterized by habits, steps, or established procedures.

me trop o lis (mə-trŏp′ə-lĭs) n.: A major city, especially a state's capital or cultural center.

mid wife (mĭd′wīf′) n.: Woman who assists women in giving birth.

min i a ture (mĭn′ē-ə-chŏŏr′, mĭn′ə-chŏŏr′, mĭn′ə-chər) adj.: Very small by comparison; scaled-down.

mis chie vous (mĭs′chə-vəs) adj.: Playful, impish, prankish.

moil (moil) v.: To work hard; to labor or toil.

mo not o nous (mə-nŏt′n-əs) adj.: Dully repetitive; lacking variation or change.

mor tar (môr′tər) n.: Mixture of cement or lime with sand and water, used to hold bricks or other building materials together.

muf fle (mŭf′əl) v.: To wrap up, in order to protect or hide.

mur mur (mûr′mər) v.: To say in a low, whispering tone; to mutter.

mu tu al (myōō′chōō-əl) adj.: Equally shared.

muz zle (mŭz′əl) n.: **1.** Upper lip and nose of a horse. **2.** Front portion of a gun's barrel.

mys tic (mĭs′tĭk) *adj.*: Mysterious, wondrous, or baffling in nature.

N

nat u ral ist (năch′ər-ə-lĭst, năch′rə-lĭst) *n.*: An expert in natural history (the study of natural objects), especially in botany (the study of plants).

ne go ti a tion (nĭ-gō′shē-ā′shən) *n.*: Act of bargaining, or reaching an agreement.

nod ule (nŏj′ool) *n.*: Small rounded lump or swelling.

no ta ry (nō′tə-rē) *n.* [short for notary public]: Person authorized to certify legal documents (such as contracts).

no ta tion (nō-tā′shən) *n.*: Brief written comment; a note.

nu ance (noo-äns′, nyoo-äns′, noo′äns′, nyoo′äns′) *n.*: Slight variation; a shade's difference.

nub (nŭb) *n.*: Small piece or knob.

O

o bliv i ous (ə-blĭv′ē-əs) *adj.*: Completely unaware.

ob sti nate ly (ŏb′stə-nĭt-lē) *adv.*: Stubbornly; in a headstrong or pigheaded way.

ob vi ous ly (ŏb′vē-əs-lē) *adv.*: Evidently, apparently.

off spring (ôf′sprĭng′, ŏf′sprĭng′) *n.*: Young born to a person, animal, or plant.

o rang u tan (ō-răng′ə-tăn′, ə-răng′ə-tăn′) *n.*: Tree-living, manlike ape that has shaggy, reddish-brown hair and very long arms.

o rig i nate (ə-rĭj′ə-nāt′) *v.*: To begin; to come into being.

o ver se er (ō′vər-sē′ər) *n.*: One who supervises, or watches over and directs the work of others; a supervisor.

P

pag eant ry (păj′ən-trē) *n.*: Pageants, or colorful public rituals or displays; usually, historical or traditional ceremonies.

pan de mo ni um (păn′də-mō′nē-əm) *n.*: Wild confusion or disorder.

pan to mime (păn′tə-mīm′) *n.*: An acting style that uses gestures, rather than words, to express feelings and ideas. —*v.*: To use pantomime.

par a lyze (păr′ə-līz′) *v.*: To make unable to move, either through injury or fear.

par a troop er (păr′ə-troo′pər) *n.*: Member of a troop trained to parachute. —*adj.*: Of or pertaining to paratroopers.

pa thet ic (pə-thĕt′ĭk) *adj.*: Pitiful; able to arouse sympathy.

pe ri od i cal ly (pîr′ē-ŏd′ĭ-kəl-ē) *adv.*: Frequently; at regular intervals.

per plex (pər-plĕks′) *v.*: To confuse, baffle, or bewilder.

per se cu tion (pûr′sə-kyoo′shən) *n.*: Oppression; continual mistreatment or abuse.

pet ri fy (pĕt′rə-fī′) *v.*: To become stiff and motionless, like stone. —**pet ri fied**, *adj.*

phan tom (făn′təm) *adj.*: Ghostlike, unreal, imaginary.

phe nom e non (fĭ-nŏm′ə-non′) *n.*: An unusual occurrence; an observable event for which there is no apparent explanation. —**phe nom e nal**, *adj.*

pig ment (pĭg′mənt) *n.*: Substance giving color to plant or animal tissue.

pil fer (pĭl′fər) *v.*: To steal by taking a small amount each time. —**pil fer er**, *n.*

pi ña ta (pēn-yät′ə) *n.*: Decorated container filled with sweets and gifts that is hung from the ceiling to be broken open during a festival.

piv ot (pĭv′ət) *v.*: To rotate, or swing around.

plague (plāg) *v.*: To torment, annoy, or afflict in a persistent fashion.

plain clothes man (plān′klōz′mən) *n.*: Policeman or detective who wears street clothes while on duty.

plas ma (plăz′mə) *n.*: Clear-fluid, protein part of blood; used in transfusions.

pla za (plä′zə, plăz′ə) *n.*: A public square, or an open, cemented area in a city for public use.

por cu pine (pôr′kyə-pīn′) *n.*: A type of rodent covered with bristles or quills.

pre car i ous ly (prĭ-kâr′ē-əs-lē) *adv.*: In an unsafe or reckless fashion; dangerously; on the brink, or at the edge.

pred a to ry (prĕd′ə-tôr′ē, prĕd′ə-tōr′ē) *adj.*: Pertaining to hunting and feeding off other animals.

pre dic a ment (prĭ-dĭk′ə-mənt) n.: Plight or diffi-culty.

preen (prēn) v.: To take obvious satisfaction in one's own appearance.

pre his tor ic (prē′hĭs-tôr′ĭk, prē′hĭs-tŏr′ĭk) adj.: Pertaining to the period before written histo-ry.

prej u dice (prĕj′ə-dĭs) n.: Unjustified hatred for a particular group, race, or religion.

pre lim i nary (prĭ-lĭm′ə-nĕr′ē) adj.: Introductory; occurring just prior to a main action or event.

pre side (prĭ-zīd′) v.: To hold command; to assume the role of chairperson or president.

pre sup pose (prē′sə-pōz′) v.: To assume before-hand; to take for granted.

pre view (prē′vyōō′) n.: Advance showing or dis-play.

pri or i ty (prĭ-ôr′ə-tē, prĭ-ŏr′ə-tē) n.: Thing that must be accomplished before anything else. —adj.: Of or pertaining to a priority.

pro ces sion (prə-sĕsh′ən) n.: A group that is mov-ing along in an orderly fashion, usually in a line.

pro fu sion (prə-fyōō′zhən, prō-fyōō′zhən) n.: Abundance, or an ample supply.

prop o si tion (prŏp′ə-zĭsh′ən) n.: Plan or scheme presented for discussion or consideration; a proposal.

pros pect (prŏs′pĕkt′) n.: Possibility or likelihood; outlook or expectation.

pros per i ty (prŏs-pĕr′ə-tē) n.: Success or good fortune.

pudg y (pŭj′ē) adj.: Chubby; short and plump.

pueb lo (pwĕb′lō) n.: Terraced dwellings of cer-tain Indian tribes of the southwestern United States made from stone and adobe, or dried clay.

puf fin (pŭf′ĭn) n.: Sea bird, found in northern regions, that has black and white plumage and a colorful, flat-sided beak.

pu ri fy (pyōōr′ə-fī′) v.: To cleanse of flaws, or make pure. —**pu ri fying**, adj.

Q

quaint (kwānt) adj.: Charmingly old-fashioned.

quest (kwĕst) n.: Act of pursuing something; a search.

quick sand (kwĭk′sănd′) n.: Deep, wet sand in which a person or object will sink.

quiv er (kwĭv′ər) n.: A slight shaking or trembling. —v.: To tremble.

R

ram bunc tious (răm-bŭngk′shəs) adj.: Boisterous, unruly, rowdy.

ram shack le (răm′shăk′əl) adj.: Broken-down, old-looking, rickety.

ra tion al ize (răsh′ən-əl-īz′) v.: To explain away one's behavior with false reasons or argu-ments.

rav en ous ly (răv′ən-əs-lē) adv.: In a terribly hun-gry or craving fashion.

realm (rĕlm) n.: Range or area.

re as sure (rē′ə-shōōr′) v.: To lend support to, or to make confident again. —**re as sur ance**, n. —**re as sur ing**, adj.

re cede (rĭ-sēd′) v.: To draw back or move away from.

reck on (rĕk′ən) v.: To think or suppose.

re flect (rĭ-flĕkt′) v.: To mirror, or form a picture of.

re flec tive ly (rĭ-flĕk′tĭv-lē) adv.: In a thoughtful or reappraising way.

re flex (rē′flĕks′) n.: Automatic, or spontaneous reaction or response.

re frain (rĭ-frān′) n.: Phrase or verse that is con-stantly repeated during a story or song.

ref u gee (rĕf′yōō-jē′) n.: One who flees from per-secution or danger.

re in force (rē′ĭn-fôrs′, rē′ĭn-fōrs′) v.: To strength-en; to give extra support to.

re li a ble (rĭ-lī′ə-bəl) adj.: Dependable, or able to be relied upon.

rem i nisce (rĕm′ə-nĭs′) v.: To recall events from one's past.

re mote (rĭ-mōt′) adj.: Distant, far-removed, out-of-the-way; isolated.

ren der (rĕn′dər) v.: To make, or cause to become.

re pel lent (rĭ-pĕl′ənt) n.: **1.** Something that repels or drives away something else. **2.** A chemical solution used to drive away animals or insects.

re pose (rĭ-pōz′) v.: To rest, recline, or relax.

res er va tion (rĕz′ər-vā′shən) n.: Arrangement to secure something in advance, such as an airplane ticket or a hotel room.

re solve (rĭ-zŏlv′) v.: To decide or determine to do something. —**re solve,** n. —**res o lu tion,** n.

re strict (rĭ-strĭkt′) v.: To impose limits; to restrain. —**re stric tion,** n.

retch (rĕch) v.: To attempt to vomit.

rib ald (rĭb′əld) adj.: Pertaining to crude or vulgar humor.

rig or ous (rĭg′ər-əs) adj.: Very strict, severe, or demanding.

rit u al (rĭch′o͞o-əl) n.: A regularly followed procedure; a rite or ceremony.

rud dy (rŭd′ē) adj.: Having a rosy color.

rus set (rŭs′ĭt) adj.: Reddish-brown.

S

sa fa ri (sə-fä′rē) n.: Journey or expedition, usually to hunt animals in East Africa.

sa ga (sä′gə) n.: Long, detailed story about some historical event or legend.

sar cas tic (sär-kăs′tĭk) adj.: Scornful or mocking in tone. —**sar cas ti cal ly,** adv.

sat el lite (săt′l-īt′) n.: Manmade object in orbit around a planet or star.

scant (skănt) adj.: Lacking in quantity; meager, inadequate.

scoff (skôf, skŏf) v.: To mock, or laugh at scornfully.

scorch (skôrch) v.: To shrivel or wither something by using extreme heat; to burn or singe.

scraw ny (skrô′nē) adj.: Skinny.

scu ba (sko͞o′bə) n. [s(elf) c(ontained) u(nderwater) b(reathing) a(pparatus)]: Breathing equipment used while swimming underwater. —adj.: Of or pertaining to scuba.

scuff (skŭf) v.: To tread or shuffle.

sear (sîr) v.: To scorch, or burn the surface of.

sec tor (sĕk′tər, sĕk′tôr′) n.: A division or zone; a group, segment, or section.

seg re ga tion (sĕg′rə-gā′shən) n.: Policy of isolating a race from the rest of society, by providing separate housing facilities, schooling, etc.

self-right eous (sĕlf′rī′chəs) adj.: Convinced of one's own righteousness or morality.

se ren i ty (sĭ-rĕn′ə-tē) n.: Peacefulness; calm. —**se rene,** adj.

shale (shāl) n.: Type of rock made up of layers of clay or other sediments.

sheep ish ly (shēp′ĭsh-lē) adv.: In a shy or embarrassed manner.

shift less (shĭft′lĭs) adj.: Lazy; lacking in ambition.

shil ling (shĭl′ĭng) n.: British coin worth twelve pence, or one-twentieth of a pound.

siege (sēj) n.: Act of surrounding something, usually a town or fortress, in order to capture it.

sim mer (sĭm′ər) v.: To be filled with anger; to almost reach the boiling point.

si mul ta ne ous ly (sī′məl-ta′nē-əs-lē) adv.: At the same time.

sit u a tion (sĭch′o͞o-ā′shən) n.: A particular set of circumstances or state of affairs.

skit tish (skĭt′ĭsh) adj.: Easily spooked or frightened.

slate (slāt) n.: Fine-grained rock produced from clay or shale.

smirk (smûrk) v.: To smile in a smug, knowing, or insulting fashion.

snor kel (snôr′kəl) v.: To swim underwater by using a tube-like breathing device.

so lic i tous ly (sə-lĭs′ə-təs-lē) adv.: Attentively; in a way that shows concern.

sol stice (sŏl′stəs, sôl′stəs) n.: Either of two days during the year when the sun is farthest north or farthest south of the equator, around June 22 and December 22.

so nar (sō′när′) n. [so(und) na(vigation) r(anging)]: Device that uses sound waves to locate underwater objects. —adj.: Of or pertaining to such a device.

sor rel (sôr′əl) n.: Light, bright reddish-brown color. —adj.: Sorrel-colored.

spec i men (spĕs′ə-mən) n.: Something representative of a whole; an example or sample.

spec tac u lar (spĕk-tăk′yə-lər) adj.: Sensational; amazing or astonishing.

spec tral (spĕk′trəl) adj.: Ghostly.

spell bound (spĕl′bound′) adj.: Held as if by magic; fascinated, entranced.

spon sor (spŏn′sər) n.: One who finances or supports someone else; a backer or patron.

sprint er (sprĭnt′ər) n.: Person who runs a short race at top speed.

spurn (spûrn) v.: To turn down or reject; usually in a contemptuous manner.

stac ca to (stə-kä′tō) *adj.:* Marked by sharp, abrupt sounds.

stam pede (stăm′pēd′) *n.:* Sudden flight of panicked animals; usually refers to cattle.

state ly (stāt′lē) *adj.:* Dignified; majestic.

stealth i ly (stĕlth′ĭ-lē) *adv.:* In a secretive, sneaky, or unnoticeable way.

steth o scope (stĕth′ə-skōp′) *n.:* Instrument used to hear sounds inside the body.

stim u late (stĭm′yə-lāt′) *v.:* To excite, rouse, or spur to action.

stock y (stŏk′ē) *adj.:* Sturdy of build; thick-set.

stout (stout) *adj.:* Sturdy; solid; thick-set.

stra te gic (strə-tē′jĭk) *adj.:* Planned or designed to deceive an enemy; having to do with a military maneuver.

stren u ous (strĕn′yoo-əs) *adj.:* Energetic, demanding; requiring great effort.

suc ces sion (sək-sĕsh′ən) *n.:* Act of following in order or sequence.

suc tion (sŭk′shən) *n.:* Act or process of sucking, or drawing in. —*adj.:* Pertaining to suction, or having its properties.

suf fo ca tion (sŭf′ə-kā′shən) *n.:* Death due to smothering, or lack of oxygen.

sul len ness (sŭl′ən-nĕs) *n.:* Gloominess; ill humor.

su per sti tion (soo′pər-stĭsh′ən) *n.:* Irrational belief or practice; for example, the belief that walking under a ladder brings bad luck.

sup ple men ta ry (sŭp′lə-mən′tə-rē) *adj.:* Additional.

sur vey (sər-vā′, sûr′vā) *v.:* **1.** To look at or inspect carefully. **2.** To determine the area or boundaries of a piece of property. —**sur vey or,** *n.*

sus cep ti ble (sə-sĕp′tə-bəl) *adj.:* Incapable of resisting; easily influenced.

swathe (swäth) *v.:* To wrap in bandages.

sym bol ic (sĭm-bŏl′ĭk) *adj.:* Pertaining to a symbol, something that represents or suggests something else.

sym bol ize (sĭm′bə-līz′) *v.:* To represent or express or stand for something.

T

ta ma le (tə-mä′lē) *n.:* Mexican dish of highly seasoned cornmeal, meat, and peppers wrapped in corn husks.

tan gi ble (tăn′jə-bəl) *adj.:* Real, substantial; able to be treated as fact; visible.

ta pir (tā′pər, tə-pîr′) *n.:* A type of large, hoofed, hoglike mammal found in tropical America or southern Asia that has short limbs and a fleshy snout.

tar nish (tär′nĭsh) *v.:* To stain or disgrace.

taut (tôt) *adj.:* Tightly stretched or pulled.

teem (tēm) *v.:* To swarm or abound with activity.

tem per (tĕm′pər) *v.:* To adjust; to fit to a situation.

tem po (tĕm′pō) *n.:* Rhythm; pace.

te nac i ty (tə-năs′ə-tē) *n.:* Steadfastness or persistence; an unwillingness to give up; stubbornness, or a firm holding on to.

ten don (tĕn′dən) *n.:* Tough band of tissue connecting muscles to bones.

tes ti mo ny (tĕs′tə-mō′nē) *n.:* Proof; evidence.

tet a nus (tĕt′n-əs) *n.:* Acute infectious disease characterized by muscle spasms and caused by a bacteria, which usually enters the body through a wound. —*adj.:* Of or pertaining to tetanus.

teth er (tĕth′ər) *v.:* To tie up; to use a short rope or chain to restrict an animal's movements or to keep it within certain boundaries.

thresh old (thrĕsh′ōld′, thrĕsh′hōld′) *n.:* Doorway; entrance.

throng (thrŏng) *v.:* To crowd into or fill; to press in upon or surround with a large group.

till (tĭl) *v.:* To plow and fertilize land in order to plant crops.

tink er (tĭng′kər) *n.:* Traveling repairman who mends metal pots and pans.

tor na do (tôr-nā′dō) *n.:* Whirling column of air, several hundred yards wide, that moves destructively at speeds up to 300 miles per hour.

tra di tion al (trə-dĭsh′ən-əl) *adj.:* **1.** Passed down from generation to generation. **2.** Pertaining to a custom.

trag e dy (trăj′ə-dē) *n.:* A serious and disastrous event.

trag ic (trăj′ĭk) *adj.:* Characterized by tragedy.

trans form (trăns-fôrm′) *v.:* To change the appearance of; to convert.

trans mis sion (trăns-mĭsh′ən, trănz-mĭsh′ən) *n.:* Message being sent by wire or radio.

trans par ent (trăns-pâr′ənt, trăns-păr′ənt) *adj*.: Able to be seen through; sheer.

trem ble (trĕm′bəl) *v*.: To shake or shiver, especially from fear or excitement.

tu mult (tōō′məlt, tyōō′məlt) *n*.: Disturbance, uproar, commotion.

tweez ers (twē′zərz) *n*.: Small tool used for plucking or picking up small objects.

U

un can ny (ŭn′kăn′ē) *adj*.: Strangely inexplicable; unearthly.

un con scious ness (ŭn′kŏn′shəs-nəs) *n*.: Lack of full awareness; state of having fainted or blacked out.

un ham pered (ŭn-hăm′pərd) *adj*.: Not impaired or restricted; unrestrained.

un kempt (ŭn′kĕmpt′) *adj*.: Not combed; messy.

un pro voked (ŭn′prə-vōkt′) *adj*.: Not forced or urged to act.

un seem ly (ŭn′sēm′lē) *adj*.: In bad taste; unbecoming or improper.

un sur passed (ŭn′sər-păst′, ŭn′sər-päst′) *adj*.: Unexcelled.

un war y (ŭn′wâr′ē) *adj*.: Not alert to danger; incautious, unguarded.

up draft (ŭp′drăft′, ŭp′drăft′) *n*.: Upward movement, particularly of air.

V

vague ly (vāg′lē) *adv*.: In an unclear or indecisive way.

van i ty (văn′ə-tē) *n*.: Excessive pride or conceit.

var i a tion (vâr′ē-ā′shən) *n*.: A slightly different version.

ven ti la tor (vĕnt′l-ā′tər) *n*.: Fan-like device that supplies fresh air to a room. —*adj*.: Of or pertaining to a ventilator.

ve ran da(h) (və-răn′də) *n*.: Type of porch or balcony, usually roofed.

ver dict (vûr′dĭkt) *n*.: Final judgment or decision.

vim (vĭm) *n*.: Great energy; vigor.

voile (voĭl) *n*.: A sheer, finely-textured fabric.

W

war i ness (wăr′ē-nĕs) *n*.: Watchfulness, cautiousness.

wean (wēn) *v*.: To deprive of mother's milk and substitute solid foods.

wea sel (wē′zəl) *n*.: Small mammal with a long, slender body and, usually, reddish-brown fur, that is noted for its sneaky or cowardly behavior.

wend (wĕnd) *v*.: To proceed or move along.

whet (hwĕt) *v*.: To sharpen.

whit tle (hwĭt′l) *v*.: To carve from wood.

wild fire (wīld′fīr′) *n*.: Rapidly spreading fire that burns out of control.

win some (wĭn′səm) *adj*.: Pleasing, charming.

wretch ed (rĕch′ĭd) *adj*.: Awful, miserable, dismal.

Y

yarn (yärn) *n*.: Long, involved adventure story, particularly a tall tale.

INDEX OF CONTENTS BY TYPE

ILLUSTRATION AND PHOTO CREDITS

Illustration

Almquist, Don, p. 56
Echevarria, Abe, pp. 204-205, 320-321, 323
Esteves, Jan, pp. 100, 328-329, 332
Eubanks, Tony, pp. 16-17, 156, 159, 161, 162, 269, 271, 275, 276-277, 368-369, 410
Geyer, Jackie, pp. 42-43, 44, 74-75, 248-249, 253, 256, 375, 377, 408-409
Karchin, Steve, pp. 210-211, 214, 216-217, 223, 225, 227, 233, 236-237, 239, 241, 312
Krepel, Richard, pp. 448-449, 454, 458, 446-467, 474-475
Lyall, Dennis, pp. 80-81, 82, 302-303, 305, 384, 388-389, 391, 418, 421
Newson, Tom, pp. 116-117, 118-119, 184-185, 186-187, 360-361, 363, 396, 400
Palucian, Dickran, pp. 182-183
Radigan, Bob, pp. 2, 5, 61, 168, 172, 174, 177
Tamura, David, pp. 108-109, 111, 284-285, 287
Wolin, Ron, pp. 192-193, 348-349, 352, 355, 426

Photo

p. xiv–1, Four By Five, Inc.; 10, © David Doubilet; 18,21,24, from the motion picture *The Invisible Man,* Courtesy of Universal Pictures; 32,34,35, © Michael Mauney; 41, © Marcia Keegan; 52, Shostal Associates/© Ray Manley; 52-53, Pictorial Parade; 54, Photo Researchers, Inc./ © Russ Kinne; 58-59, Stock Photos Unlimited, Inc., New York; 66,68, Black Star/© Charles Bonnay; 86, Schomberg Center for Research in Black Culture, New York Library, Astor, Lenox, and Tilden Foundations; 89, United States Post Office; 90,94, The Bettmann Archive; 99, Four By Five, Inc.; 124-125, © James Gilmour; 127, Black Star/© Robert Eckert, Jr.; 129, H. Armstrong Roberts; 139, © Lisa Heinzman; 140, © James Gilmour; 144-145, Stock Photos Unlimited, Inc., New York; 147-148, Los Angeles Zoo; 151-152, Los Angeles Zoo/© Sy Oskeroff; 246-247, Stock Photos Unlimited, Inc., New York; 282-283, Earth Scenes/© Zig Leszczynski; 292, H. Armstrong Roberts; 297, Movie Star News; 310-311, Black Star/© Ira Berger; 342-343,344, Courtesy of the Museum of the American Indian, Heye Foundation, New York; 346-347, Rhea Goodman, Quilt Gallery, Inc.; 383, Black Star/© Fred Zimmerman; 432-433,435, Courtesy of ABC; 444-445, Shostal Associates/© Ed Cooper; 446, Four By Five, Inc.

Design: Taurins Design Associates
Cover: © Earl Roberge, Photo Researchers, Inc. *Riders in British Columbia*

INDEX OF AUTHORS AND TITLES

C 3
D 4
E 5
F 6
G 7
H 8
I 9
J 0